VIZ GRAPHIC NOVEL

ANGEL OF VICTORY

A BATTLE ANGEL ALITA™ GRAPHIC NOVEL

STORY AND ART BY

YUKITO KISHIRO

CONTENTS

This volume contains BATTLE ANGEL ALITA PART THREE
issues #7 through #13 in their entirety.

STORY AND ART BY YUKITO KISHIRO

English Adaptation/Fred Burke & Toshifumi Yoshida
Touch-Up Art & Lettering/Wayne Truman
Cover Design/Viz Graphics
Editors/Trish Ledoux & Annette Roman
Assistant Editor/Toshifumi Yoshida

Managing Editor/Satoru Fujii
Executive Editor/Seiji Horibuchi
Publisher/Keizo Inoue

First published as *Gunnm* by Shueisha, Inc. in Japan

Printed in Canada

Published by Viz Communications, Inc.
P.O. Box 77010 • San Francisco, CA 94107

10 9 8 7 6 5 4 3 2 1
First Printing, August 1995

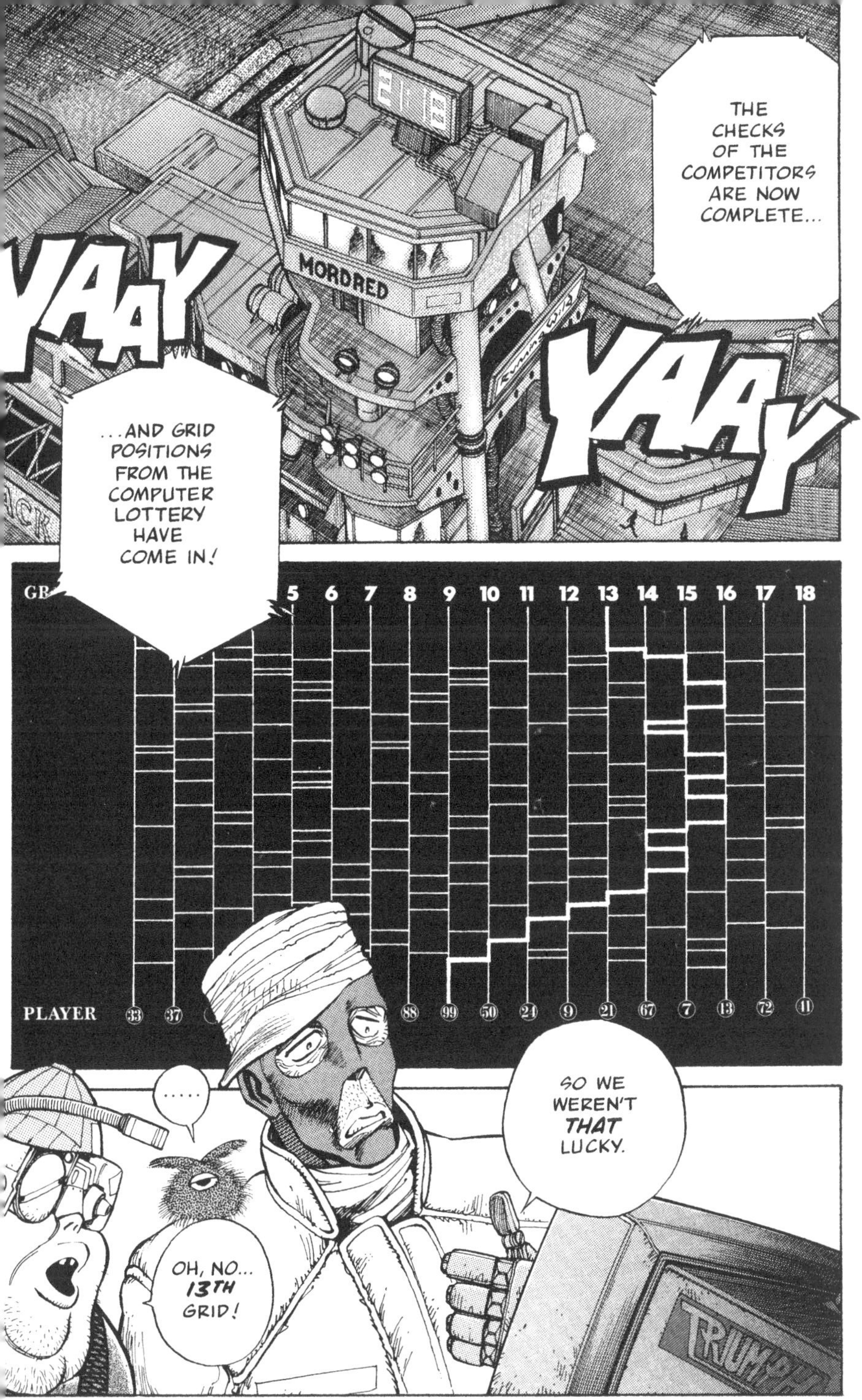
YAAAY
MORDRED
THE CHECKS OF THE COMPETITORS ARE NOW COMPLETE...
YAAAY
...AND GRID POSITIONS FROM THE COMPUTER LOTTERY HAVE COME IN!
5 6 7 8 9 10 11 12 13 14 15 16 17 18
PLAYER 33 37 88 99 50 24 9 21 67 7 13 72 11
.....
SO WE WEREN'T *THAT* LUCKY.
OH, NO... *13TH* GRID!

HEADBANGER'S BALL
Race 1: Face of Evil/Touch of Cruelty

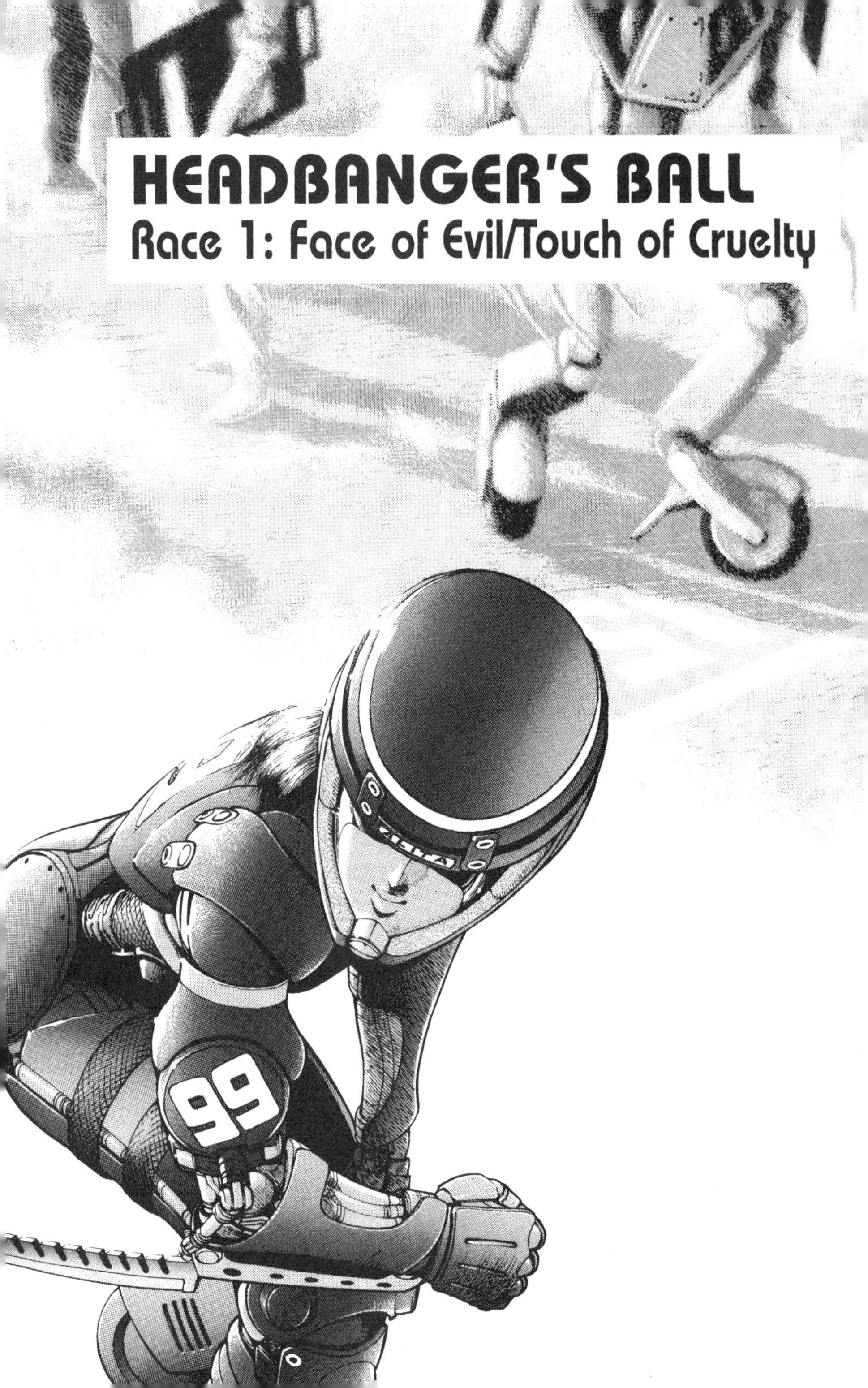

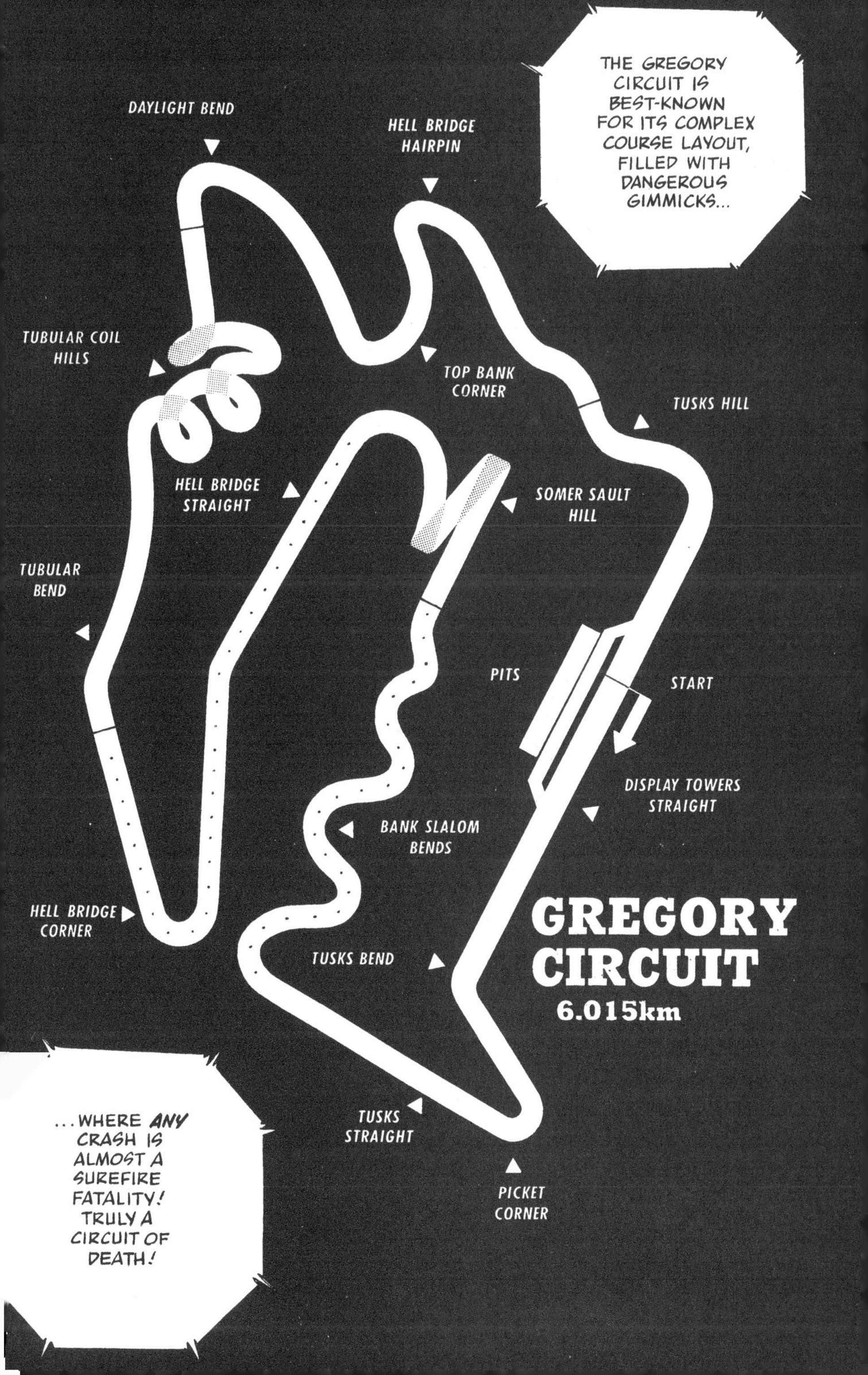
THE GREGORY CIRCUIT IS BEST-KNOWN FOR ITS COMPLEX COURSE LAYOUT, FILLED WITH DANGEROUS GIMMICKS...
DAYLIGHT BEND
HELL BRIDGE HAIRPIN
TUBULAR COIL HILLS
TOP BANK CORNER
TUSKS HILL
HELL BRIDGE STRAIGHT
SOMER SAULT HILL
TUBULAR BEND
PITS
START
DISPLAY TOWERS STRAIGHT
BANK SLALOM BENDS
HELL BRIDGE CORNER
GREGORY CIRCUIT
6.015km
TUSKS BEND
TUSKS STRAIGHT
PICKET CORNER
...WHERE ANY CRASH IS ALMOST A SUREFIRE FATALITY! TRULY A CIRCUIT OF DEATH!

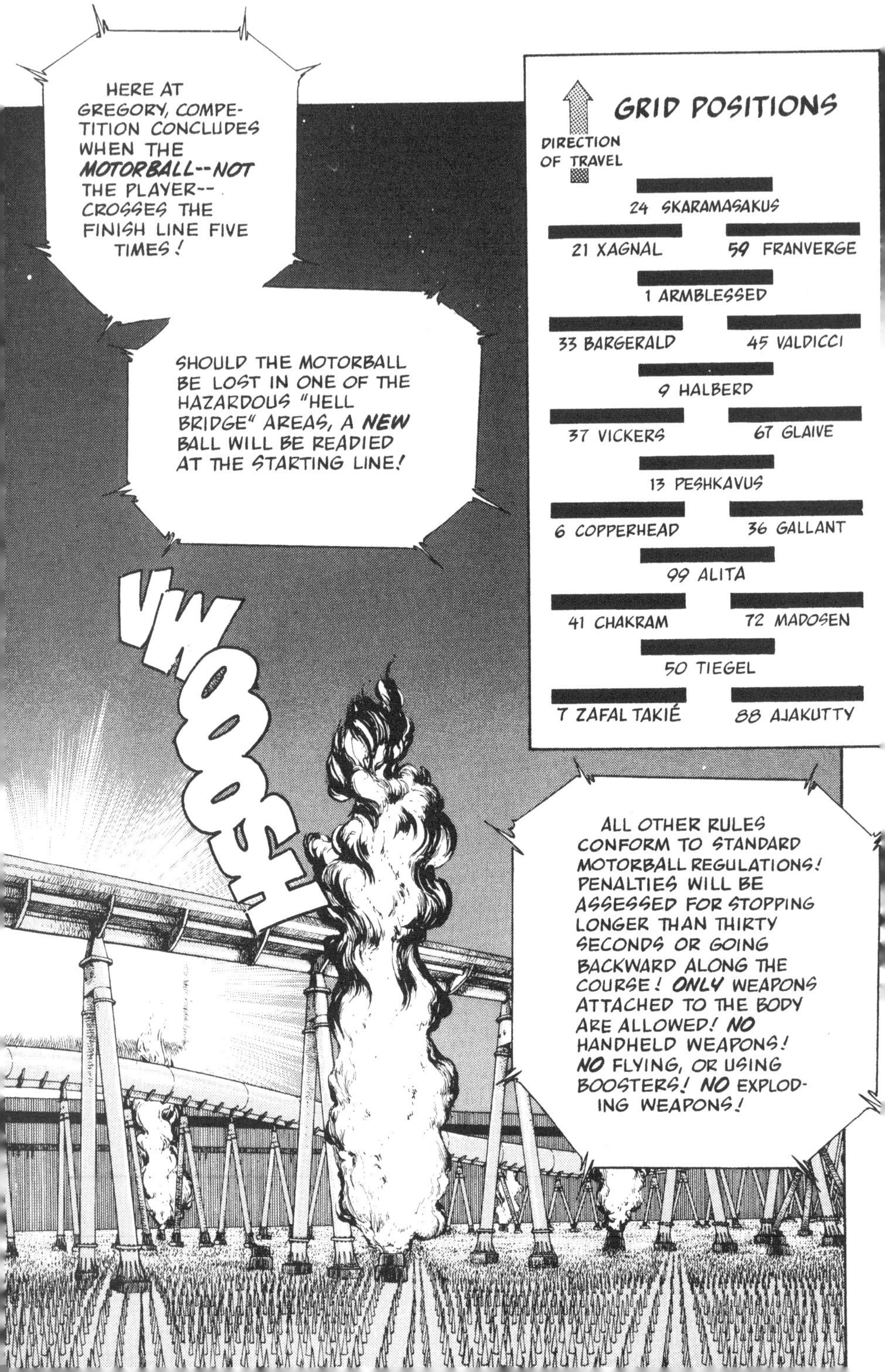
HERE AT GREGORY, COMPETITION CONCLUDES WHEN THE MOTORBALL--NOT THE PLAYER--CROSSES THE FINISH LINE FIVE TIMES!
GRID POSITIONS
DIRECTION OF TRAVEL
24 SKARAMASAKUS
21 XAGNAL
59 FRANVERGE
1 ARMBLESSED
33 BARGERALD
45 VALDICCI
9 HALBERD
37 VICKERS
67 GLAIVE
13 PESHKAVUS
6 COPPERHEAD
36 GALLANT
99 ALITA
41 CHAKRAM
72 MADOSEN
50 TIEGEL
7 ZAFAL TAKIÉ
88 AJAKUTTY
SHOULD THE MOTORBALL BE LOST IN ONE OF THE HAZARDOUS "HELL BRIDGE" AREAS, A NEW BALL WILL BE READIED AT THE STARTING LINE!
VWOOOSH
ALL OTHER RULES CONFORM TO STANDARD MOTORBALL REGULATIONS! PENALTIES WILL BE ASSESSED FOR STOPPING LONGER THAN THIRTY SECONDS OR GOING BACKWARD ALONG THE COURSE! ONLY WEAPONS ATTACHED TO THE BODY ARE ALLOWED! NO HANDHELD WEAPONS! NO FLYING, OR USING BOOSTERS! NO EXPLODING WEAPONS!

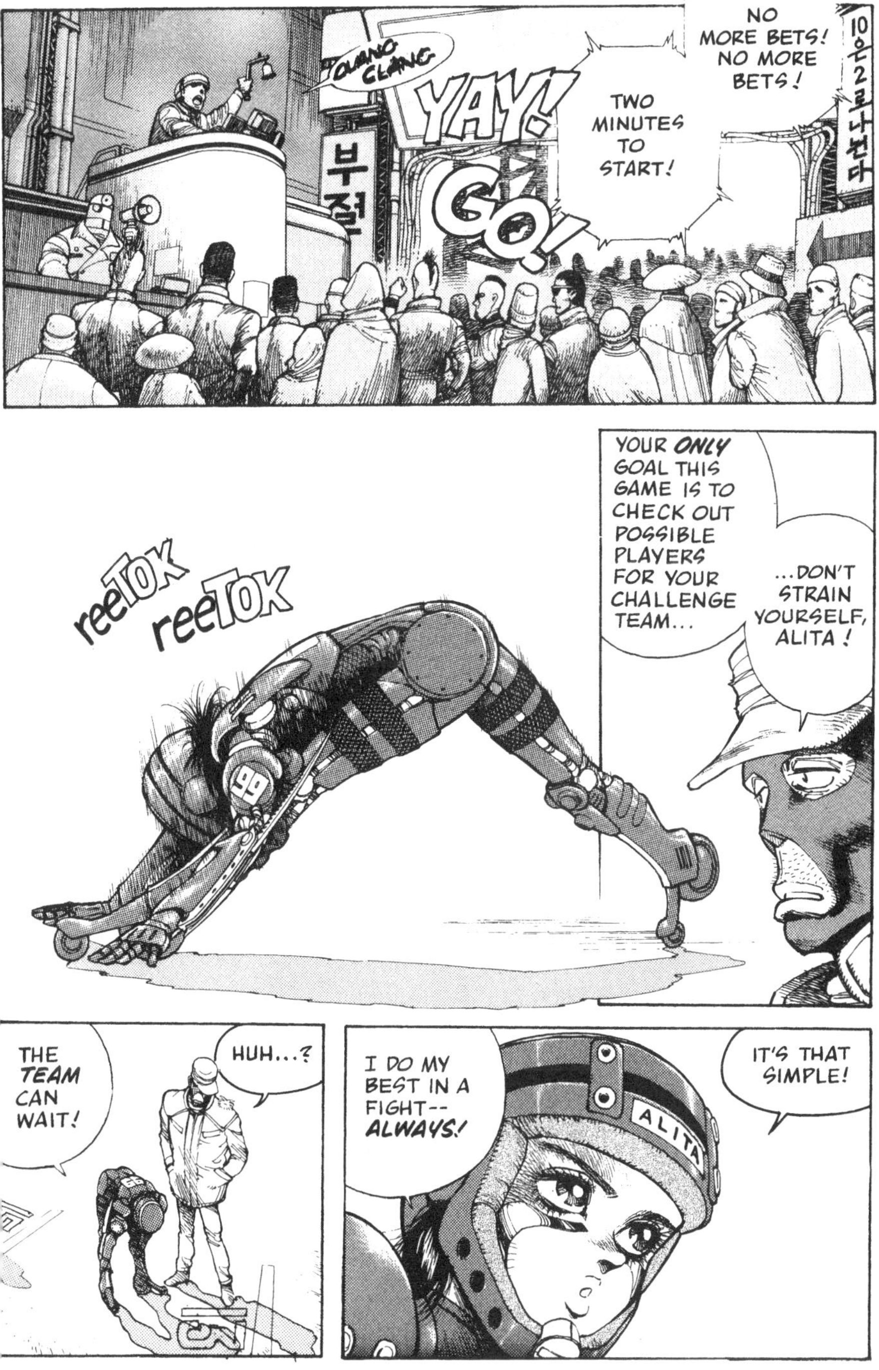
CLANG CLANG
YAY!
GO!
부절
TWO MINUTES TO START!
NO MORE BETS! NO MORE BETS!
reeTOK reeTOK
YOUR ONLY GOAL THIS GAME IS TO CHECK OUT POSSIBLE PLAYERS FOR YOUR CHALLENGE TEAM...
...DON'T STRAIN YOURSELF, ALITA!
THE TEAM CAN WAIT!
HUH...?
I DO MY BEST IN A FIGHT-- ALWAYS!
ALITA
IT'S THAT SIMPLE!

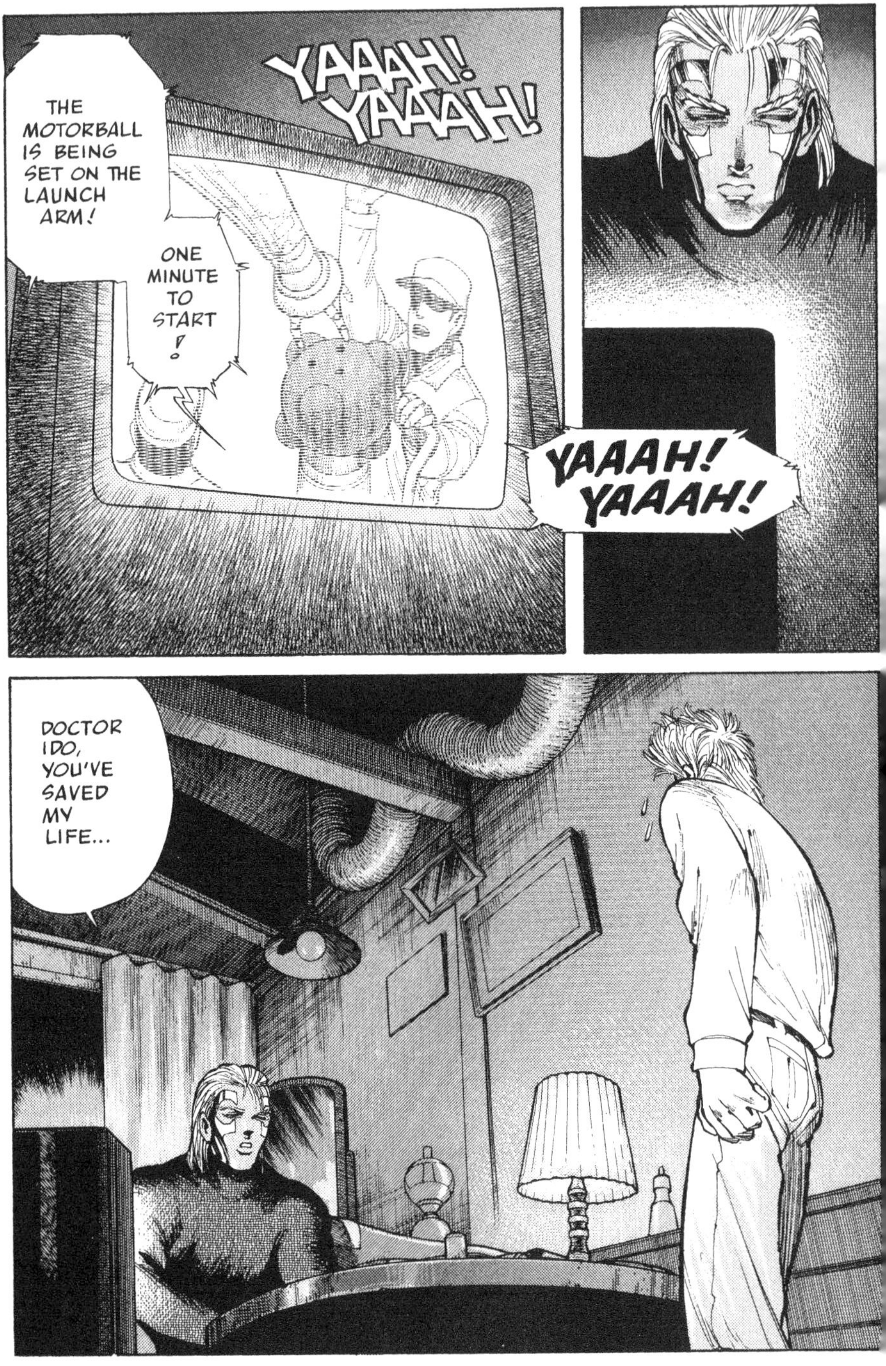
THE MOTORBALL IS BEING SET ON THE LAUNCH ARM!
YAAAH! YAAAH!
ONE MINUTE TO START!
YAAAH! YAAAH!
DOCTOR IDO, YOU'VE SAVED MY LIFE...

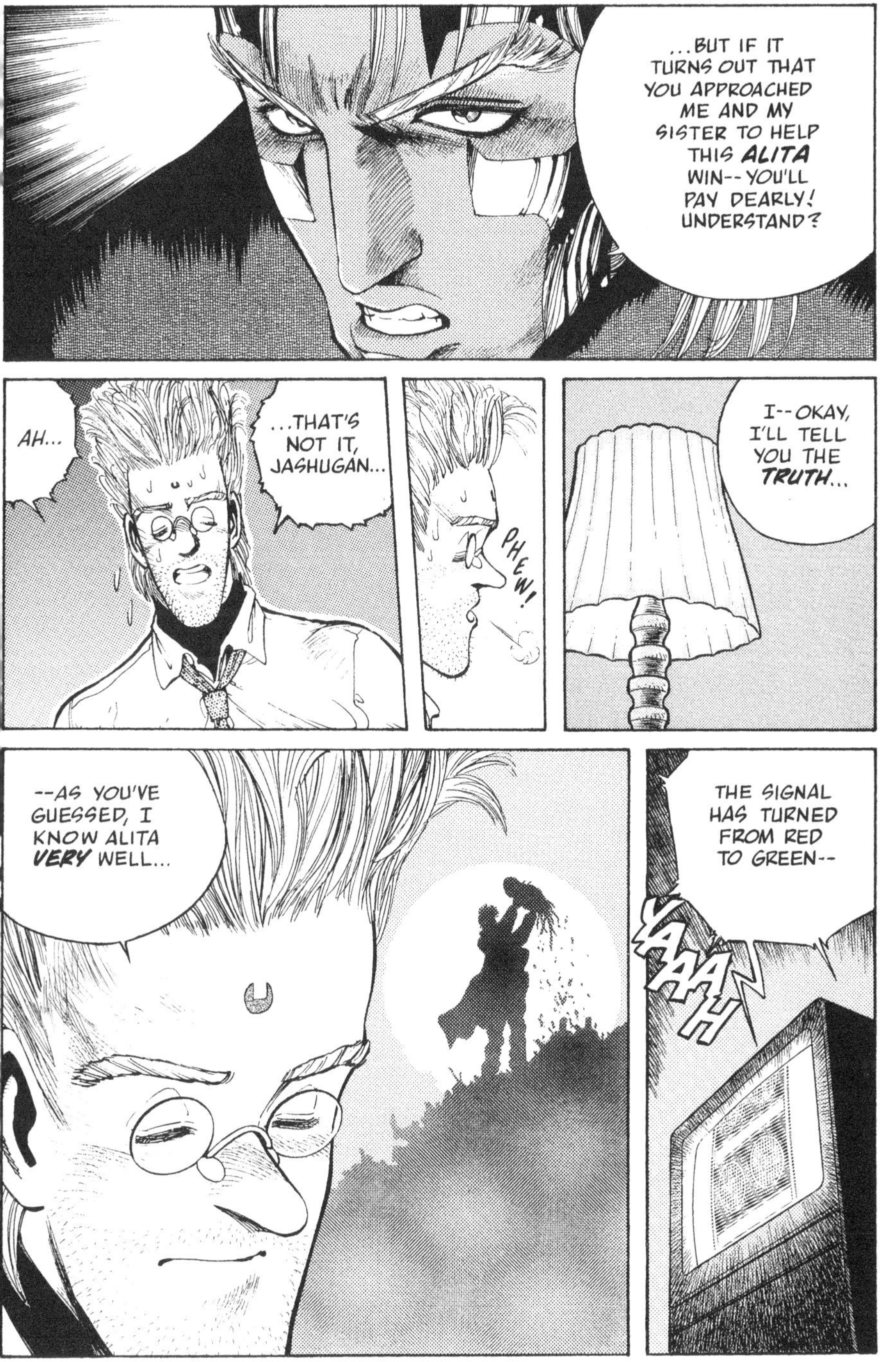
...BUT IF IT TURNS OUT THAT YOU APPROACHED ME AND MY SISTER TO HELP THIS ALITA WIN--YOU'LL PAY DEARLY! UNDERSTAND?
AH...
...THAT'S NOT IT, JASHUGAN...
PHEW!
I--OKAY, I'LL TELL YOU THE TRUTH...
--AS YOU'VE GUESSED, I KNOW ALITA VERY WELL...
THE SIGNAL HAS TURNED FROM RED TO GREEN--
YAAAH

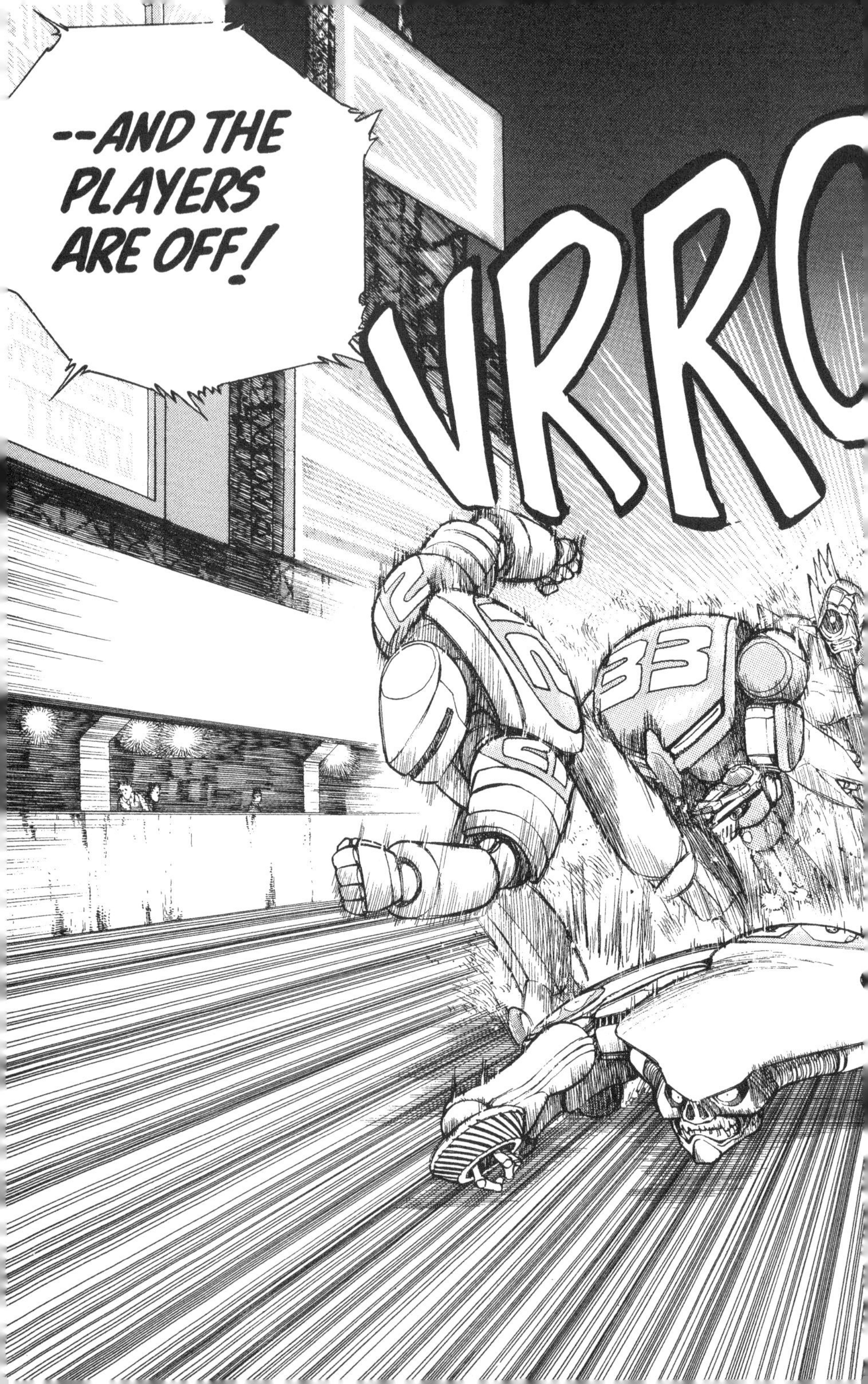
--AND THE PLAYERS ARE OFF!
VRRO

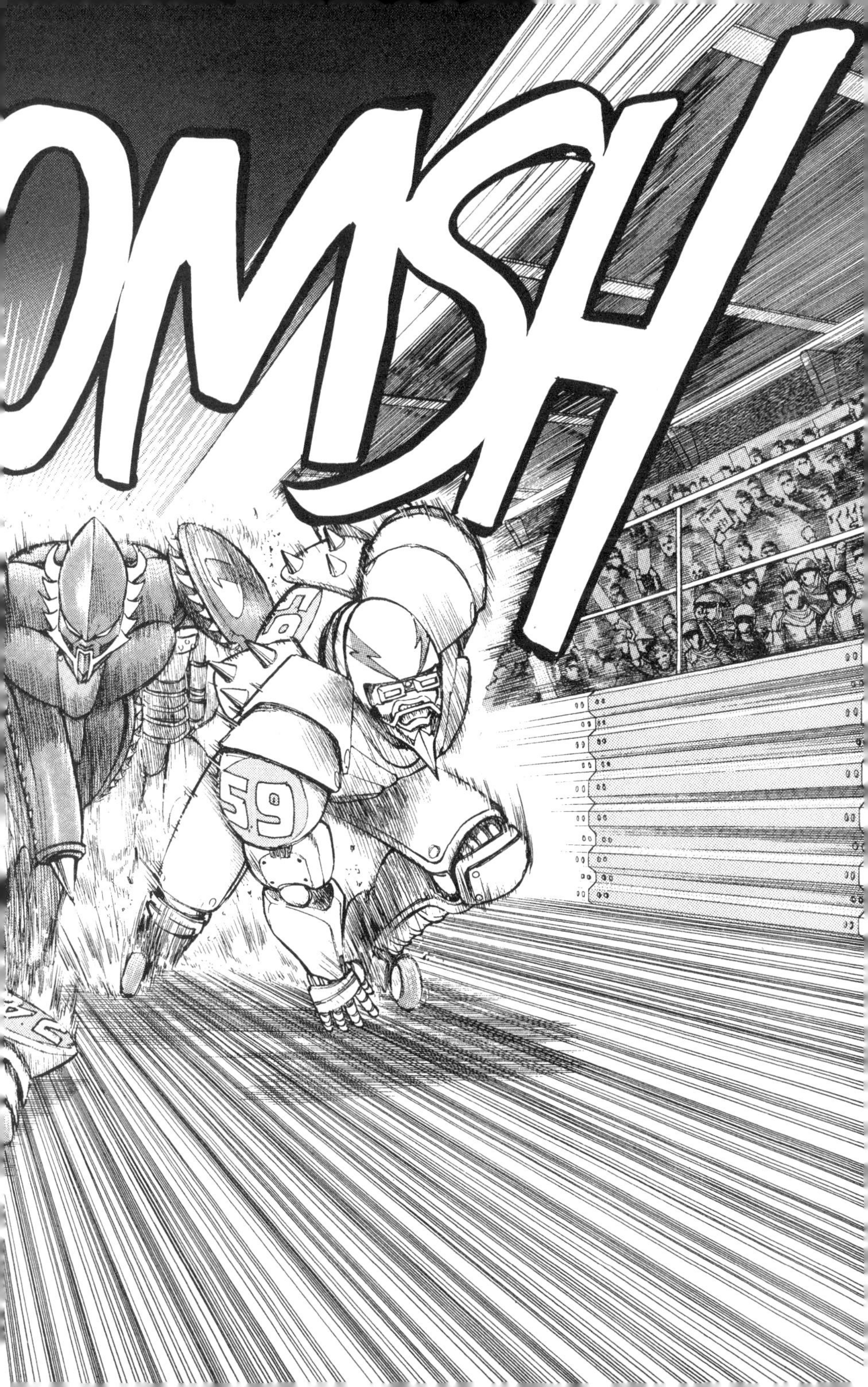
OMSH

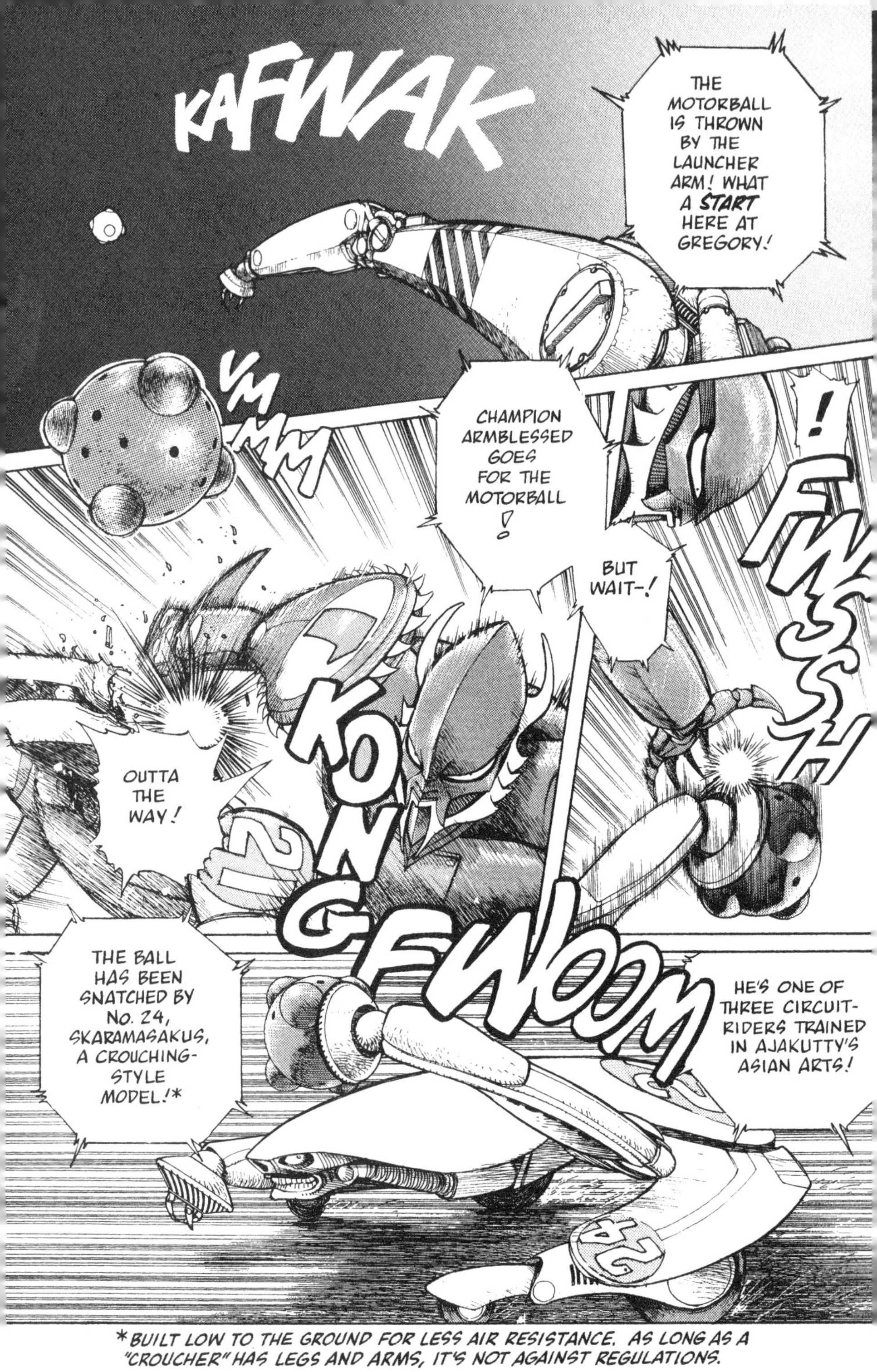
KAFWAK
THE MOTORBALL IS THROWN BY THE LAUNCHER ARM! WHAT A **START** HERE AT GREGORY!
VMMM
CHAMPION ARMBLESSED GOES FOR THE MOTORBALL!
!
FWSSSH
BUT WAIT-!
KONG
OUTTA THE WAY!
GFWOOM
THE BALL HAS BEEN SNATCHED BY No. 24, SKARAMASAKUS, A CROUCHING-STYLE MODEL!*
HE'S ONE OF THREE CIRCUIT-RIDERS TRAINED IN AJAKUTTY'S ASIAN ARTS!

*BUILT LOW TO THE GROUND FOR LESS AIR RESISTANCE. AS LONG AS A "CROUCHER" HAS LEGS AND ARMS, IT'S NOT AGAINST REGULATIONS.

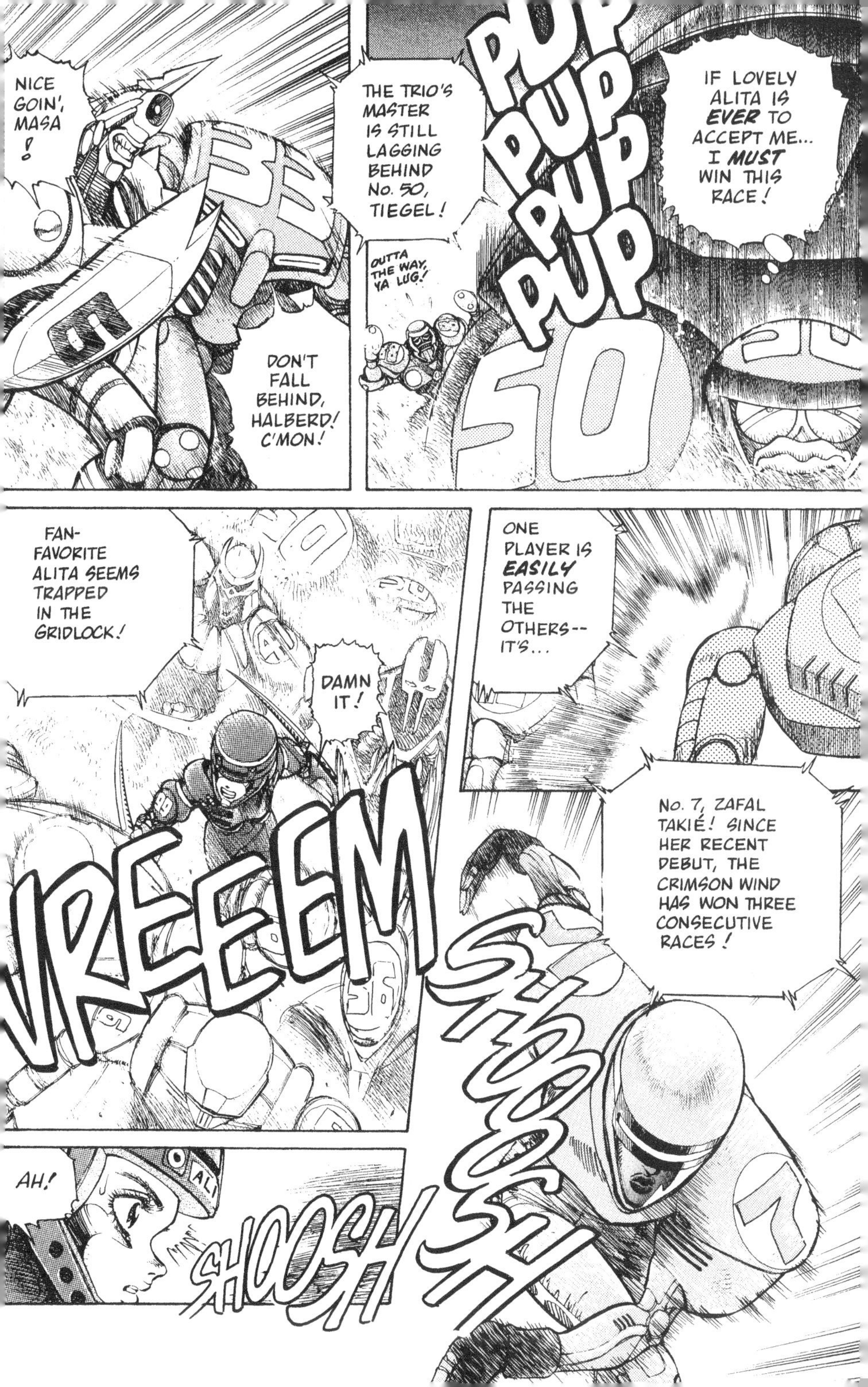
NICE GOIN', MASA!
DON'T FALL BEHIND, HALBERD! C'MON!
THE TRIO'S MASTER IS STILL LAGGING BEHIND No. 50, TIEGEL!
OUTTA THE WAY, YA LUG!
PUP PUP PUP PUP PUP
IF LOVELY ALITA IS **EVER** TO ACCEPT ME... I **MUST** WIN THIS RACE!
FAN-FAVORITE ALITA SEEMS TRAPPED IN THE GRIDLOCK!
DAMN IT!
VREEEM
ONE PLAYER IS **EASILY** PASSING THE OTHERS-- IT'S...
No. 7, ZAFAL TAKIÉ! SINCE HER RECENT DEBUT, THE CRIMSON WIND HAS WON THREE CONSECUTIVE RACES!
SHOOOOSH
AH!
SHOOSH

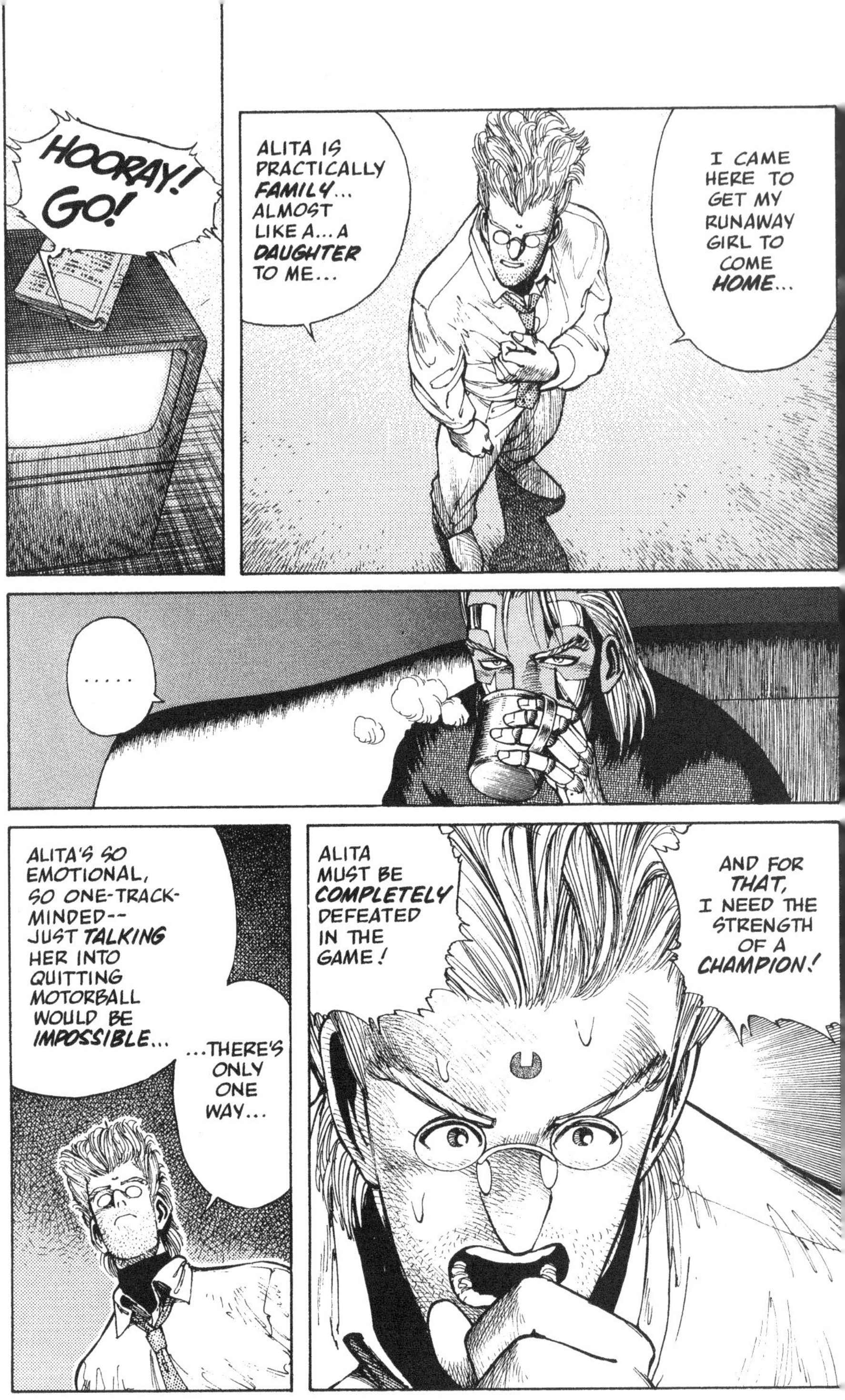
HOORAY! GO!
ALITA IS PRACTICALLY FAMILY... ALMOST LIKE A... A DAUGHTER TO ME...
I CAME HERE TO GET MY RUNAWAY GIRL TO COME HOME...
.....
ALITA'S SO EMOTIONAL, SO ONE-TRACK-MINDED-- JUST TALKING HER INTO QUITTING MOTORBALL WOULD BE IMPOSSIBLE...
...THERE'S ONLY ONE WAY...
ALITA MUST BE COMPLETELY DEFEATED IN THE GAME!
AND FOR THAT, I NEED THE STRENGTH OF A CHAMPION!

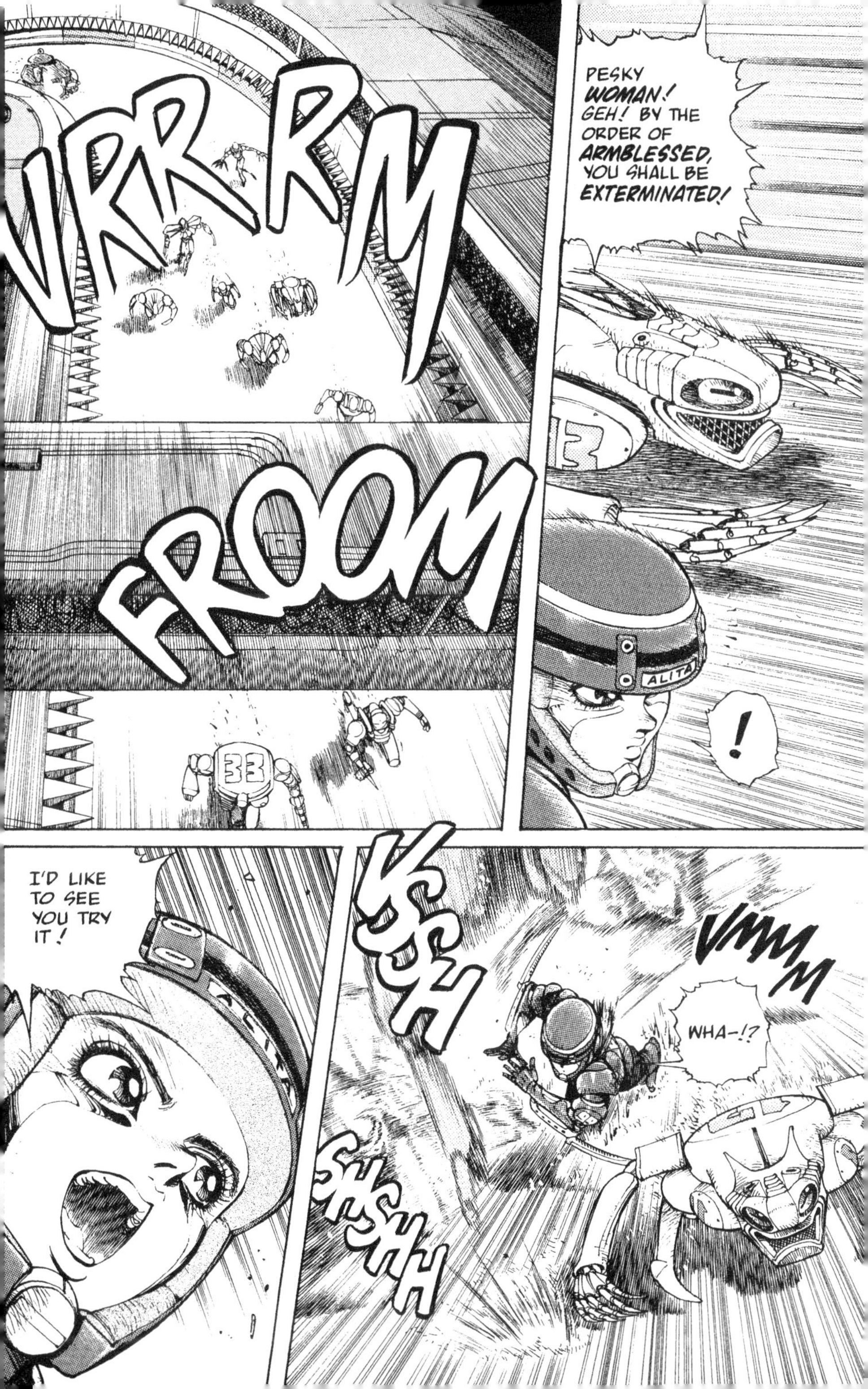
VRR RM
FROOM
PESKY WOMAN! GEH! BY THE ORDER OF ARMBLESSED, YOU SHALL BE EXTERMINATED!
ALITA
!
I'D LIKE TO SEE YOU TRY IT!
VSSH
SHSHH
VMMM
WHA-!?

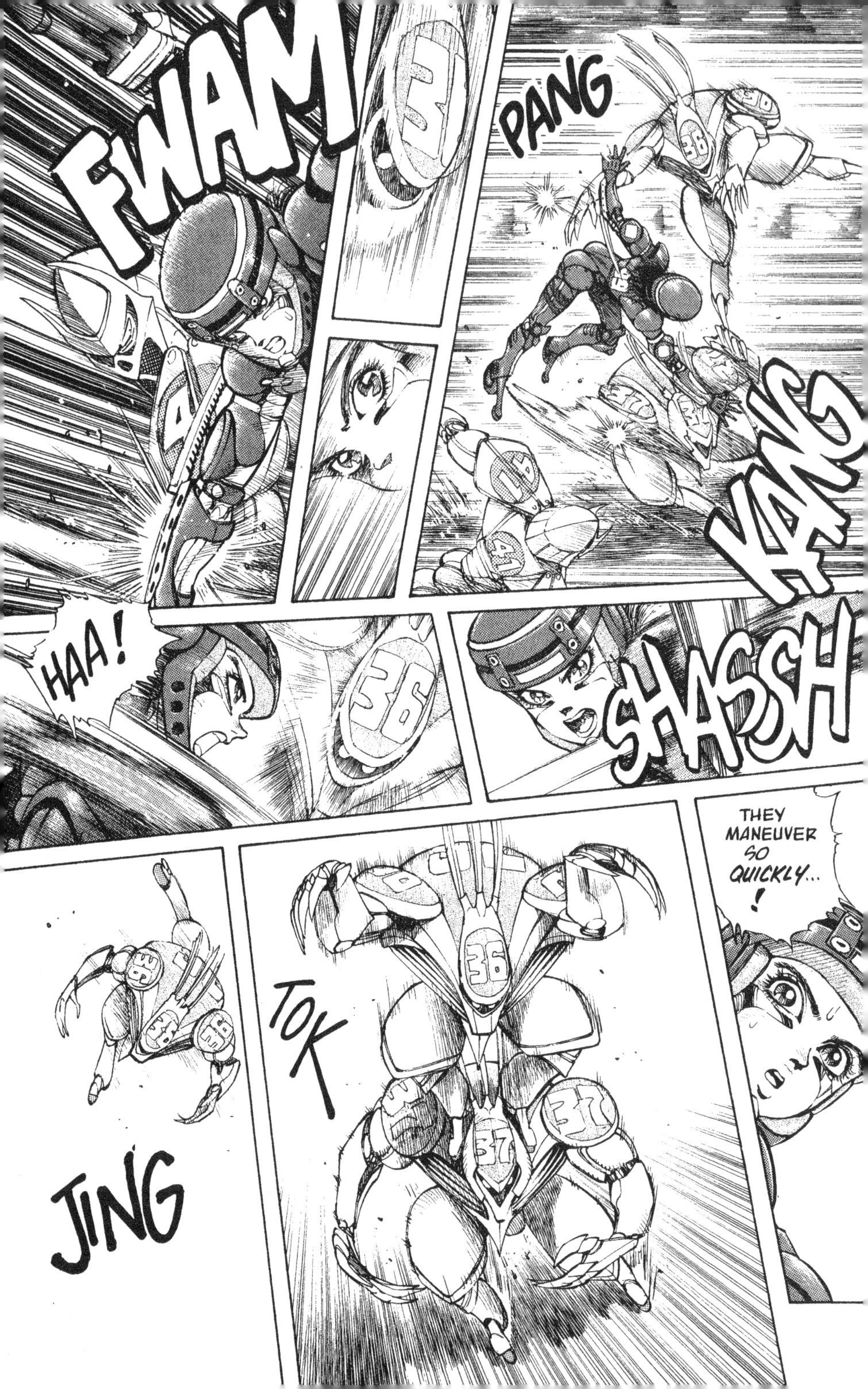
FWAM!
PANG
KANG
HAA!
SHASSH
JING
TOK
THEY MANEUVER SO QUICKLY... !

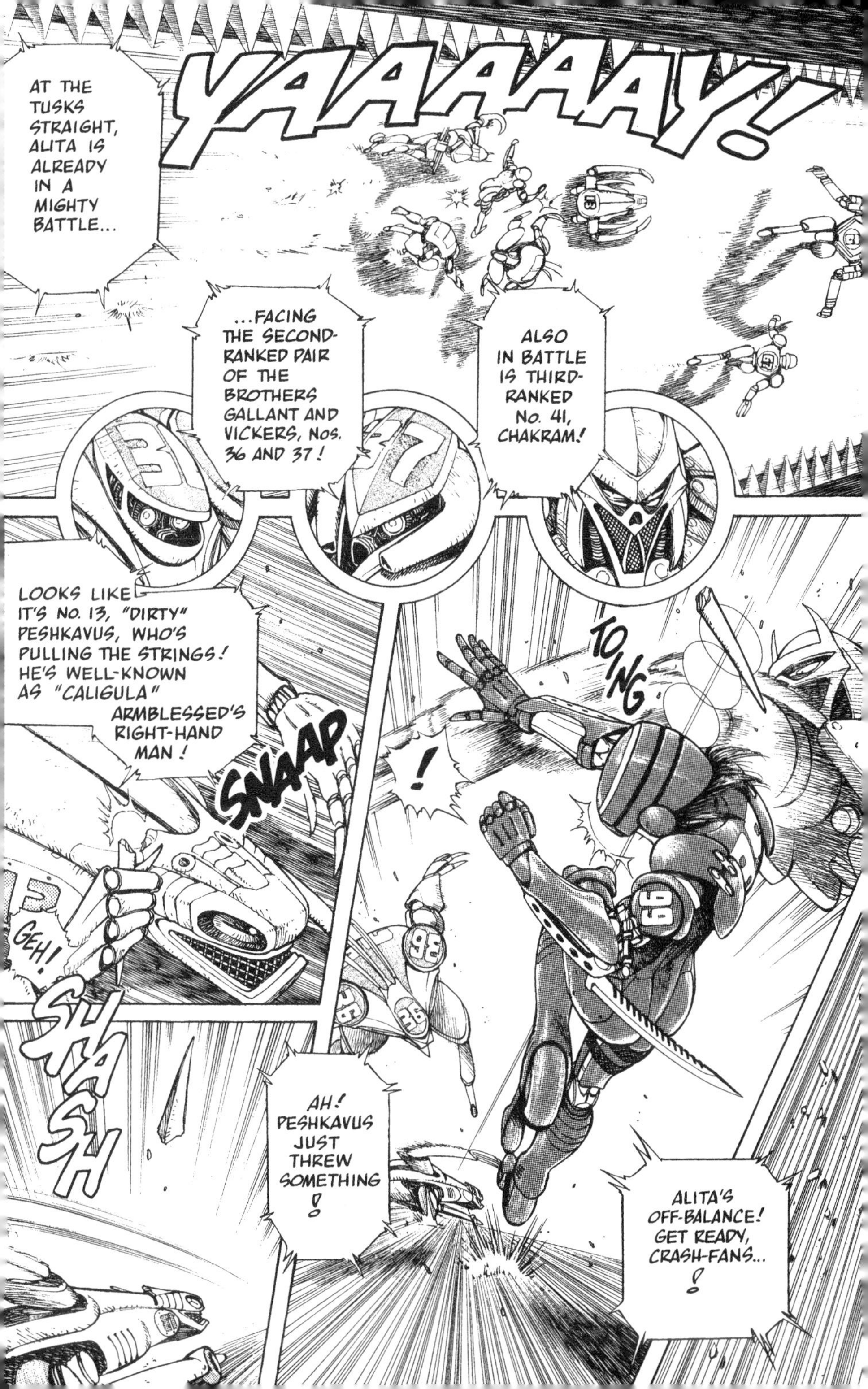
YAAAAAY!
AT THE TUSKS STRAIGHT, ALITA IS ALREADY IN A MIGHTY BATTLE...
...FACING THE SECOND-RANKED PAIR OF THE BROTHERS GALLANT AND VICKERS, NOS. 36 AND 37!
ALSO IN BATTLE IS THIRD-RANKED NO. 41, CHAKRAM!
LOOKS LIKE IT'S NO. 13, "DIRTY" PESHKAVUS, WHO'S PULLING THE STRINGS! HE'S WELL-KNOWN AS "CALIGULA" ARMBLESSED'S RIGHT-HAND MAN!
SNAAP
GEH!
TOING
!
SHASH
AH! PESHKAVUS JUST THREW SOMETHING!
ALITA'S OFF-BALANCE! GET READY, CRASH-FANS...!

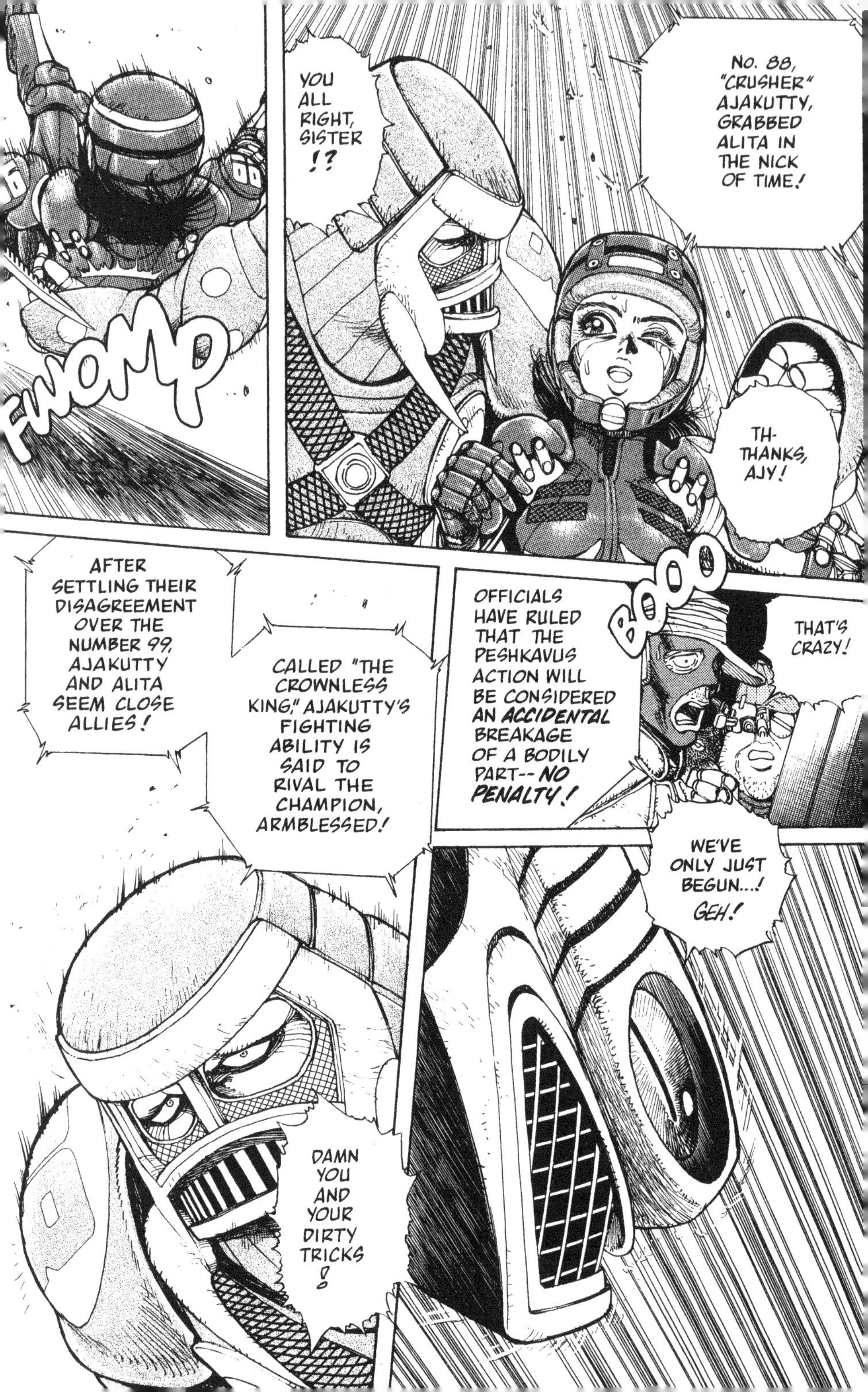
FWOMP
YOU ALL RIGHT, SISTER !?
NO. 88, "CRUSHER" AJAKUTTY, GRABBED ALITA IN THE NICK OF TIME!
TH-THANKS, AJY!
AFTER SETTLING THEIR DISAGREEMENT OVER THE NUMBER 99, AJAKUTTY AND ALITA SEEM CLOSE ALLIES!
CALLED "THE CROWNLESS KING," AJAKUTTY'S FIGHTING ABILITY IS SAID TO RIVAL THE CHAMPION, ARMBLESSED!
OFFICIALS HAVE RULED THAT THE PESHKAVUS ACTION WILL BE CONSIDERED AN ACCIDENTAL BREAKAGE OF A BODILY PART-- NO PENALTY!
BOOO
THAT'S CRAZY!
DAMN YOU AND YOUR DIRTY TRICKS !
WE'VE ONLY JUST BEGUN...! GEH!

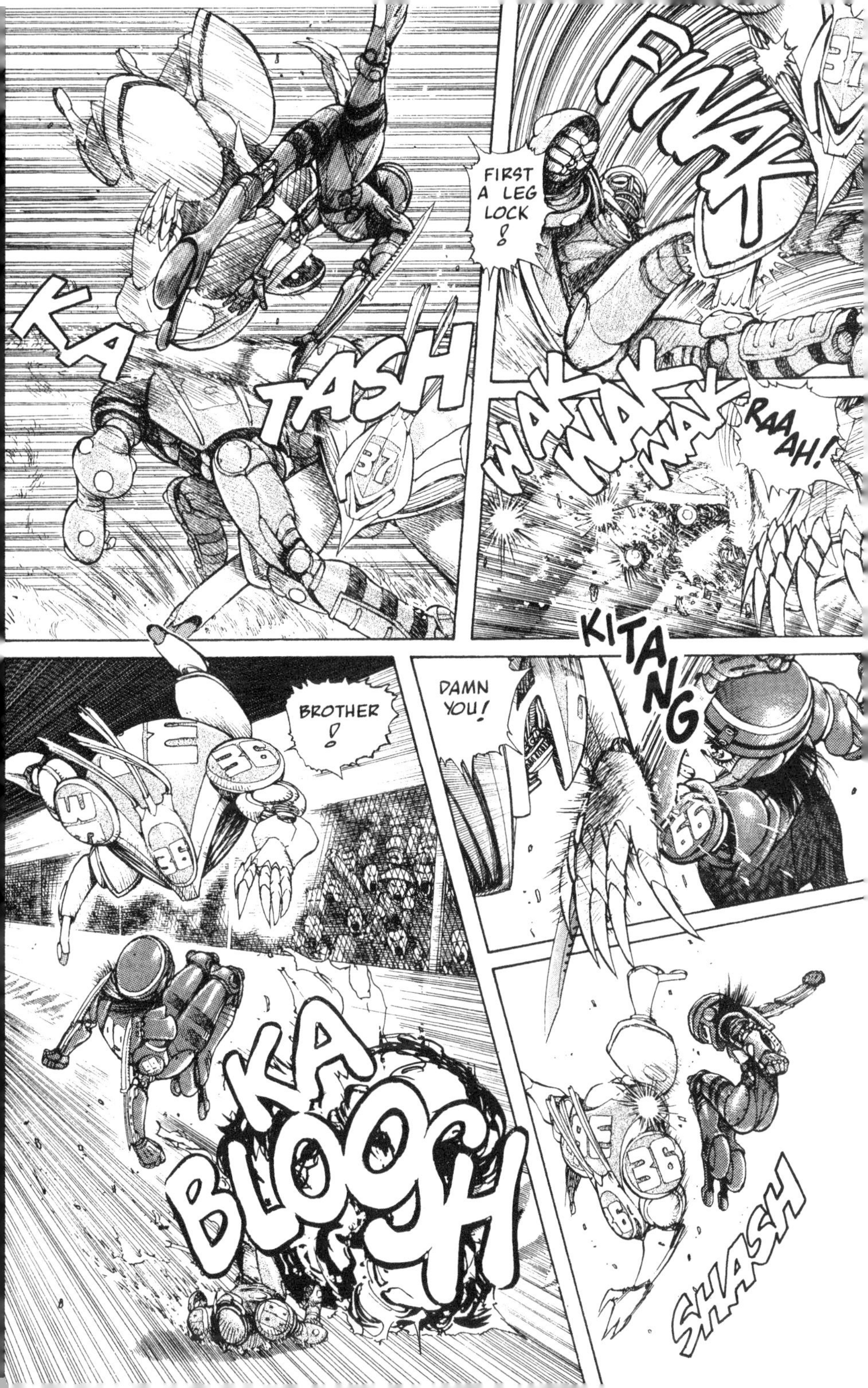
KA
TASH
FIRST A LEG LOCK!
FINAK
WAK WAK WAK
RAAAH!
KITANG
BROTHER!
DAMN YOU!
KA BLOOOH
SHASH

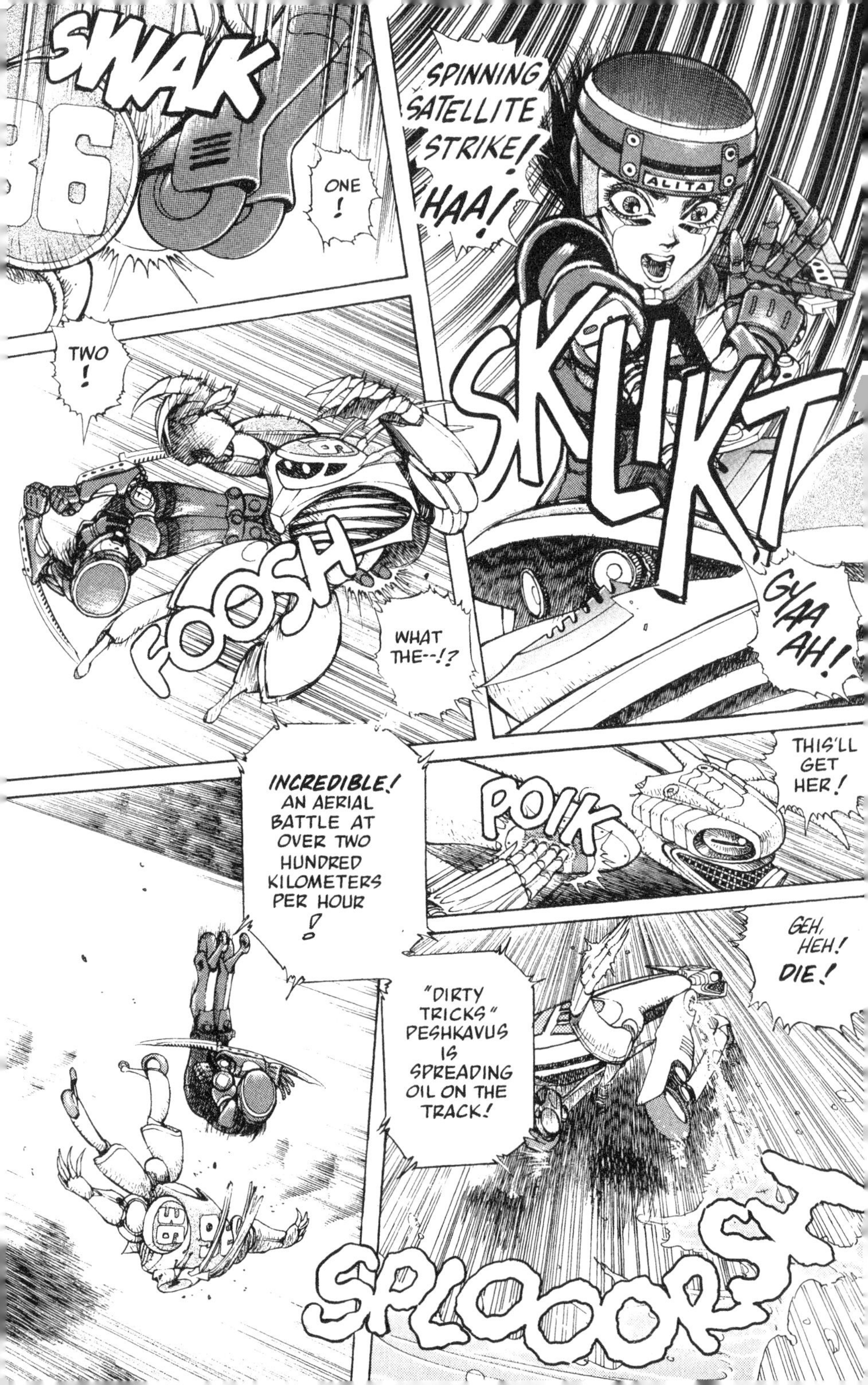
SWAK
ONE!
TWO!
FOOSH
WHAT THE--!?
SPINNING SATELLITE STRIKE!
HAA!
SKLIKT
GYAAAH!
INCREDIBLE! AN AERIAL BATTLE AT OVER TWO HUNDRED KILOMETERS PER HOUR!
THIS'LL GET HER!
POIK
GEH, HEH! DIE!
"DIRTY TRICKS" PESHKAVUS IS SPREADING OIL ON THE TRACK!
SPLOOORSH

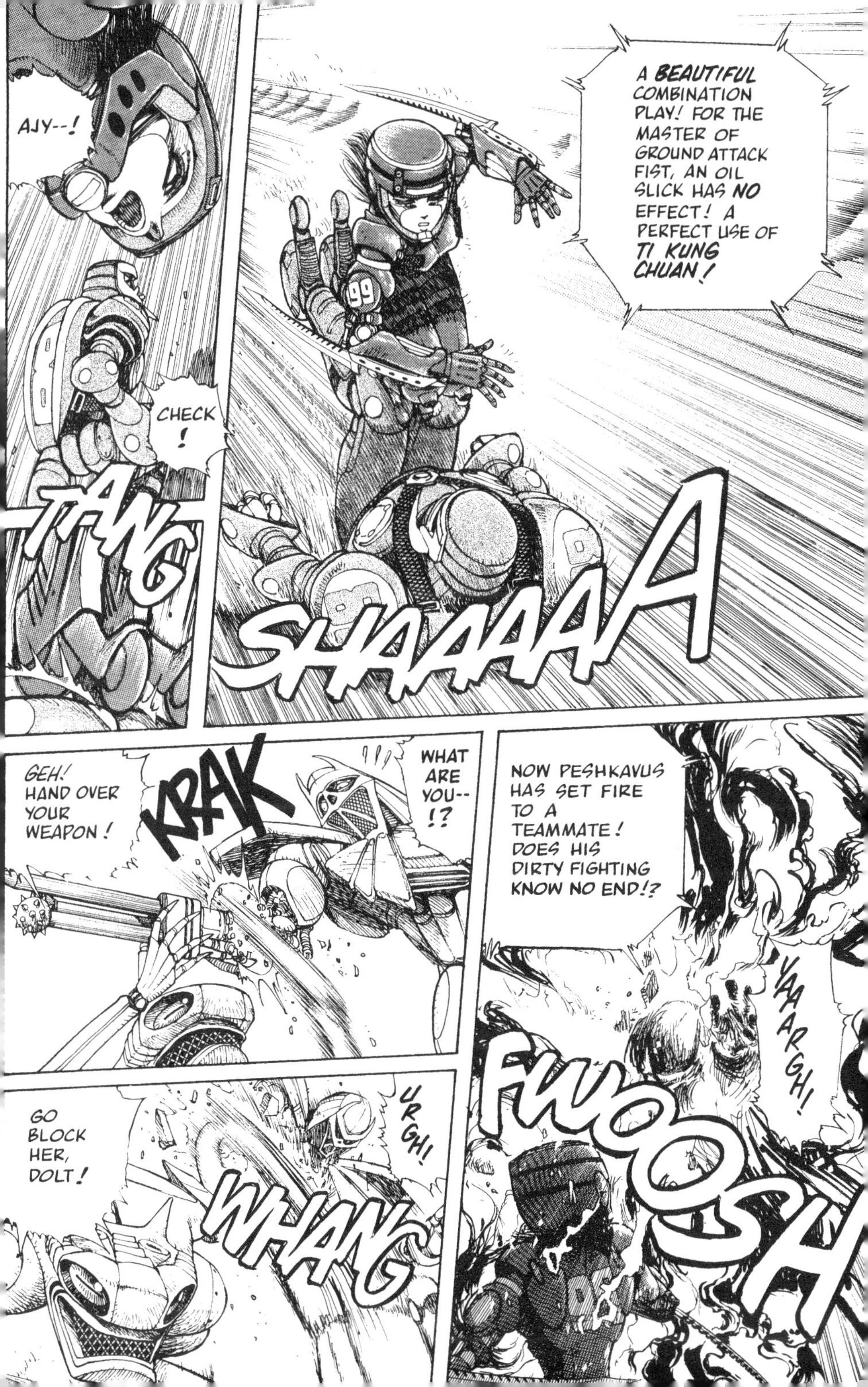
AJY--!
CHECK!
TANG
A BEAUTIFUL COMBINATION PLAY! FOR THE MASTER OF GROUND ATTACK FIST, AN OIL SLICK HAS NO EFFECT! A PERFECT USE OF TI KUNG CHUAN!
SHAAAAAA
GEH! HAND OVER YOUR WEAPON!
KRAK
WHAT ARE YOU--!?
NOW PESHKAVUS HAS SET FIRE TO A TEAMMATE! DOES HIS DIRTY FIGHTING KNOW NO END!?
YAAARGH!
FWOOOSH
GO BLOCK HER, DOLT!
URGH!
WHANG

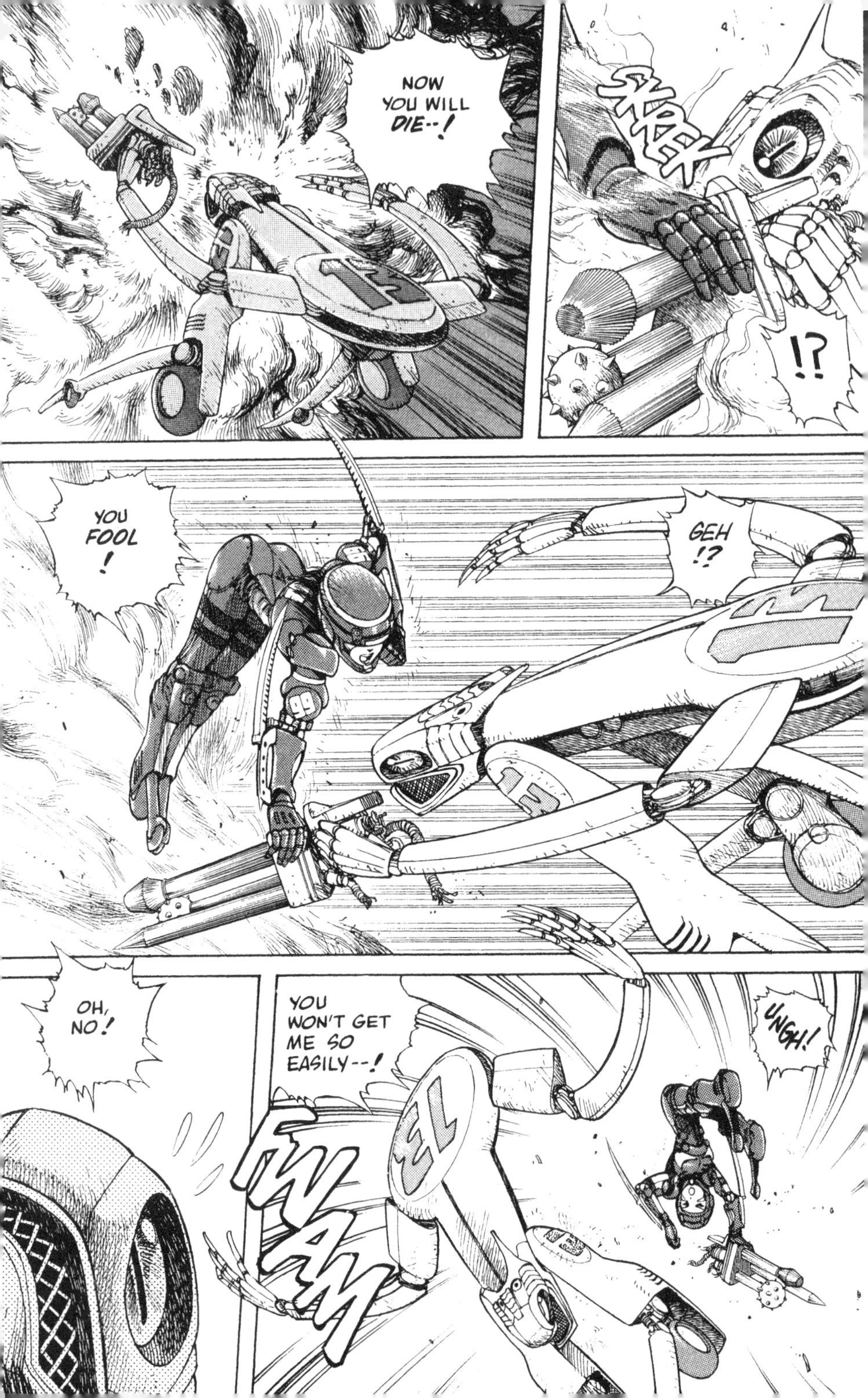
NOW YOU WILL DIE--!
SKREEK
!?
YOU FOOL !
GEH !?
OH, NO!
YOU WON'T GET ME SO EASILY--!
WAM
UNGH!

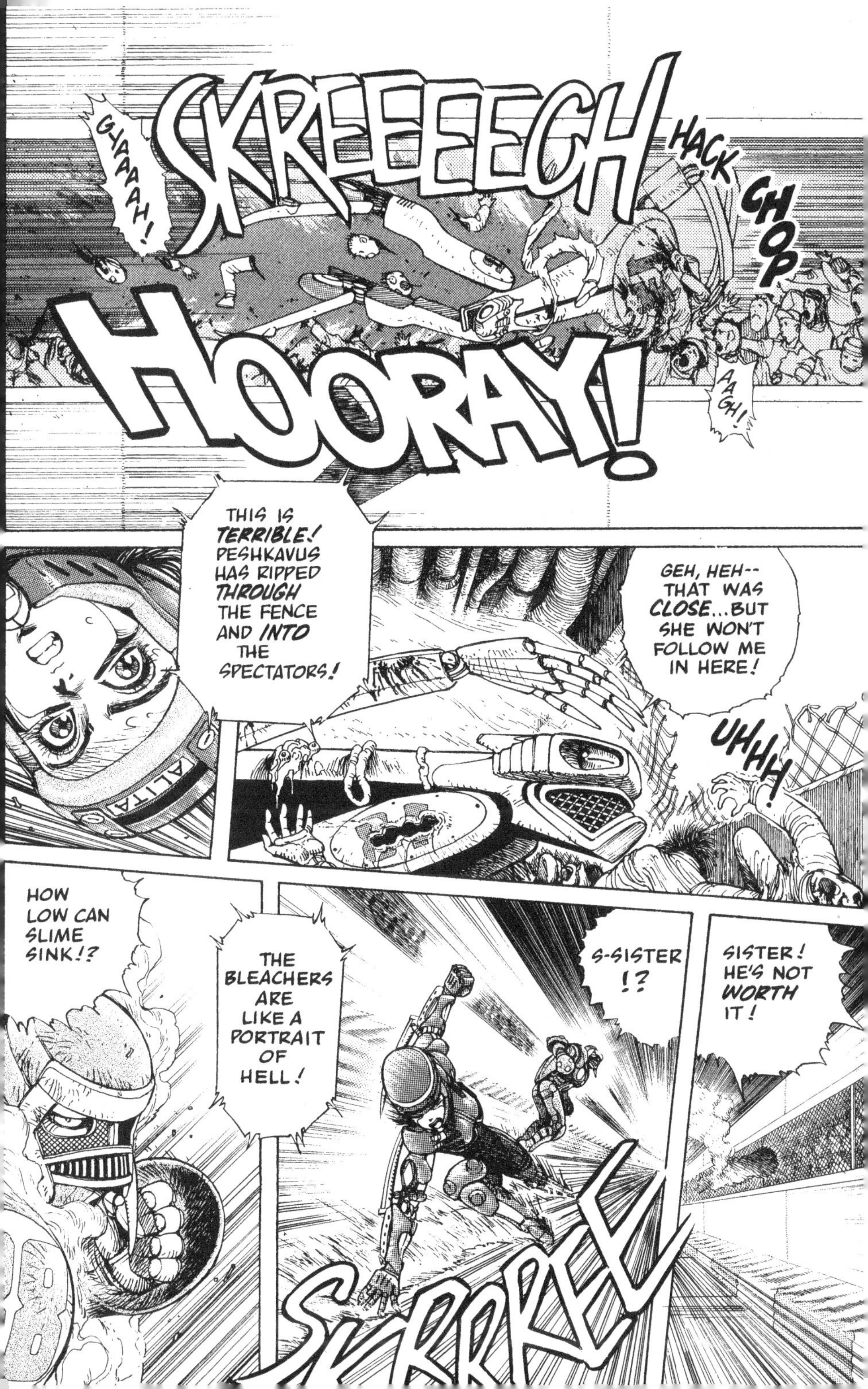
GYAAAAH!
SKREEEECH
HACK
CHOP
HOORAY!
AAGH!
THIS IS TERRIBLE! PESHKAVUS HAS RIPPED THROUGH THE FENCE AND INTO THE SPECTATORS!
ALITA
GEH, HEH-- THAT WAS CLOSE...BUT SHE WON'T FOLLOW ME IN HERE!
UHHH
HOW LOW CAN SLIME SINK!?
THE BLEACHERS ARE LIKE A PORTRAIT OF HELL!
S-SISTER !?
SISTER! HE'S NOT WORTH IT!
SKRRREE

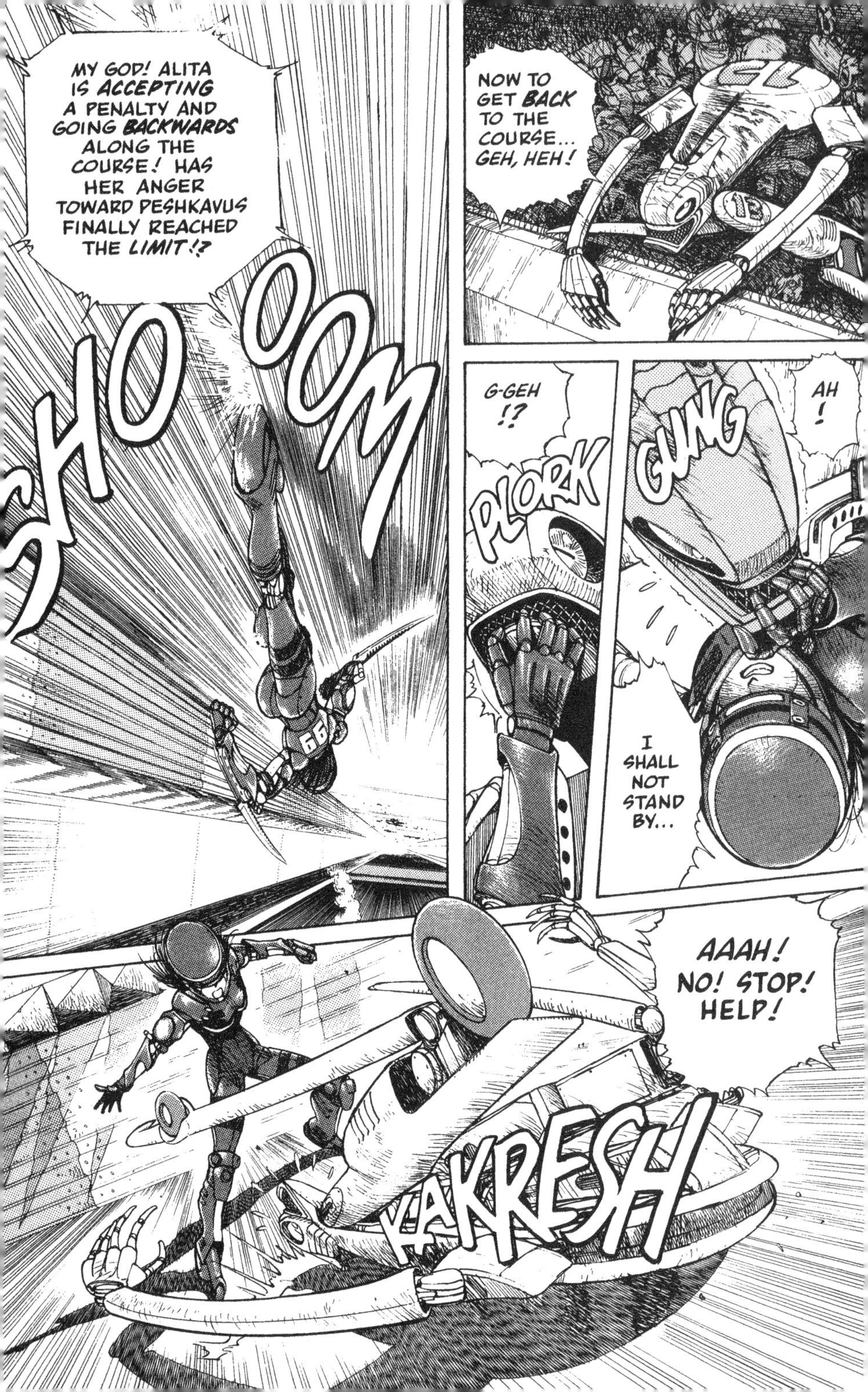
MY GOD! ALITA IS *ACCEPTING* A PENALTY AND GOING *BACKWARDS* ALONG THE COURSE! HAS HER ANGER TOWARD PESHKAVUS FINALLY REACHED THE *LIMIT*!?
SHOOOOM
NOW TO GET *BACK* TO THE COURSE... GEH, HEH!
G-GEH !?
PLORK
GUNG
AH !
I SHALL NOT STAND BY...
AAAH! NO! STOP! HELP!
KAKRESH

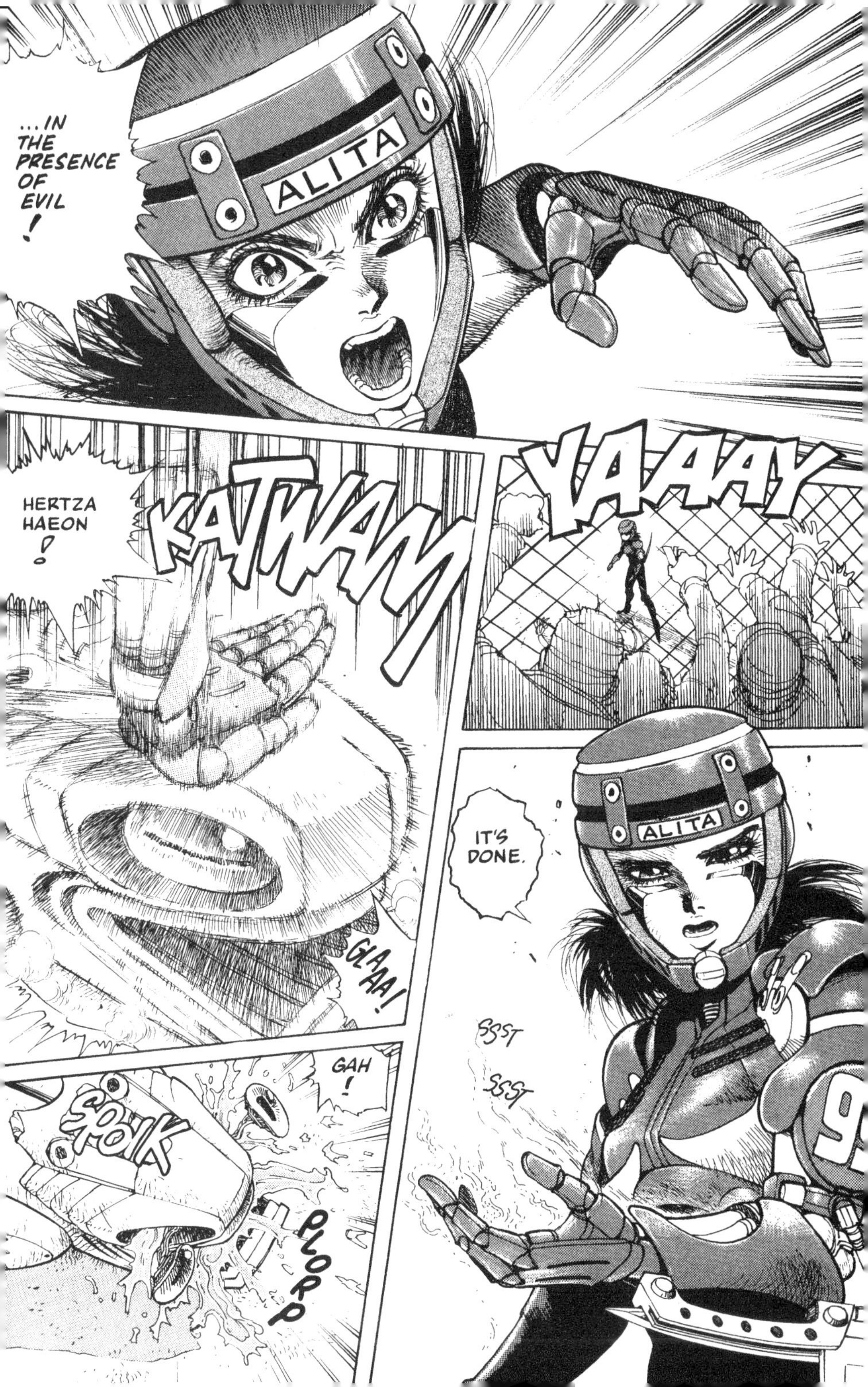
...IN THE PRESENCE OF EVIL!
HERTZA HAEON!
KATWAM
YAAAY
GLAAA!
IT'S DONE.
SSST
SSST
GAH!
SPOIK
PLORP

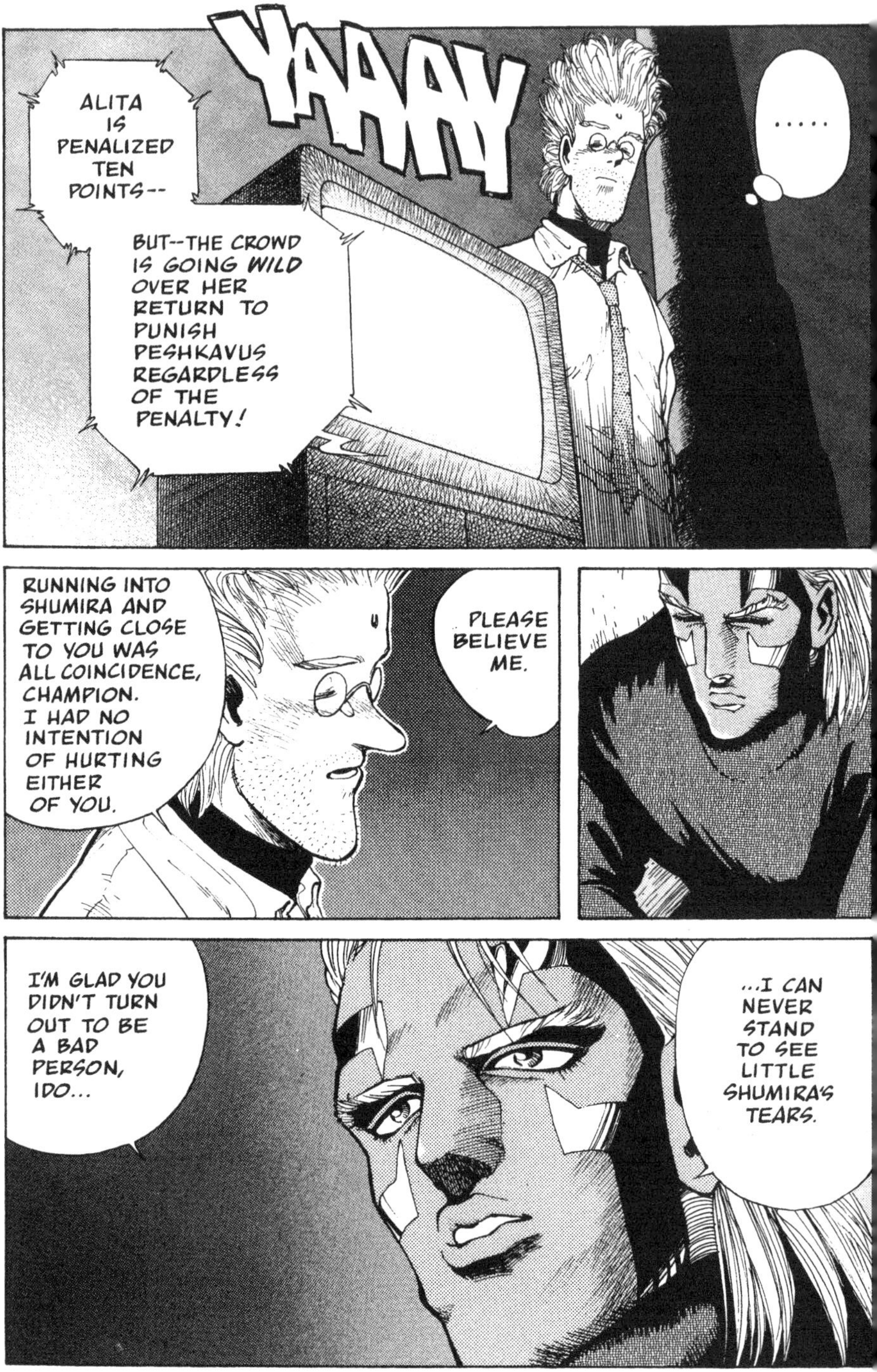
YAAAY
ALITA IS PENALIZED TEN POINTS--
BUT--THE CROWD IS GOING WILD OVER HER RETURN TO PUNISH PESHKAVUS REGARDLESS OF THE PENALTY!
.....
RUNNING INTO SHUMIRA AND GETTING CLOSE TO YOU WAS ALL COINCIDENCE, CHAMPION. I HAD NO INTENTION OF HURTING EITHER OF YOU.
..PLEASE BELIEVE ME.
I'M GLAD YOU DIDN'T TURN OUT TO BE A BAD PERSON, IDO...
...I CAN NEVER STAND TO SEE LITTLE SHUMIRA'S TEARS.

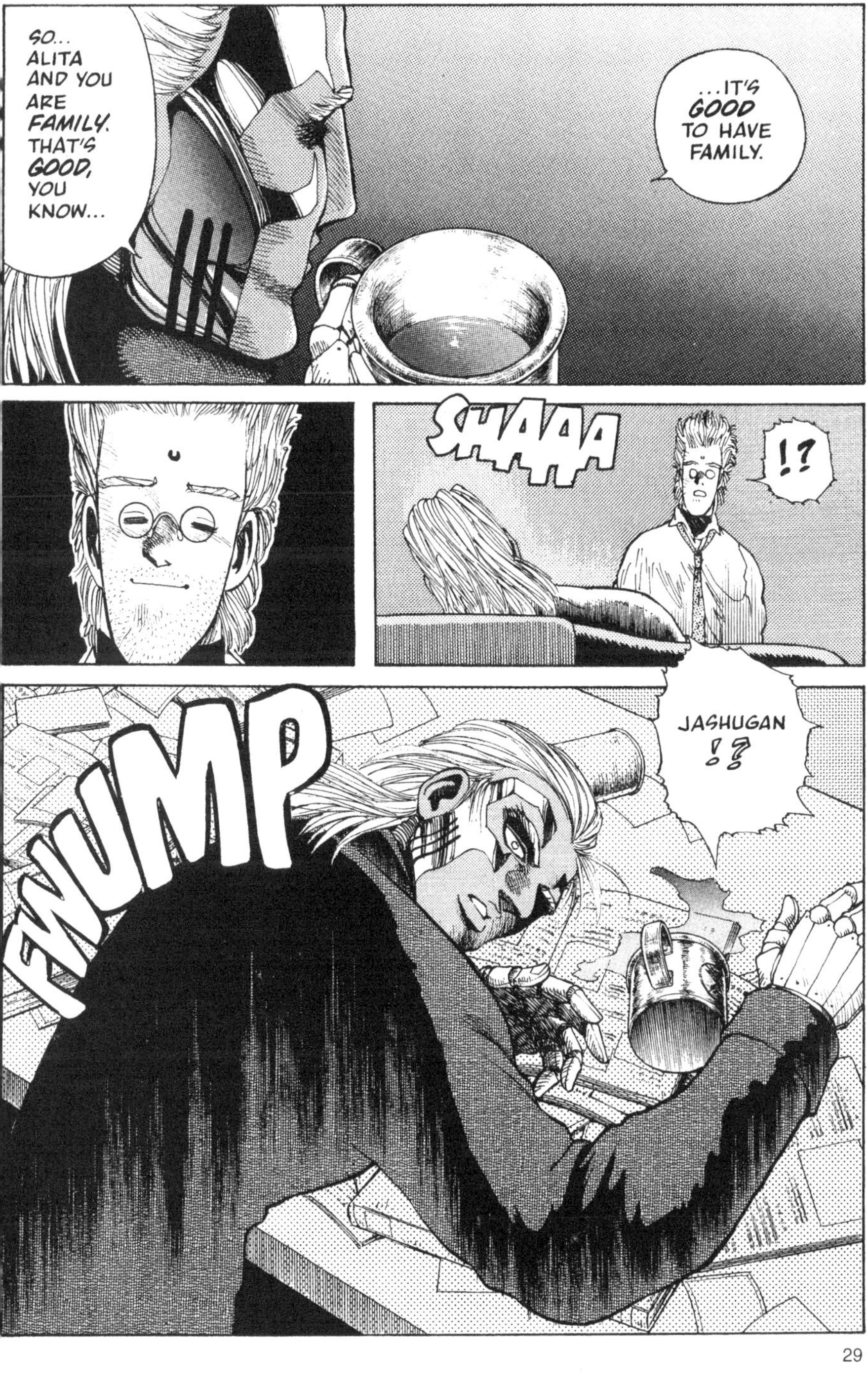
SO... ALITA AND YOU ARE FAMILY. THAT'S GOOD, YOU KNOW...
...IT'S GOOD TO HAVE FAMILY.
SHAAAA
!?
FWUMP
JASHUGAN !?

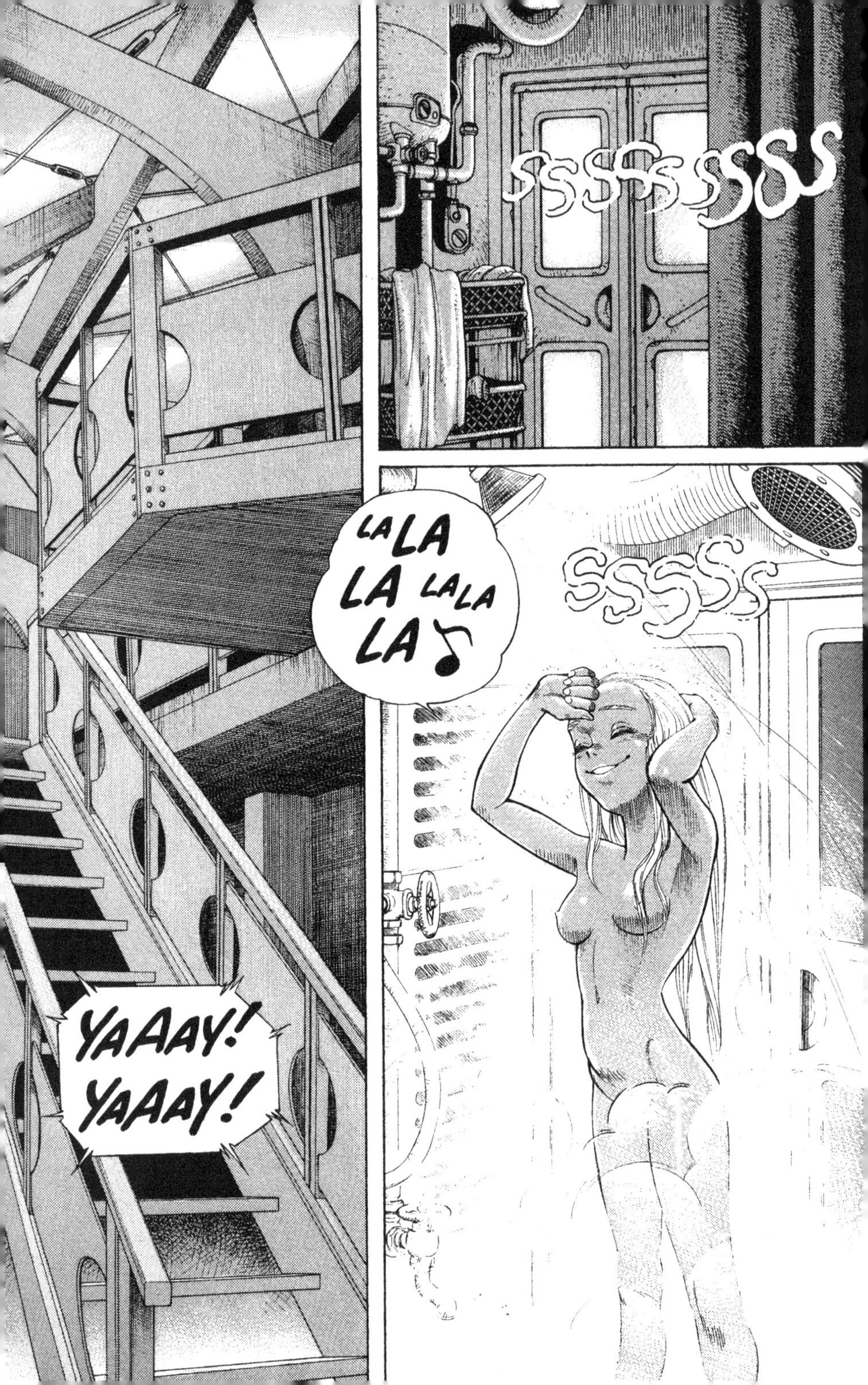
YAAAY! YAAAY!
SSSSSSSSS
LA LA LA LA LA LA ♪
SSSSS

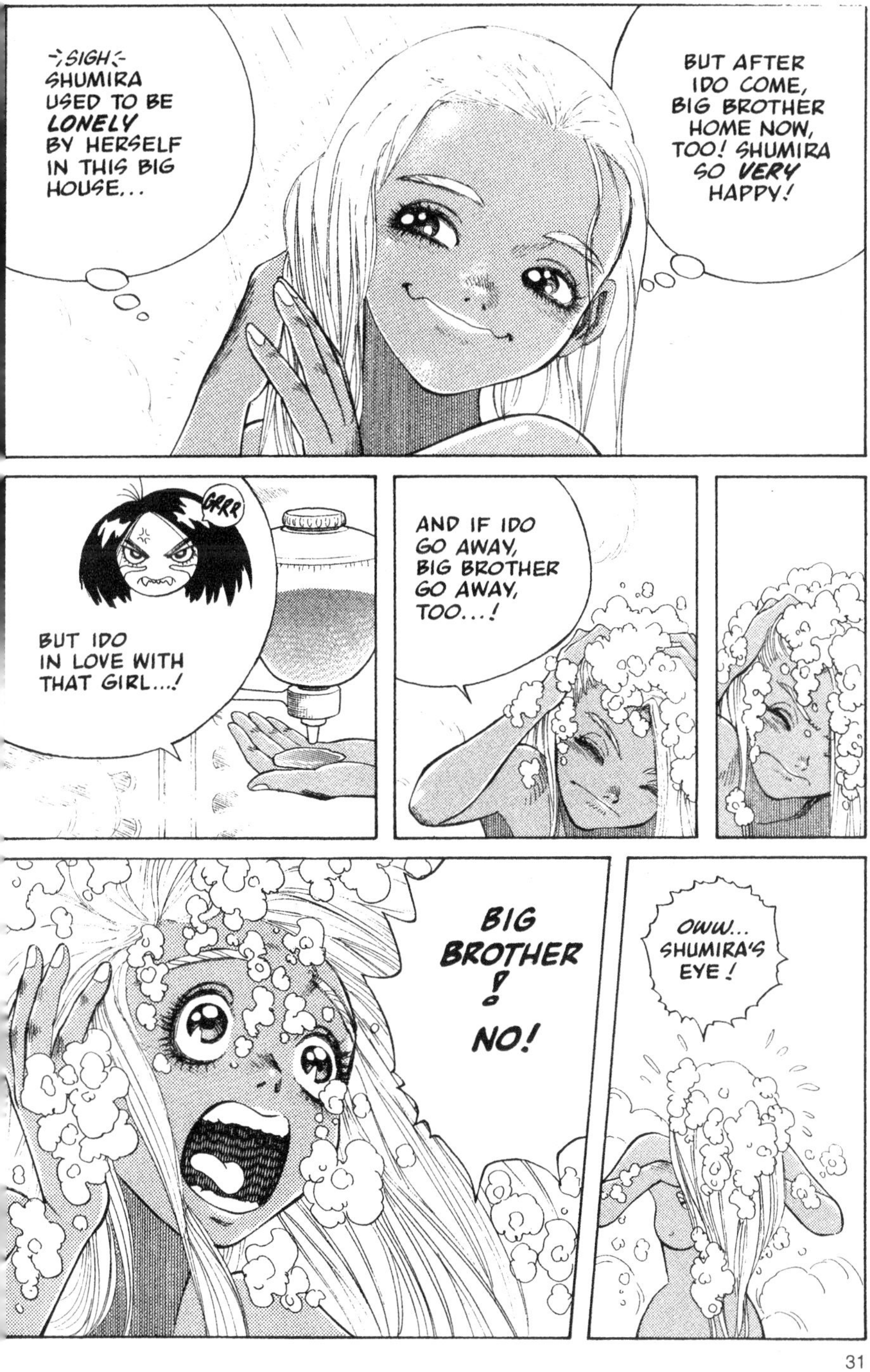

SIGH
SHUMIRA USED TO BE LONELY BY HERSELF IN THIS BIG HOUSE...
BUT AFTER IDO COME, BIG BROTHER HOME NOW, TOO! SHUMIRA SO VERY HAPPY!
GRRR
BUT IDO IN LOVE WITH THAT GIRL...!
AND IF IDO GO AWAY, BIG BROTHER GO AWAY, TOO...!
BIG BROTHER! NO!
OWW... SHUMIRA'S EYE!

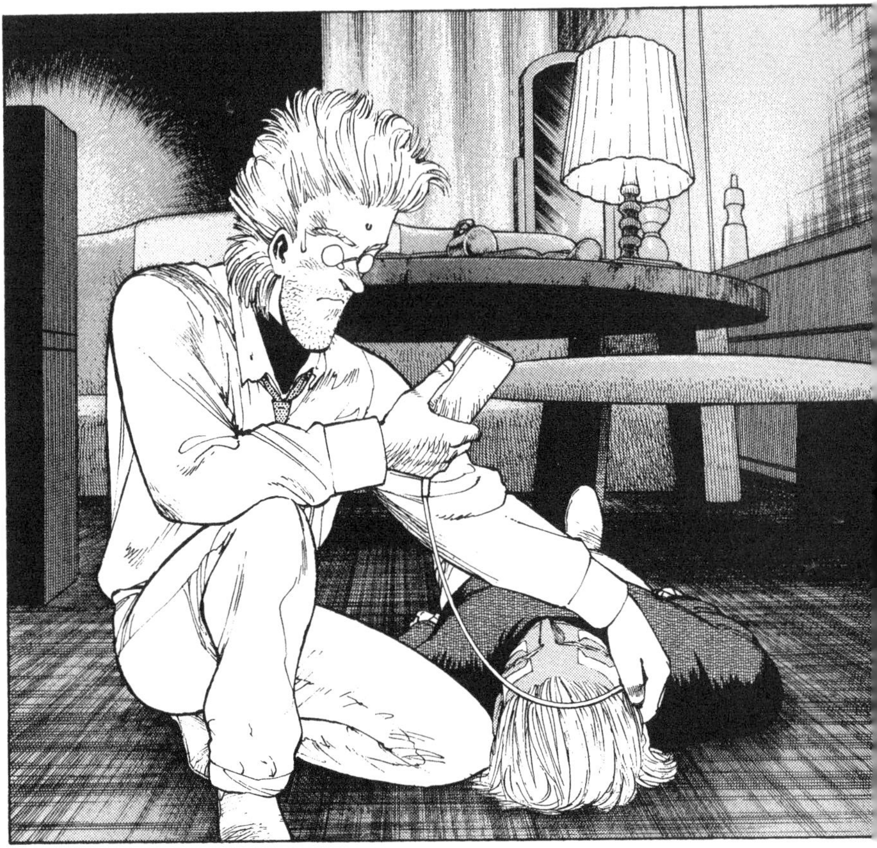

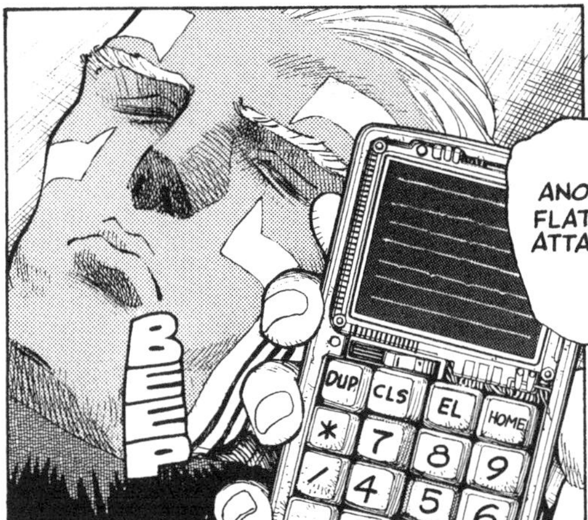
BEEP
DUP
CLS
EL
HOME
ANOTHER FLATLINE ATTACK...!

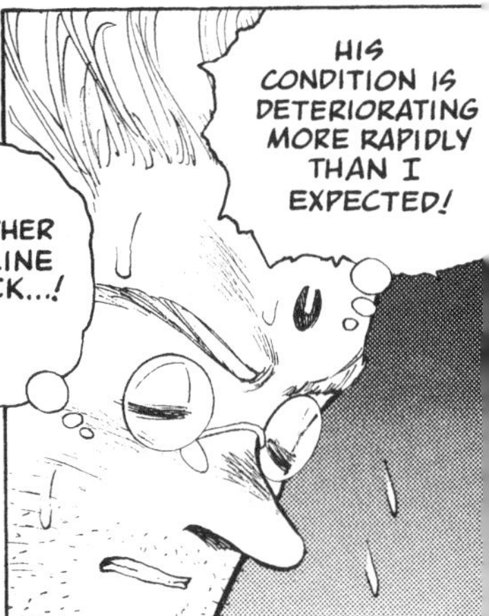
HIS CONDITION IS DETERIORATING MORE RAPIDLY THAN I EXPECTED!

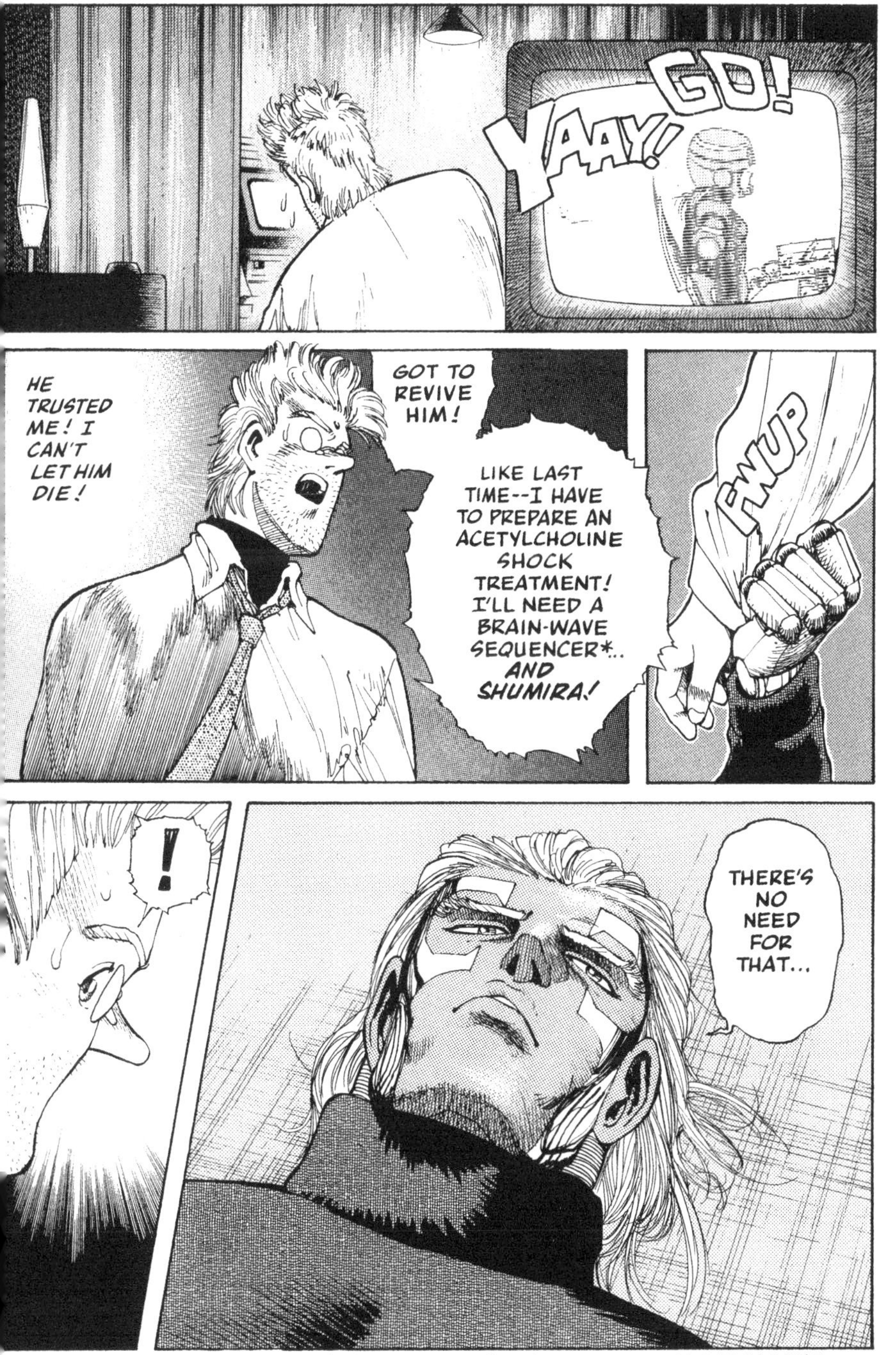
YAAY!
GO!
HE TRUSTED ME! I CAN'T LET HIM DIE!
GOT TO REVIVE HIM!
LIKE LAST TIME--I HAVE TO PREPARE AN ACETYLCHOLINE SHOCK TREATMENT! I'LL NEED A BRAIN-WAVE SEQUENCER*... AND SHUMIRA!
FWUP
!
THERE'S NO NEED FOR THAT...

*USED TO TAKE A PRE-SAMPLED BRAIN WAVE, MODIFY IT, AND OUTPUT IT TO THE PATIENT.

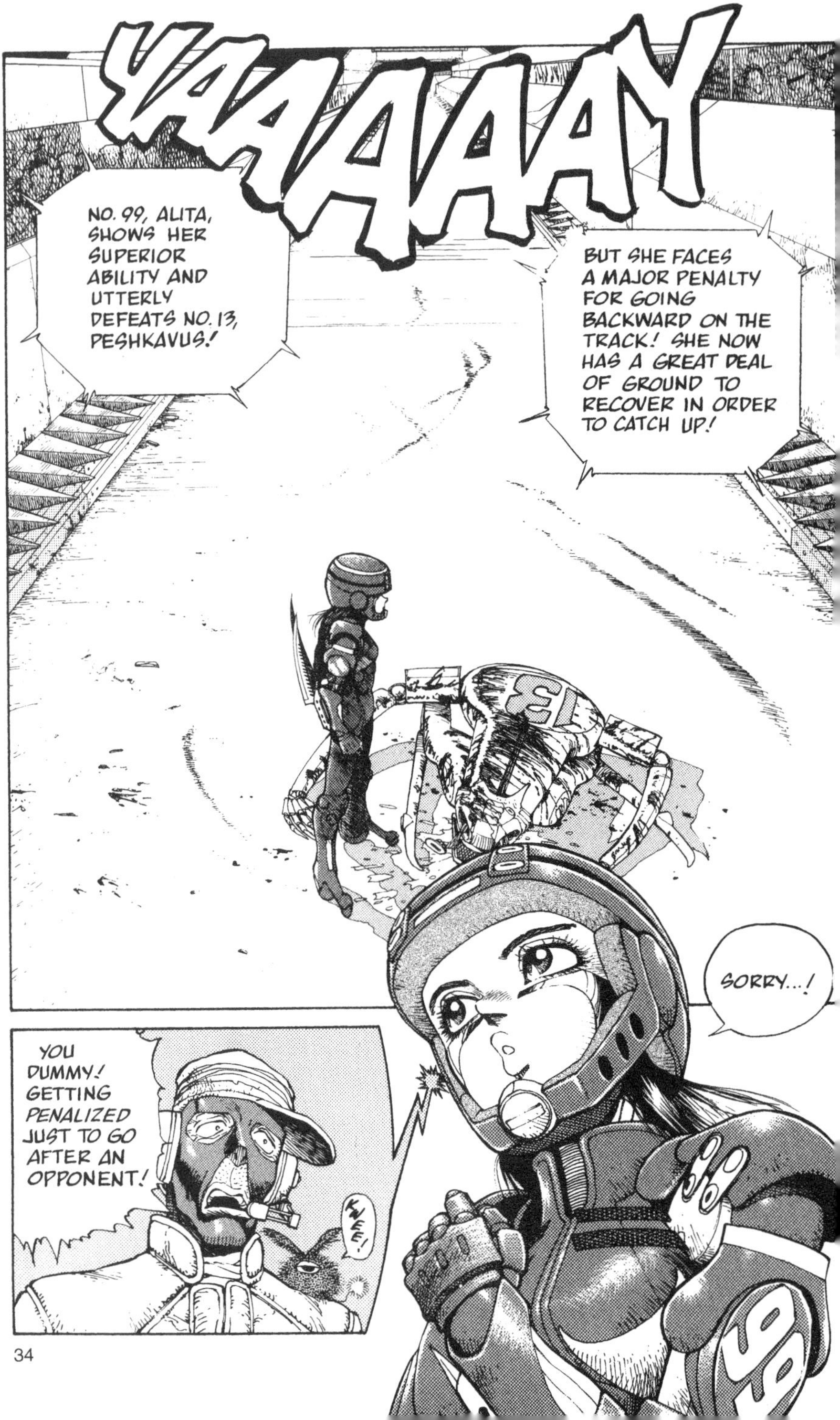
YAAAAAAY
NO. 99, ALITA, SHOWS HER SUPERIOR ABILITY AND UTTERLY DEFEATS NO. 13, PESHKAVUS!
BUT SHE FACES A MAJOR PENALTY FOR GOING BACKWARD ON THE TRACK! SHE NOW HAS A GREAT DEAL OF GROUND TO RECOVER IN ORDER TO CATCH UP!
SORRY...!
YOU DUMMY! GETTING PENALIZED JUST TO GO AFTER AN OPPONENT!
KWEE!

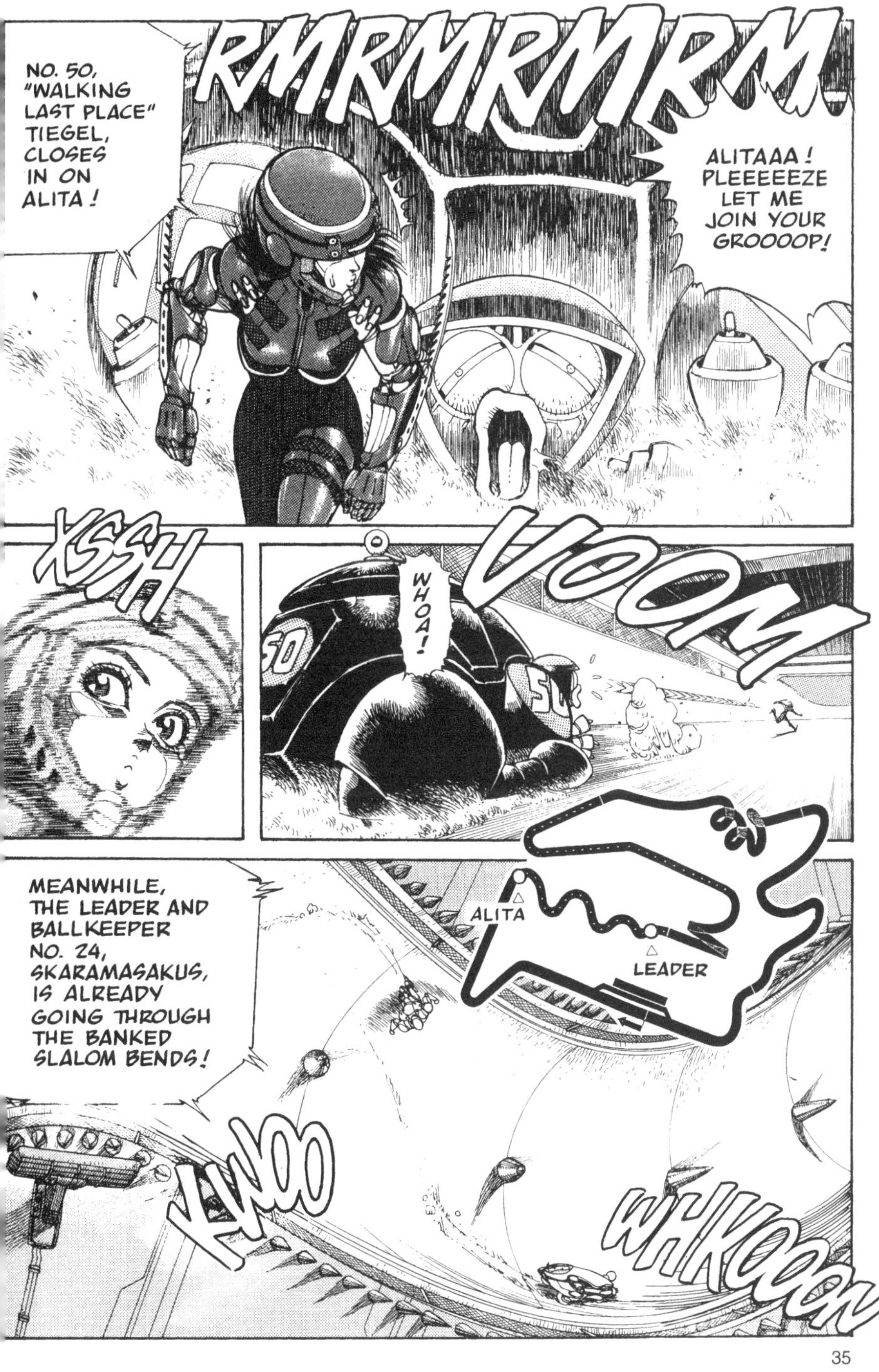
NO. 50, "WALKING LAST PLACE" TIEGEL, CLOSES IN ON ALITA!
RMRMRMRMRM
ALITAAA! PLEEEEEZE LET ME JOIN YOUR GROOOOP!
XSSH
WHOA!
VOOM
MEANWHILE, THE LEADER AND BALLKEEPER NO. 24, SKARAMASAKUS, IS ALREADY GOING THROUGH THE BANKED SLALOM BENDS!
ALITA
LEADER
KWOO
WHKOOON

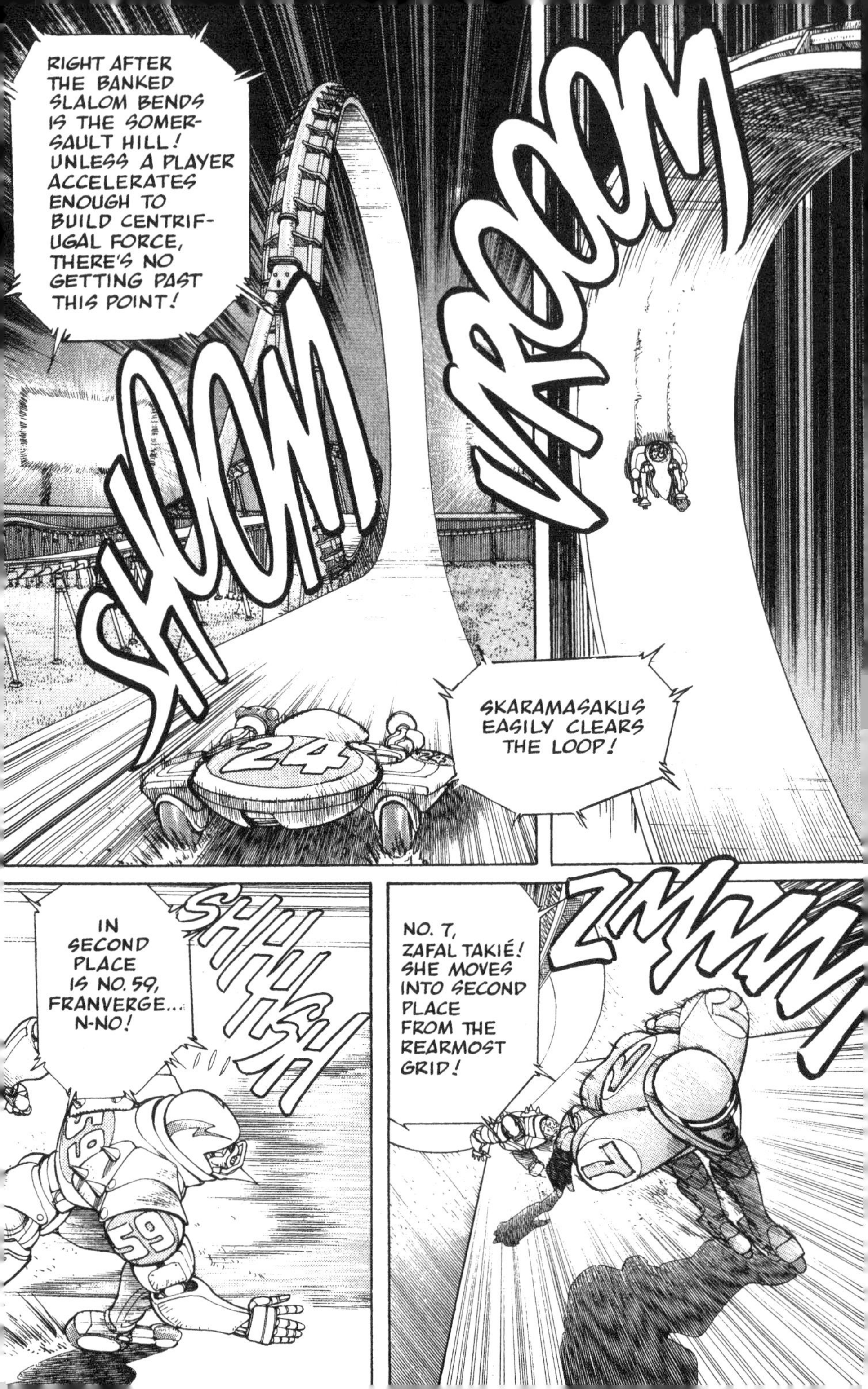
RIGHT AFTER THE BANKED SLALOM BENDS IS THE SOMER-SAULT HILL! UNLESS A PLAYER ACCELERATES ENOUGH TO BUILD CENTRIF-UGAL FORCE, THERE'S NO GETTING PAST THIS POINT!
SHOOM
VROOOM
SKARAMASAKUS EASILY CLEARS THE LOOP!
IN SECOND PLACE IS NO. 59, FRANVERGE... N-NO!
SHHHH
NO. 7, ZAFAL TAKIÉ! SHE MOVES INTO SECOND PLACE FROM THE REARMOST GRID!
ZMMM

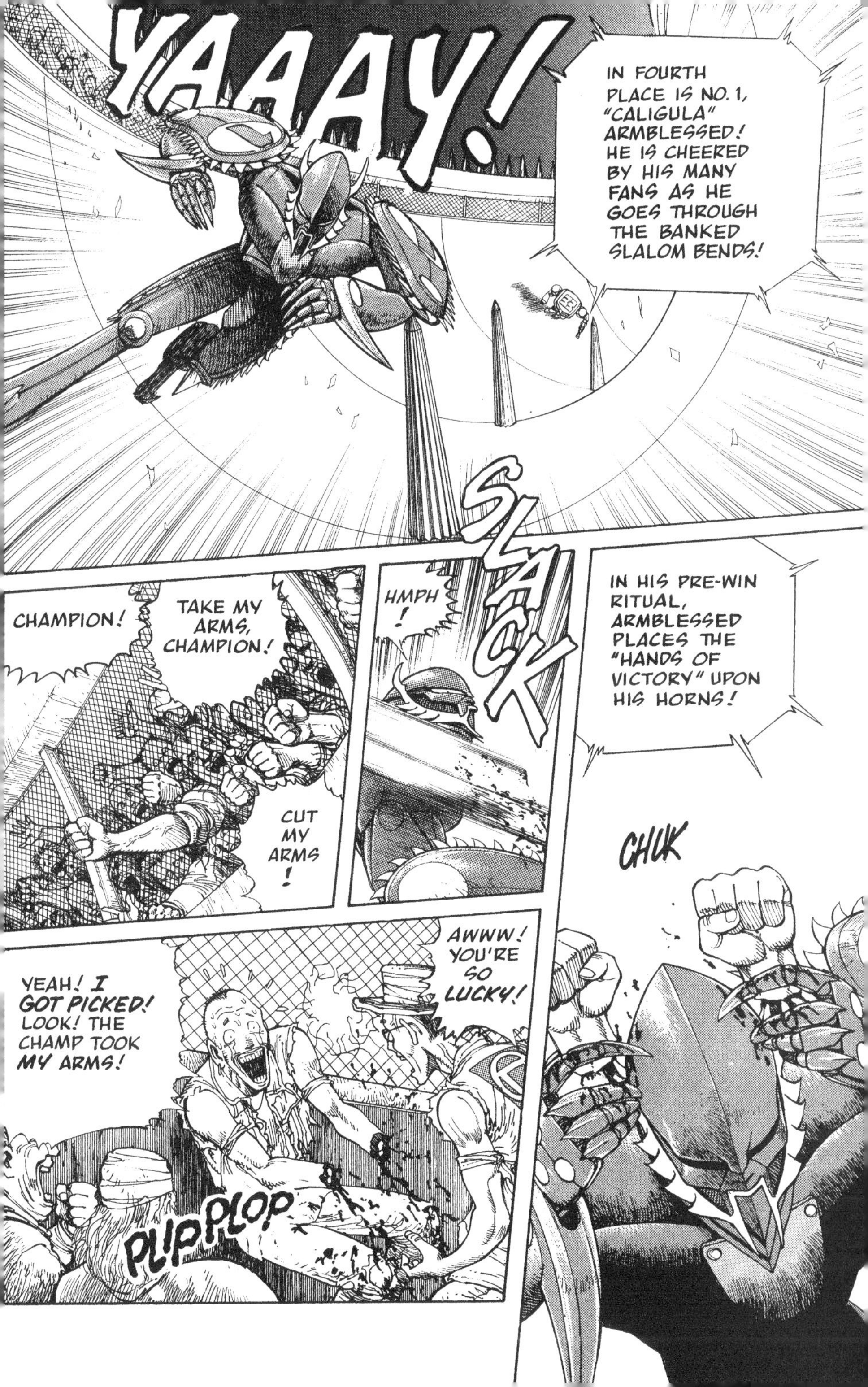
YAAAY!
IN FOURTH PLACE IS NO. 1, "CALIGULA" ARMBLESSED! HE IS CHEERED BY HIS MANY FANS AS HE GOES THROUGH THE BANKED SLALOM BENDS!
SLAACK
CHAMPION!
TAKE MY ARMS, CHAMPION!
CUT MY ARMS!
HMPH!
IN HIS PRE-WIN RITUAL, ARMBLESSED PLACES THE "HANDS OF VICTORY" UPON HIS HORNS!
YEAH! I GOT PICKED! LOOK! THE CHAMP TOOK MY ARMS!
AWWW! YOU'RE SO LUCKY!
PLIP PLOP
CHUK

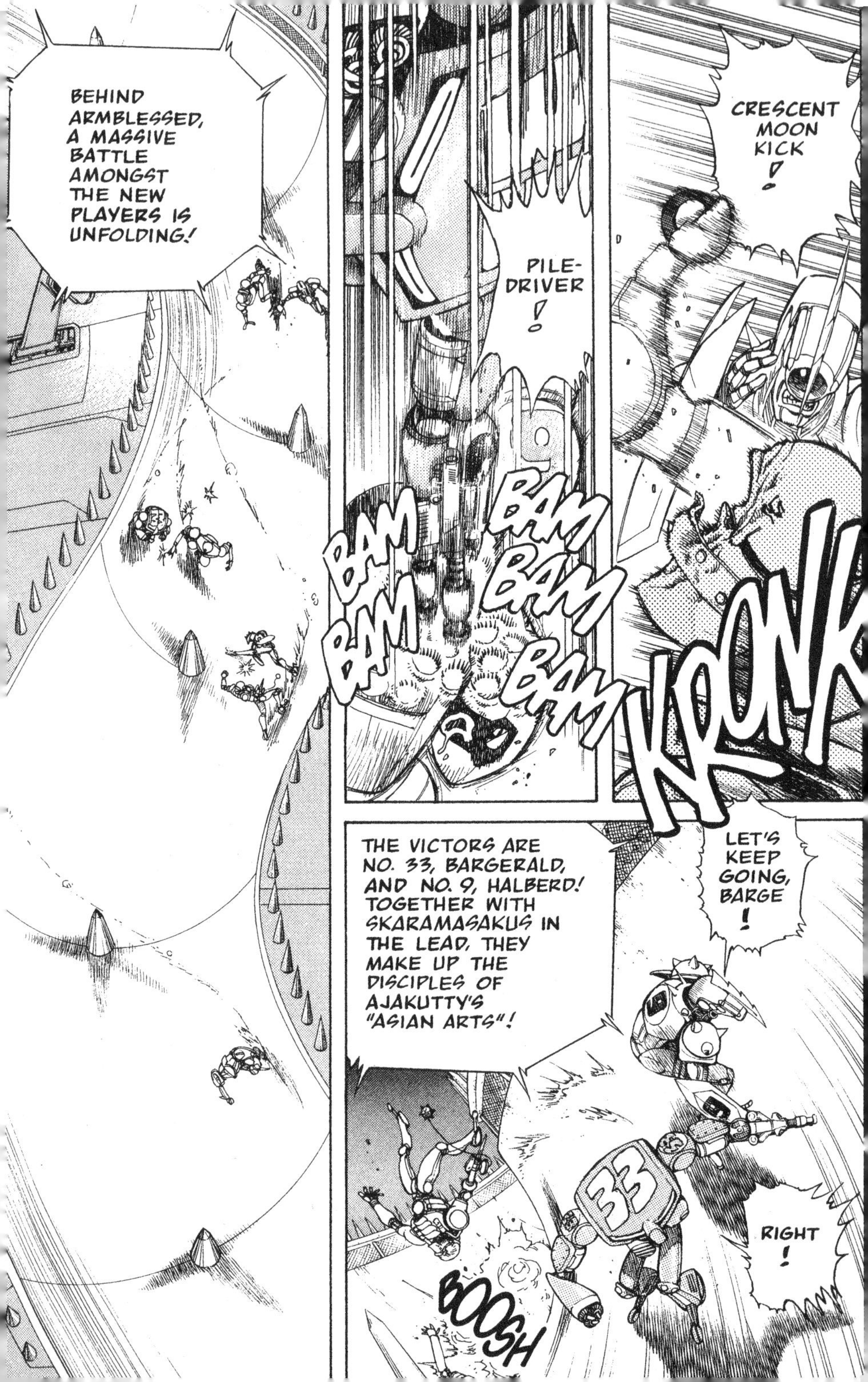
BEHIND ARMBLESSED, A MASSIVE BATTLE AMONGST THE NEW PLAYERS IS UNFOLDING!
PILE-DRIVER!
BAM BAM
BAM BAM BAM BAM
CRESCENT MOON KICK!
KRONK
THE VICTORS ARE NO. 33, BARGERALD, AND NO. 9, HALBERD! TOGETHER WITH SKARAMASAKUS IN THE LEAD, THEY MAKE UP THE DISCIPLES OF AJAKUTTY'S "ASIAN ARTS"!
LET'S KEEP GOING, BARGE!
RIGHT!
BOOSH

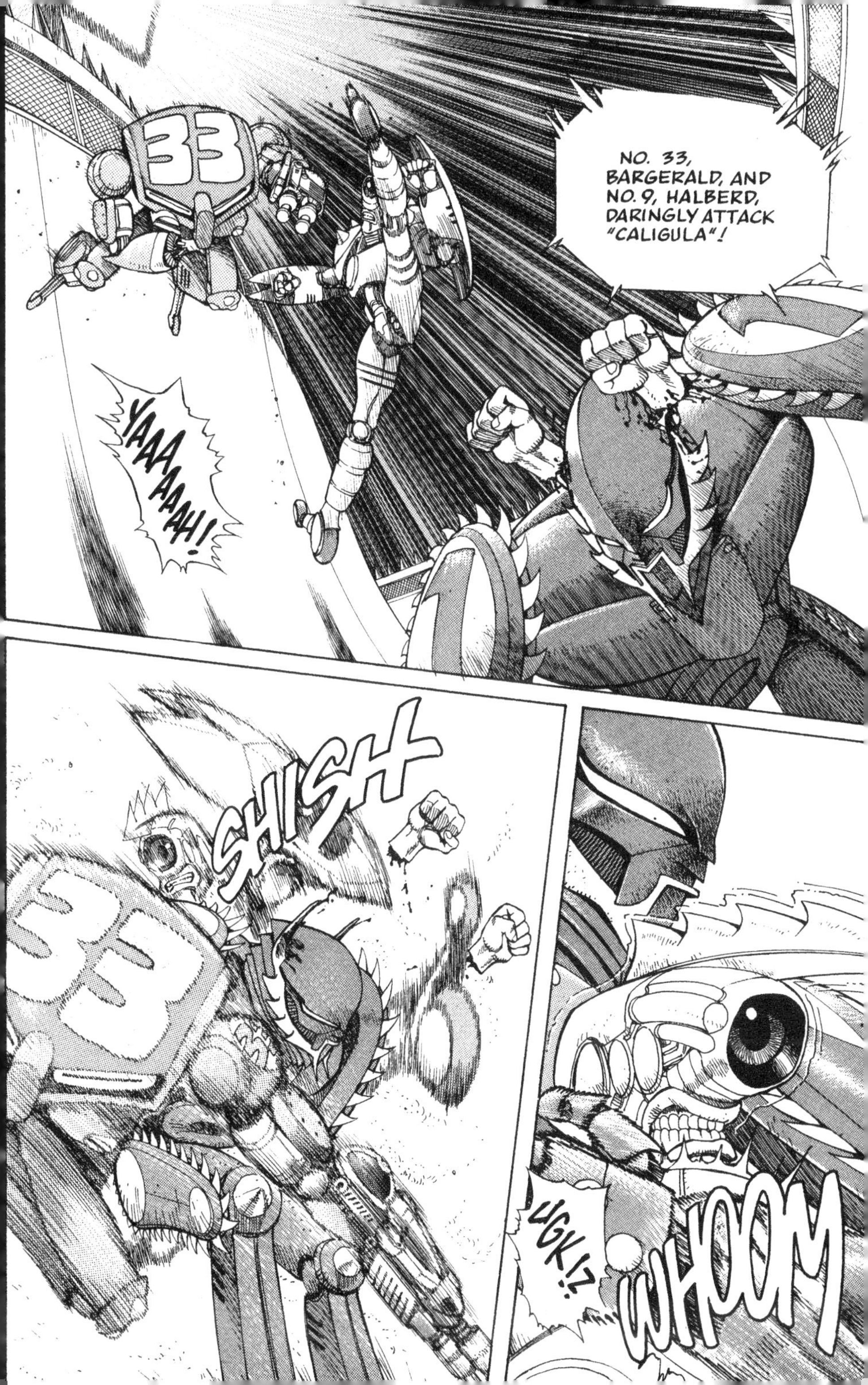
NO. 33, BARGERALD, AND NO. 9, HALBERD, DARINGLY ATTACK "CALIGULA"!
YAAAAAAAH!
SHISH
UGK!?
WHOOM

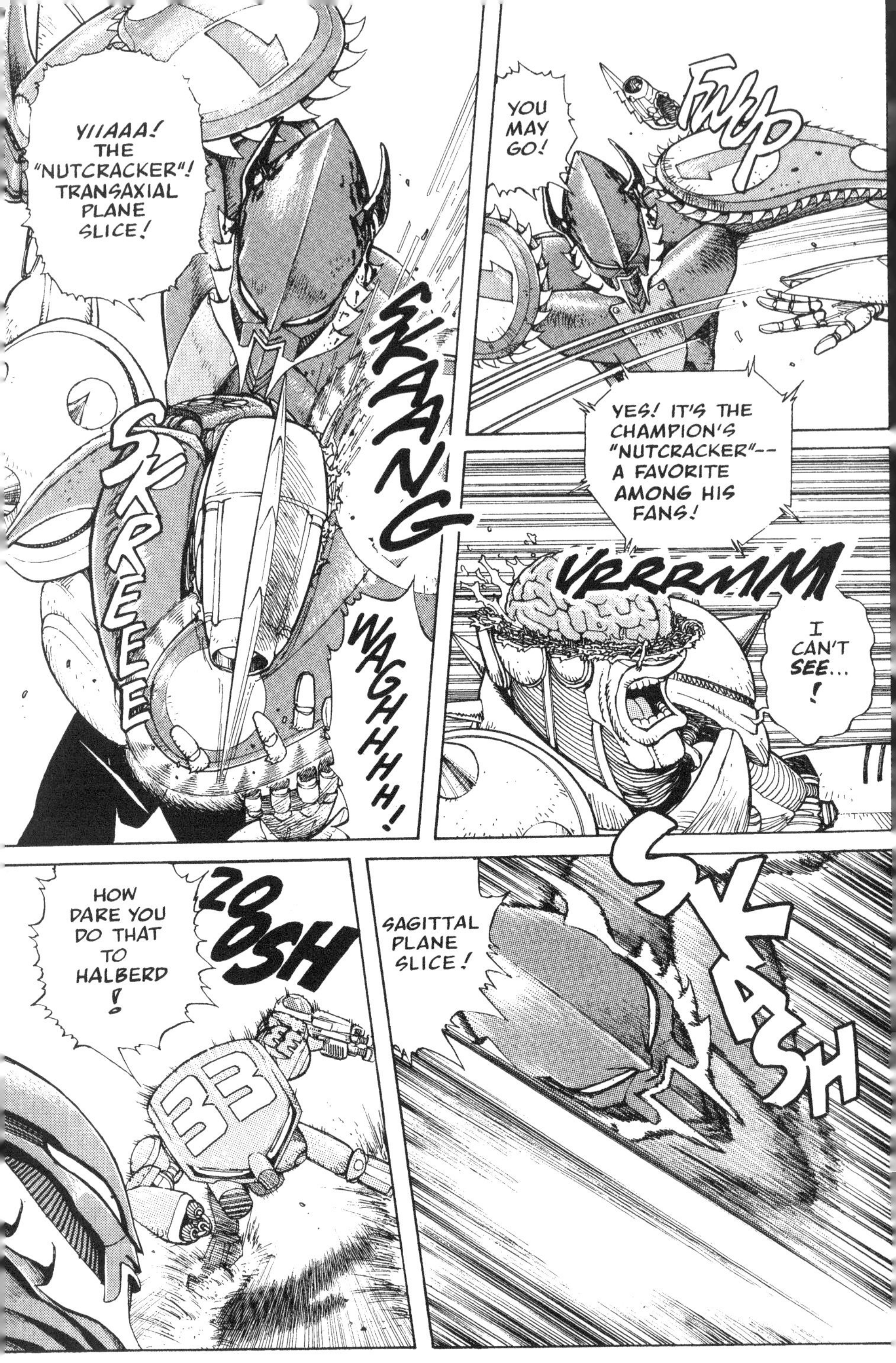
YIIAAA! THE "NUTCRACKER"! TRANSAXIAL PLANE SLICE!
SKRAANG
SKREEEE
WAGHHHHH!
YOU MAY GO!
FWUP
YES! IT'S THE CHAMPION'S "NUTCRACKER"-- A FAVORITE AMONG HIS FANS!
VRRRMM
I CAN'T SEE...!
HOW DARE YOU DO THAT TO HALBERD!
ZOOSH
SAGITTAL PLANE SLICE!
SKASH

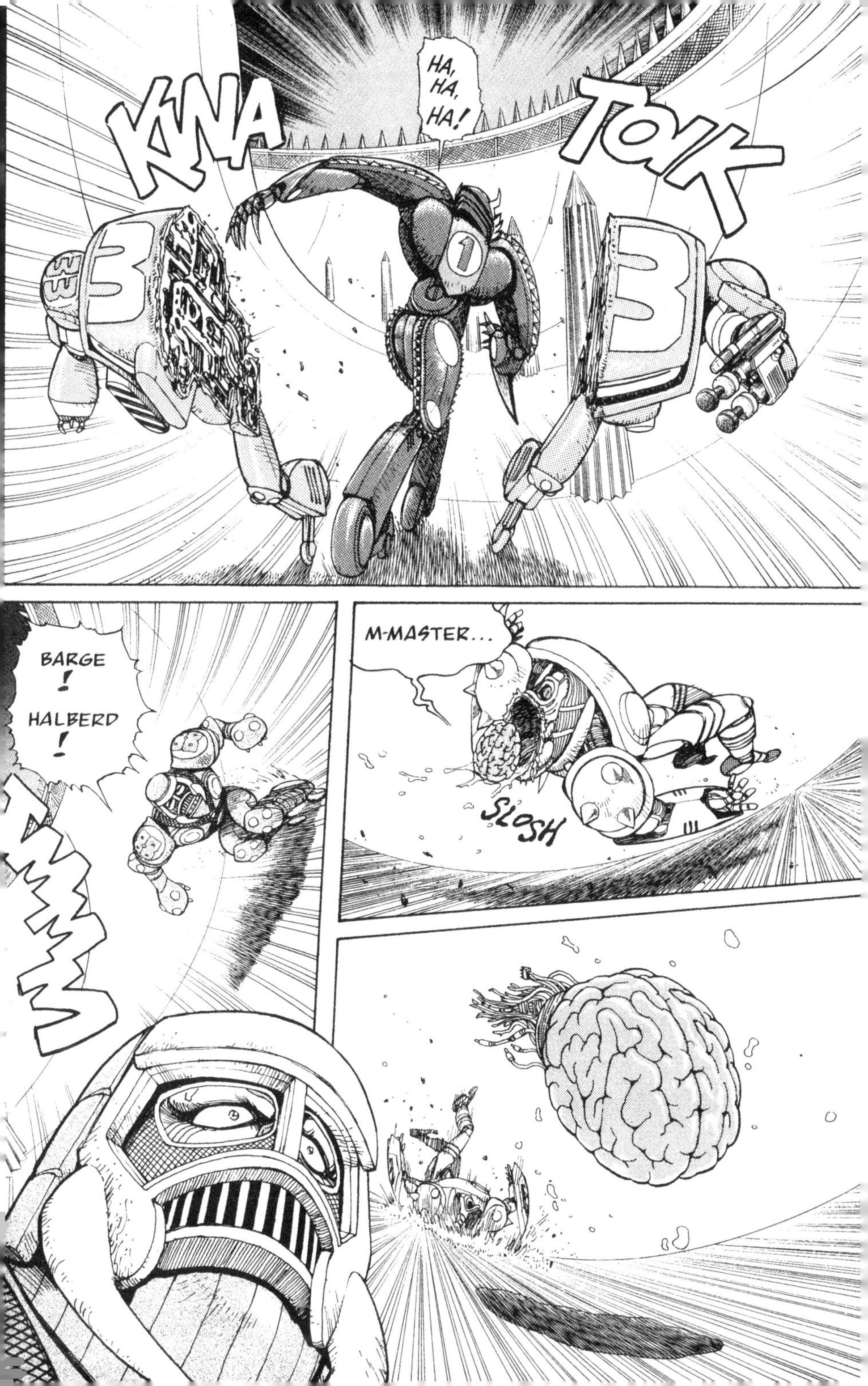
KWA
HA, HA, HA!
TOK
BARGE! HALBERD!
M-MASTER...
SLOSH

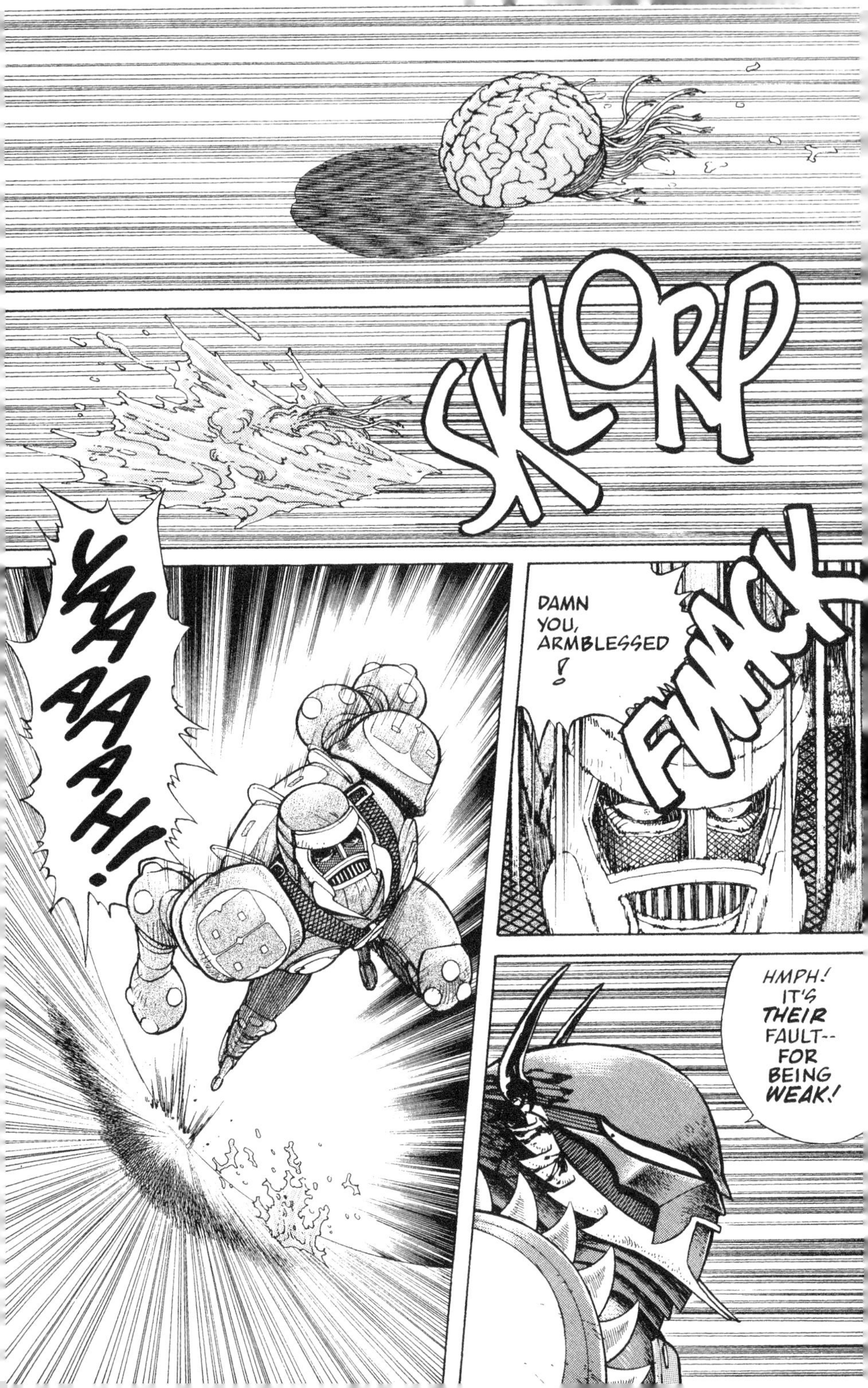
SKLORP
YAAAAAAH!!
DAMN YOU, ARMBLESSED!
FWACK
HMPH! IT'S **THEIR** FAULT-- FOR BEING **WEAK!**

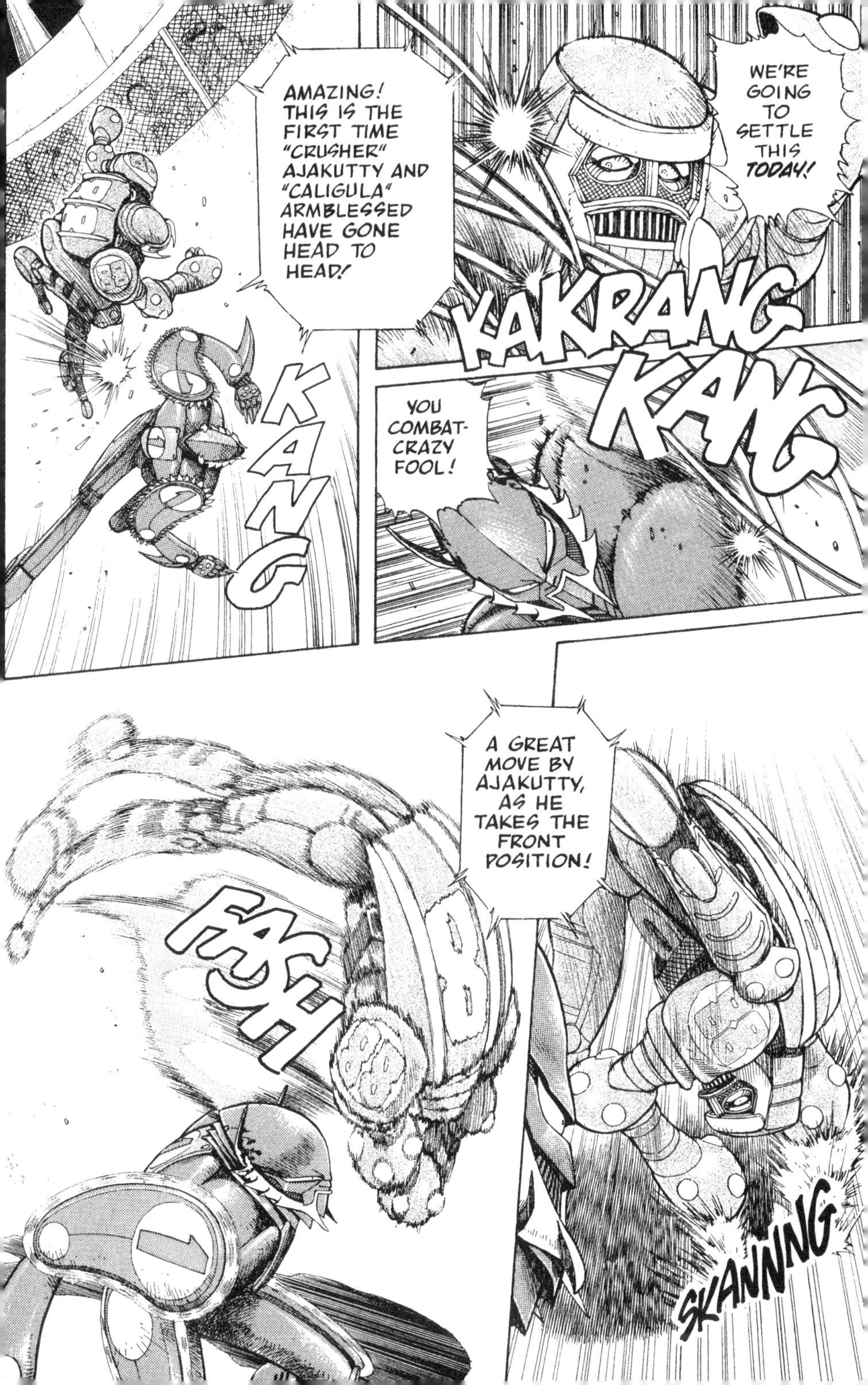
AMAZING! THIS IS THE FIRST TIME "CRUSHER" AJAKUTTY AND "CALIGULA" ARMBLESSED HAVE GONE HEAD TO HEAD!
KANG
WE'RE GOING TO SETTLE THIS *TODAY!*
KAKRANG
KANG
YOU COMBAT-CRAZY FOOL!
FASH
A GREAT MOVE BY AJAKUTTY, AS HE TAKES THE FRONT POSITION!
SKANNNG

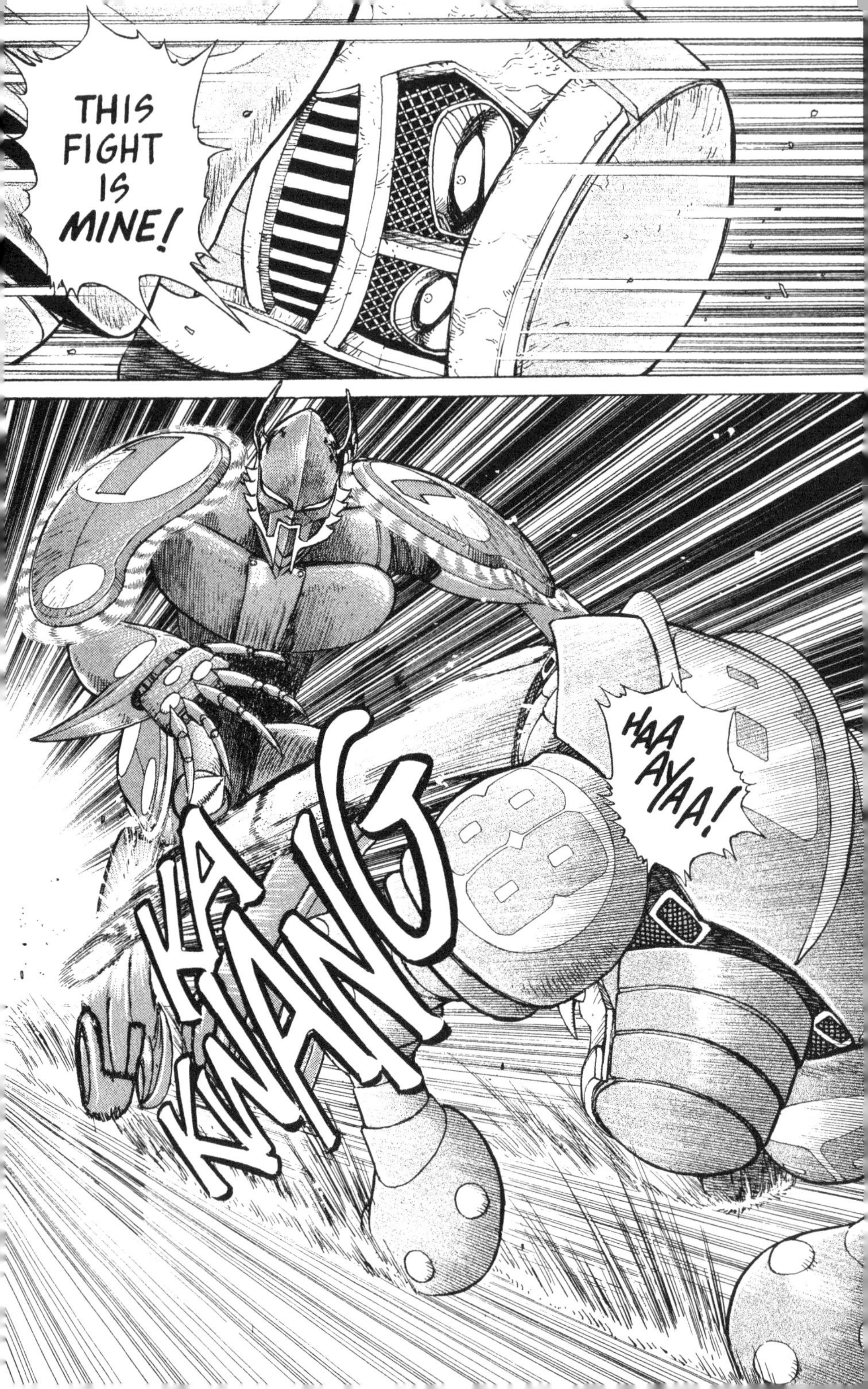
THIS FIGHT IS MINE!
HAAAYAAA!
KA KWANG

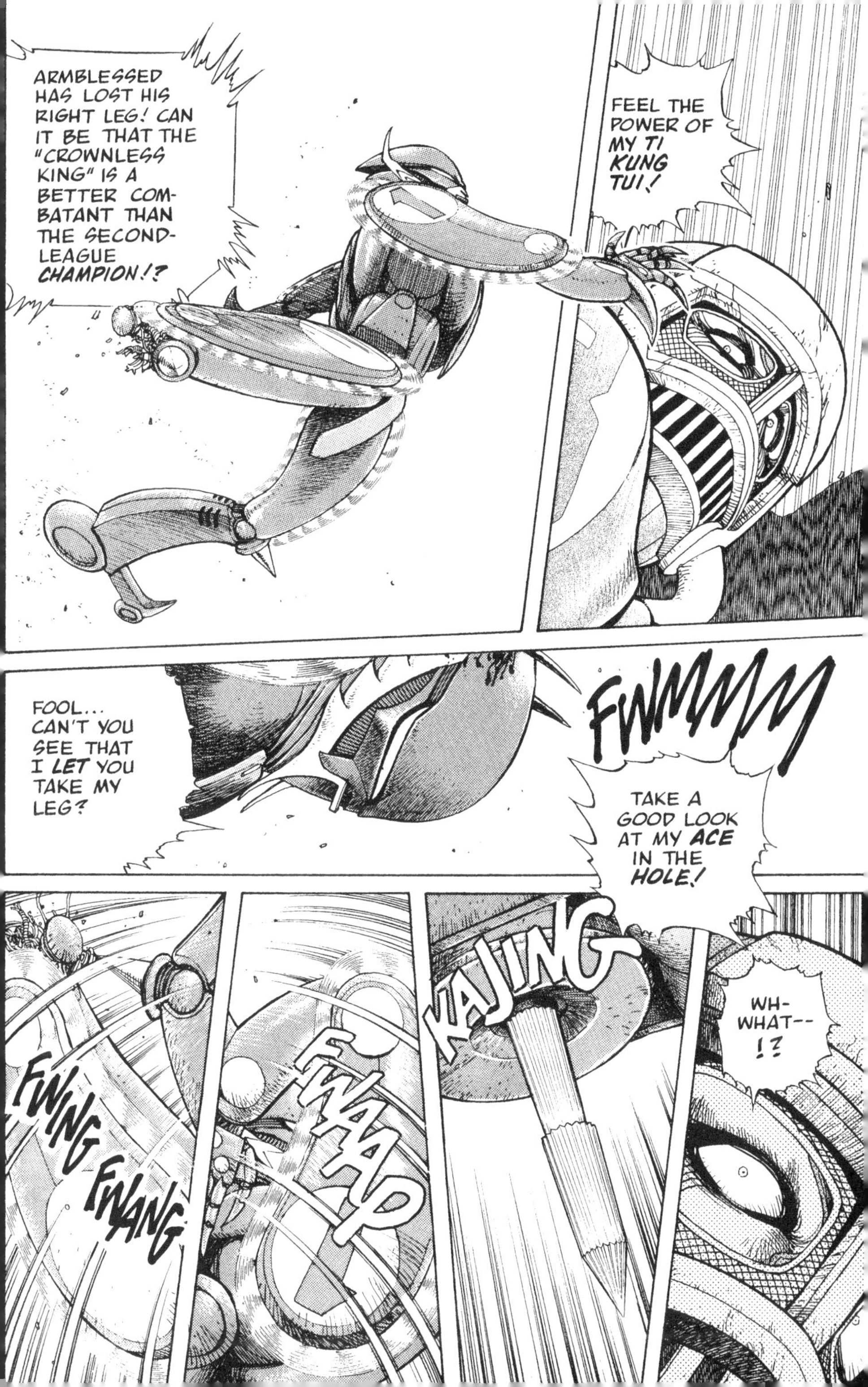
ARMBLESSED HAS LOST HIS RIGHT LEG! CAN IT BE THAT THE "CROWNLESS KING" IS A BETTER COMBATANT THAN THE SECOND-LEAGUE CHAMPION!?
FEEL THE POWER OF MY TI KUNG TUI!
FOOL... CAN'T YOU SEE THAT I LET YOU TAKE MY LEG?
FWMMM
TAKE A GOOD LOOK AT MY ACE IN THE HOLE!
FWING FWANG
FWAAP
KAJING
WH-WHAT--!?

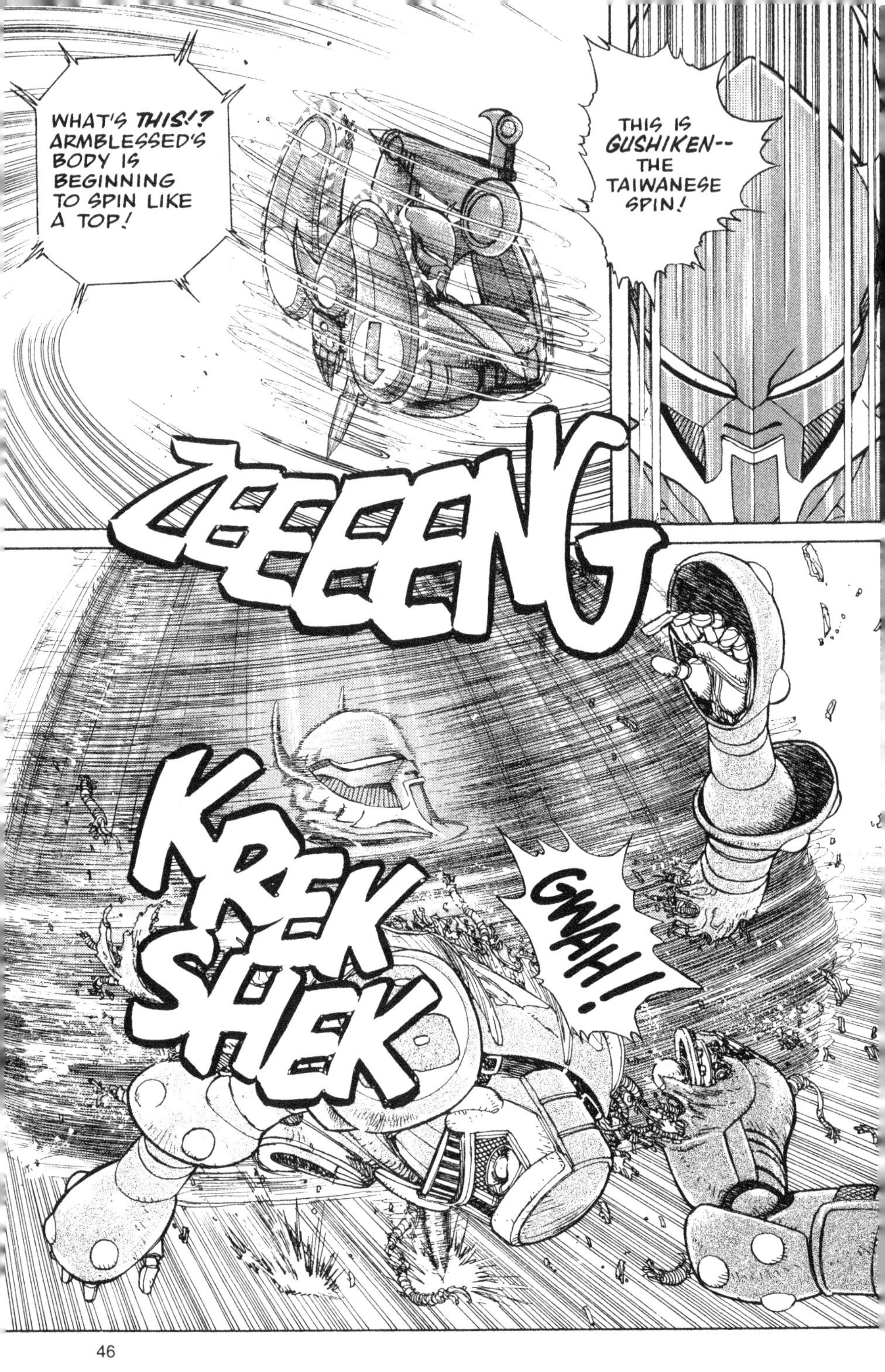
WHAT'S *THIS!?* ARMBLESSED'S BODY IS BEGINNING TO SPIN LIKE A TOP!
THIS IS *GUSHIKEN*-- THE TAIWANESE SPIN!
ZEEEEENG
KREK SHEK
GWAH!

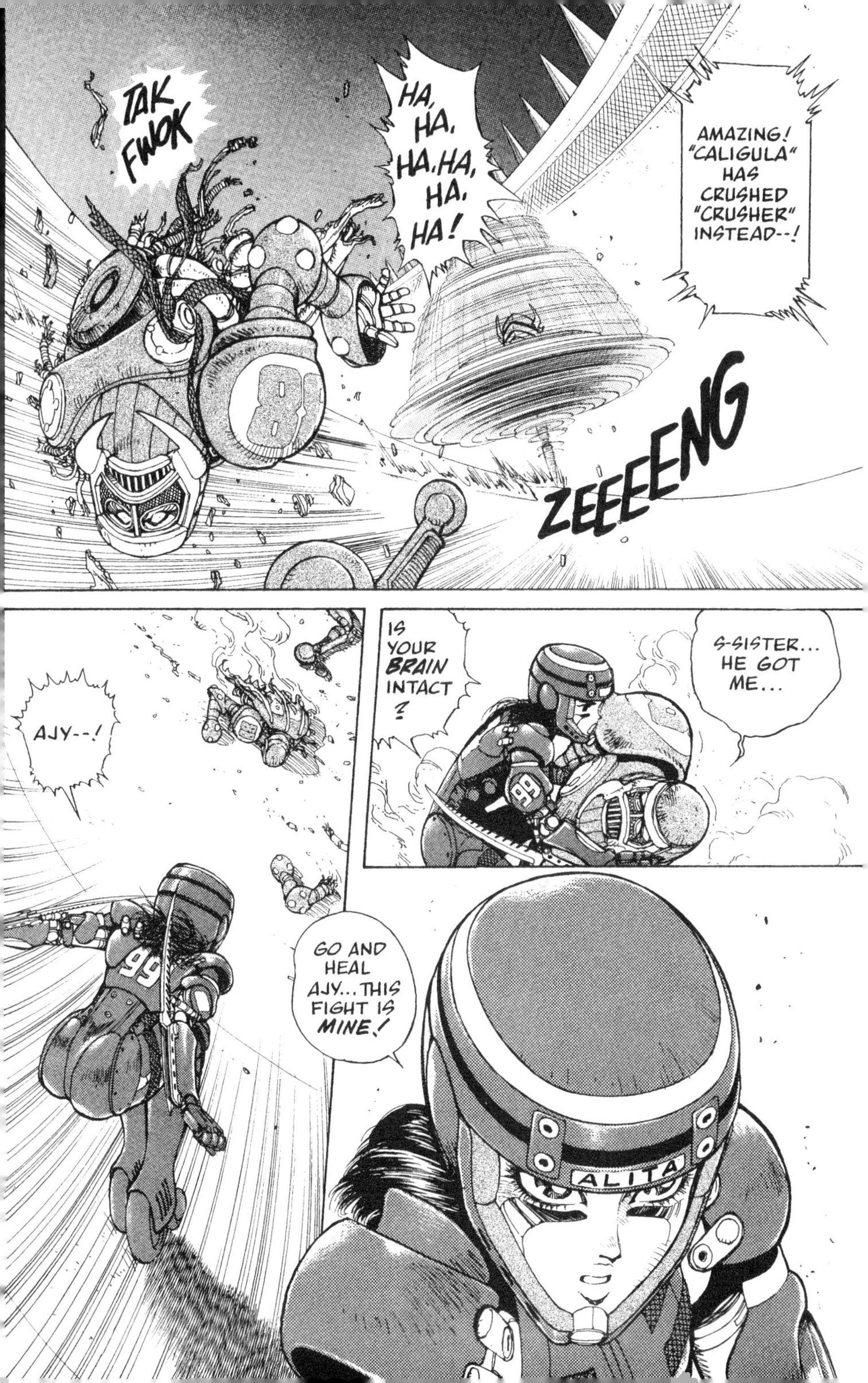
TAK
FWOK
HA, HA, HA, HA, HA, HA!
AMAZING! "CALIGULA" HAS CRUSHED "CRUSHER" INSTEAD--!
ZEEEEENG
AJY--!
IS YOUR BRAIN INTACT?
S-SISTER... HE GOT ME...
GO AND HEAL AJY... THIS FIGHT IS MINE!
ALITA

DOCTOR IDO...

IF I SHOULD EVER *NOT* COME BACK FROM A FLATLINE ATTACK...PLEASE TAKE CARE OF MY SISTER.

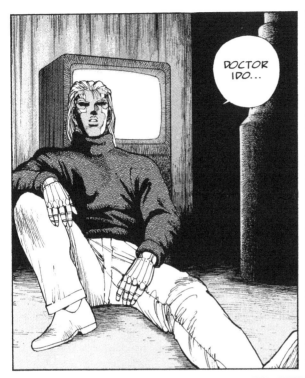

DON'T BE RIDICULOUS! YOU'RE THE IMMORTAL CHAMPION! YOU'LL *ALWAYS* COME BACK TO LIFE!

DON'T TRY TO HIDE IT...

...THE RECONSTRUCTIVE BRAIN SURGERY I HAD... IT'S KILLING ME, ISN'T IT?

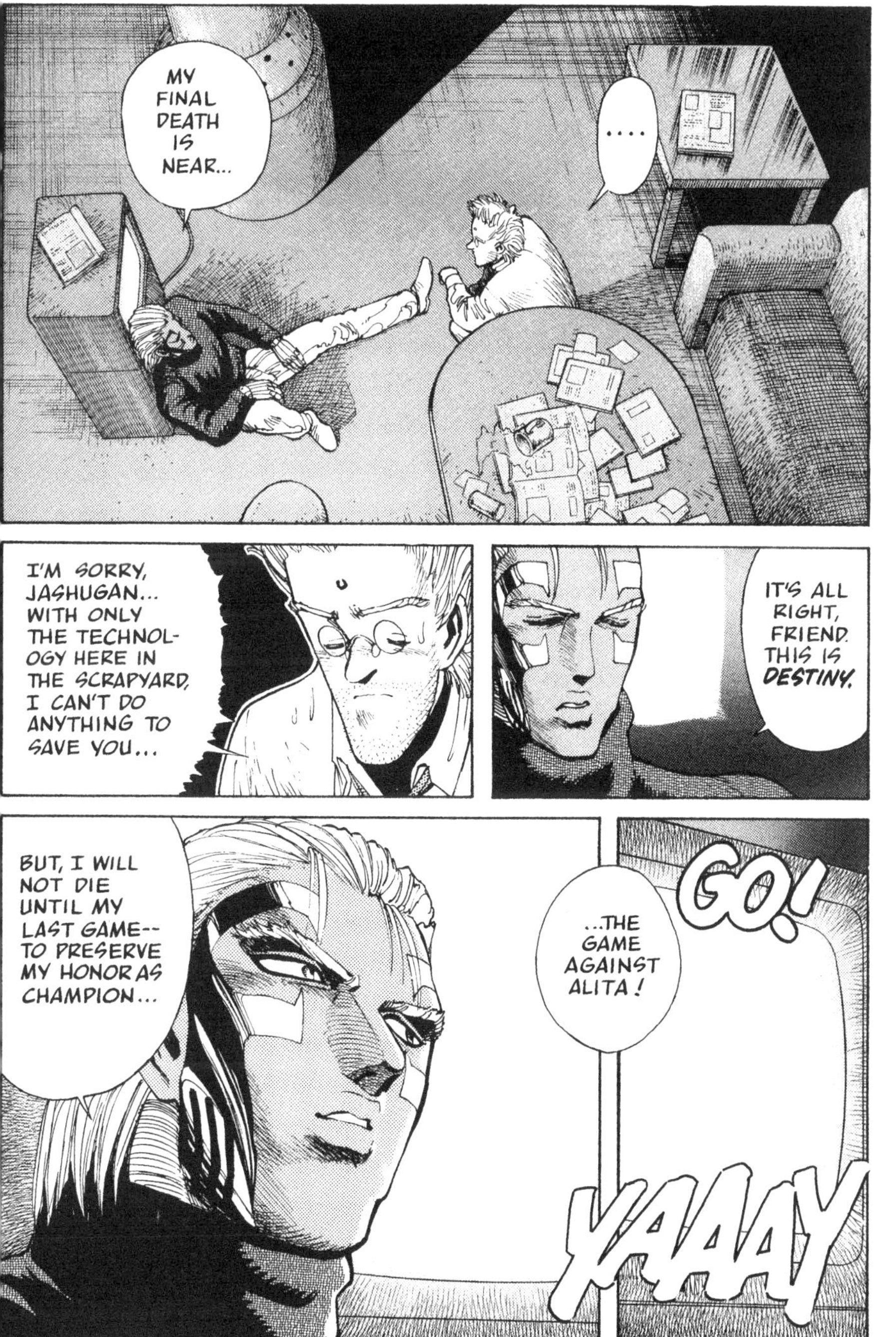
MY FINAL DEATH IS NEAR...
....
I'M SORRY, JASHUGAN... WITH ONLY THE TECHNOLOGY HERE IN THE SCRAPYARD, I CAN'T DO ANYTHING TO SAVE YOU...
IT'S ALL RIGHT, FRIEND. THIS IS DESTINY.
BUT, I WILL NOT DIE UNTIL MY LAST GAME-- TO PRESERVE MY HONOR AS CHAMPION...
...THE GAME AGAINST ALITA!
GO!
YAAAY

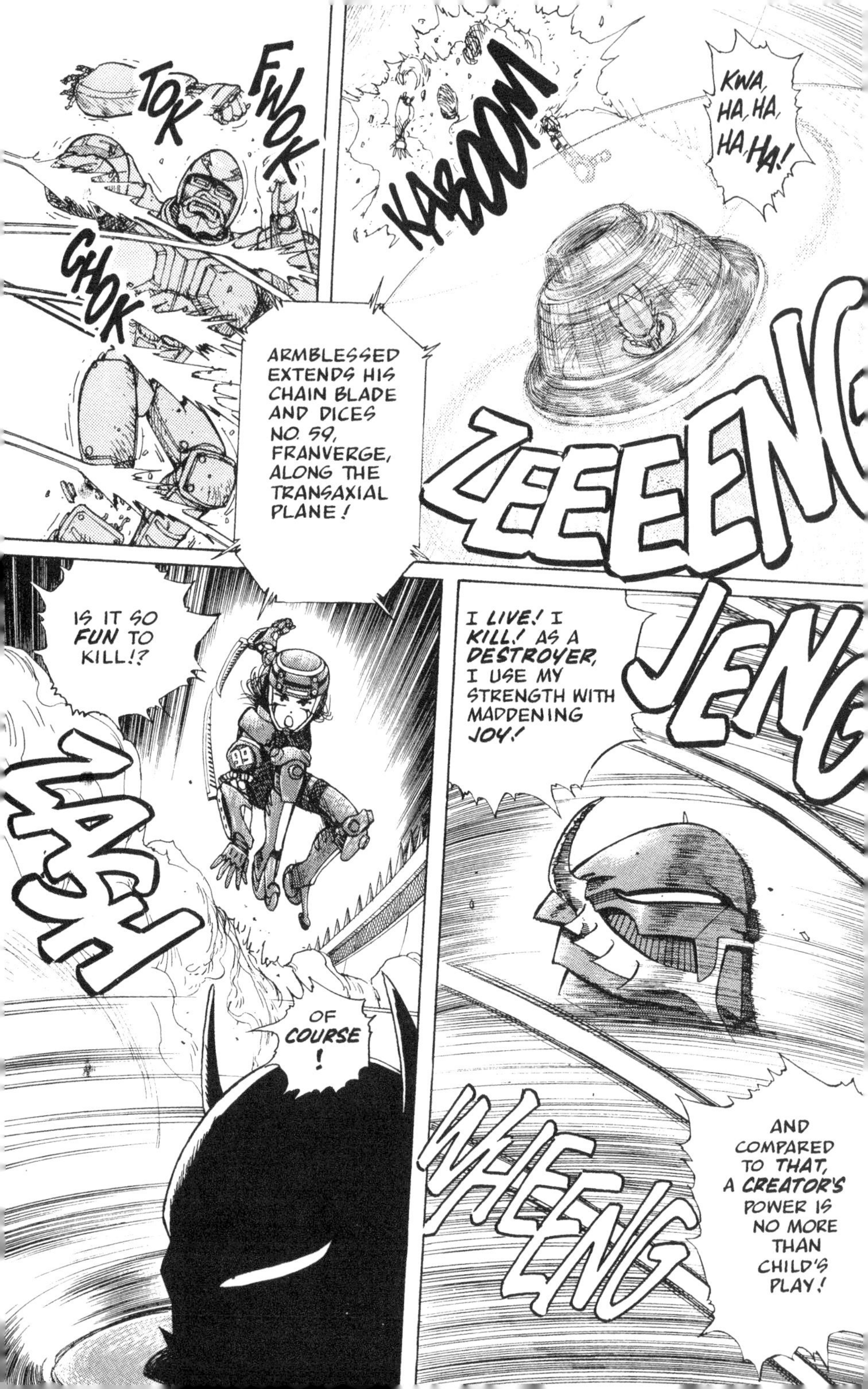
TOK
FWOK
CHOK
ARMBLESSED EXTENDS HIS CHAIN BLADE AND DICES NO. 59, FRANVERGE, ALONG THE TRANSAXIAL PLANE!
KABOOM
KWA, HA, HA, HA, HA!
ZEEEENG
IS IT SO FUN TO KILL!?
OF COURSE!
JENG
I LIVE! I KILL! AS A DESTROYER, I USE MY STRENGTH WITH MADDENING JOY!
WHEENG
AND COMPARED TO THAT, A CREATOR'S POWER IS NO MORE THAN CHILD'S PLAY!

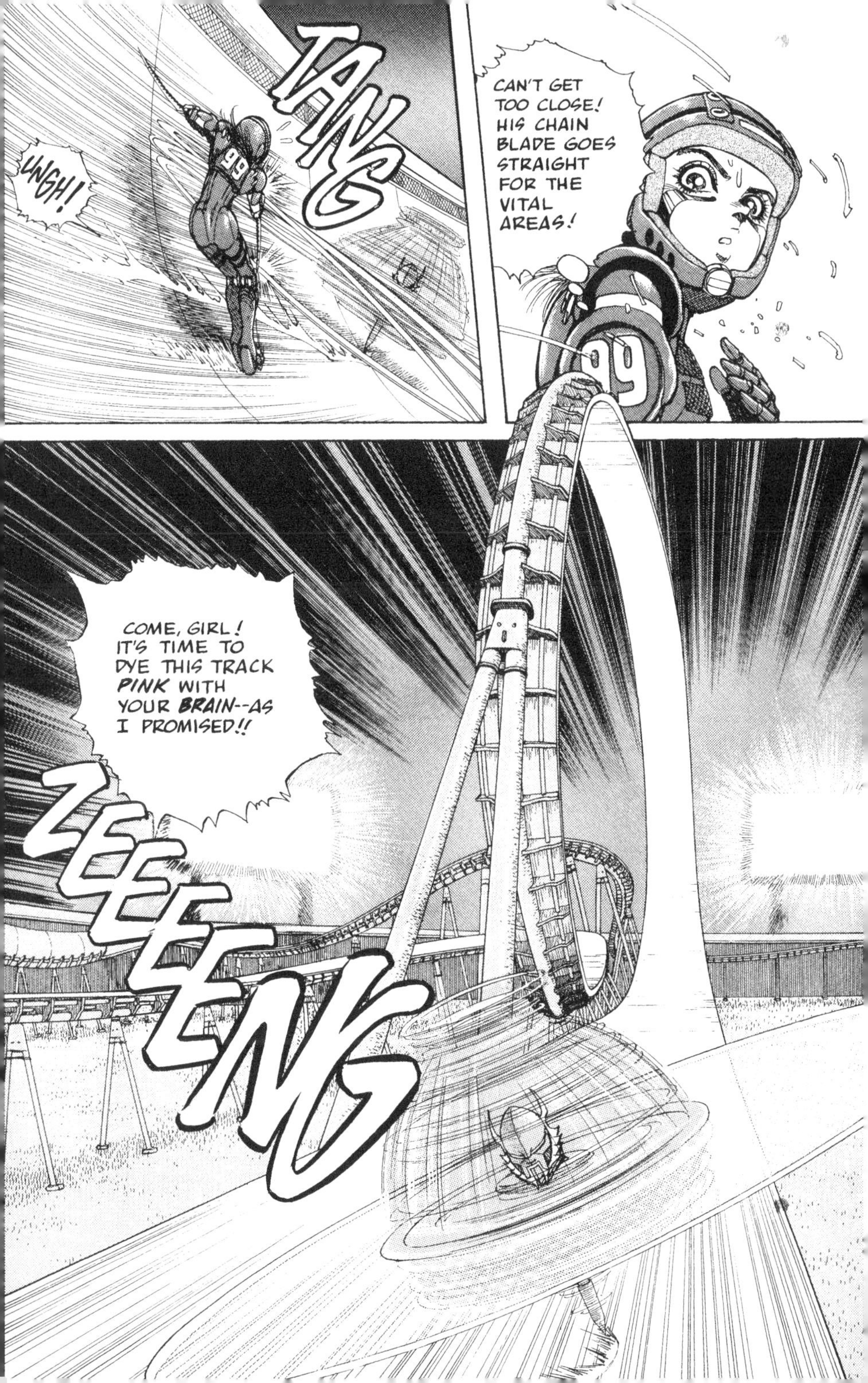
TANG
UNGH!
CAN'T GET TOO CLOSE! HIS CHAIN BLADE GOES STRAIGHT FOR THE VITAL AREAS!
COME, GIRL! IT'S TIME TO DYE THIS TRACK *PINK* WITH YOUR *BRAIN*--AS I PROMISED!!
ZEEEENG

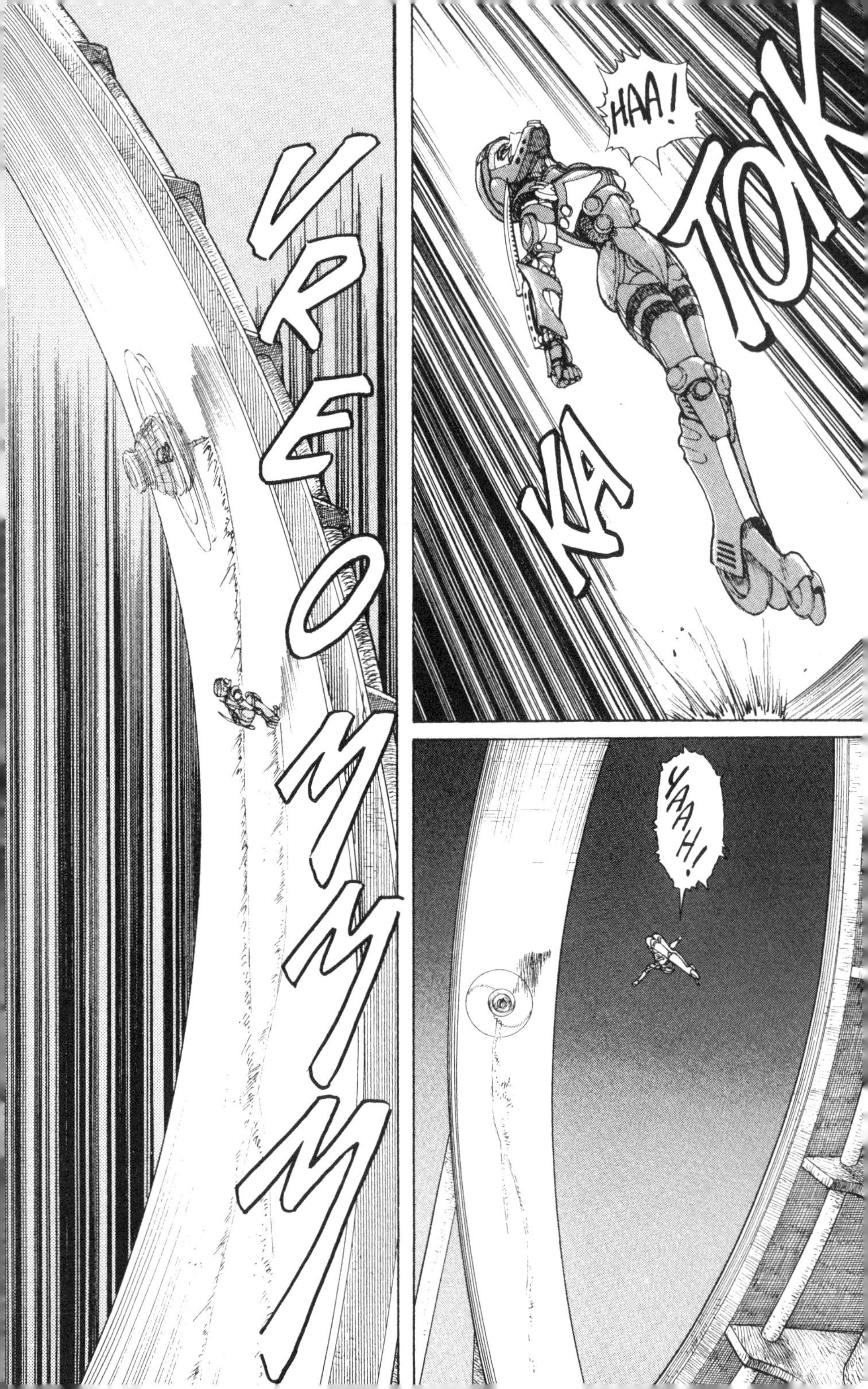
VREOMMMM
HAA!
TOK
KA
YAAAH!

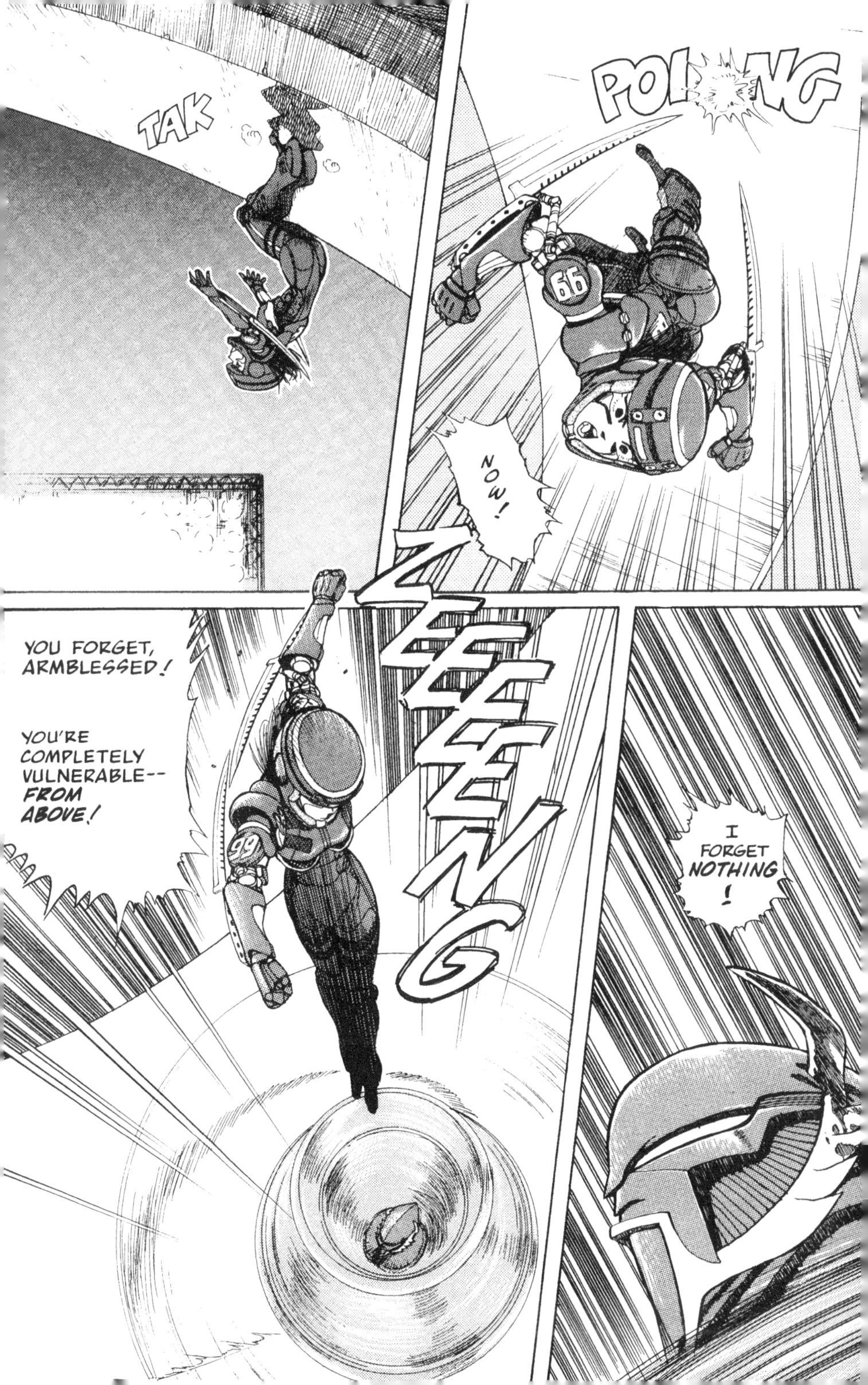
TAK
POI NG
NOW!
ZEEEEENG
YOU FORGET, ARMBLESSED!
YOU'RE COMPLETELY VULNERABLE-- *FROM ABOVE!*
I FORGET *NOTHING*!

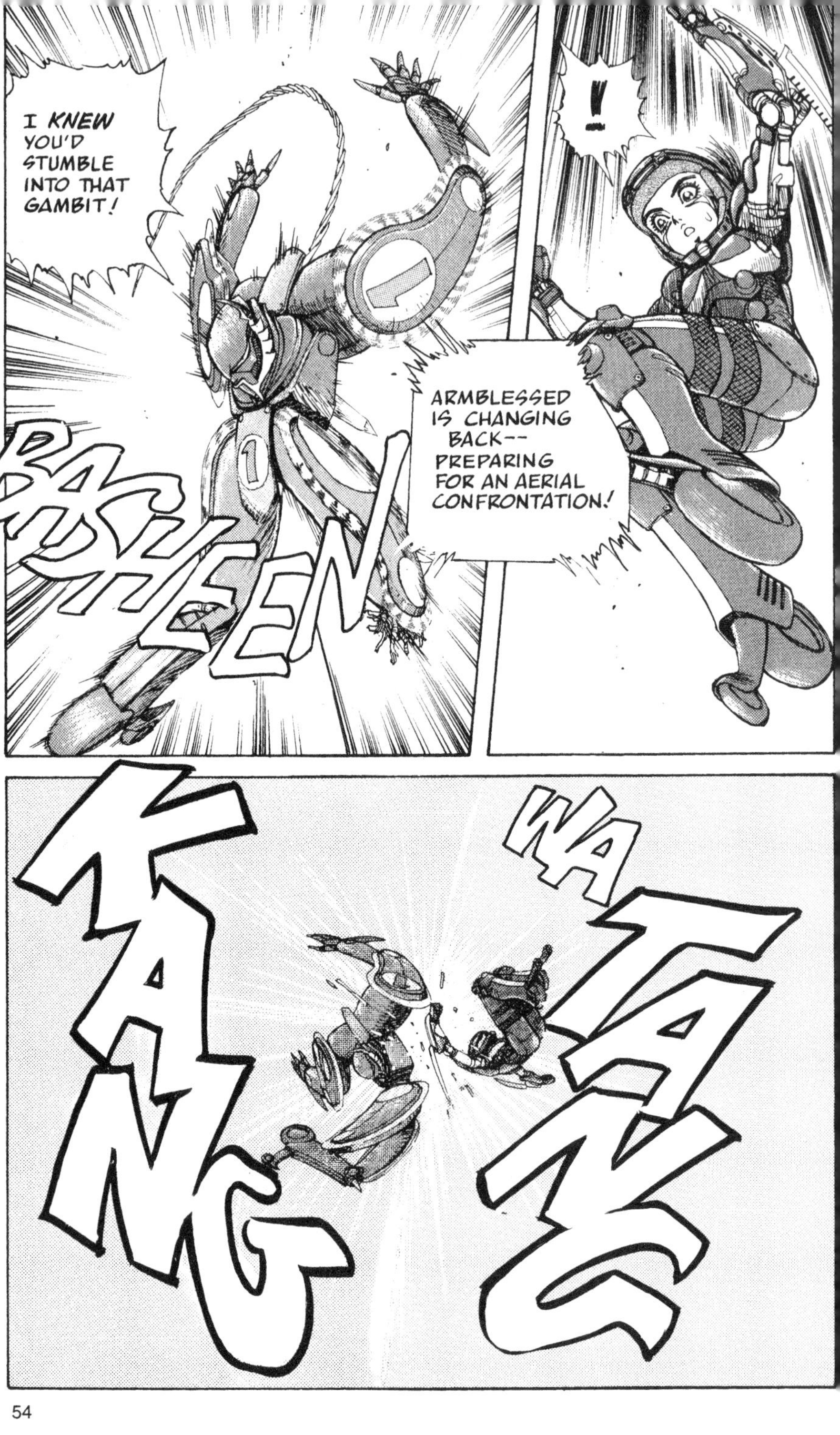
I KNEW YOU'D STUMBLE INTO THAT GAMBIT!
BASHEEN
!
ARMBLESSED IS CHANGING BACK-- PREPARING FOR AN AERIAL CONFRONTATION!
KANG
WATANG

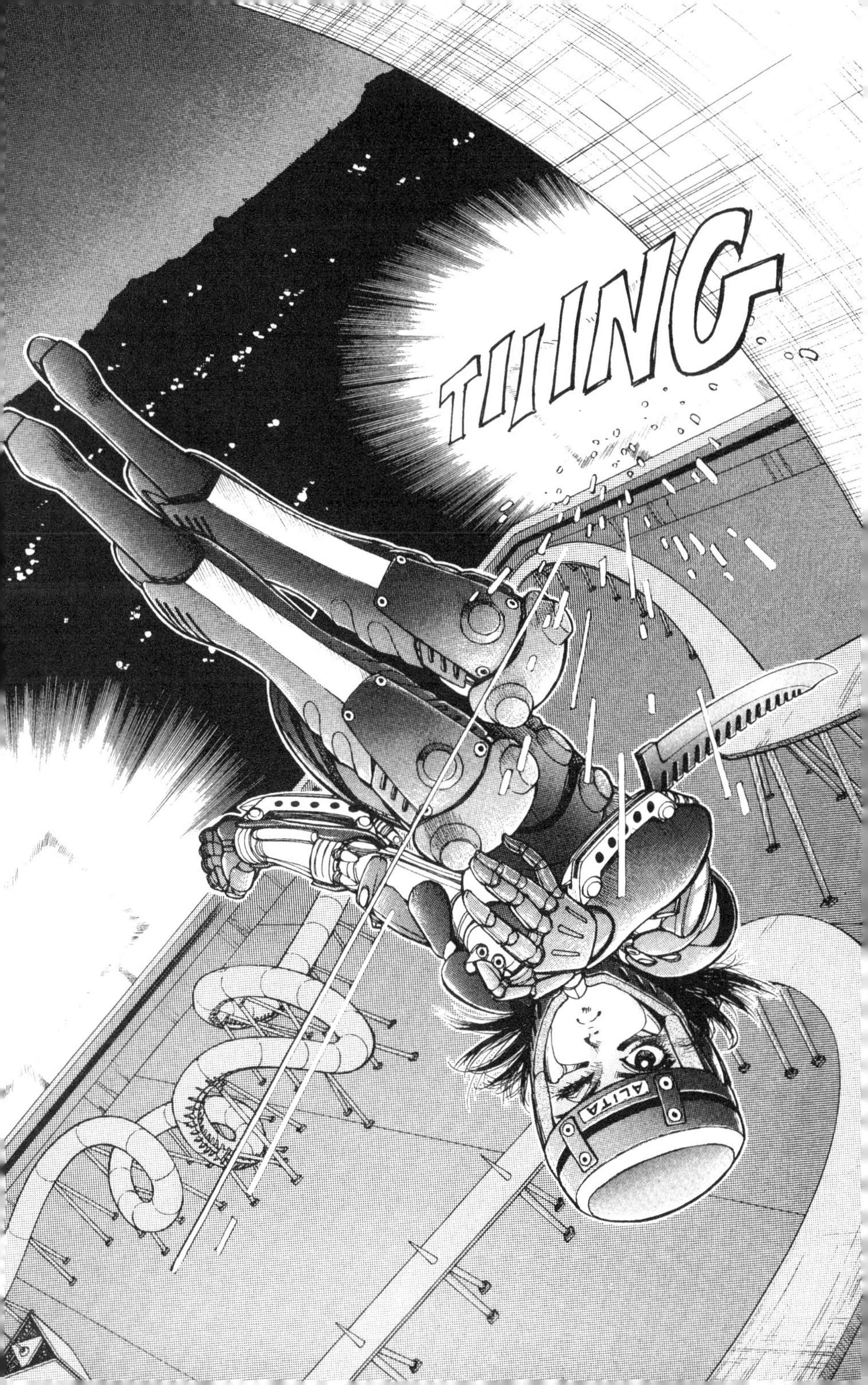
TIIING
ALITA

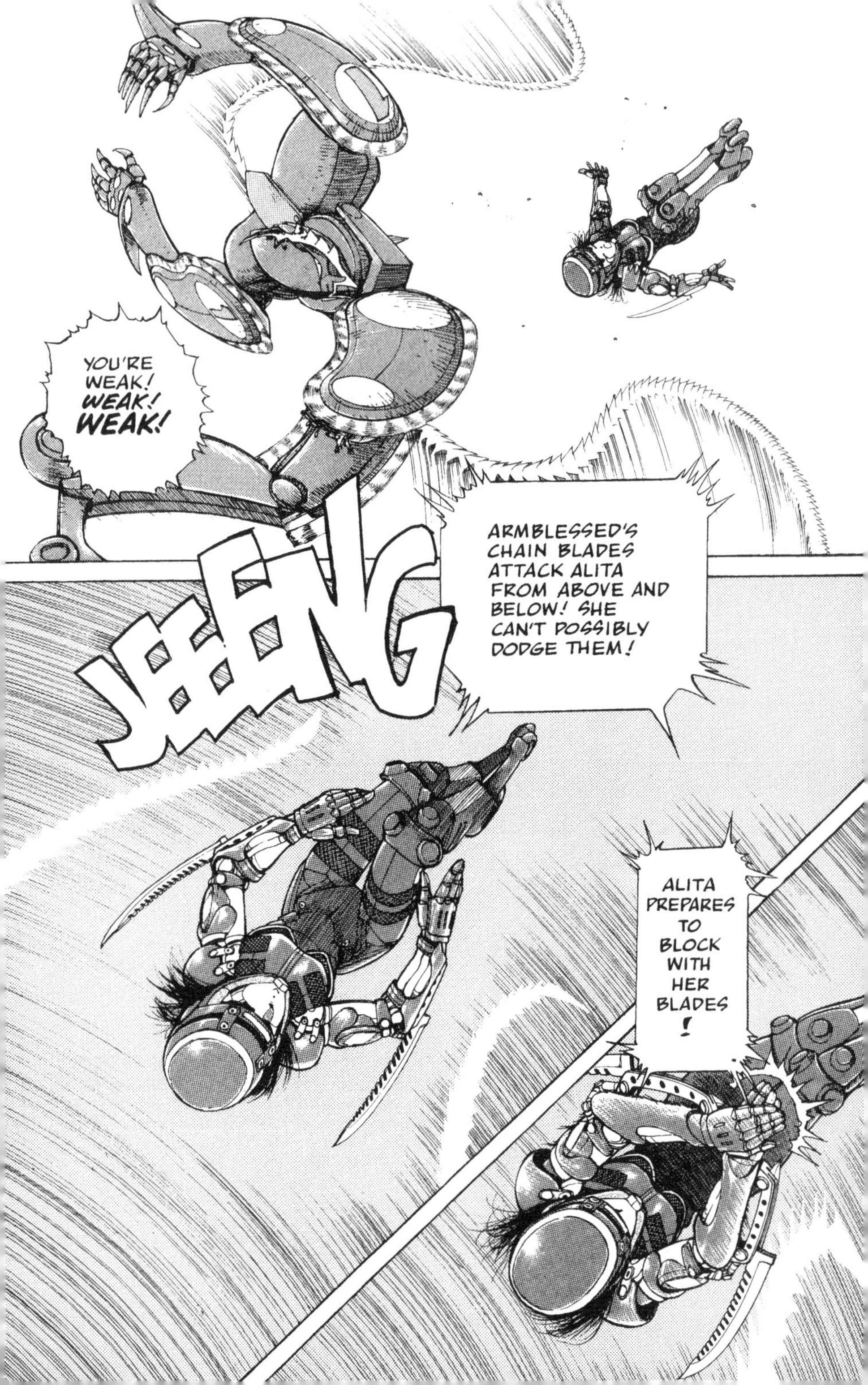
YOU'RE WEAK! **WEAK! WEAK!**
JEEENG
ARMBLESSED'S CHAIN BLADES ATTACK ALITA FROM ABOVE AND BELOW! SHE CAN'T POSSIBLY DODGE THEM!
ALITA PREPARES TO BLOCK WITH HER BLADES!

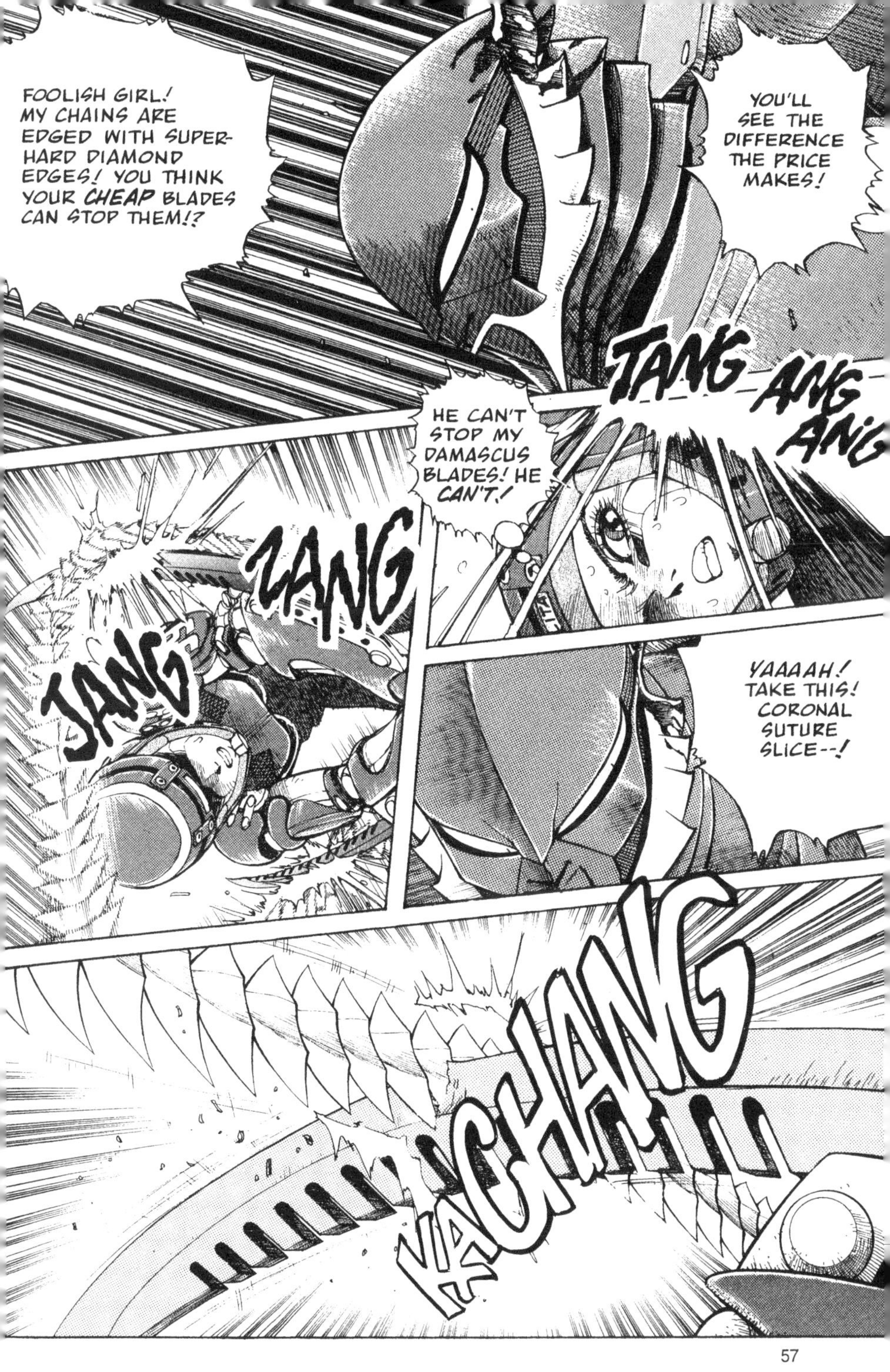
FOOLISH GIRL! MY CHAINS ARE EDGED WITH SUPER-HARD DIAMOND EDGES! YOU THINK YOUR *CHEAP* BLADES CAN STOP THEM!?
YOU'LL SEE THE DIFFERENCE THE PRICE MAKES!
TANG--ANG ANG
HE CAN'T STOP MY DAMASCUS BLADES! HE *CAN'T*!
ZANG
JANG
YAAAAH! TAKE THIS! CORONAL SUTURE SLICE--!
KACHANG!!!

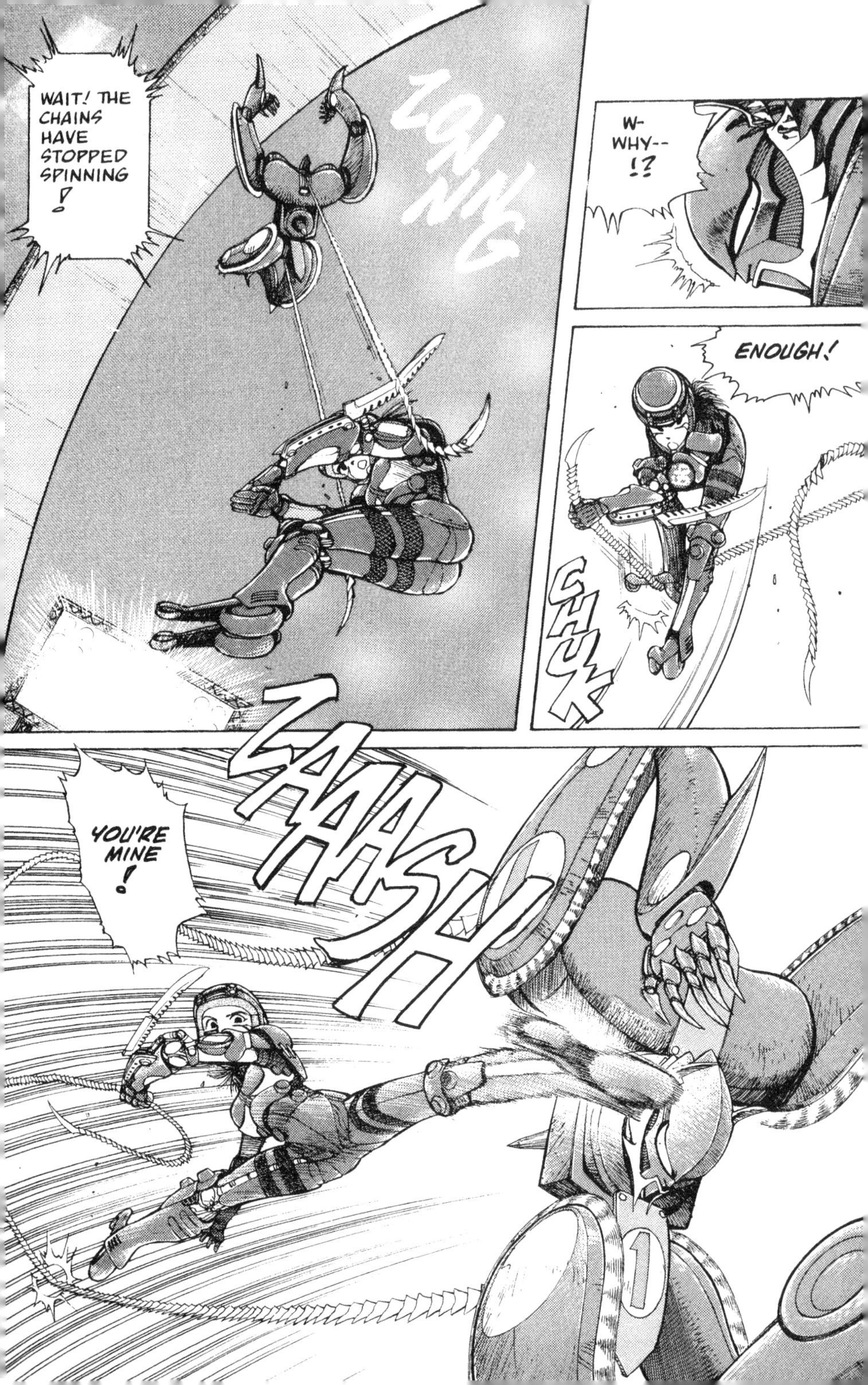
WAIT! THE CHAINS HAVE STOPPED SPINNING!
ZONNNG
W-WHY--!?
ENOUGH!
CHUCK
ZAAASH
YOU'RE MINE!

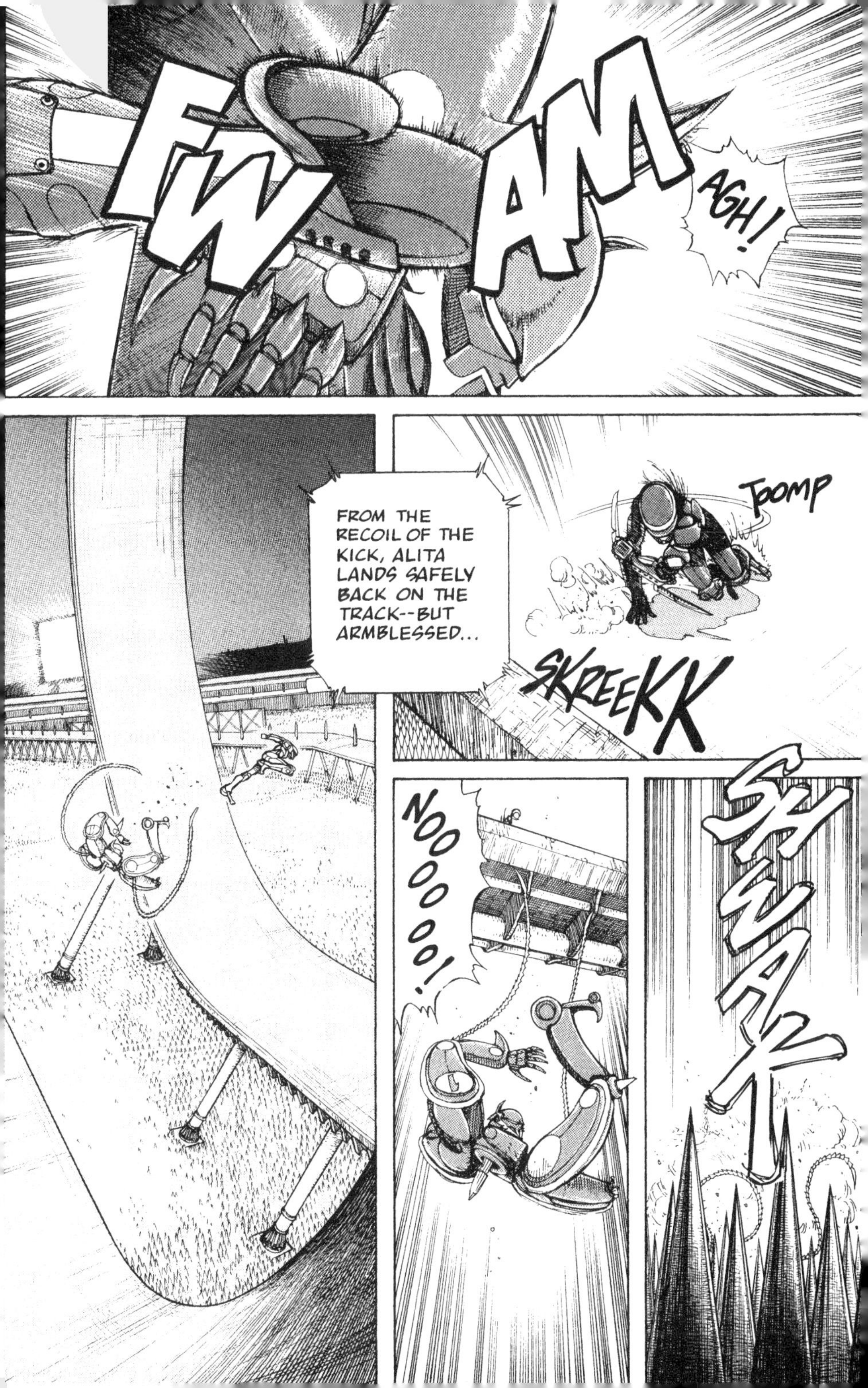
FWAM
AGH!
FROM THE RECOIL OF THE KICK, ALITA LANDS SAFELY BACK ON THE TRACK--BUT ARMBLESSED...
TOOMP
SKREEKK
NOOOOOOO!
SHWAK

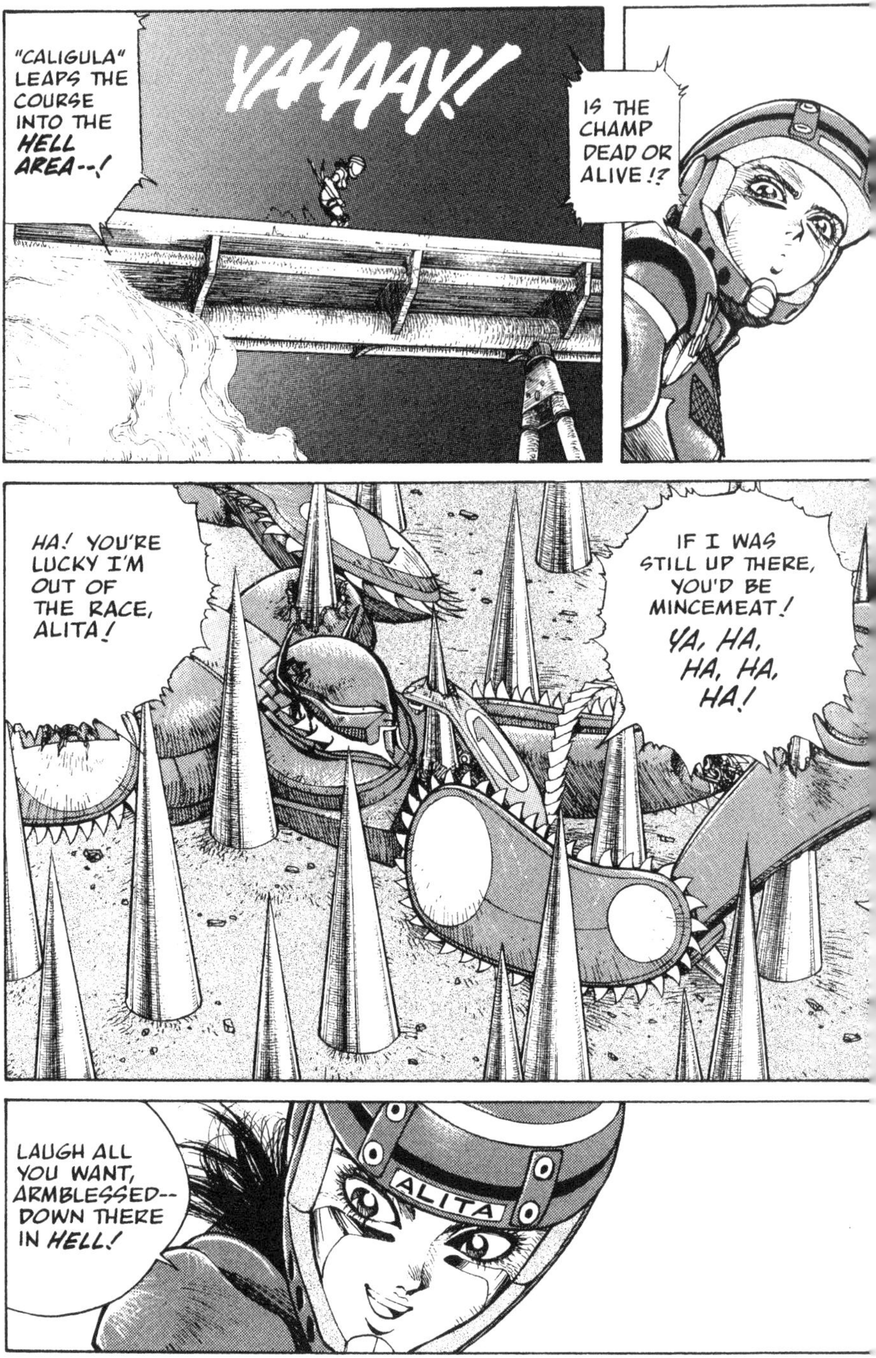
"CALIGULA" LEAPS THE COURSE INTO THE *HELL AREA*--!
YAAAAAY!
IS THE CHAMP DEAD OR ALIVE!?
HA! YOU'RE LUCKY I'M OUT OF THE RACE, ALITA!
IF I WAS STILL UP THERE, YOU'D BE MINCEMEAT! *YA, HA, HA, HA, HA!*
LAUGH ALL YOU WANT, ARMBLESSED-- DOWN THERE IN *HELL*!
ALITA

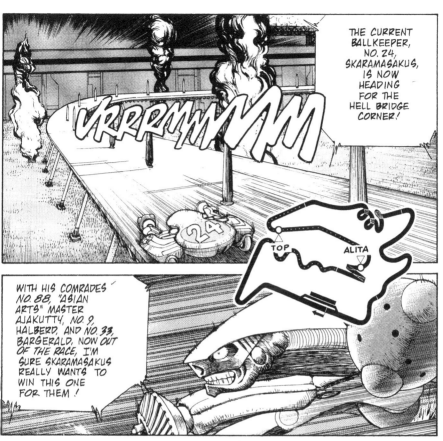

THE CURRENT BALLKEEPER, NO. 24, SKARAMASAKUS, IS NOW HEADING FOR THE HELL BRIDGE CORNER!

TOP   ALITA

WITH HIS COMRADES NO. 88, "ASIAN ARTS" MASTER AJAKUTTY, NO. 9, HALBERD, AND NO. 33, BARGERALD, NOW OUT OF THE RACE, I'M SURE SKARAMASAKUS REALLY WANTS TO WIN THIS ONE FOR THEM!

BUT FOR SOME TIME NOW, A CRIMSON SHADOW HAS BEEN TAILING SKARAMASAKUS!

SHMMM

NO. 7, ZAFAL TAKIÉ, SILENTLY CLOSES IN ON THE LEADER!

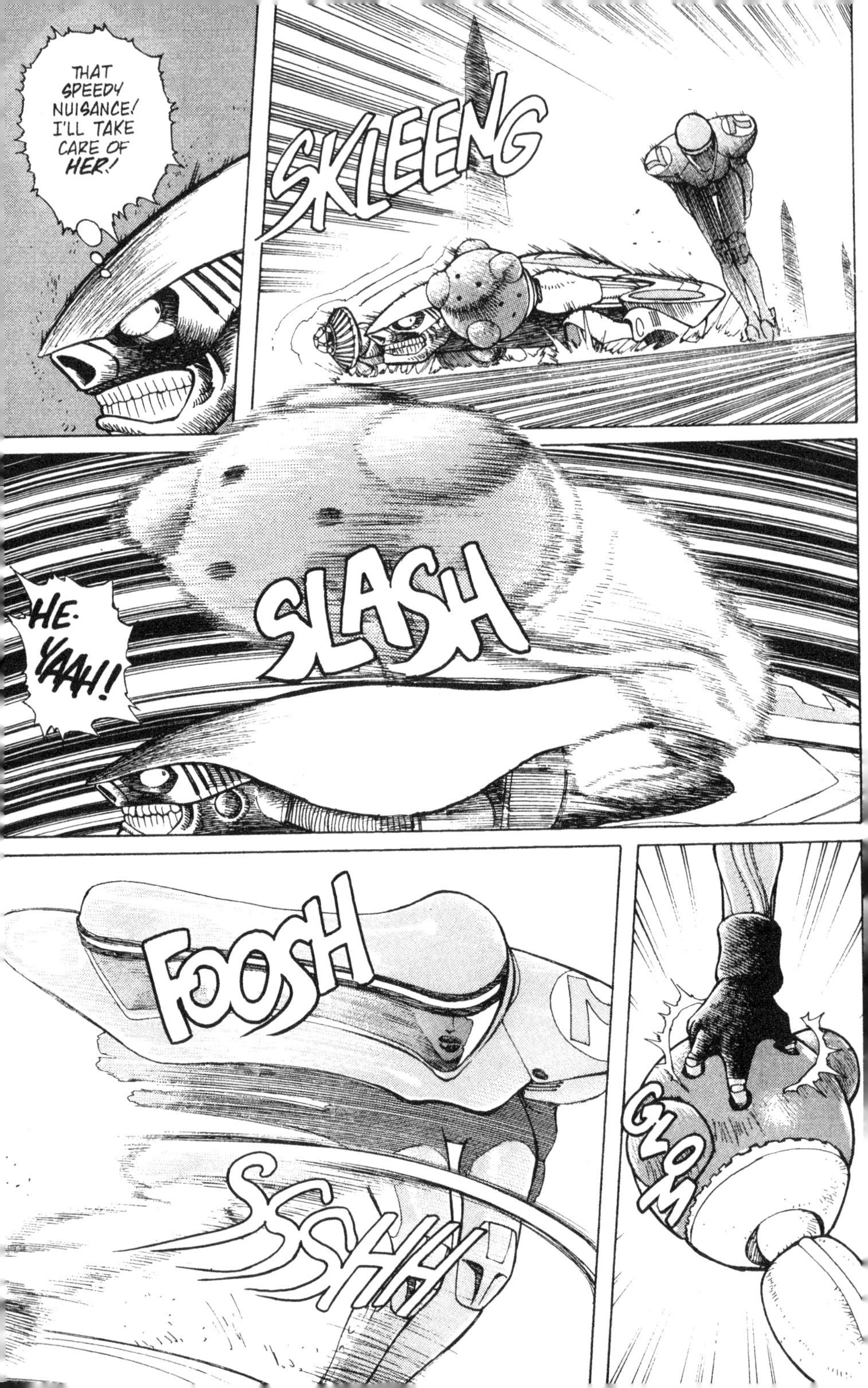
THAT SPEEDY NUISANCE! I'LL TAKE CARE OF HER!
SKLEENG
HE-YAAH!
SLASH
FOOSH
SSHH
GNOM

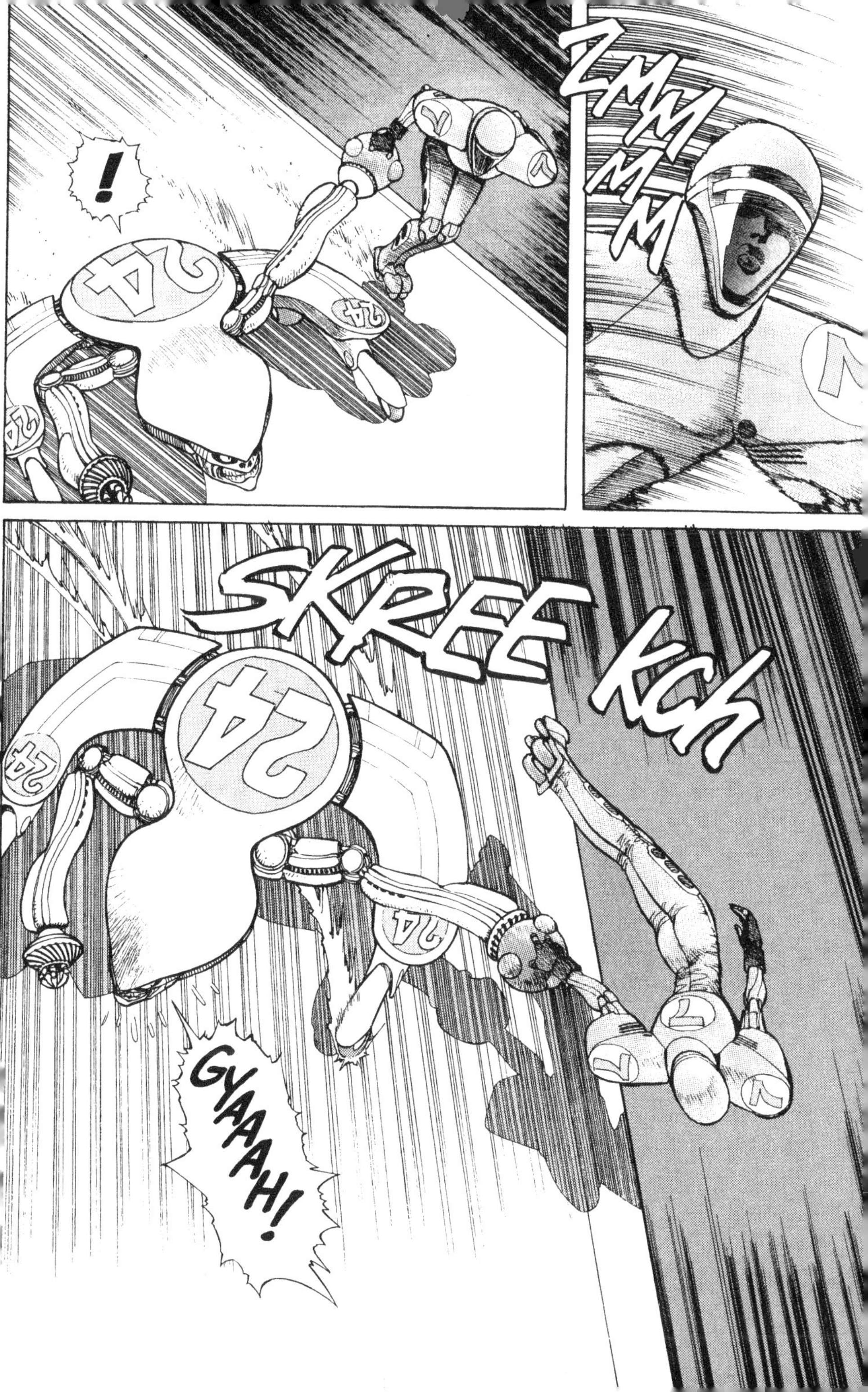
!
ZMMMMMM
SKREE KCH
GYAAAH!

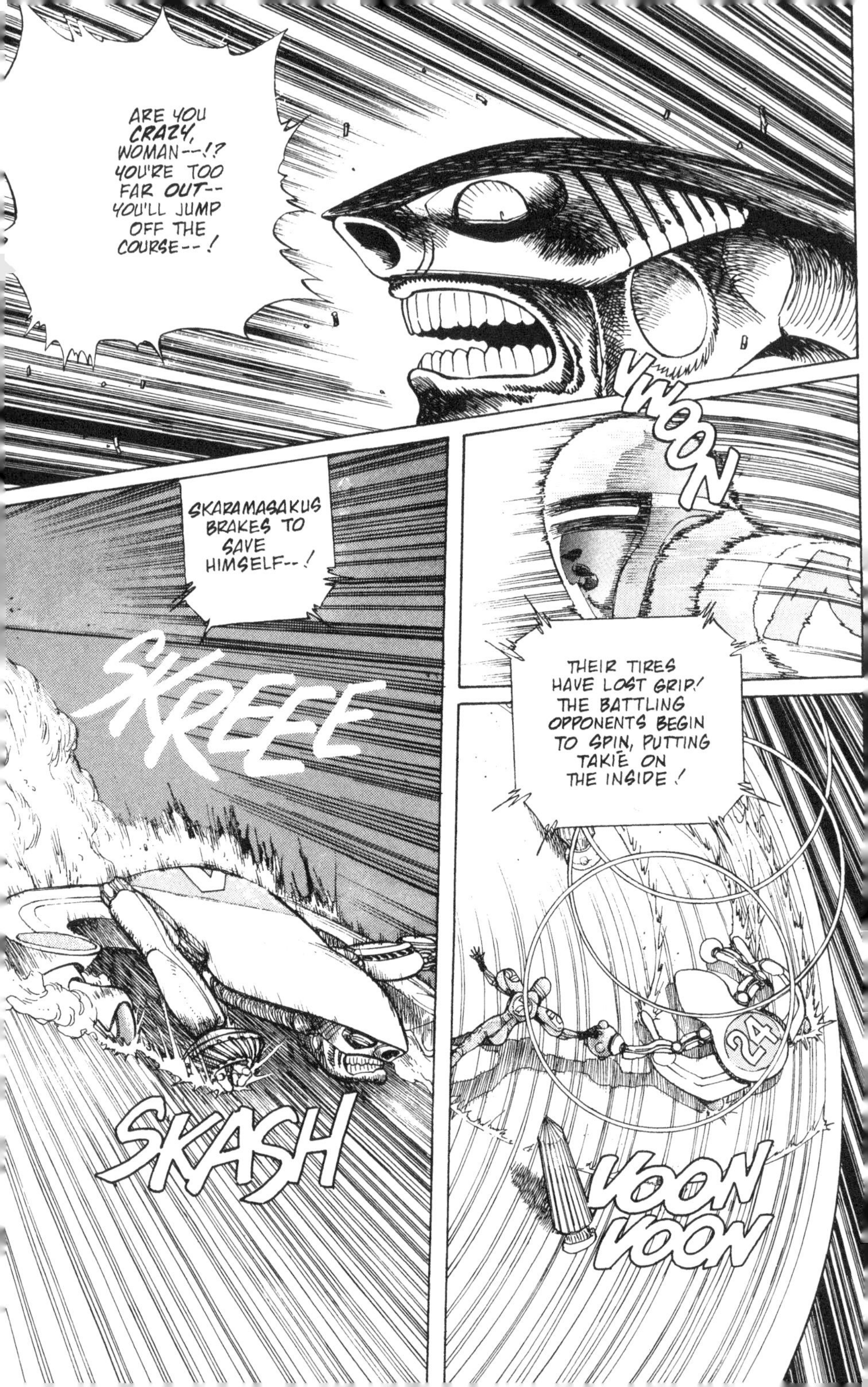
ARE YOU CRAZY, WOMAN--!? YOU'RE TOO FAR OUT-- YOU'LL JUMP OFF THE COURSE--!
VWOON
SKARAMASAKUS BRAKES TO SAVE HIMSELF--!
SKREEE
SKASH
THEIR TIRES HAVE LOST GRIP! THE BATTLING OPPONENTS BEGIN TO SPIN, PUTTING TAKIE ON THE INSIDE!
24
VOON VOON

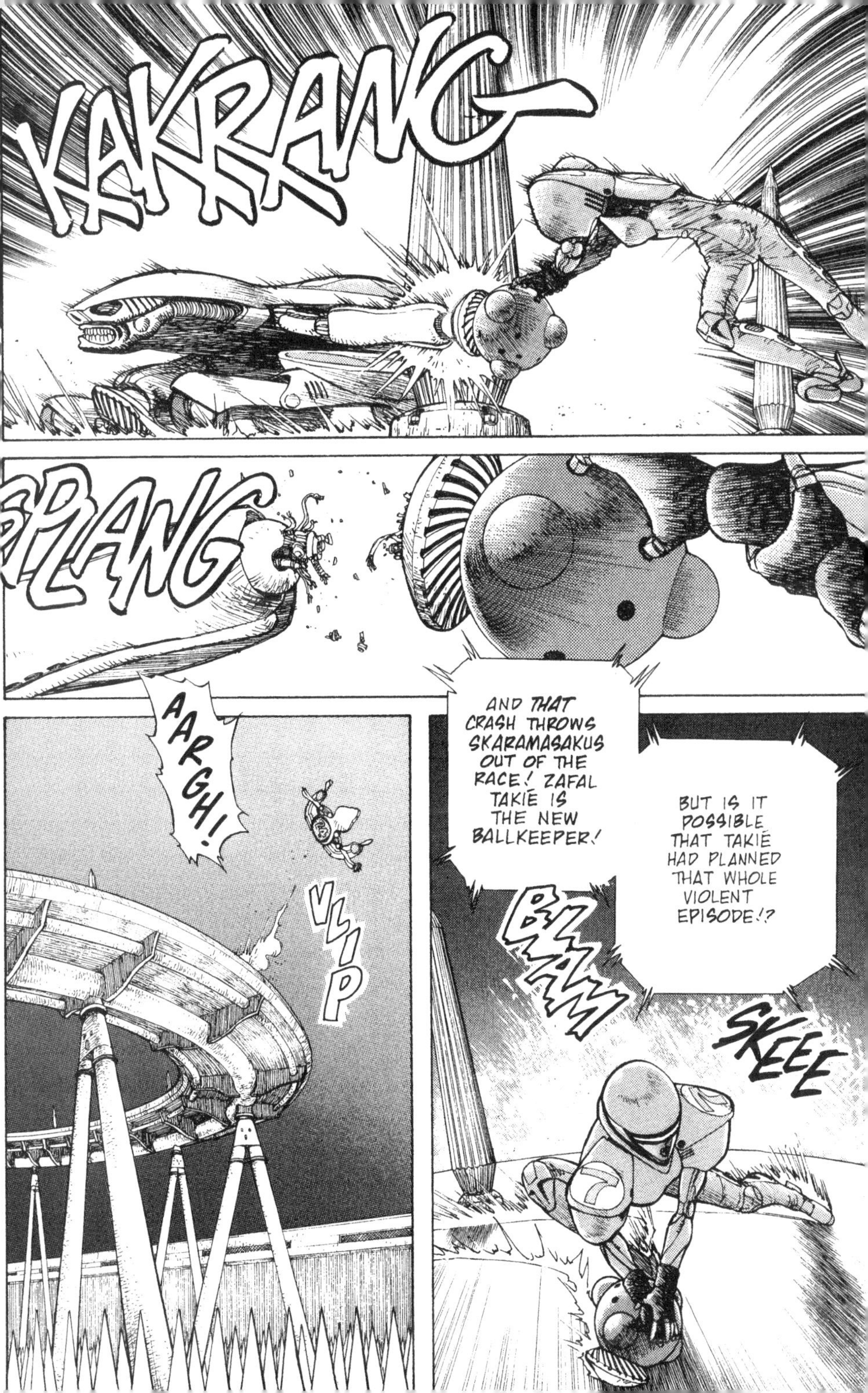
KAKRANG
SPLANG
AARGH!
VLIP
AND THAT CRASH THROWS SKARAMASAKUS OUT OF THE RACE! ZAFAL TAKIÉ IS THE NEW BALLKEEPER!
BUT IS IT POSSIBLE THAT TAKIÉ HAD PLANNED THAT WHOLE VIOLENT EPISODE!?
BLAM
SKEEE

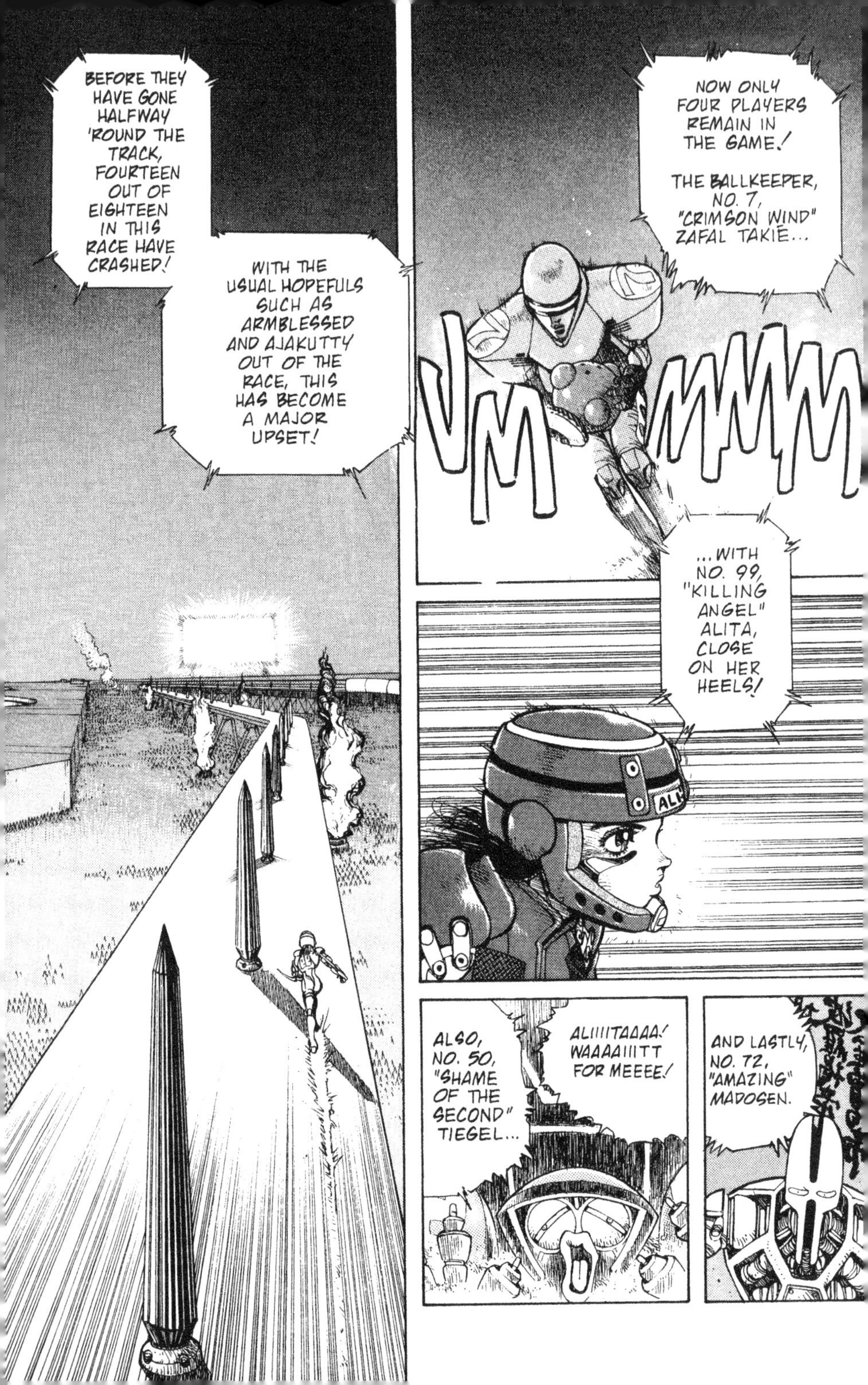

BEFORE THEY HAVE GONE HALFWAY 'ROUND THE TRACK, FOURTEEN OUT OF EIGHTEEN IN THIS RACE HAVE CRASHED!
WITH THE USUAL HOPEFULS SUCH AS ARMBLESSED AND AJAKUTTY OUT OF THE RACE, THIS HAS BECOME A MAJOR UPSET!
NOW ONLY FOUR PLAYERS REMAIN IN THE GAME!
THE BALLKEEPER, NO. 7, "CRIMSON WIND" ZAFAL TAKIE...
VMMMMM
...WITH NO. 99, "KILLING ANGEL" ALITA, CLOSE ON HER HEELS!
ALSO, NO. 50, "SHAME OF THE SECOND" TIEGEL...
ALIIIITAAAA! WAAAAIIITT FOR MEEEE!
AND LASTLY, NO. 72, "AMAZING" MADOSEN.

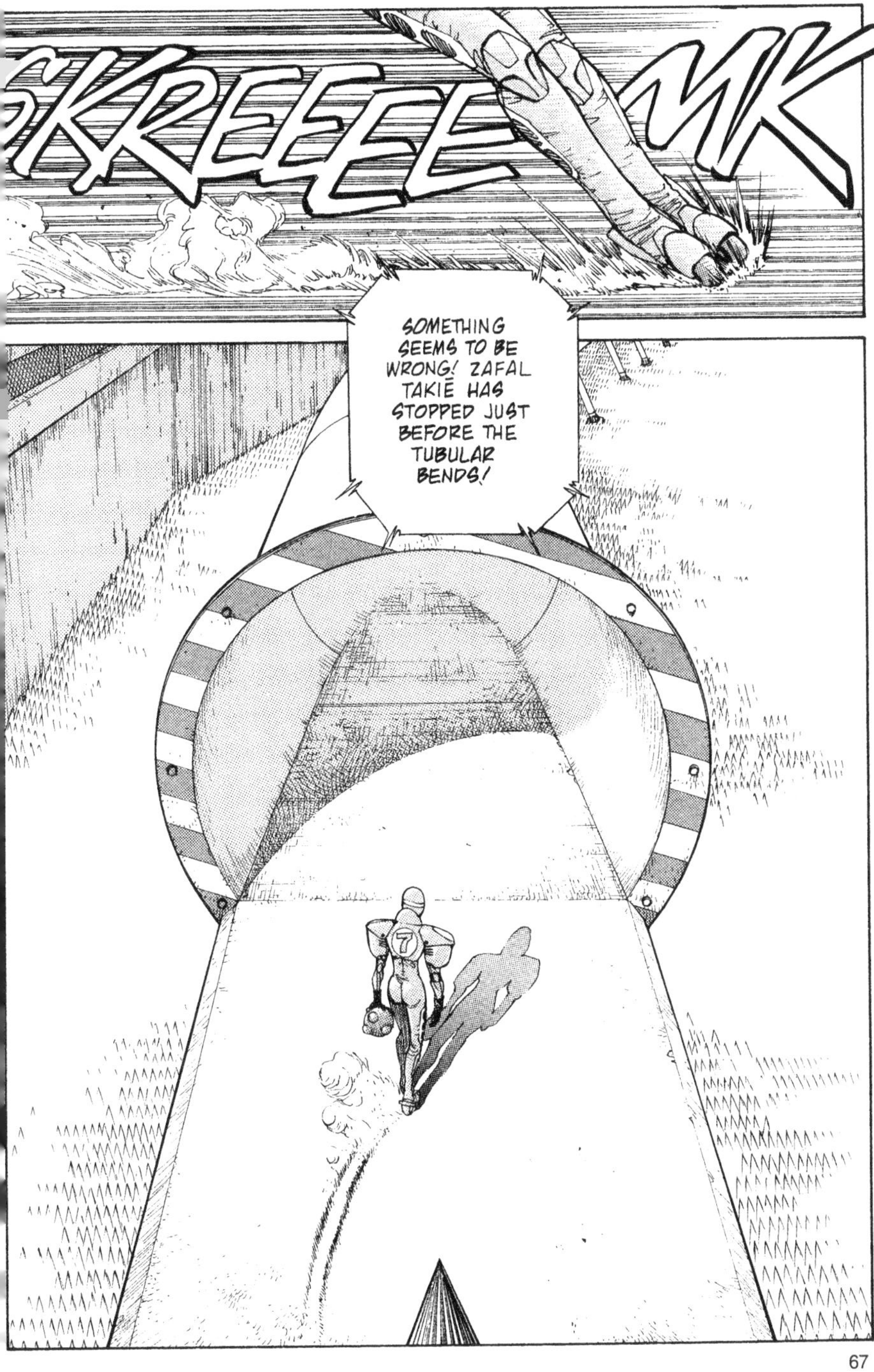
SKREEEEEMK
SOMETHING SEEMS TO BE WRONG! ZAFAL TAKIĒ HAS STOPPED JUST BEFORE THE TUBULAR BENDS!

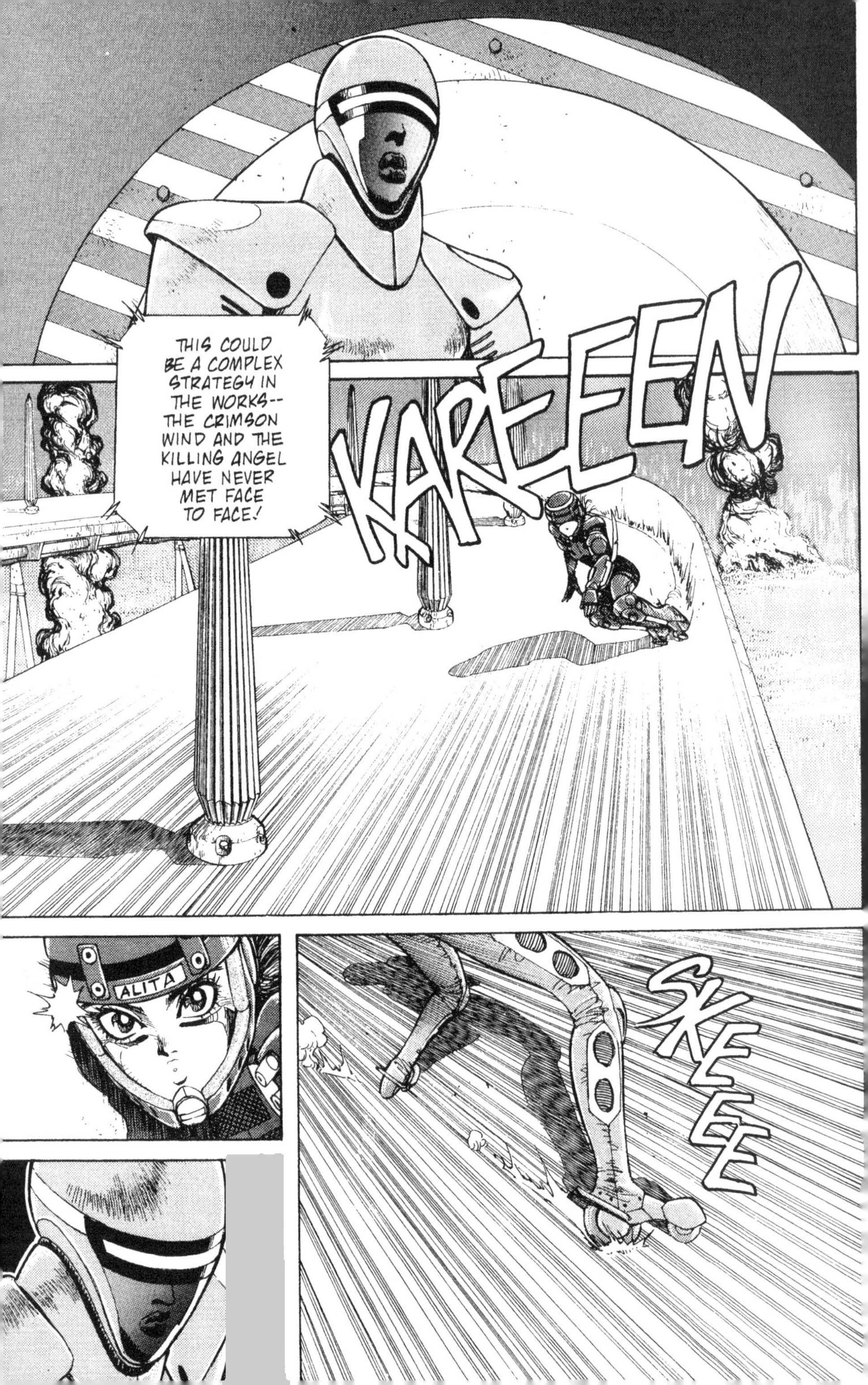
THIS COULD BE A COMPLEX STRATEGY IN THE WORKS-- THE CRIMSON WIND AND THE KILLING ANGEL HAVE NEVER MET FACE TO FACE!
KAREEEN
ALITA
SKEEE

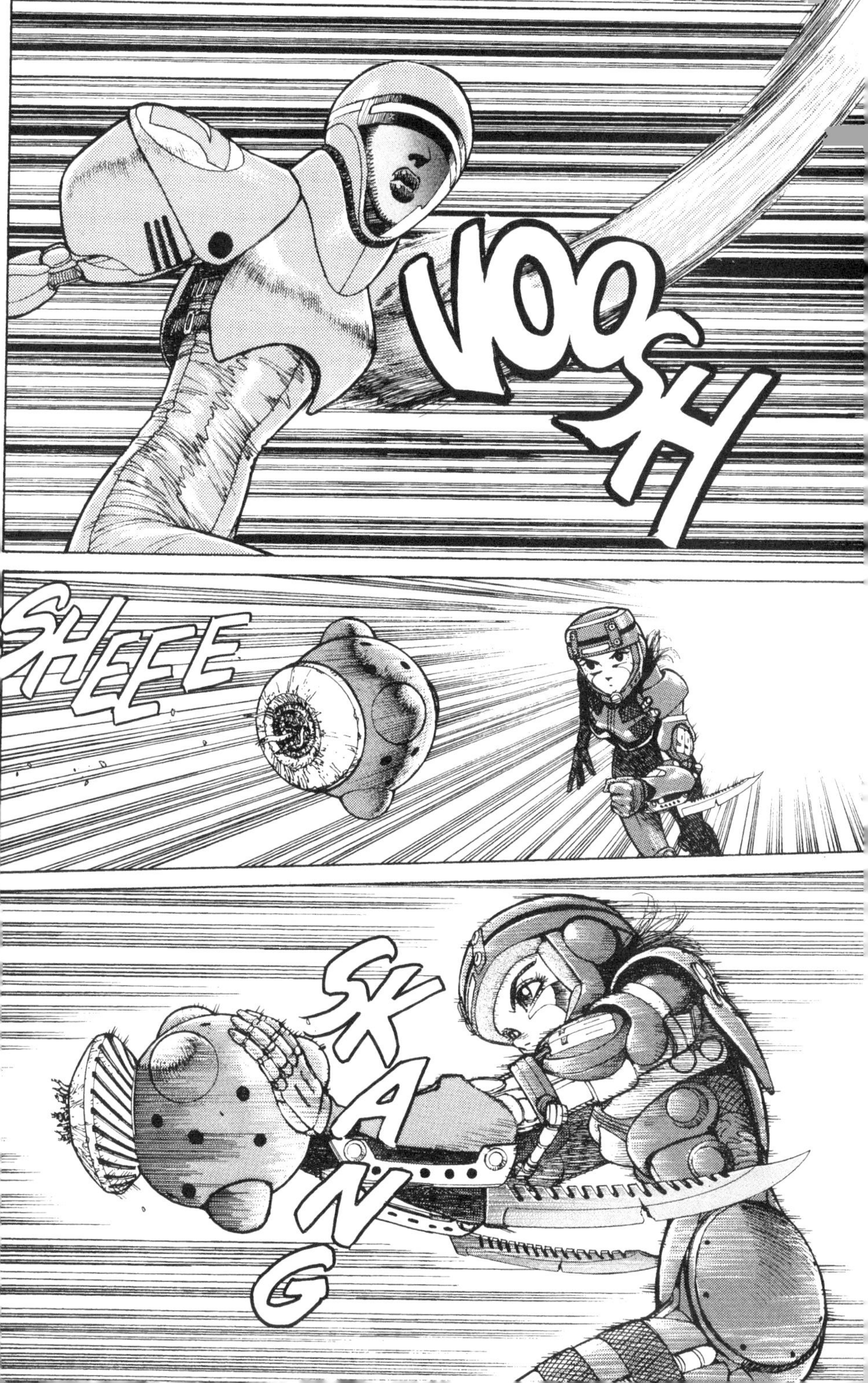
VOOSH
SHEEE
SKANG

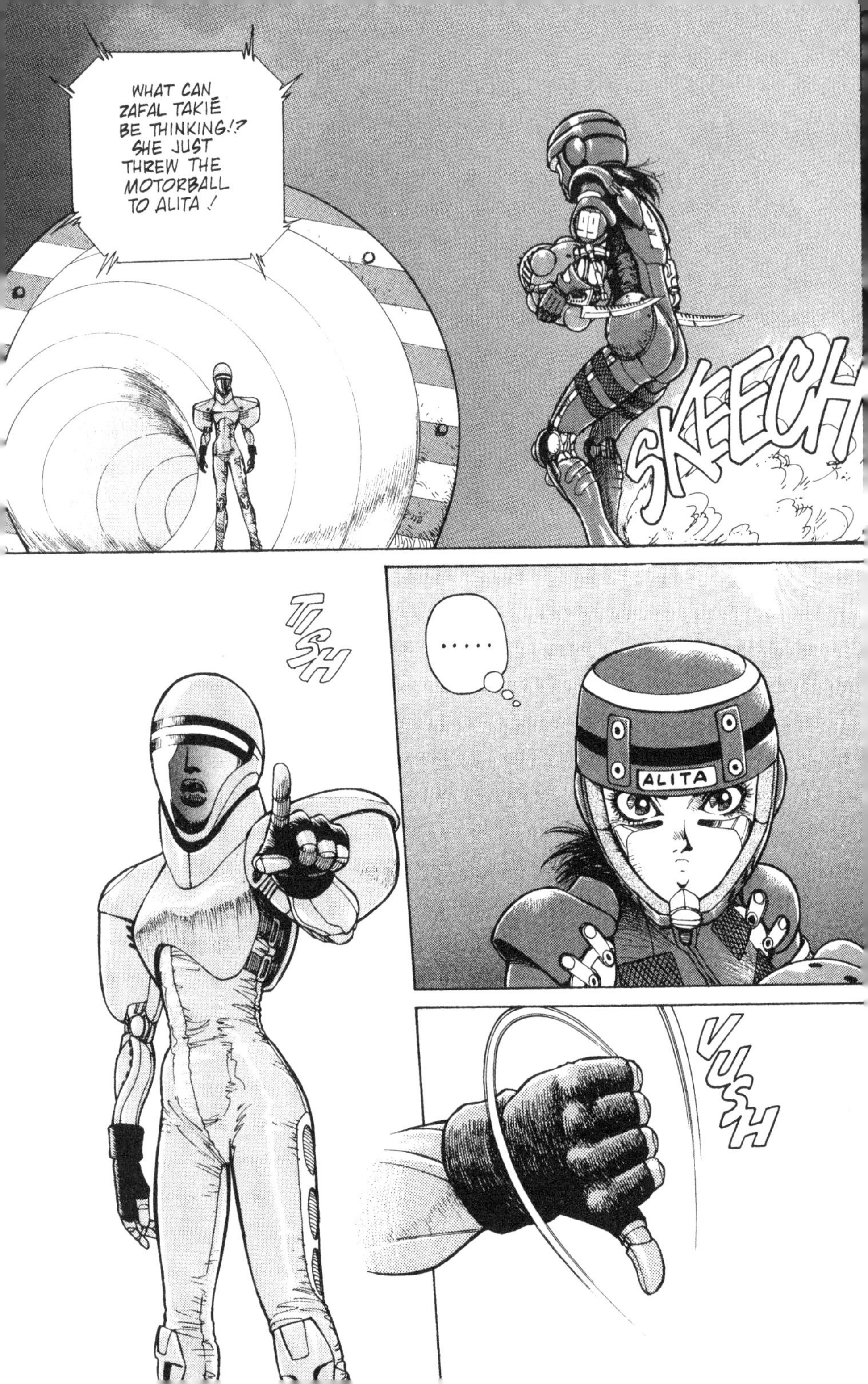
WHAT CAN ZAFAL TAKIE BE THINKING!? SHE JUST THREW THE MOTORBALL TO ALITA!
SKEECH
TISH
......
ALITA
VUSH

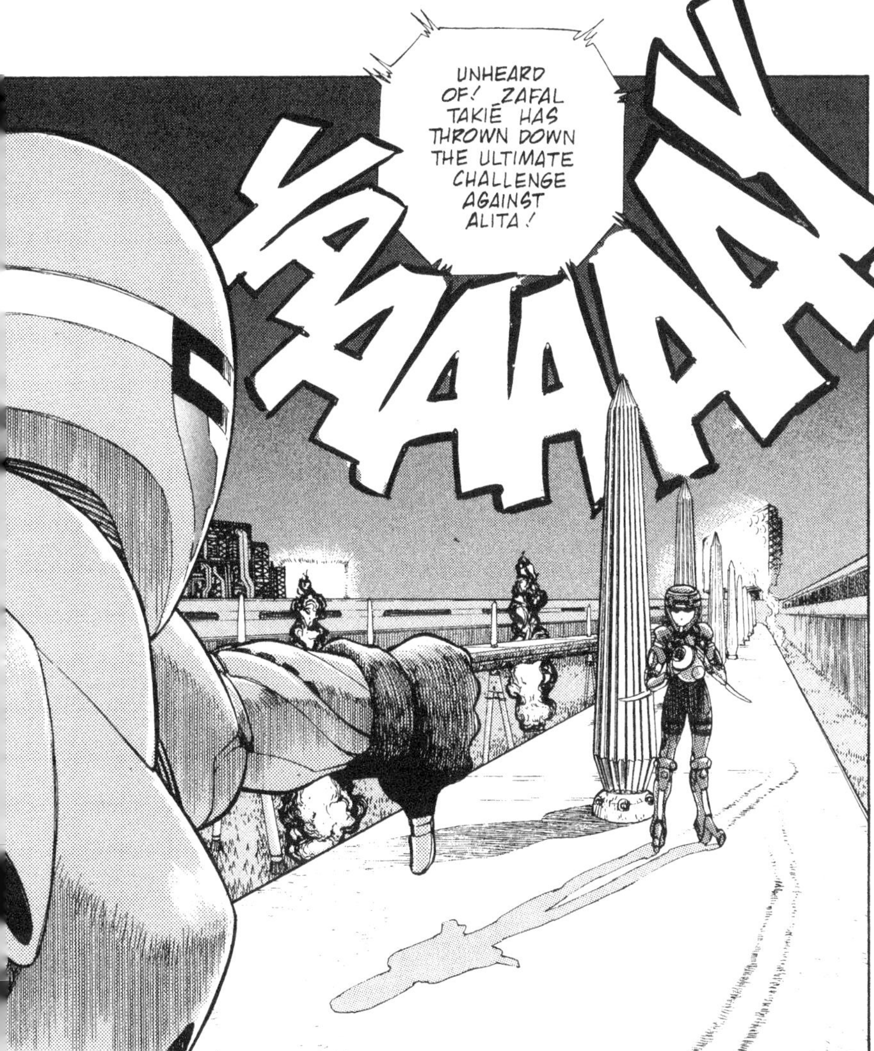
YAAAAAY
UNHEARD OF! ZAFAL TAKIÉ HAS THROWN DOWN THE ULTIMATE CHALLENGE AGAINST ALITA!

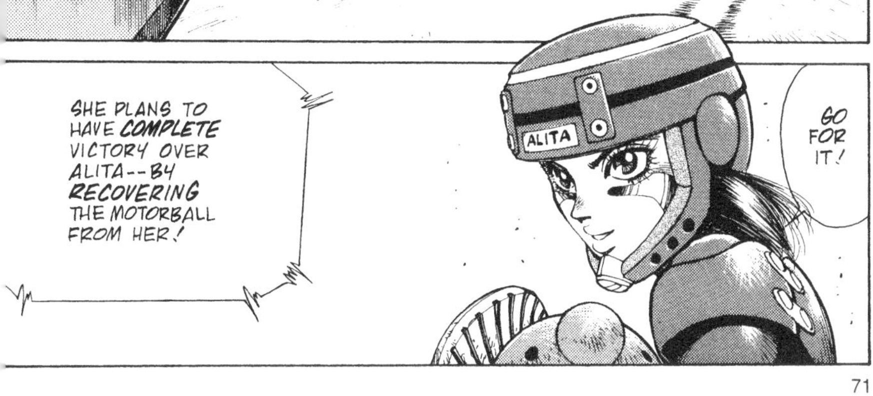
SHE PLANS TO HAVE COMPLETE VICTORY OVER ALITA--BY RECOVERING THE MOTORBALL FROM HER!
ALITA
GO FOR IT!

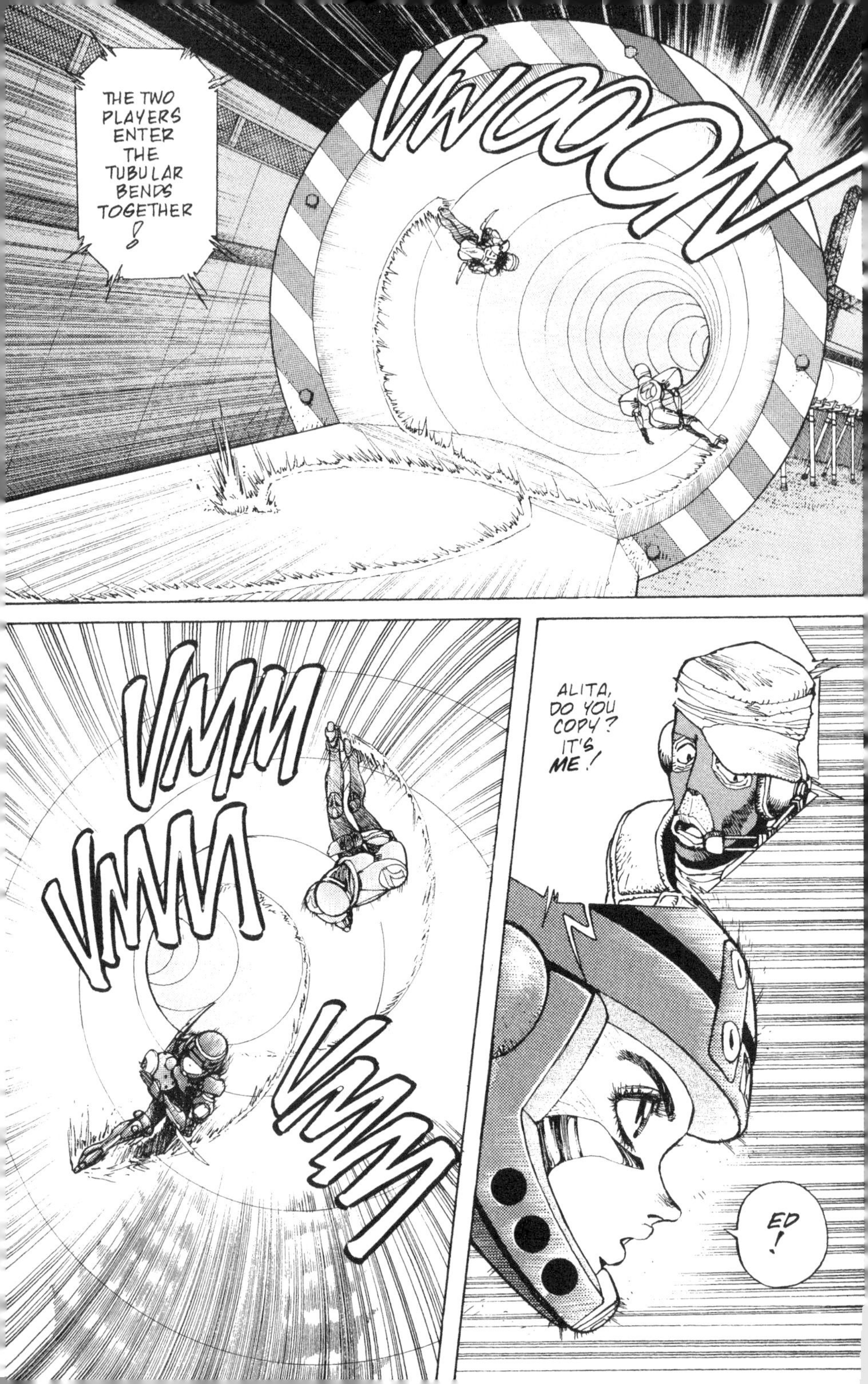
THE TWO PLAYERS ENTER THE TUBULAR BENDS TOGETHER!
VWAAON
VMM VMM VMM
ALITA, DO YOU COPY? IT'S ME!
ED!

LISTEN UP! DON'T LET ZAFAL TAKIE RILE YOU!

HER FIGHTING STYLE IS CLEAN AND SIMPLE! SHE'LL MAKE YOU ATTACK SO THAT SHE CAN DODGE-- THEN HIT YOU WHILE YOU'RE VULNERABLE! HER TECHNIQUES ARE ALL *DEFENSIVE!*

IF YOU FALL FOR HER RUSE AND ATTACK-- YOU'LL NEVER BE ABLE TO AVOID HER SPEED!

OKAY-- GOT YA!

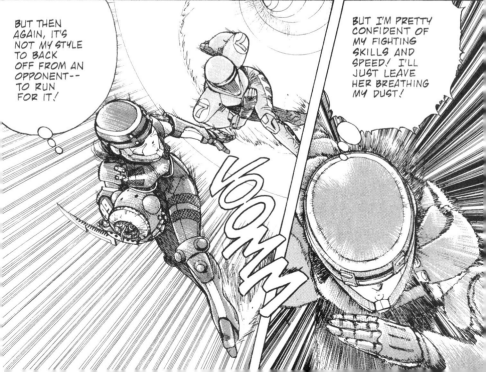

BUT THEN AGAIN, IT'S NOT MY STYLE TO BACK OFF FROM AN OPPONENT-- TO RUN FOR IT!

BUT I'M PRETTY CONFIDENT OF MY FIGHTING SKILLS AND SPEED! I'LL JUST LEAVE HER BREATHING MY DUST!

VOOMM

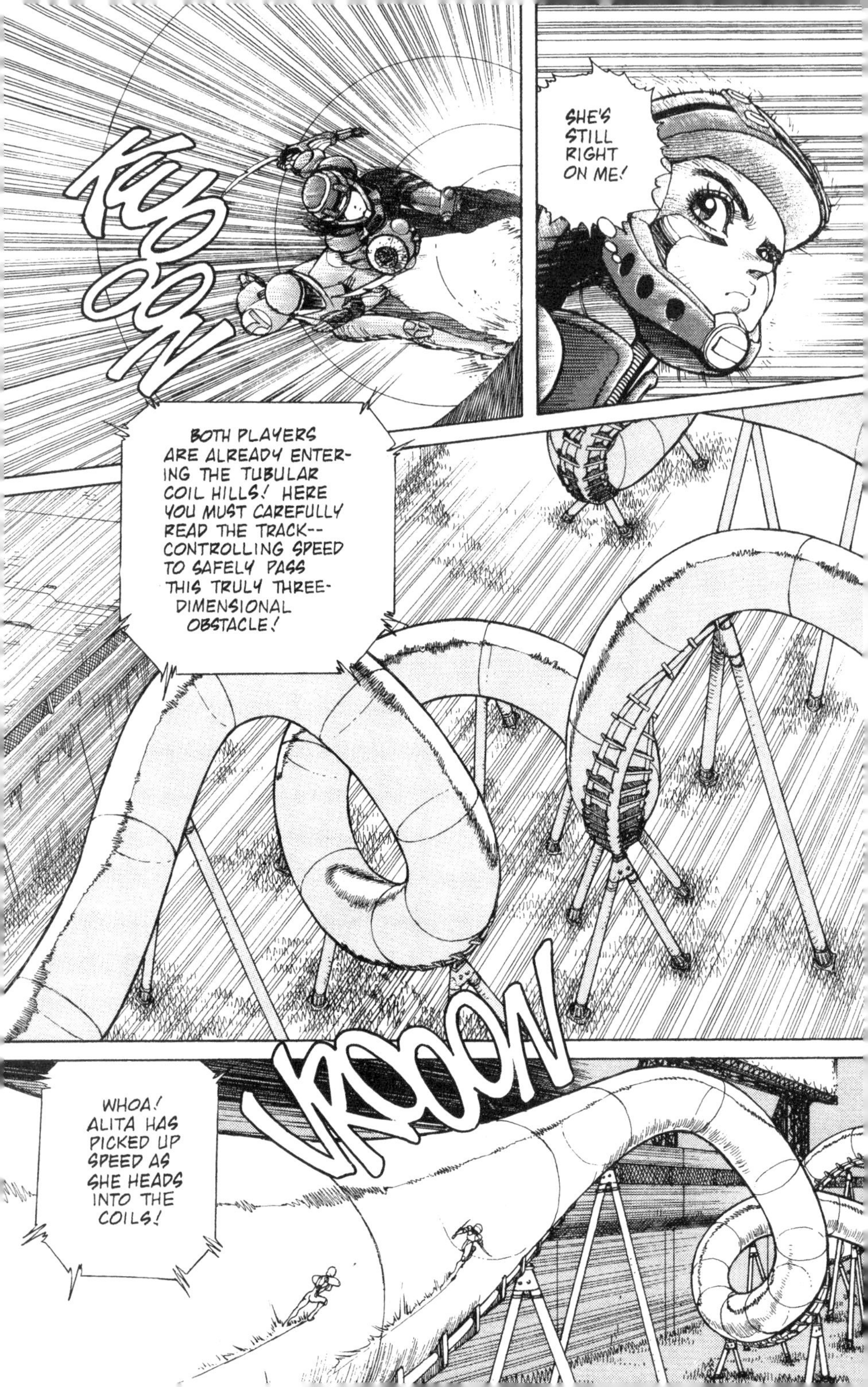
KYOOON
SHE'S STILL RIGHT ON ME!
BOTH PLAYERS ARE ALREADY ENTERING THE TUBULAR COIL HILLS! HERE YOU MUST CAREFULLY READ THE TRACK--CONTROLLING SPEED TO SAFELY PASS THIS TRULY THREE-DIMENSIONAL OBSTACLE!
VROOON
WHOA! ALITA HAS PICKED UP SPEED AS SHE HEADS INTO THE COILS!

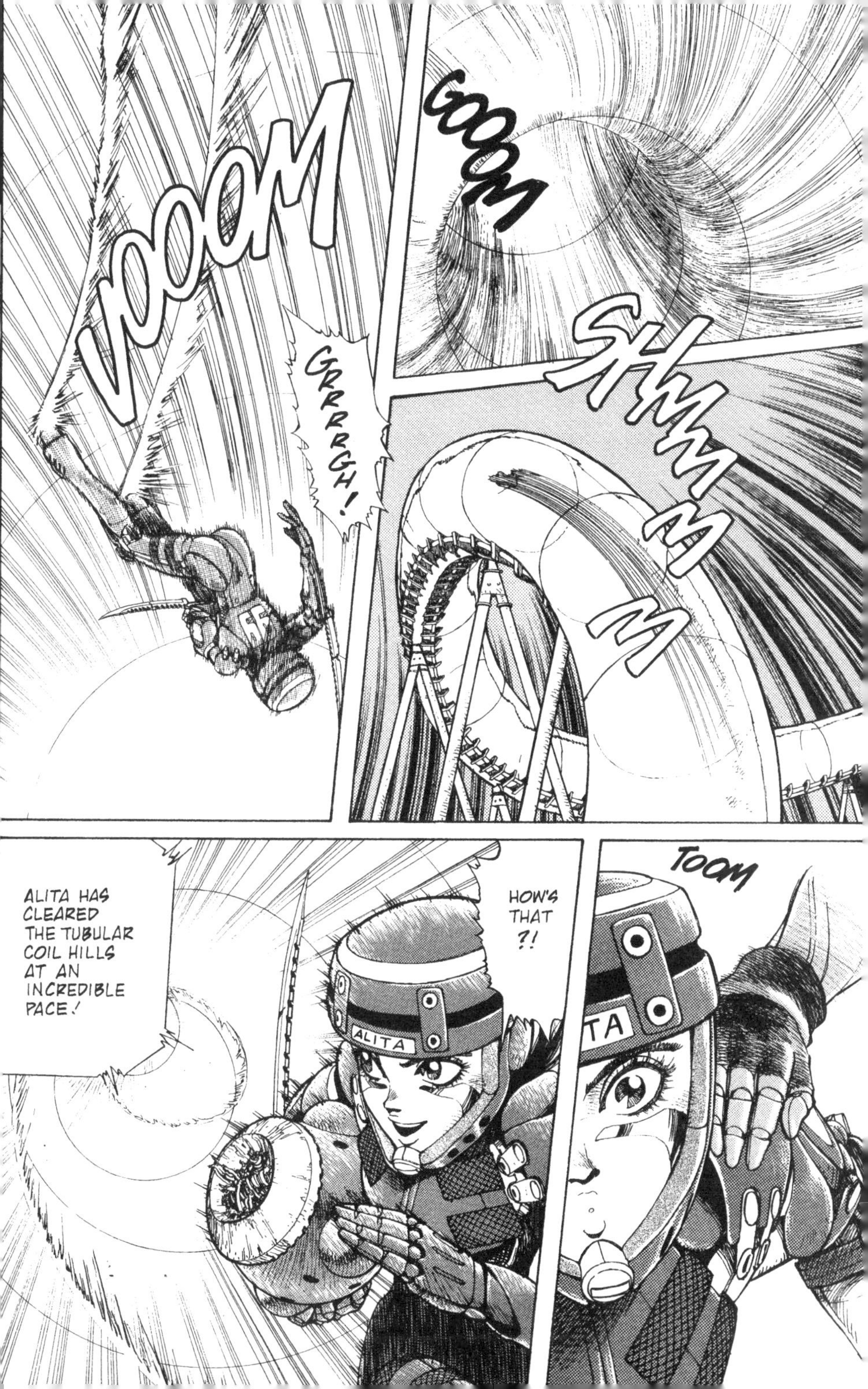
VOOOM
GRRRRGH!
GOOOM
SHMMMM
ALITA HAS CLEARED THE TUBULAR COIL HILLS AT AN INCREDIBLE PACE!
HOW'S THAT ?!
ALITA
TOOM

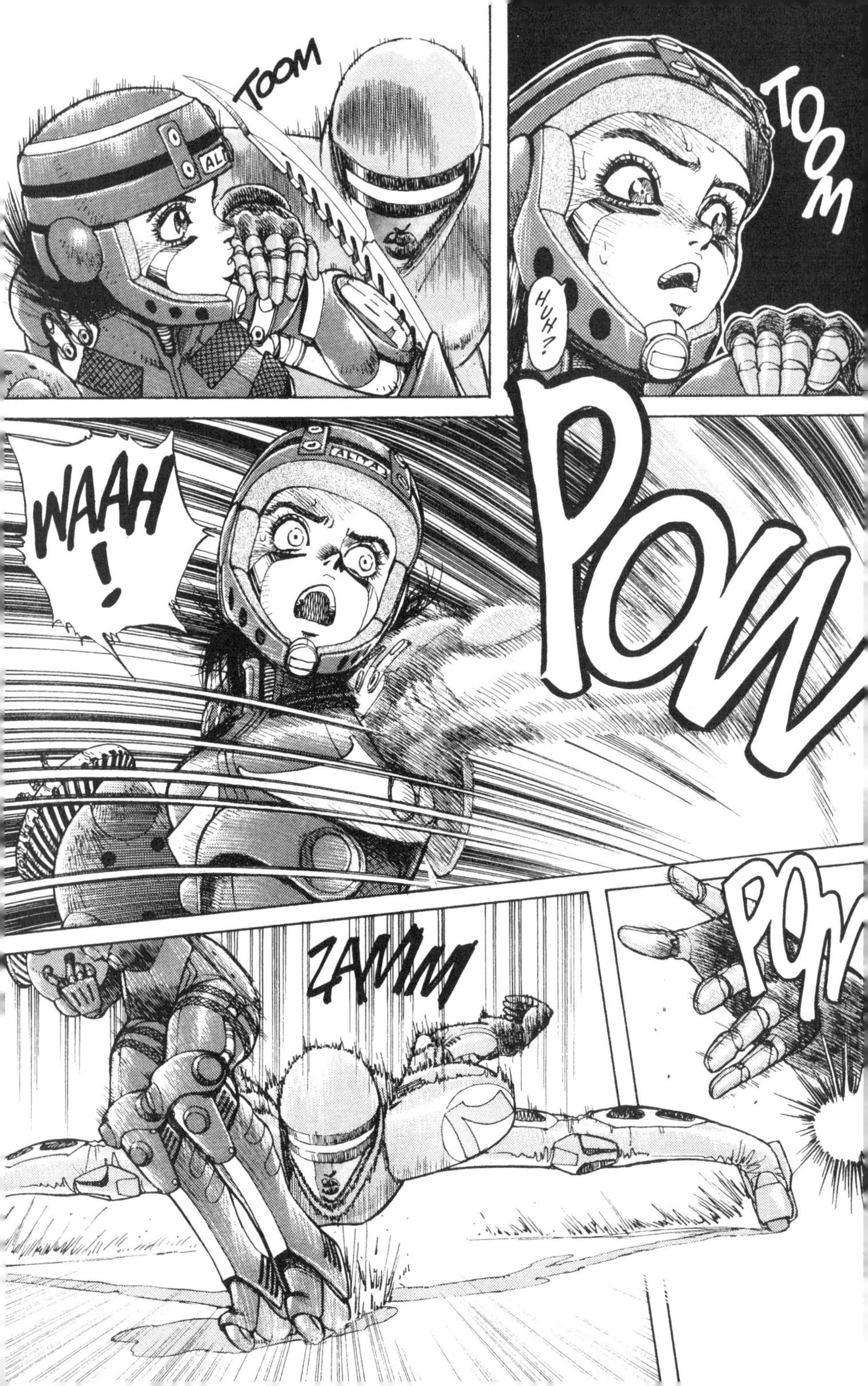

TOOM
TOOM
HUH?!
WAAH!
POW
ZAWM
PO

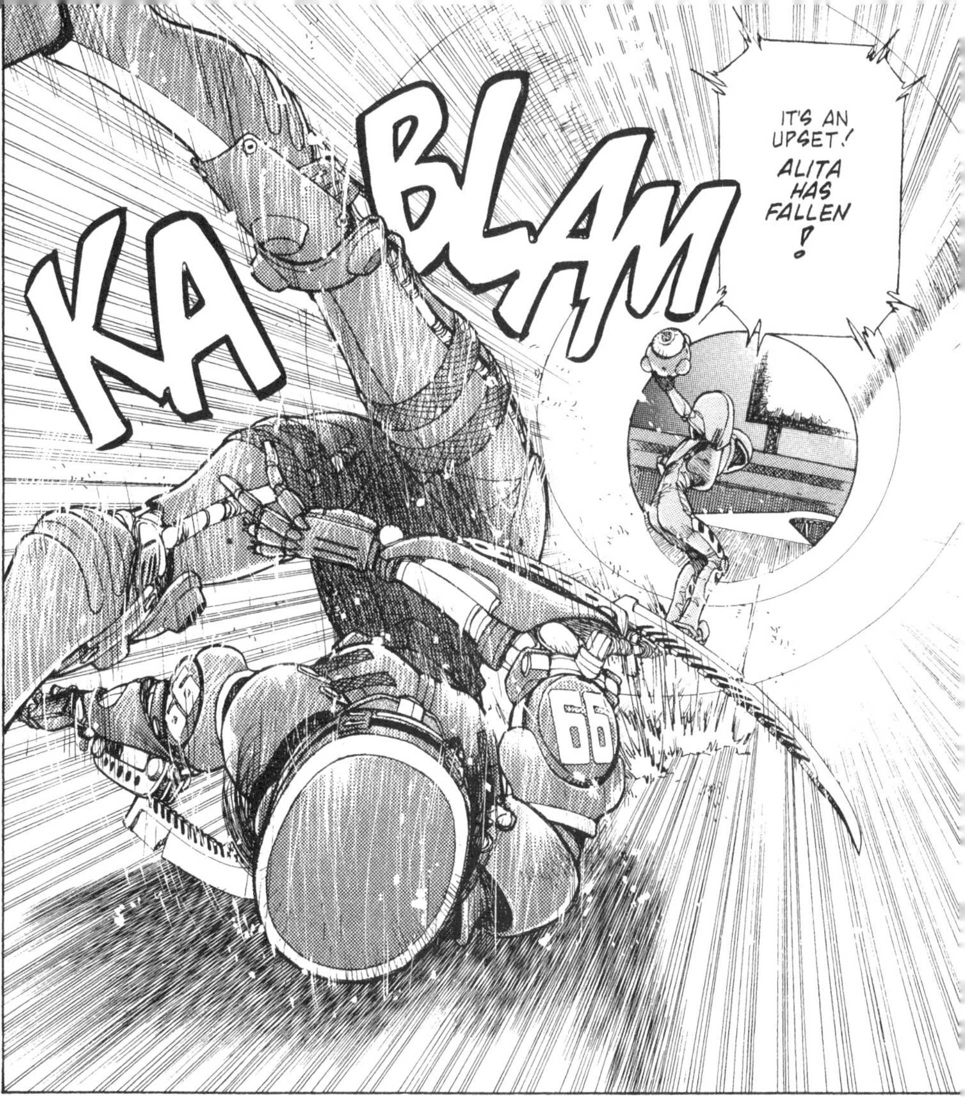
KA BLAM
IT'S AN UPSET! ALITA HAS FALLEN!

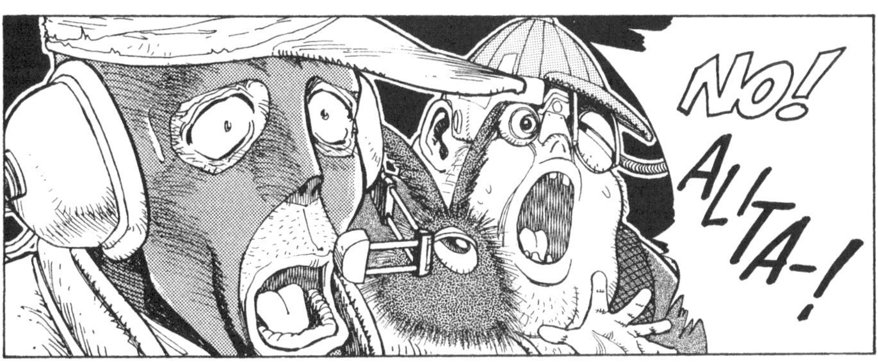
NO! ALITA-!

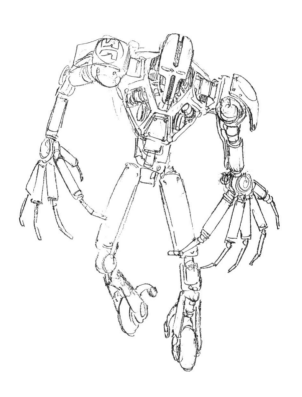

RED ZONE
Race 2: Fight Like the Wind

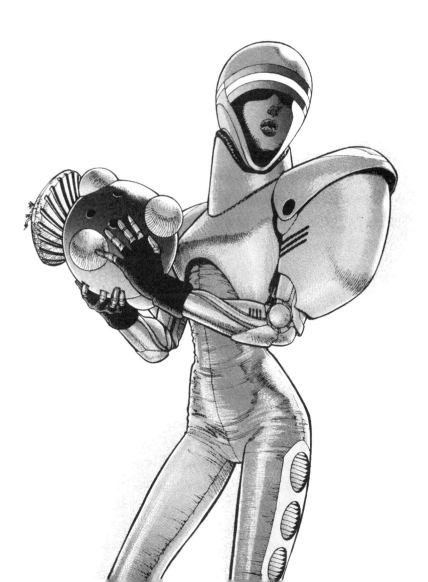

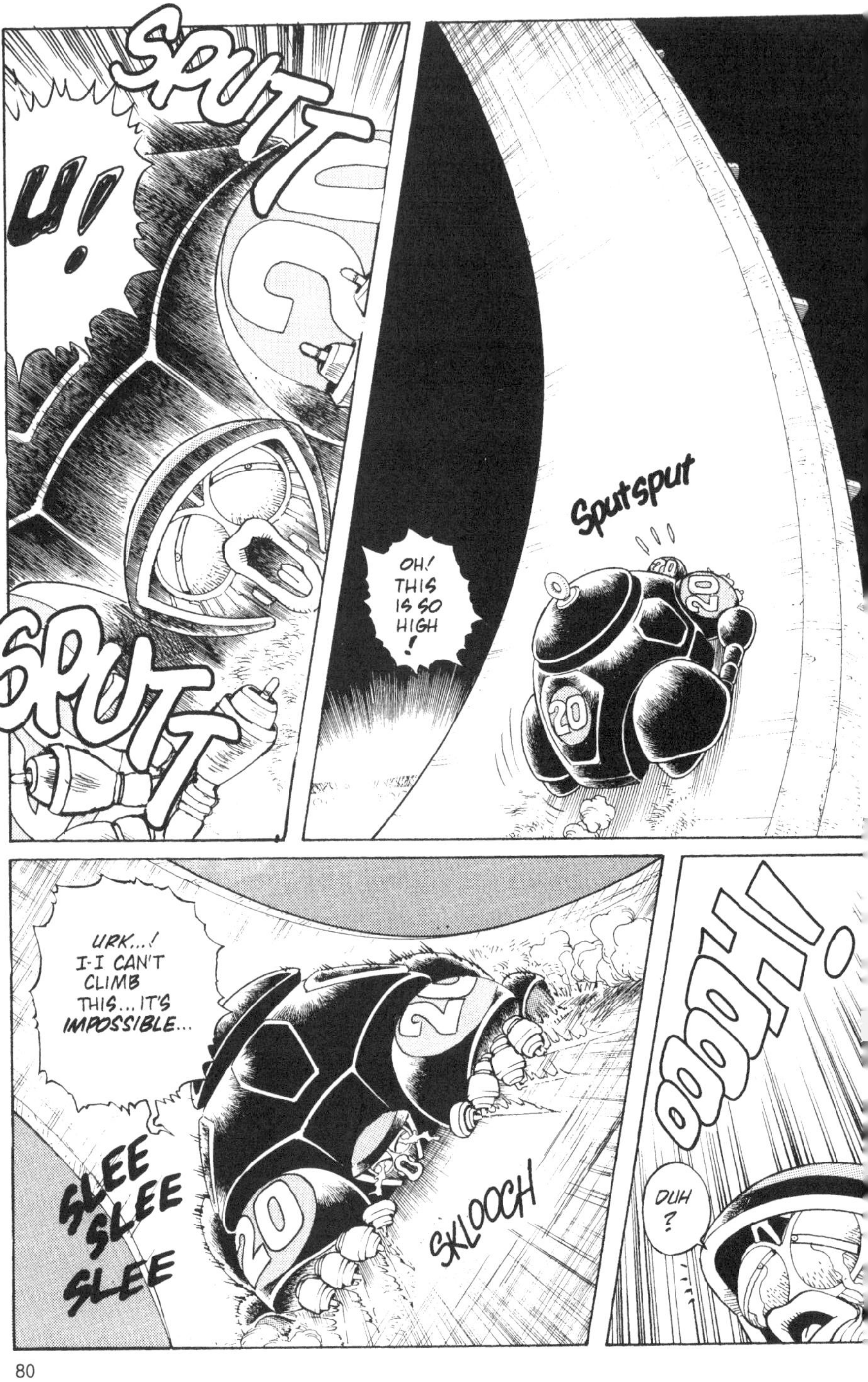
SPUTT
U!
SPUTT
Sputspur
OH! THIS IS SO HIGH!
URK...! I-I CAN'T CLIMB THIS... IT'S IMPOSSIBLE...
SLEE SLEE SLEE
SKLOOCH
OOOOH!!
DUH?

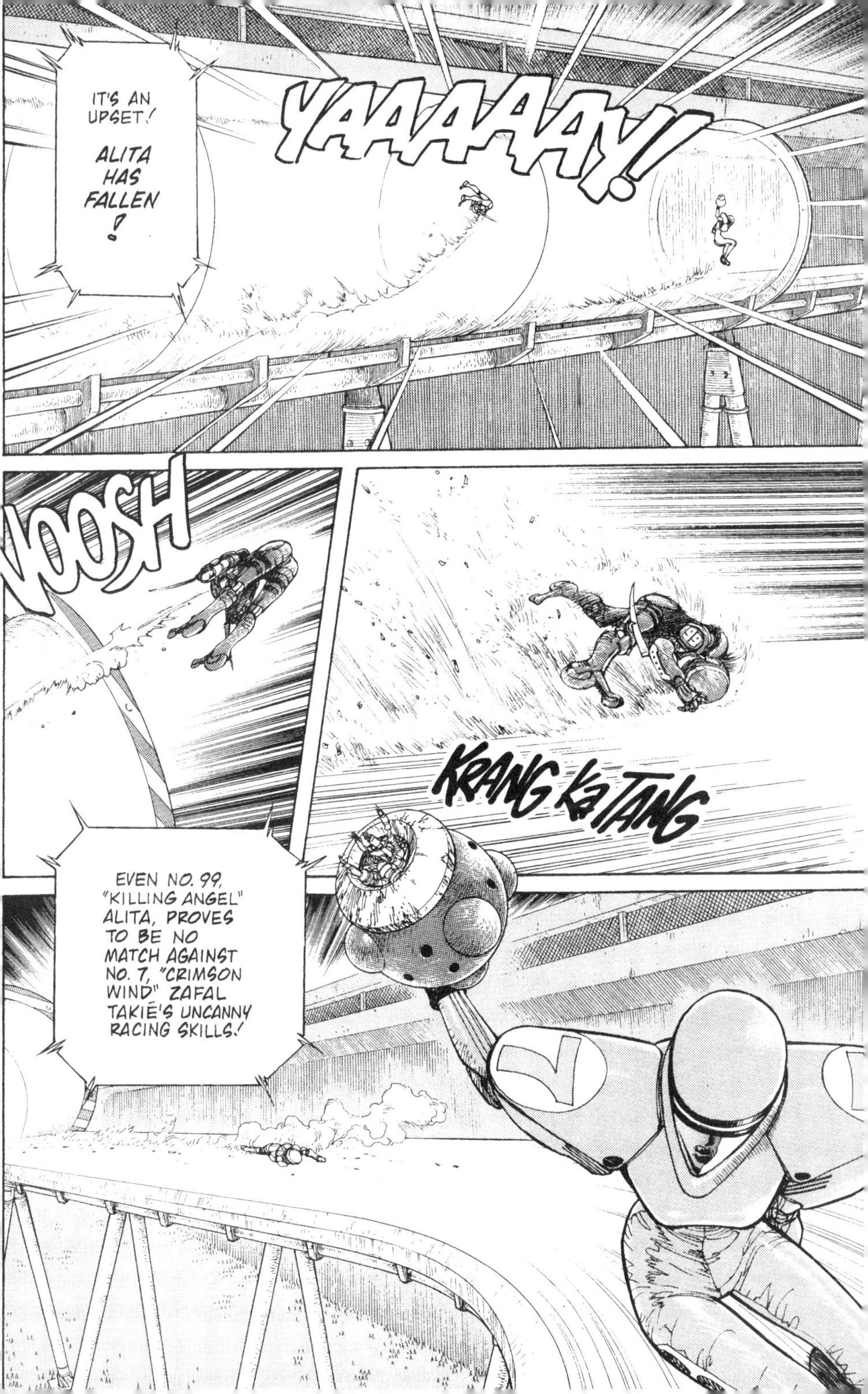
IT'S AN UPSET! ALITA HAS FALLEN !
YAAAAAAY!!
VOOSH
KRANG KA TANG
EVEN NO. 99, "KILLING ANGEL" ALITA, PROVES TO BE NO MATCH AGAINST NO. 7, "CRIMSON WIND" ZAFAL TAKIÉ'S UNCANNY RACING SKILLS!

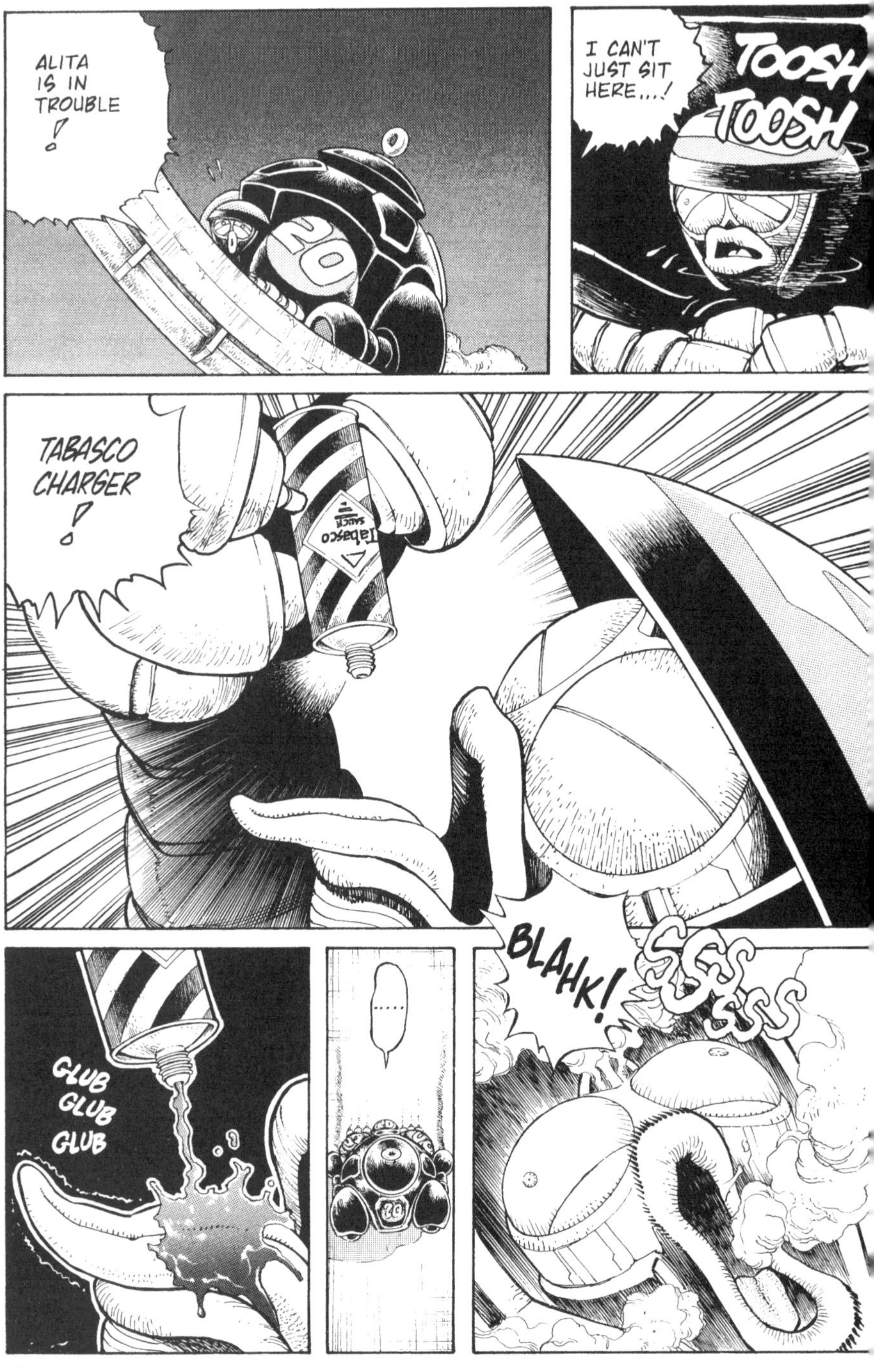
ALITA IS IN TROUBLE!
I CAN'T JUST SIT HERE...!
TOOSH
TOOSH
TABASCO CHARGER!
Tabasco SAUCE
BLAHK!
SSSSSSS
GLUB GLUB GLUB
......

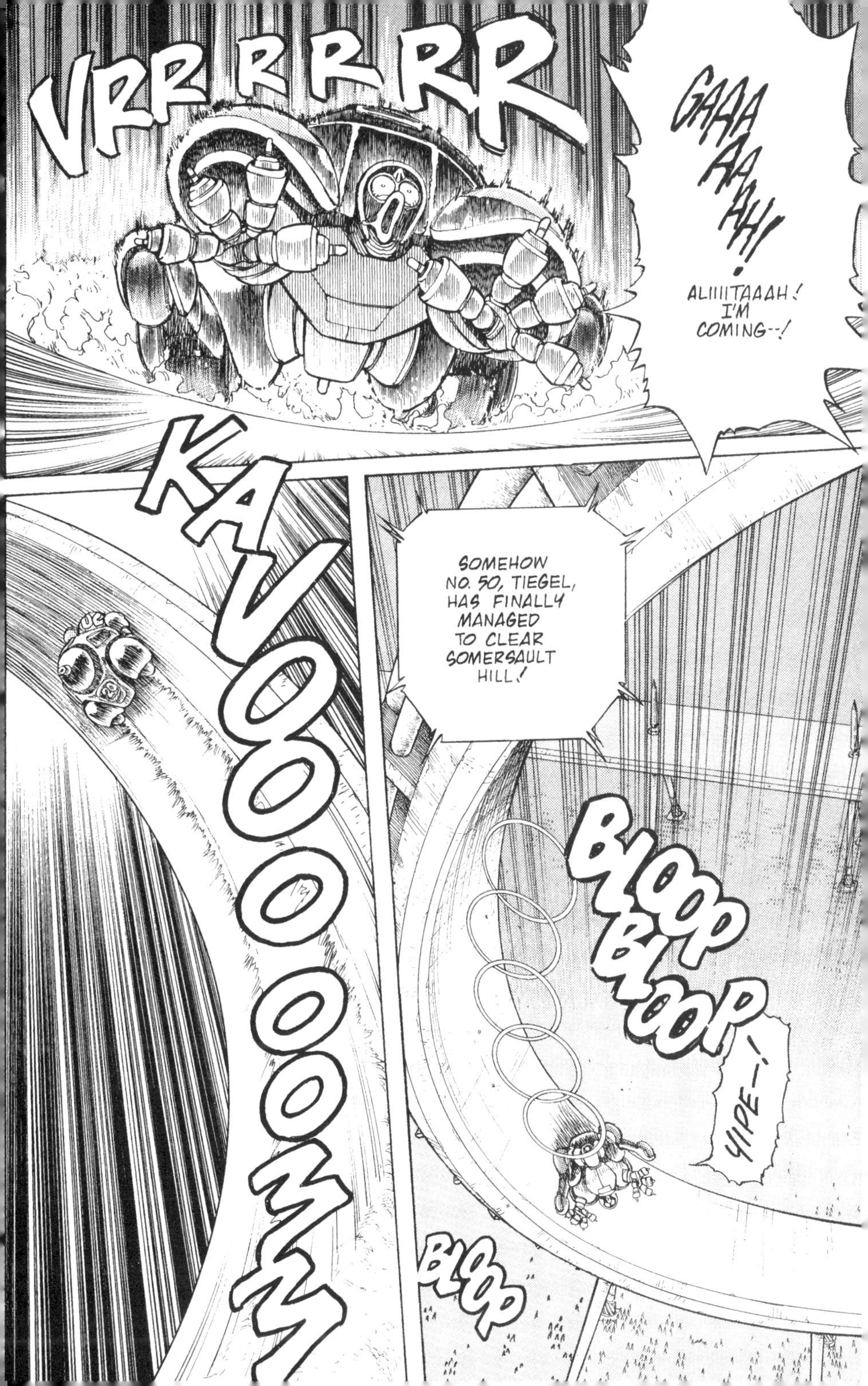
VRRRRRR
GAAAAAAAH!!
ALIIIITAAAH! I'M COMING--!
KAVOOOOOOMM
SOMEHOW NO. 50, TIEGEL, HAS FINALLY MANAGED TO CLEAR SOMERSAULT HILL!
BLOOP BLOOP BLOOP
YIPE--!
BLOOP

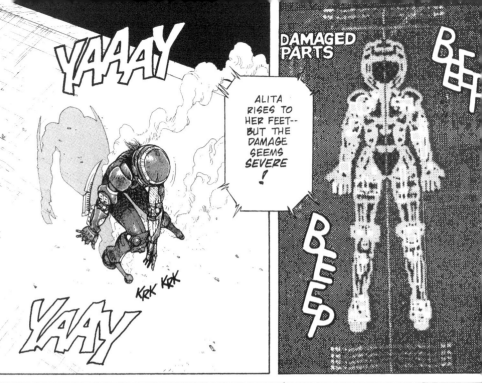

YAAAY

KRK KRK

YAAY

ALITA RISES TO HER FEET-- BUT THE DAMAGE SEEMS *SEVERE*!

DAMAGED PARTS

BEEP

BEEP

HOW IS SHE, UMBA!?

THE DATASCAN SAYS THE DAMAGE IS ONLY IN THE JOINTS. I'D SAY FIVE MINUTES TO REPLACE ALL FOUR LIMBS AND ANOTHER THREE MINUTES TO ALIGN THEM!

HEY, APPRENTICE! WHAT'S THE COURSE RECORD FOR ONE LAP OF THIS TRACK!?

TWO MINUTES, 16.392 SECONDS!

THEN YOU'VE GOT *LESS* THAN SIX MINUTES TO FINISH-- OR THERE'S *NO* CHANCE OF BEATING TAKIE!

I'LL *DO* IT!

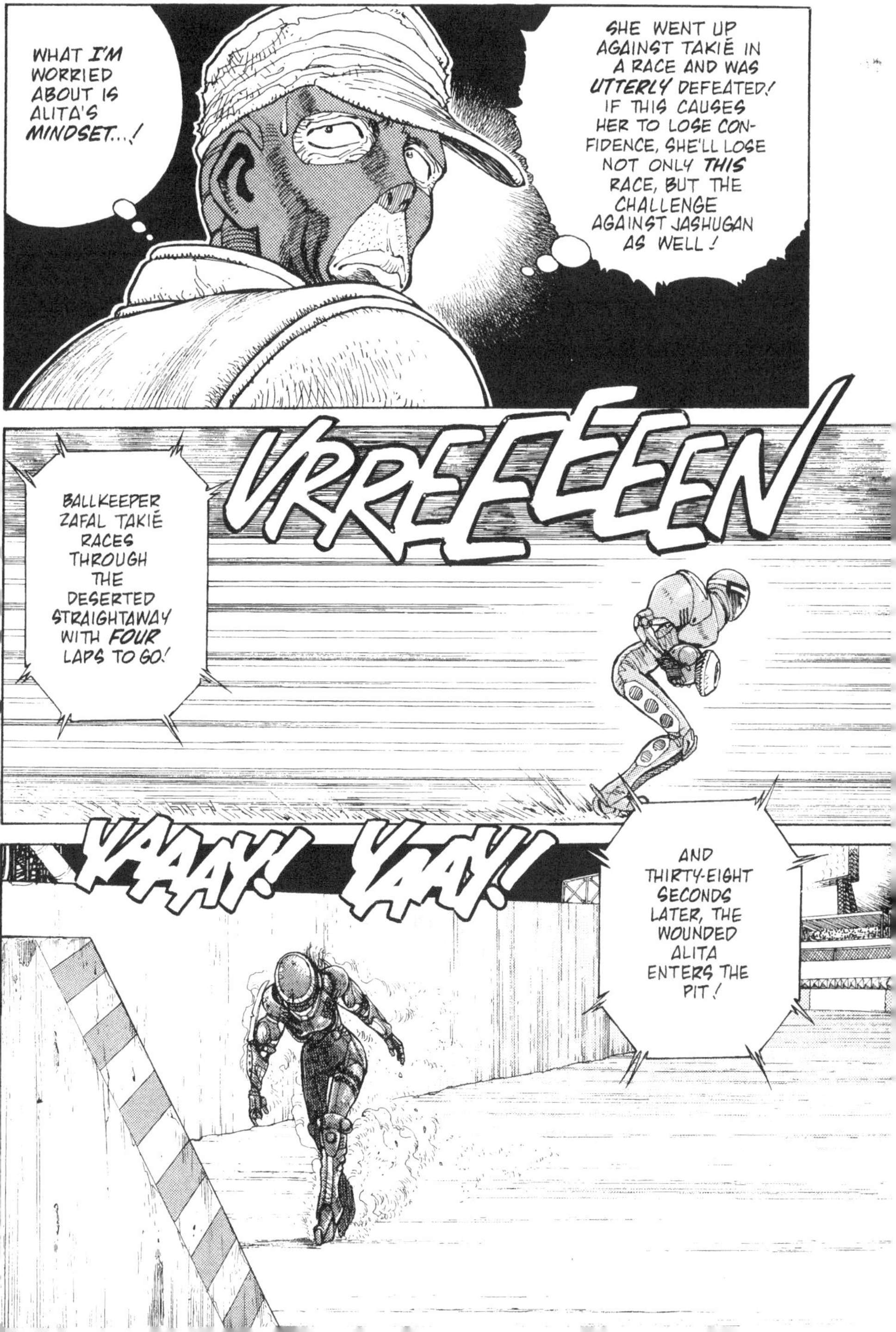
WHAT *I'M* WORRIED ABOUT IS ALITA'S *MINDSET*...!
SHE WENT UP AGAINST TAKIÉ IN A RACE AND WAS *UTTERLY* DEFEATED! IF THIS CAUSES HER TO LOSE CON-FIDENCE, SHE'LL LOSE NOT ONLY *THIS* RACE, BUT THE CHALLENGE AGAINST JASHUGAN AS WELL!
VRREEEEEN
BALLKEEPER ZAFAL TAKIÉ RACES THROUGH THE DESERTED STRAIGHTAWAY WITH *FOUR* LAPS TO GO!
YAAAY! YAAY!
AND THIRTY-EIGHT SECONDS LATER, THE WOUNDED ALITA ENTERS THE PIT!

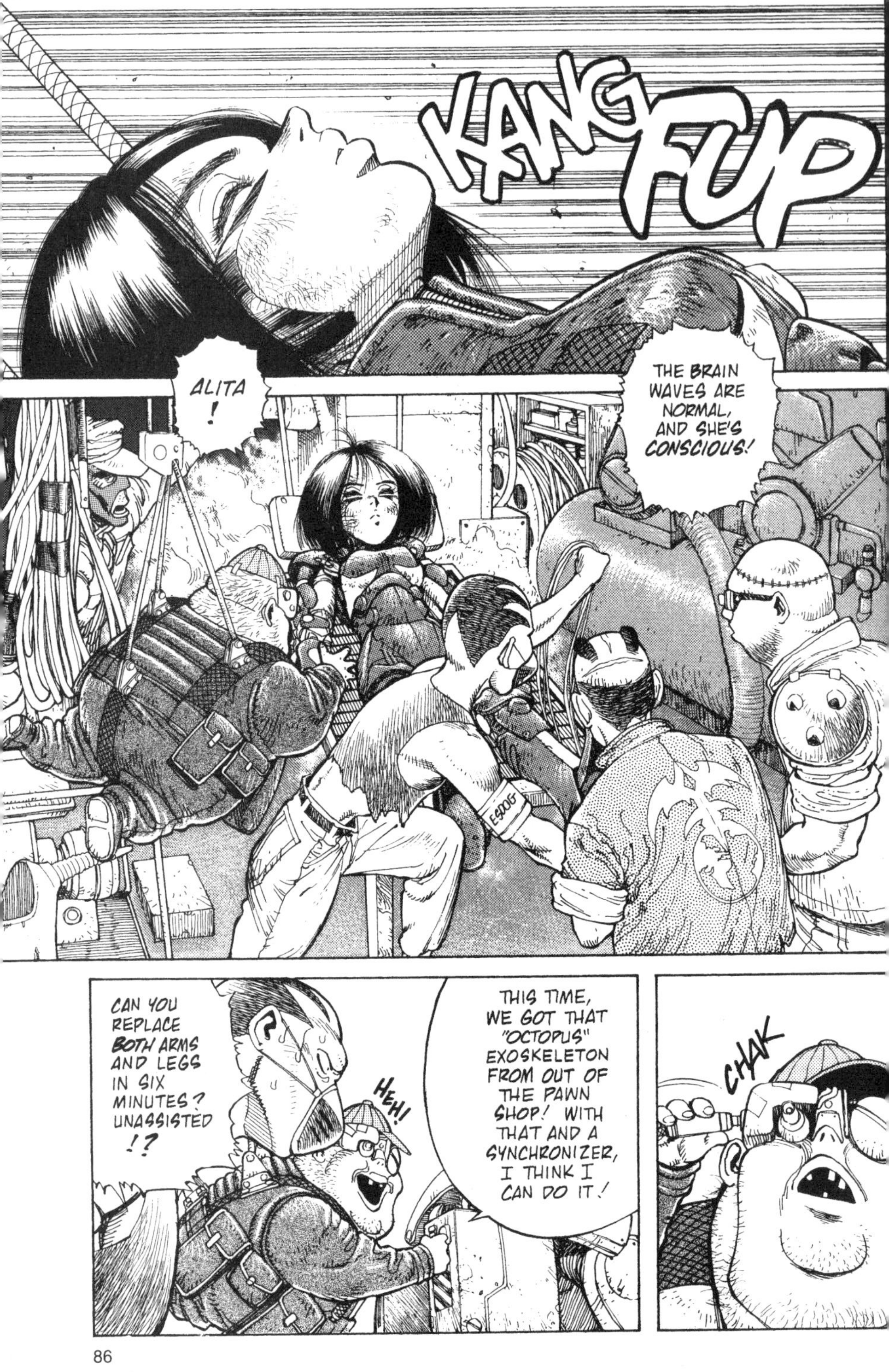
KANG FUP
ALITA!
THE BRAIN WAVES ARE NORMAL, AND SHE'S CONSCIOUS!
E-SDOG
CAN YOU REPLACE BOTH ARMS AND LEGS IN SIX MINUTES? UNASSISTED!?
HEH!
THIS TIME, WE GOT THAT "OCTOPUS" EXOSKELETON FROM OUT OF THE PAWN SHOP! WITH THAT AND A SYNCHRONIZER, I THINK I CAN DO IT!
CHAK

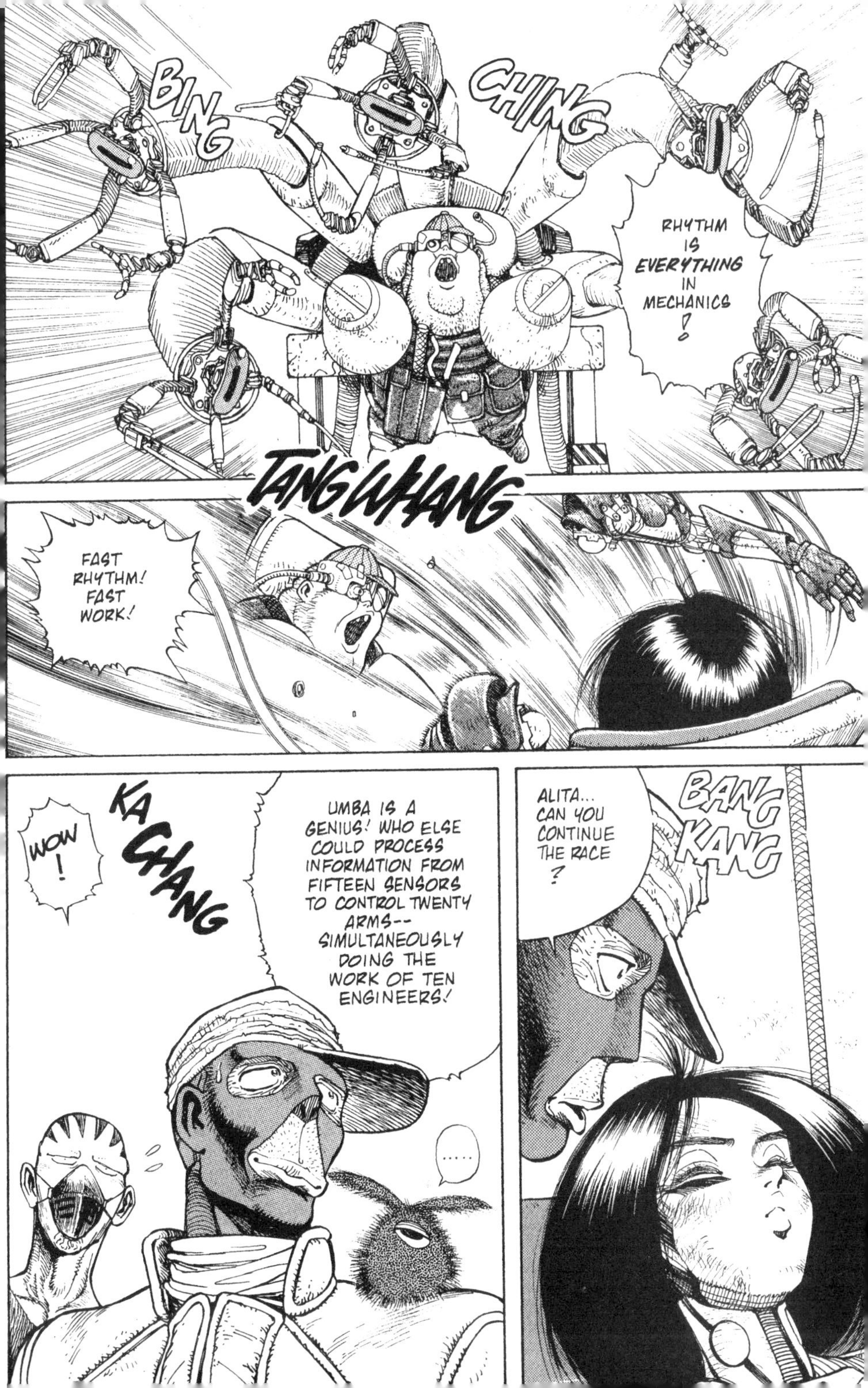
BING
CHING
RHYTHM IS **EVERYTHING** IN MECHANICS!
TANG WHANG
FAST RHYTHM! FAST WORK!
WOW!
KA CHANG
UMBA IS A GENIUS! WHO ELSE COULD PROCESS INFORMATION FROM FIFTEEN SENSORS TO CONTROL TWENTY ARMS-- SIMULTANEOUSLY DOING THE WORK OF TEN ENGINEERS!
......
ALITA... CAN YOU CONTINUE THE RACE?
BANG KANG

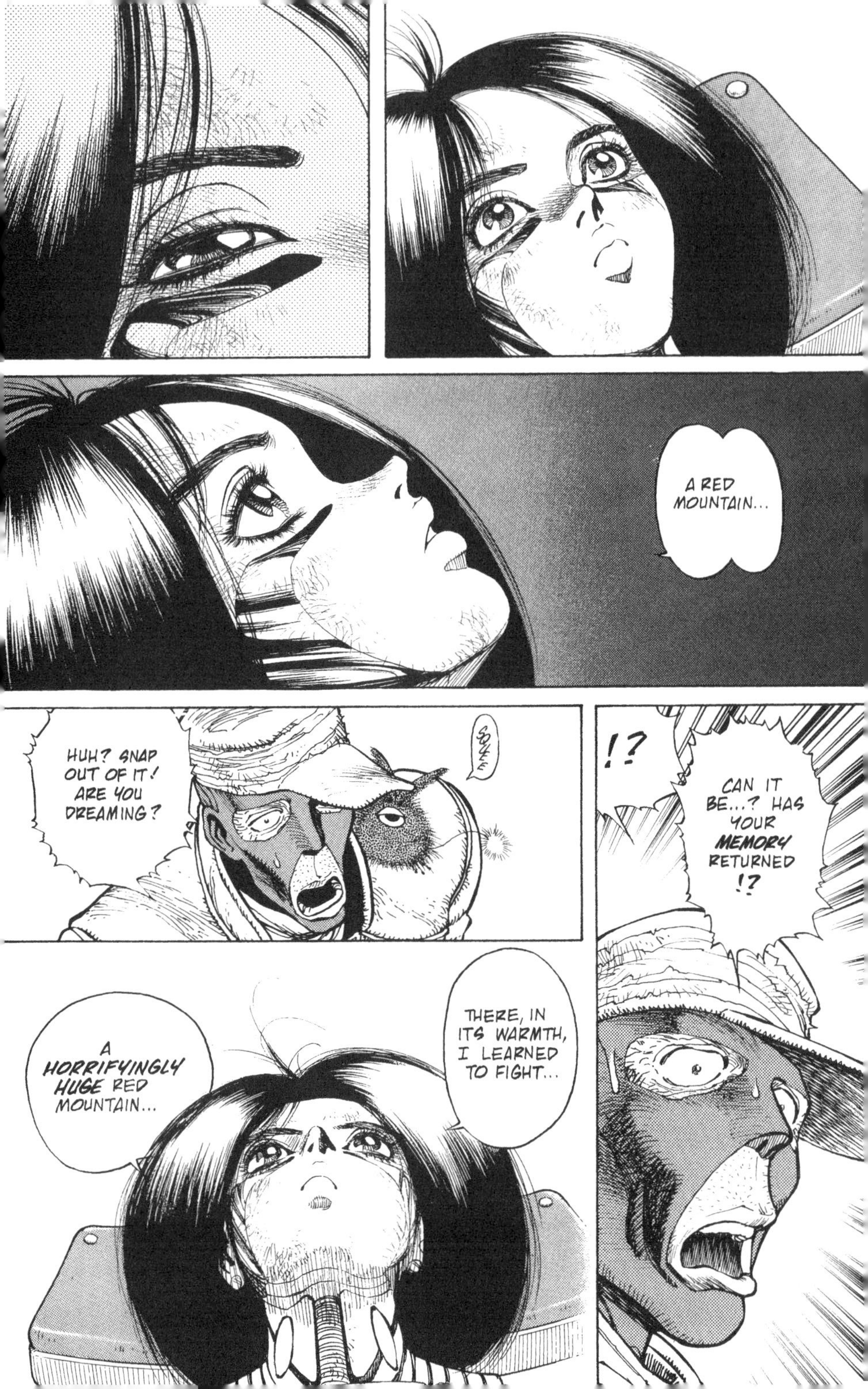
A RED MOUNTAIN...
HUH? SNAP OUT OF IT! ARE YOU DREAMING?
A HORRIFYINGLY HUGE RED MOUNTAIN...
THERE, IN ITS WARMTH, I LEARNED TO FIGHT...
!?
CAN IT BE...? HAS YOUR MEMORY RETURNED !?

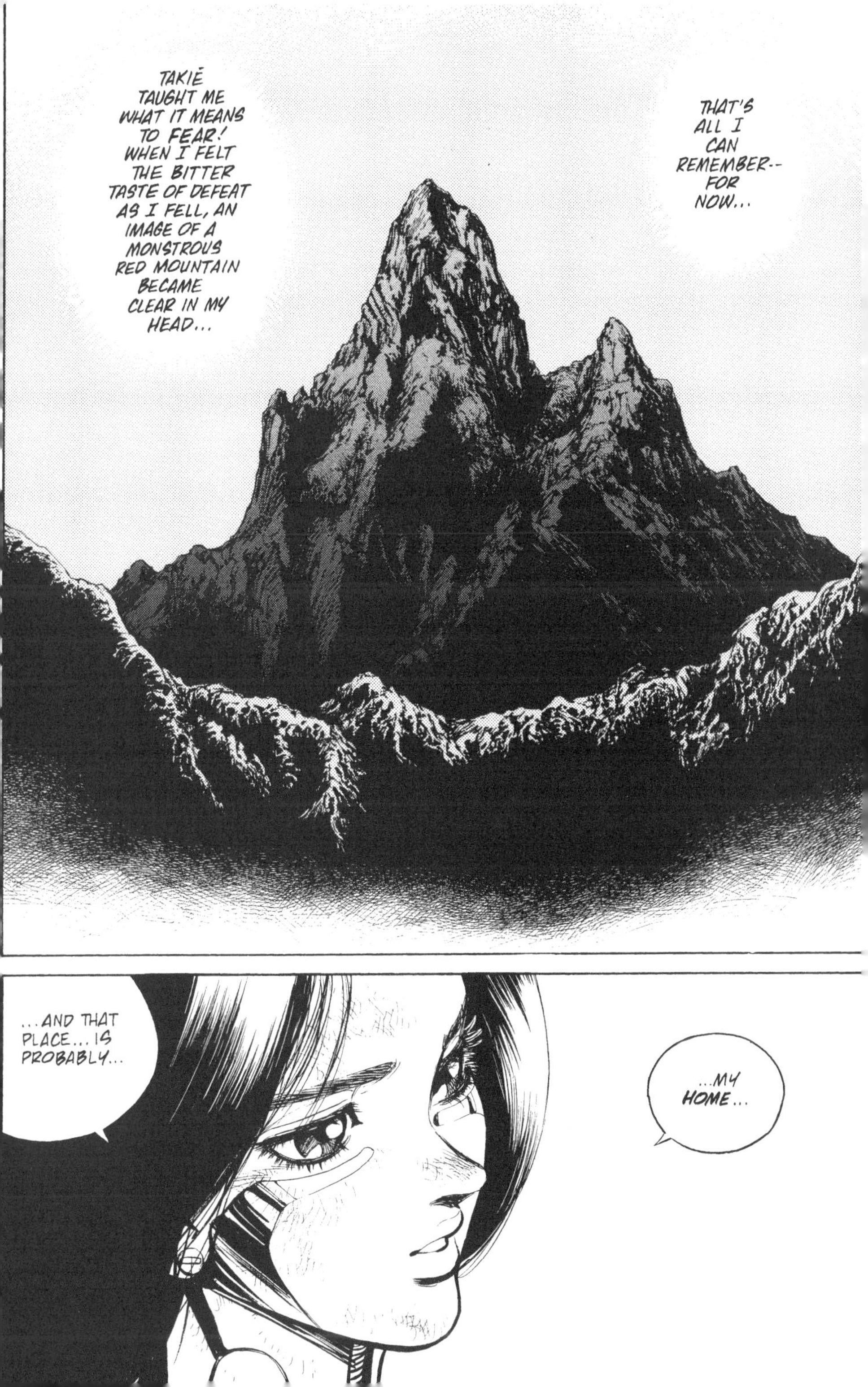
TAKIĒ TAUGHT ME WHAT IT MEANS TO FEAR! WHEN I FELT THE BITTER TASTE OF DEFEAT AS I FELL, AN IMAGE OF A MONSTROUS RED MOUNTAIN BECAME CLEAR IN MY HEAD...
THAT'S ALL I CAN REMEMBER-- FOR NOW...
...AND THAT PLACE... IS PROBABLY...
...MY HOME...

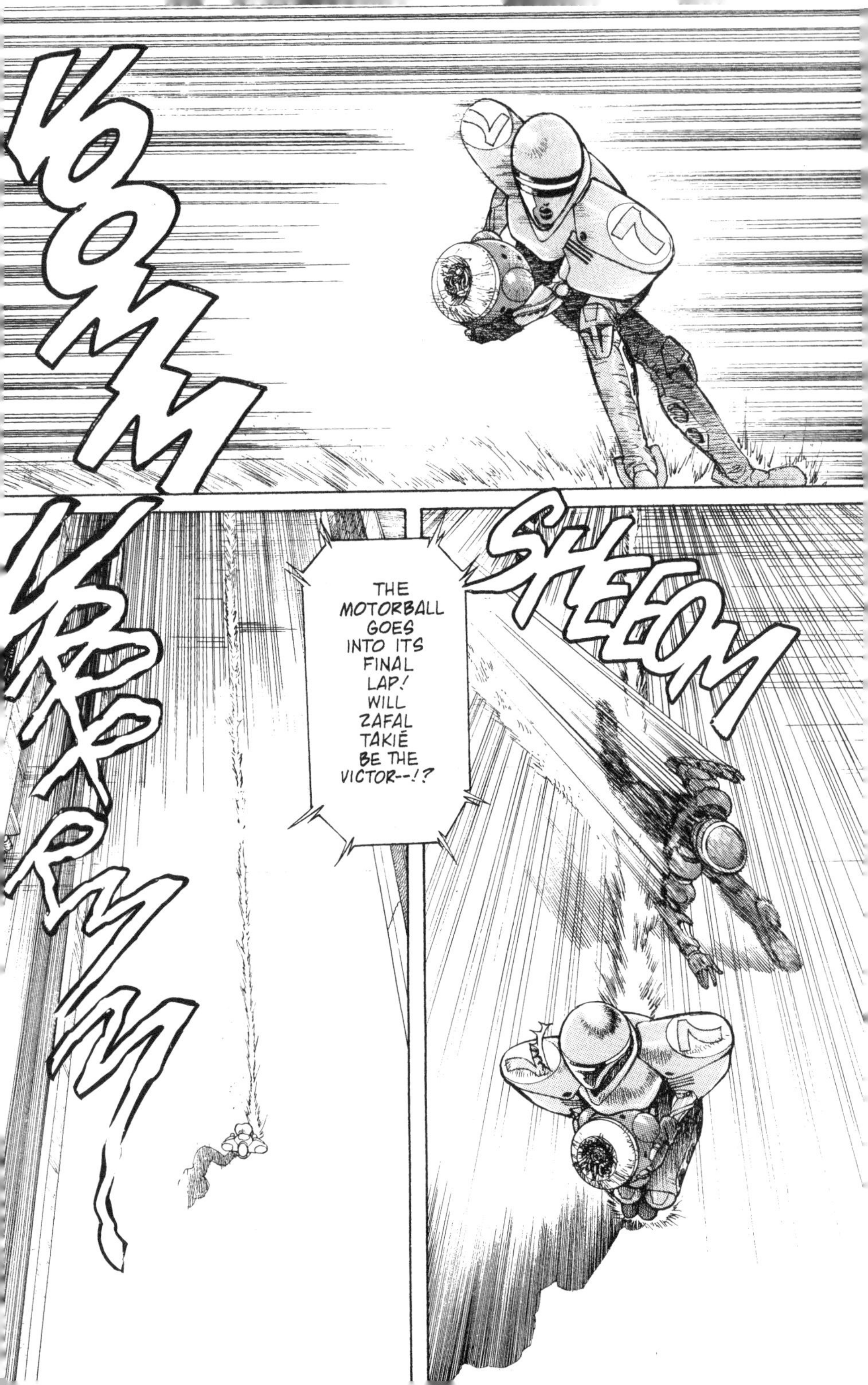
THE MOTORBALL GOES INTO ITS FINAL LAP! WILL ZAFAL TAKIÉ BE THE VICTOR--!?

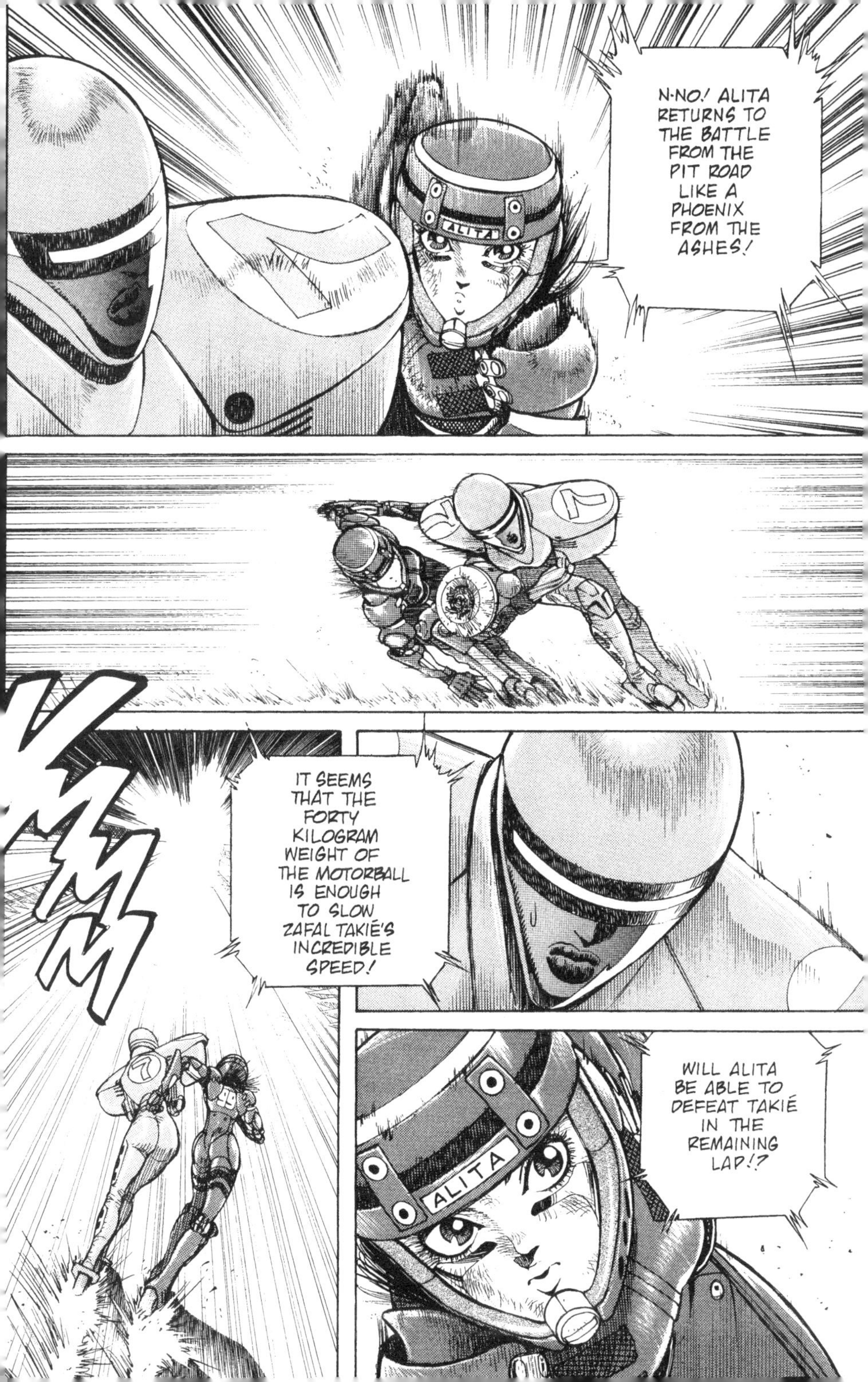
N-NO! ALITA RETURNS TO THE BATTLE FROM THE PIT ROAD LIKE A PHOENIX FROM THE ASHES!
ALITA
IT SEEMS THAT THE FORTY KILOGRAM WEIGHT OF THE MOTORBALL IS ENOUGH TO SLOW ZAFAL TAKIÉ'S INCREDIBLE SPEED!
WILL ALITA BE ABLE TO DEFEAT TAKIÉ IN THE REMAINING LAP!?
ALITA

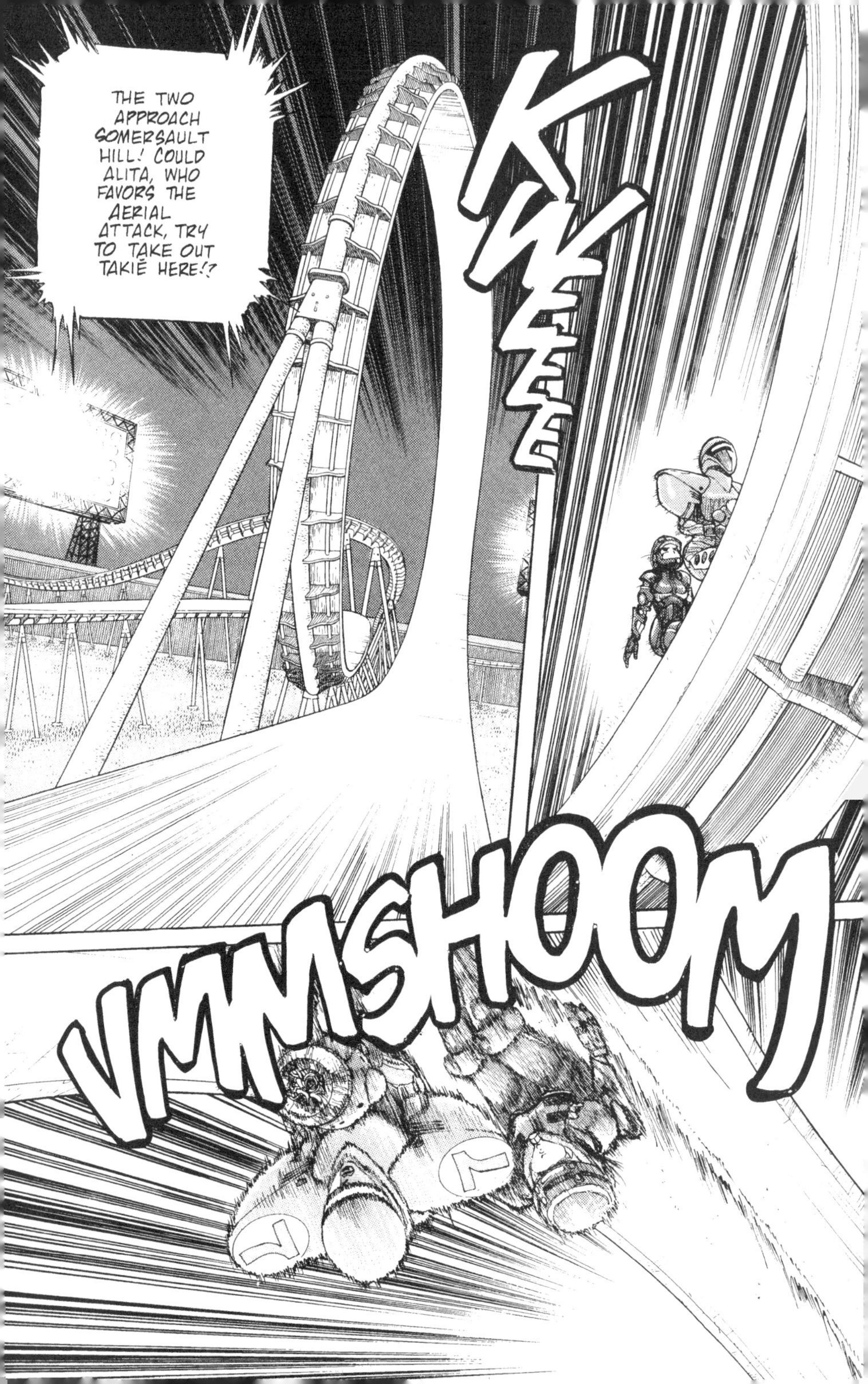
THE TWO APPROACH SOMERSAULT HILL! COULD ALITA, WHO FAVORS THE AERIAL ATTACK, TRY TO TAKE OUT TAKIË HERE!?
KWEEEE
VMMSHOOM

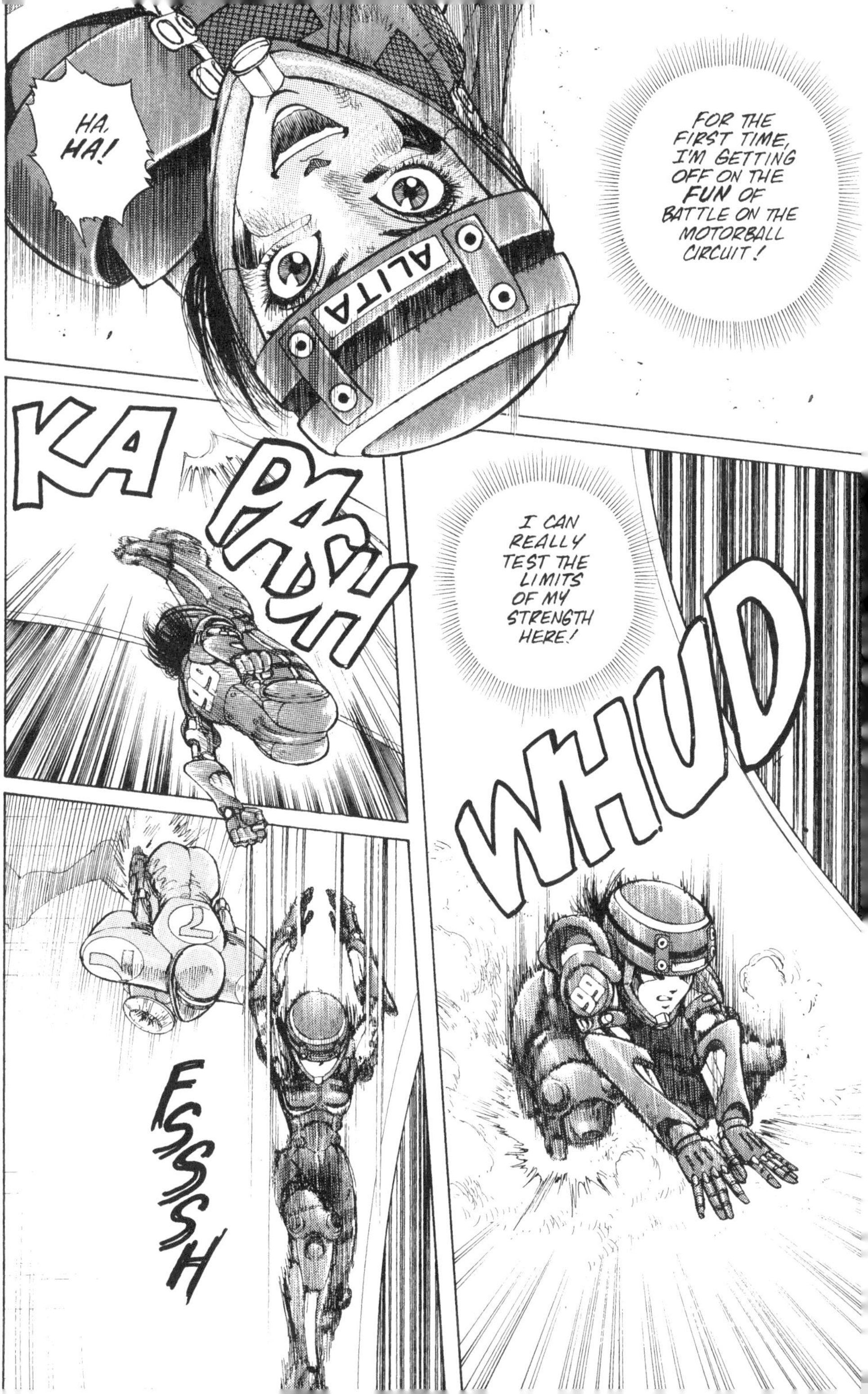
HA, HA!
FOR THE FIRST TIME, I'M GETTING OFF ON THE FUN OF BATTLE ON THE MOTORBALL CIRCUIT!
KA
PASHH
I CAN REALLY TEST THE LIMITS OF MY STRENGTH HERE!
WHUD
FSSSH

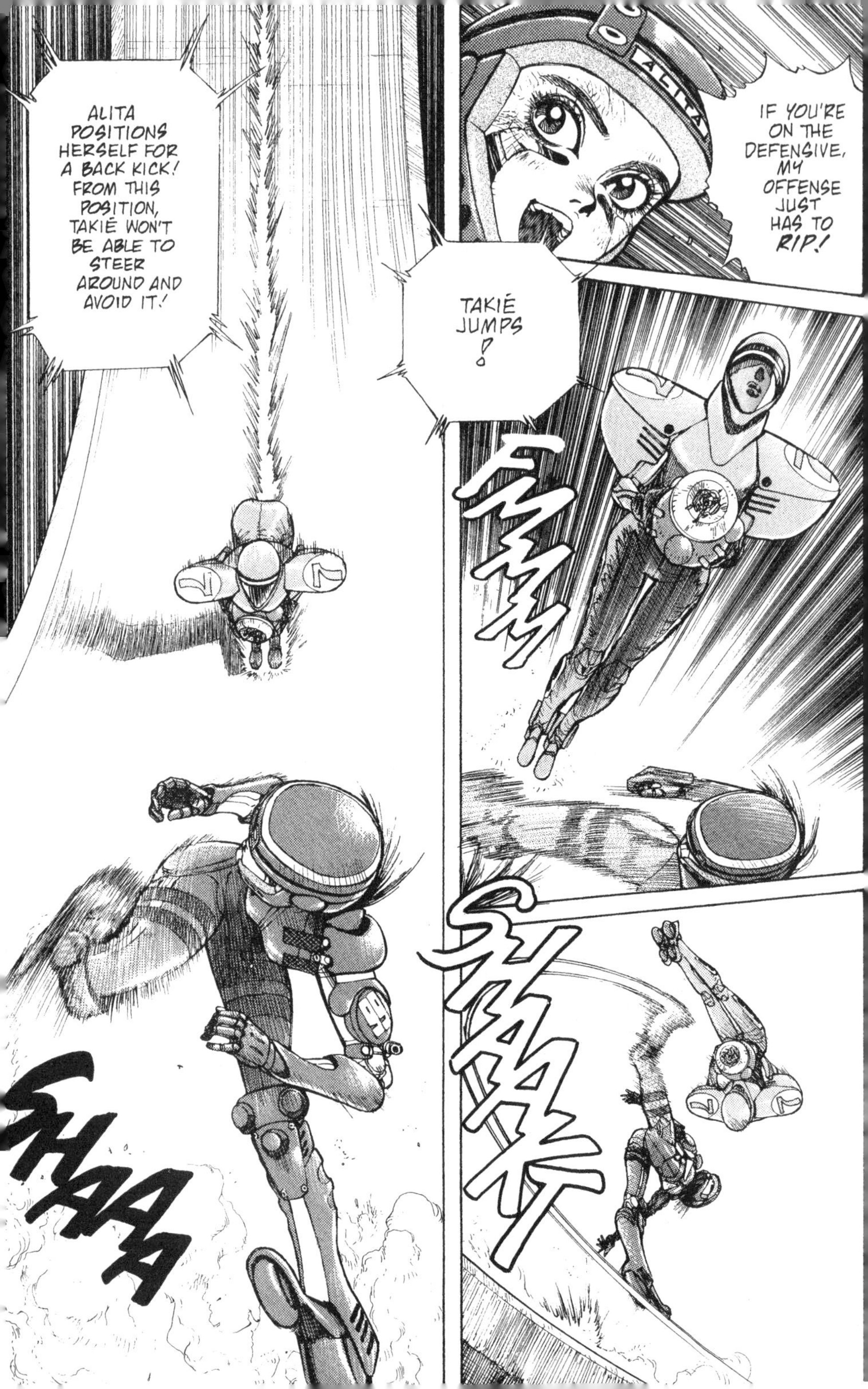
ALITA POSITIONS HERSELF FOR A BACK KICK! FROM THIS POSITION, TAKIÉ WON'T BE ABLE TO STEER AROUND AND AVOID IT!
IF YOU'RE ON THE DEFENSIVE, MY OFFENSE JUST HAS TO *RIP!*
TAKIÉ JUMPS!
FMMM
SHAAA
SHAAKT

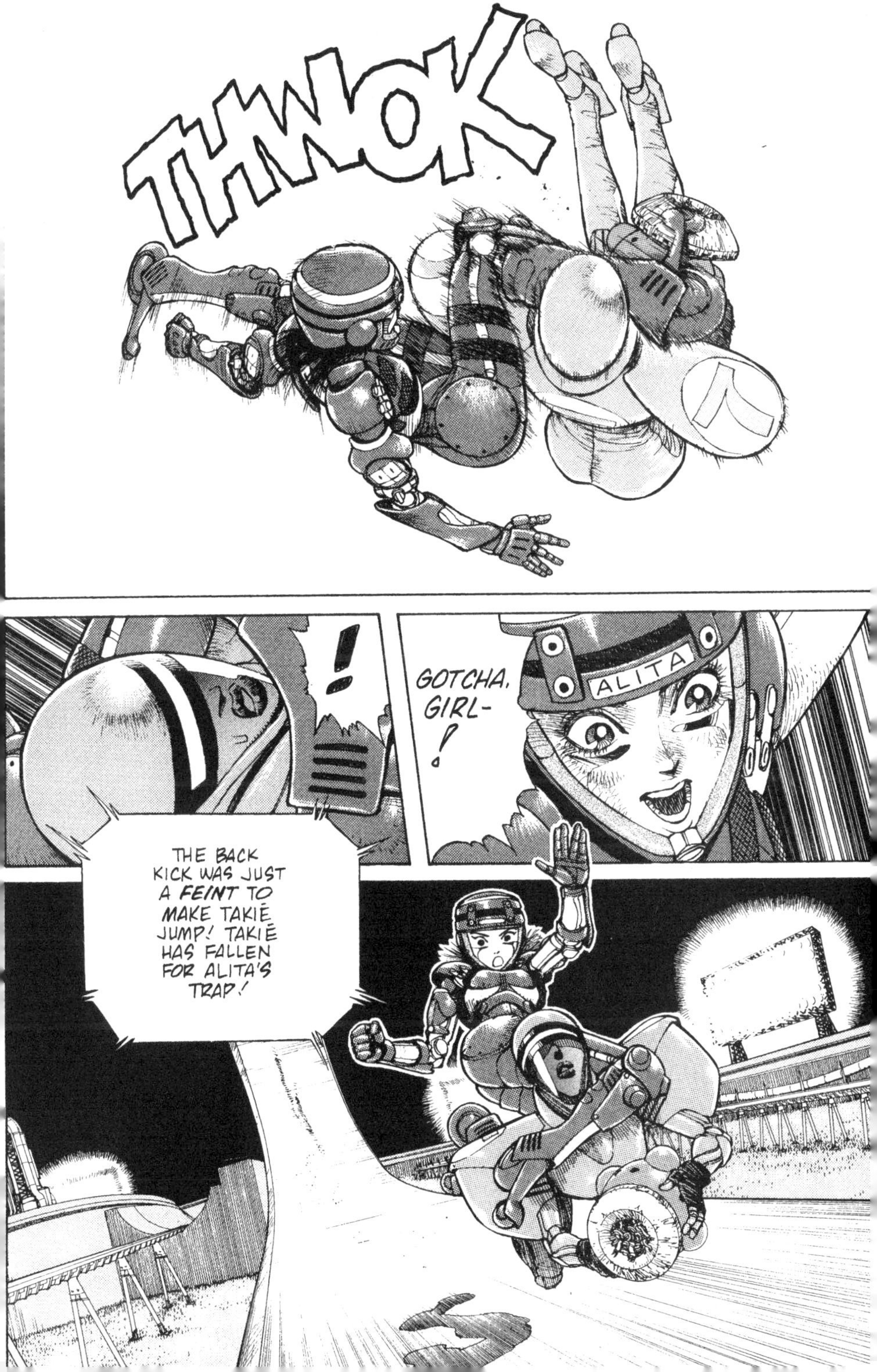
THWOK!
!
GOTCHA, GIRL-!
THE BACK KICK WAS JUST A FEINT TO MAKE TAKIE JUMP! TAKIE HAS FALLEN FOR ALITA'S TRAP!

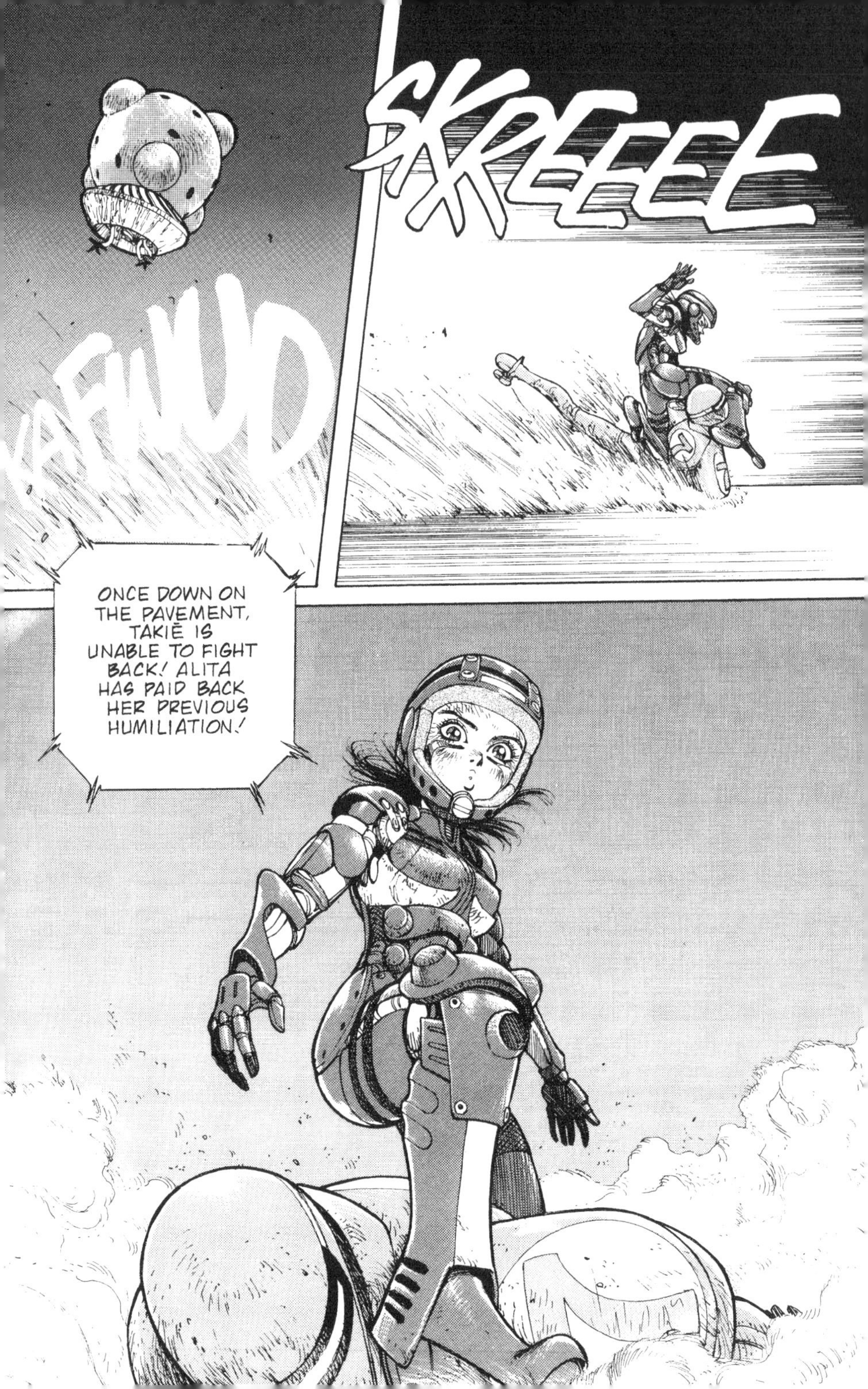
KAFWUD
SKREEEE
ONCE DOWN ON THE PAVEMENT, TAKIĒ IS UNABLE TO FIGHT BACK! ALITA HAS PAID BACK HER PREVIOUS HUMILIATION!

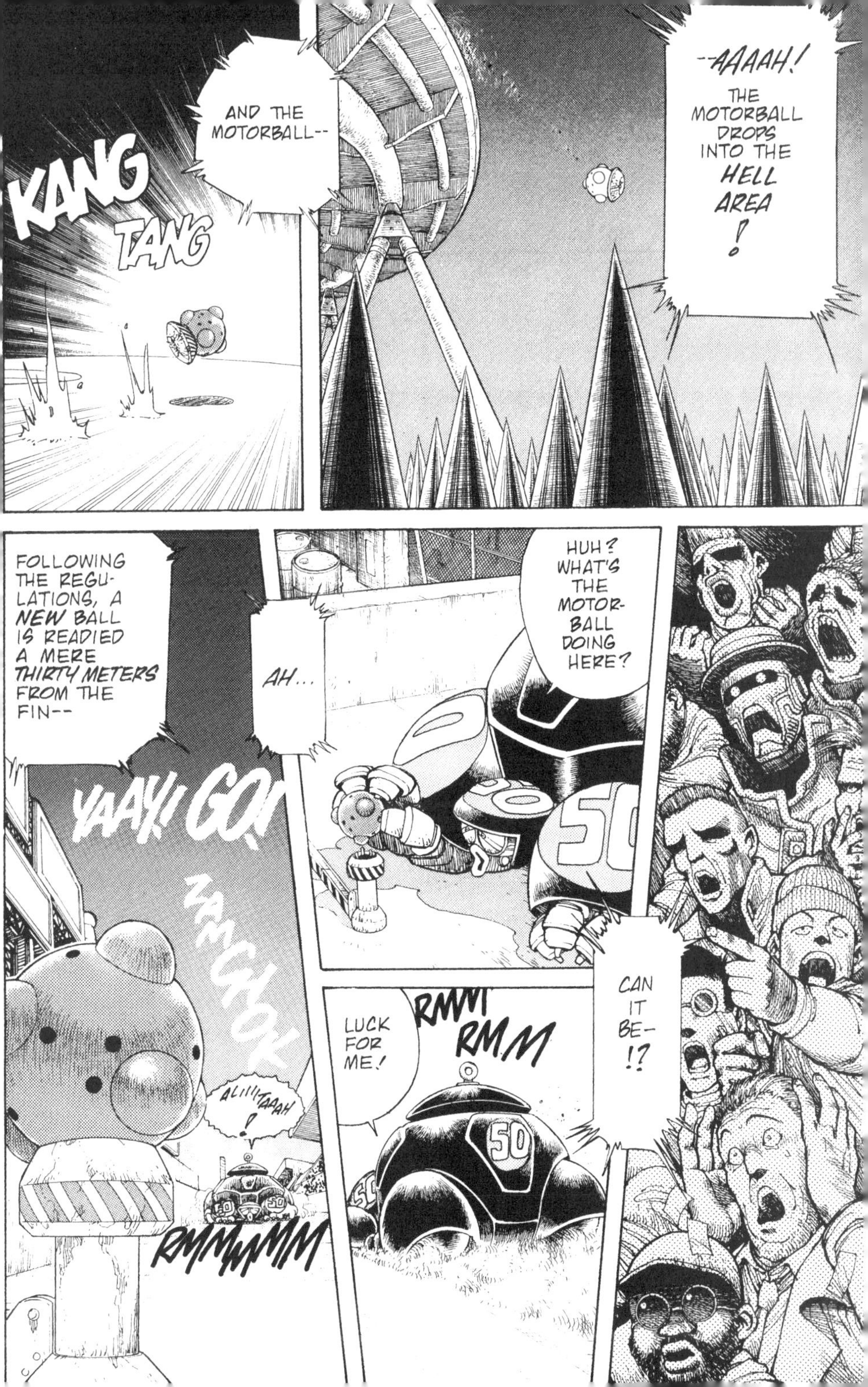
AND THE MOTORBALL--
KANG
TANG
--AAAAH! THE MOTORBALL DROPS INTO THE HELL AREA!
FOLLOWING THE REGULATIONS, A NEW BALL IS READIED A MERE THIRTY METERS FROM THE FIN--
YAAY! GO!
ALIIIITAAAH!
RMMMMMM
AH...
HUH? WHAT'S THE MOTORBALL DOING HERE?
LUCK FOR ME!
RMM
RMM
CAN IT BE-!?

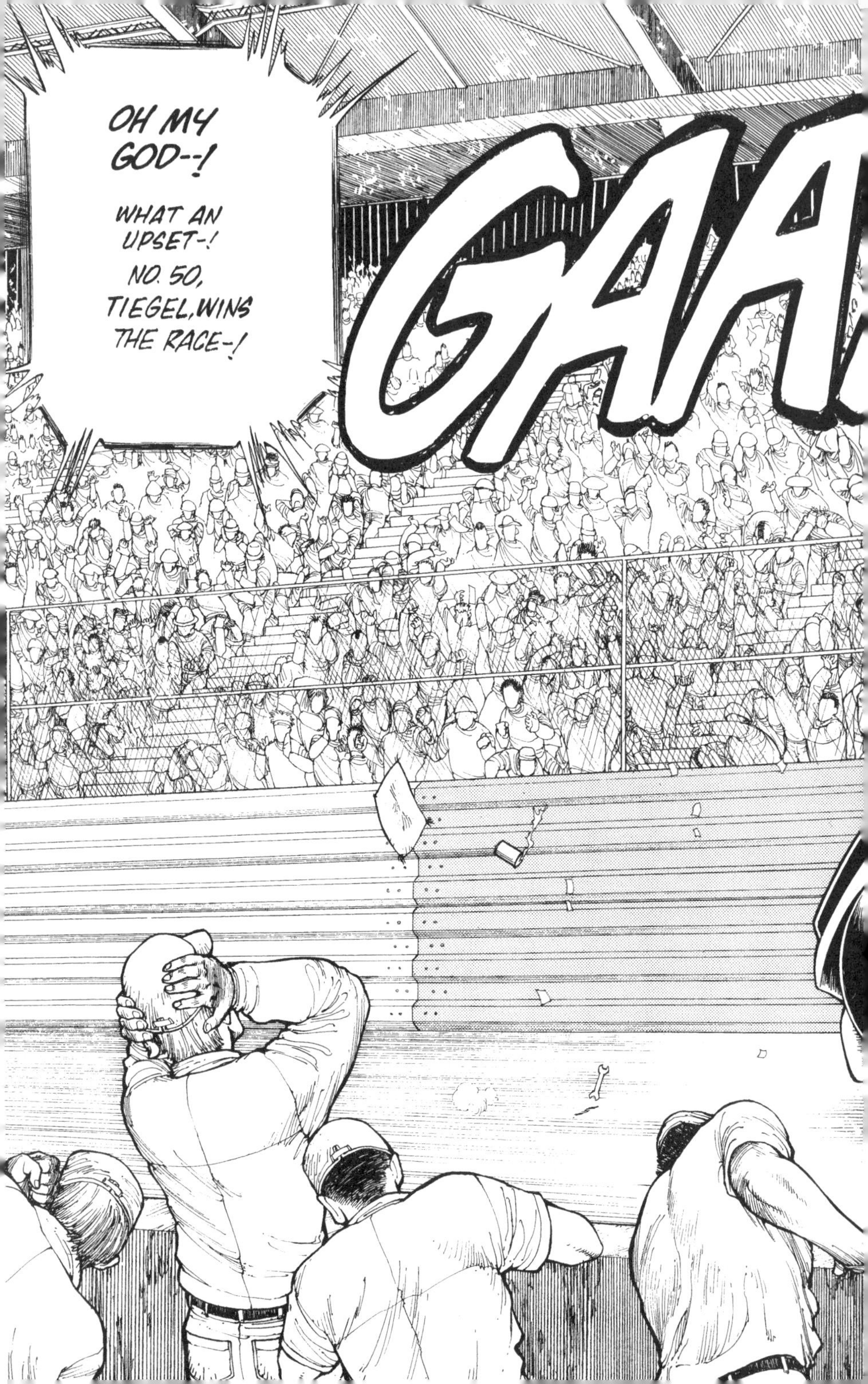
OH MY GOD--!
WHAT AN UPSET-! NO. 50, TIEGEL, WINS THE RACE-!
GAA

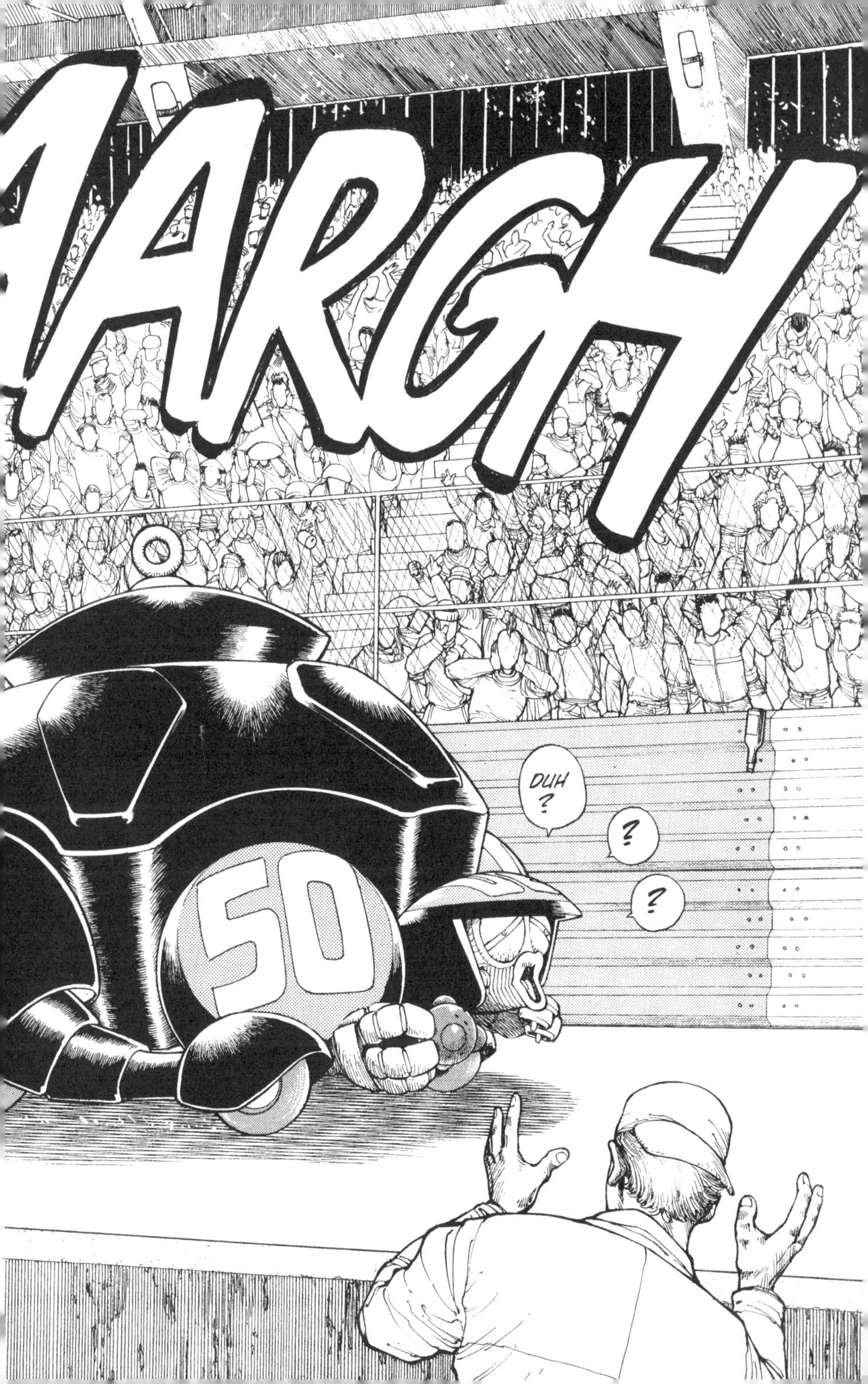
AARGH
DUH ?
?
?

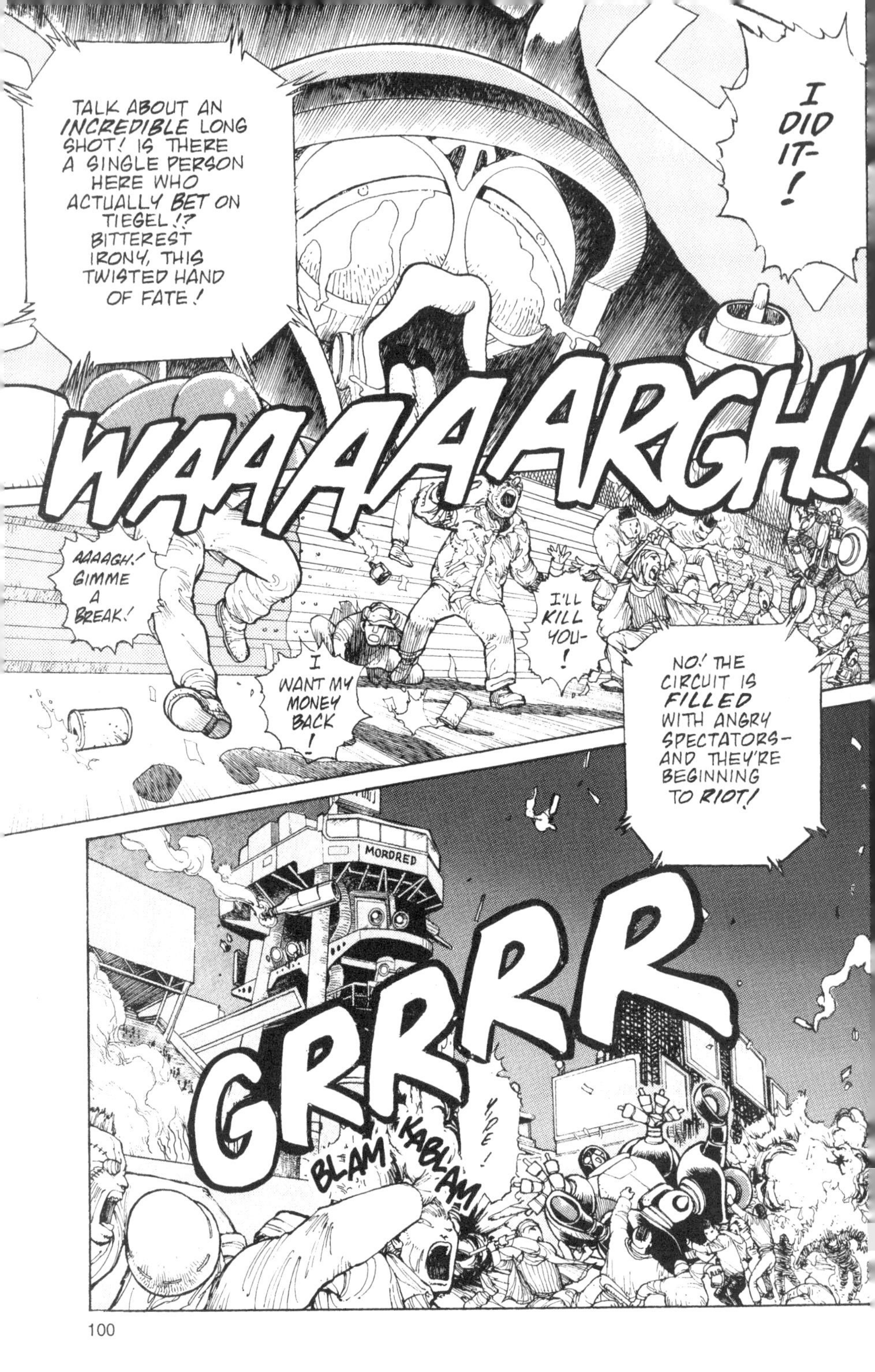
TALK ABOUT AN *INCREDIBLE* LONG SHOT! IS THERE A SINGLE PERSON HERE WHO ACTUALLY *BET* ON TIEGEL!? BITTEREST IRONY, THIS TWISTED HAND OF FATE!
I DID IT-!
WAAAAARGH!
AAAAGH! GIMME A BREAK!
I WANT MY MONEY BACK!
I'LL KILL YOU-!
NO! THE CIRCUIT IS *FILLED* WITH ANGRY SPECTATORS- AND THEY'RE BEGINNING TO *RIOT*!
MORDRED
GRRRR
BLAM
KABLAM
YIPE!

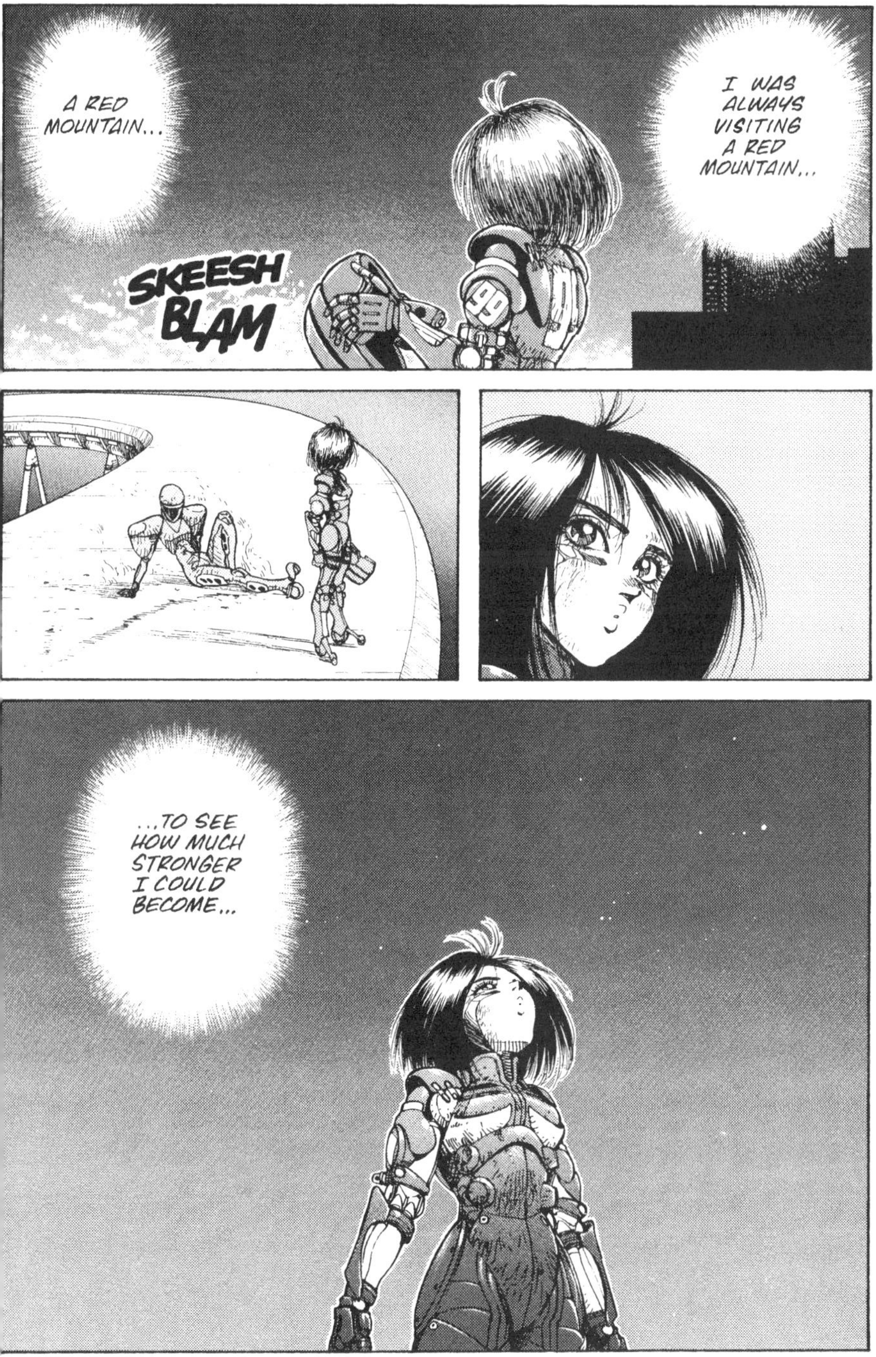
A RED MOUNTAIN...
I WAS ALWAYS VISITING A RED MOUNTAIN...
SKEESH
BLAM
...TO SEE HOW MUCH STRONGER I COULD BECOME...

CARRY ON THE DREAM

Race 3: Tradition

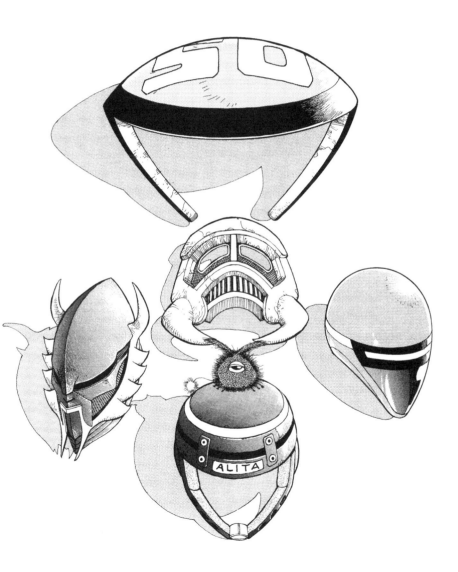

ESDOC MOTORS, HOME OF NO. 99, "KILLING ANGEL" ALITA, IS PLEASED TO ANNOUNCE THE NAMES OF THE FOUR MEMBERS OF HER CHALLENGE TEAM-- READY TO RISK ALL AGAINST EMPEROR JASHUGAN.

NO. 88, "CRUSHER" AJAKUTTY.

NO. 7, "CRIMSON WIND" ZAFAL TAKIE.

THIS IS A SURPRISE-- NO. 50, TIEGEL.

MY HARD WORK HAS PAID OFF--!

NO. 1, "CALIGULA" ARMBLESSED.

YOU *MOCK* ME! THERE'S NO *WAY* I'M JOINING A TEAM FULL OF *GRUNTS*--!

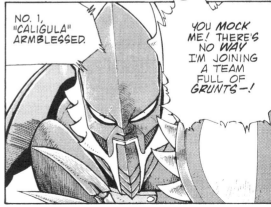

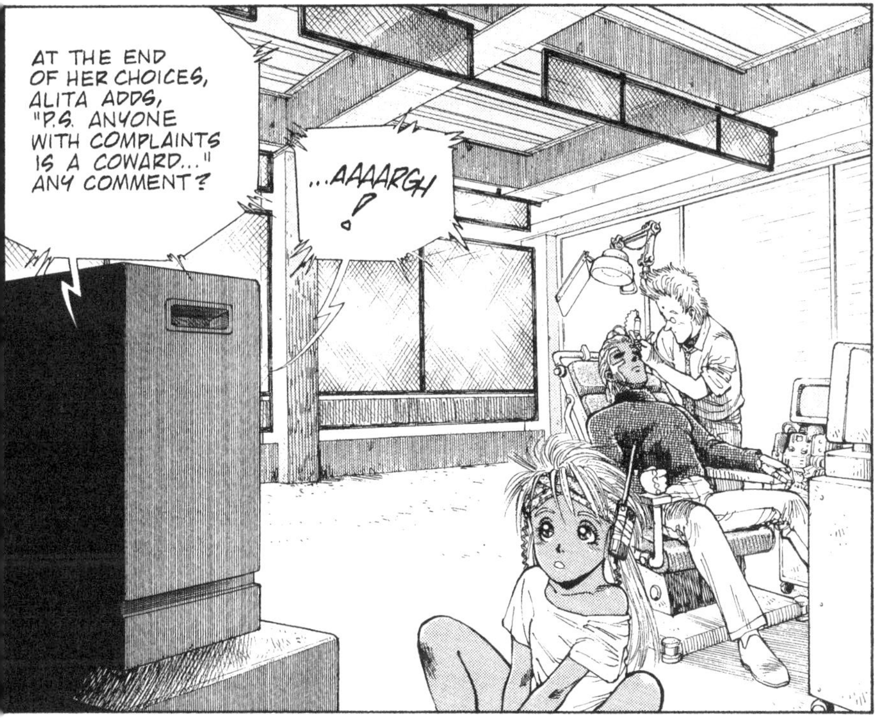
AT THE END OF HER CHOICES, ALITA ADDS, "P.S. ANYONE WITH COMPLAINTS IS A COWARD..." ANY COMMENT?
...AAAARGH!

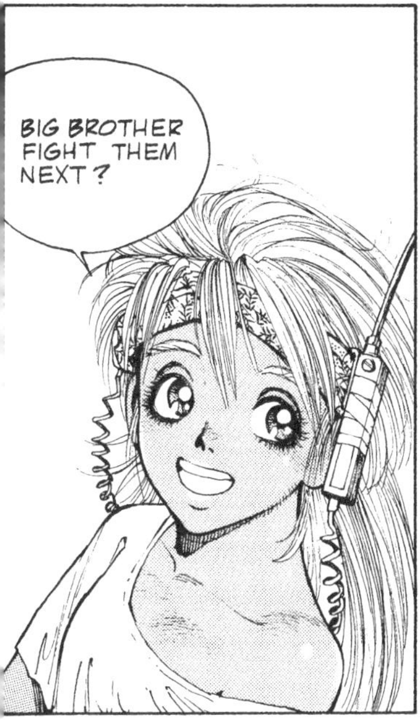
BIG BROTHER FIGHT THEM NEXT?

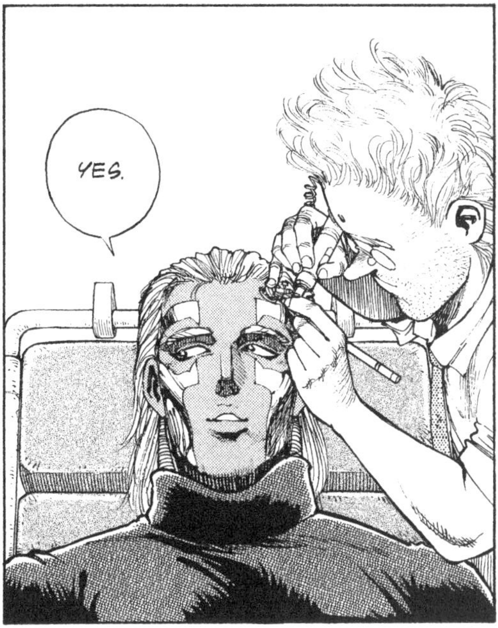
YES.

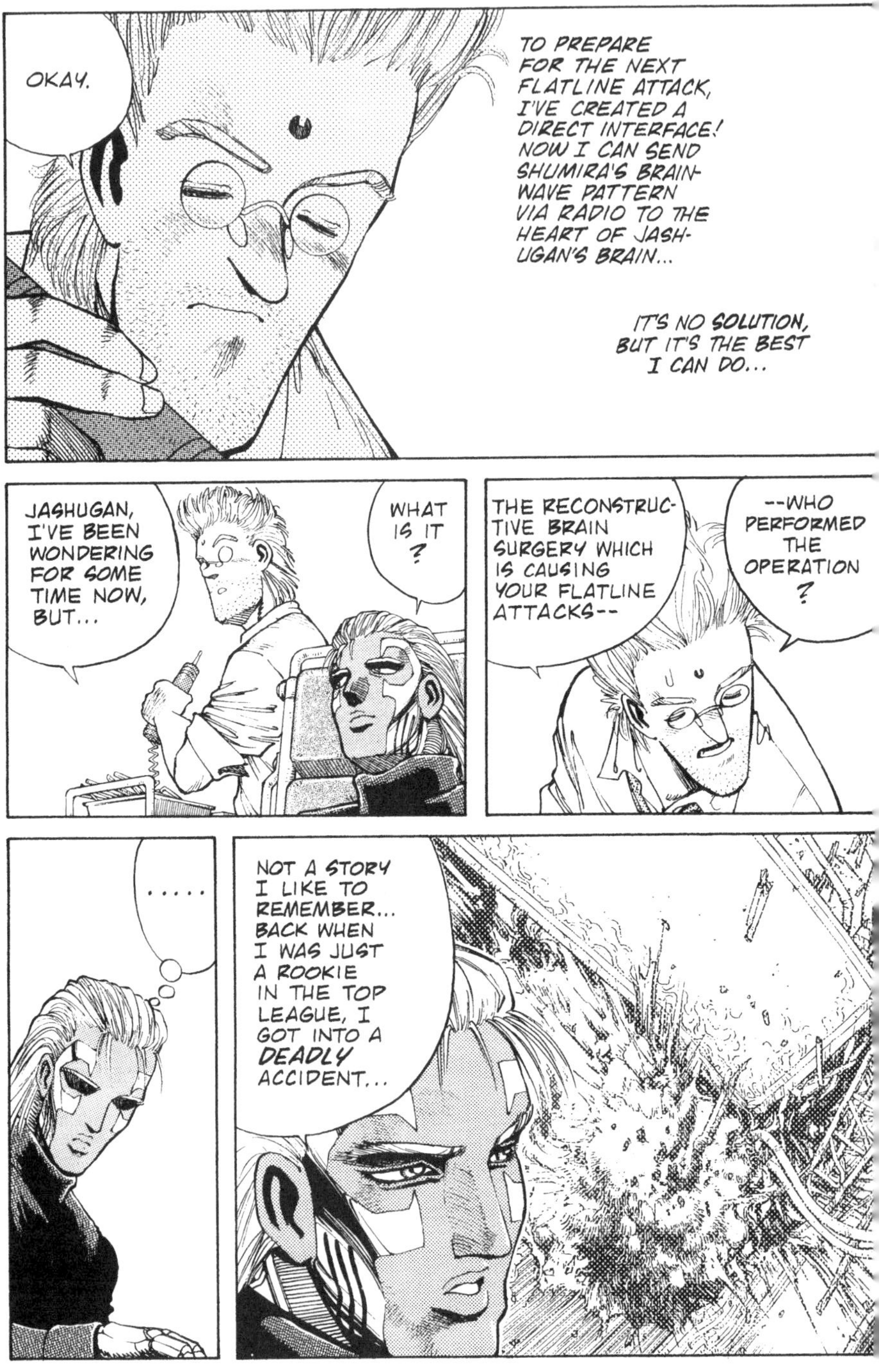
OKAY.
TO PREPARE FOR THE NEXT FLATLINE ATTACK, I'VE CREATED A DIRECT INTERFACE! NOW I CAN SEND SHUMIRA'S BRAIN-WAVE PATTERN VIA RADIO TO THE HEART OF JASHUGAN'S BRAIN...
IT'S NO SOLUTION, BUT IT'S THE BEST I CAN DO...
JASHUGAN, I'VE BEEN WONDERING FOR SOME TIME NOW, BUT...
WHAT IS IT?
THE RECONSTRUCTIVE BRAIN SURGERY WHICH IS CAUSING YOUR FLATLINE ATTACKS--
--WHO PERFORMED THE OPERATION?
.....
NOT A STORY I LIKE TO REMEMBER... BACK WHEN I WAS JUST A ROOKIE IN THE TOP LEAGUE, I GOT INTO A DEADLY ACCIDENT...

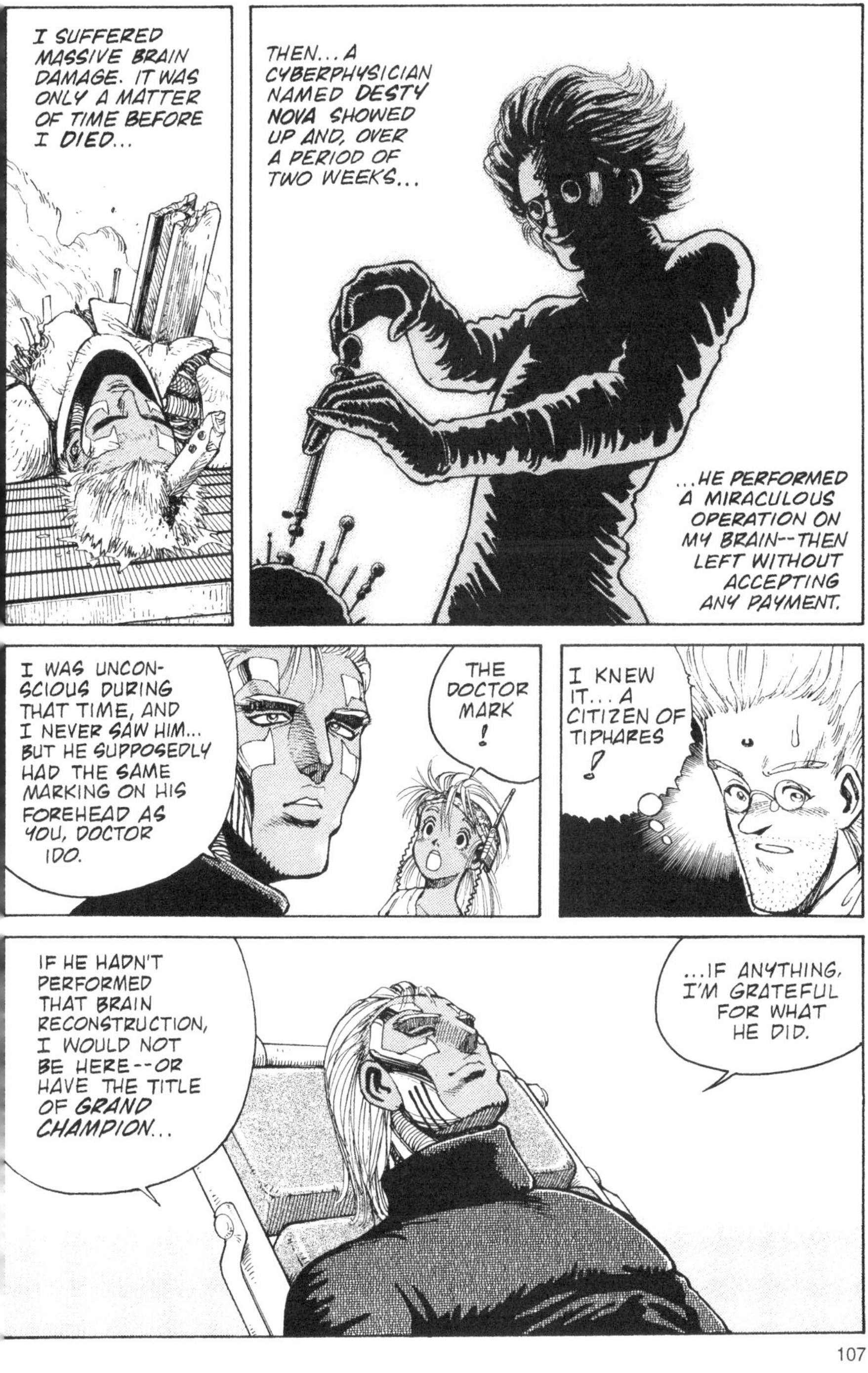

I SUFFERED MASSIVE BRAIN DAMAGE. IT WAS ONLY A MATTER OF TIME BEFORE I DIED...
THEN... A CYBERPHYSICIAN NAMED DESTY NOVA SHOWED UP AND, OVER A PERIOD OF TWO WEEKS...
...HE PERFORMED A MIRACULOUS OPERATION ON MY BRAIN--THEN LEFT WITHOUT ACCEPTING ANY PAYMENT.
I WAS UNCONSCIOUS DURING THAT TIME, AND I NEVER SAW HIM... BUT HE SUPPOSEDLY HAD THE SAME MARKING ON HIS FOREHEAD AS YOU, DOCTOR IDO.
THE DOCTOR MARK!
I KNEW IT... A CITIZEN OF TIPHARES!
IF HE HADN'T PERFORMED THAT BRAIN RECONSTRUCTION, I WOULD NOT BE HERE--OR HAVE THE TITLE OF GRAND CHAMPION...
...IF ANYTHING, I'M GRATEFUL FOR WHAT HE DID.

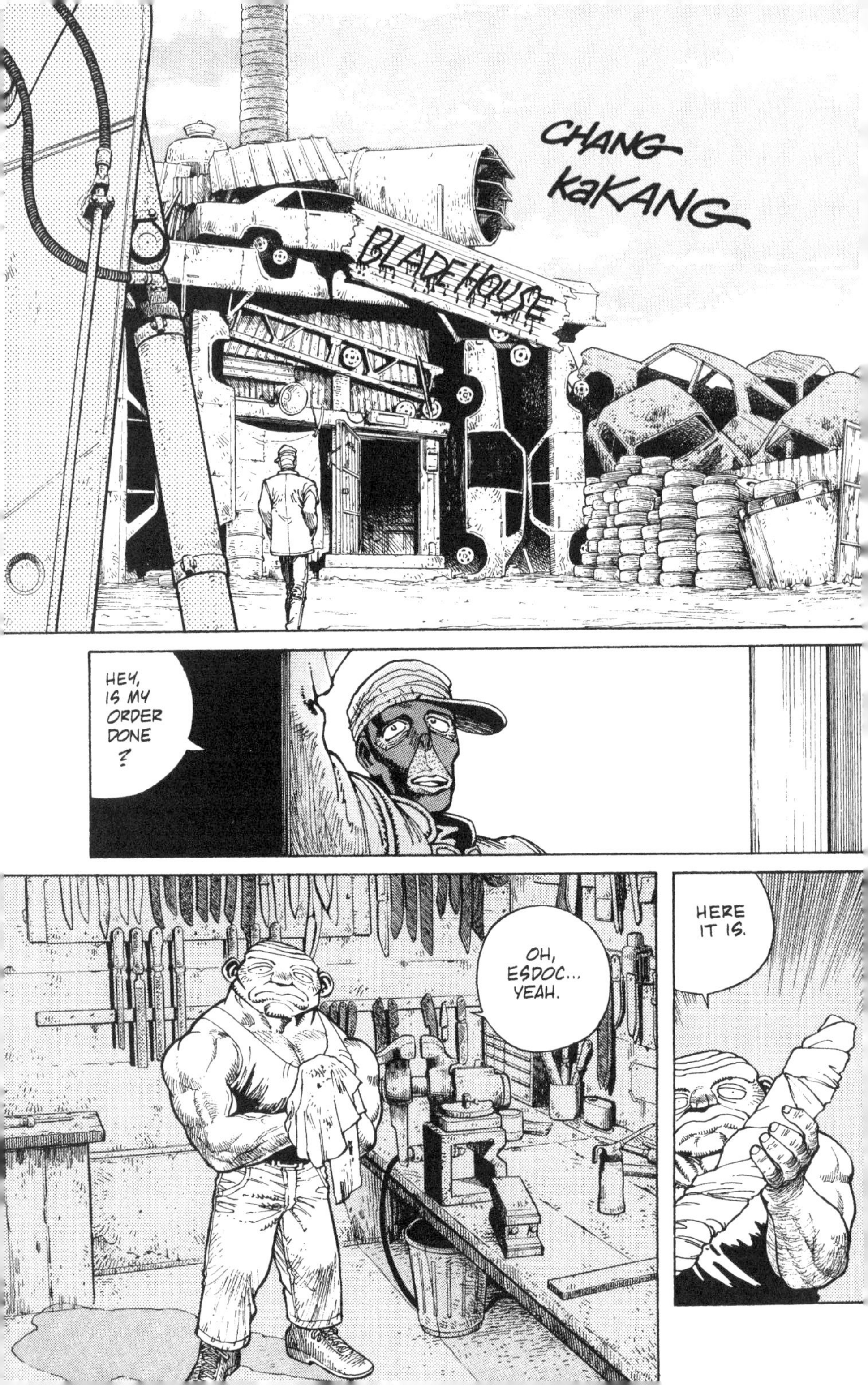
CHANG kaKANG
BLADE HOUSE
HEY, IS MY ORDER DONE?
OH, ESDOC... YEAH.
HERE IT IS.

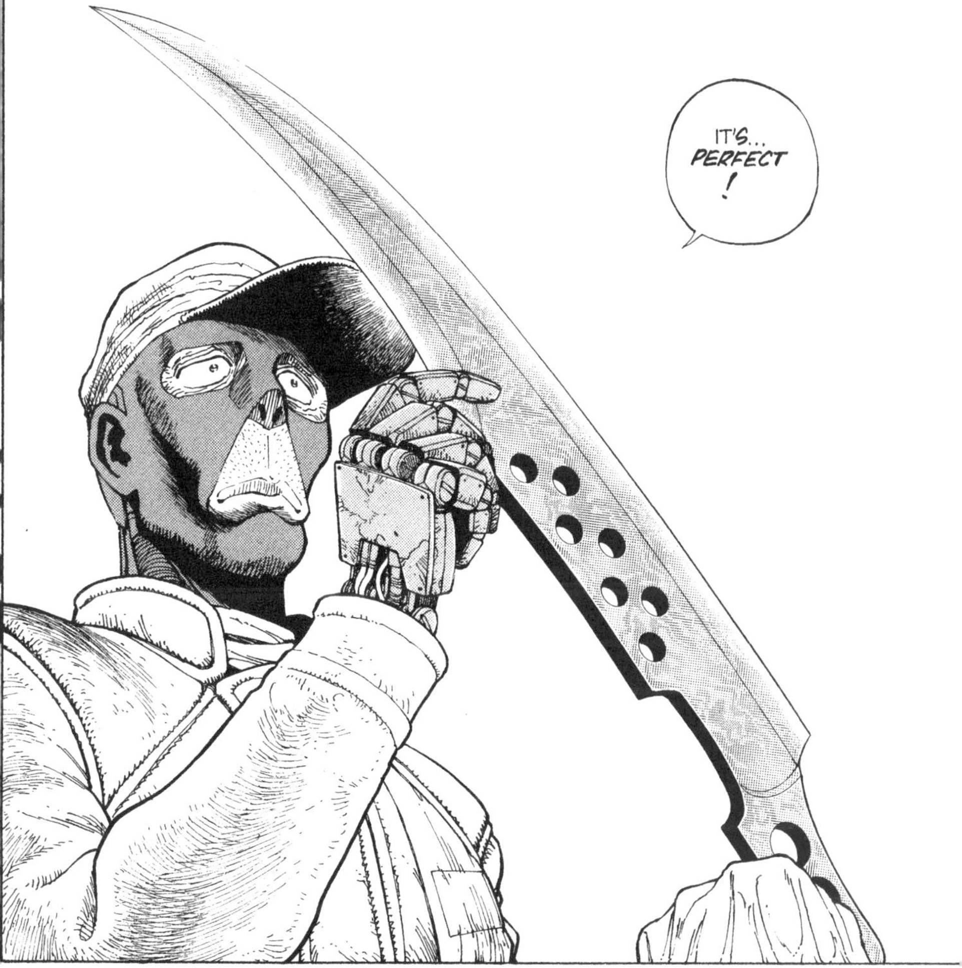
IT'S... PERFECT!

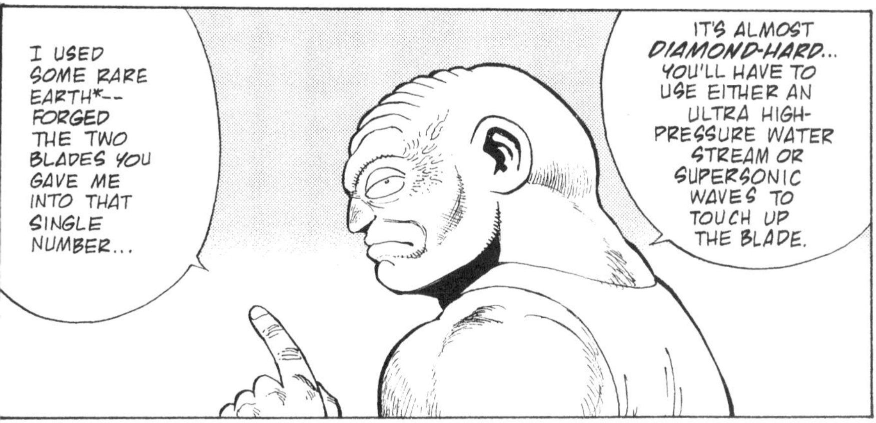
I USED SOME RARE EARTH*-- FORGED THE TWO BLADES YOU GAVE ME INTO THAT SINGLE NUMBER...
IT'S ALMOST DIAMOND-HARD... YOU'LL HAVE TO USE EITHER AN ULTRA HIGH-PRESSURE WATER STREAM OR SUPERSONIC WAVES TO TOUCH UP THE BLADE.

* RARE MATERIALS SUCH AS SCANDIUM, YTTRIUM, LUTETIUM AND OTHER BASE ELEMENTS.

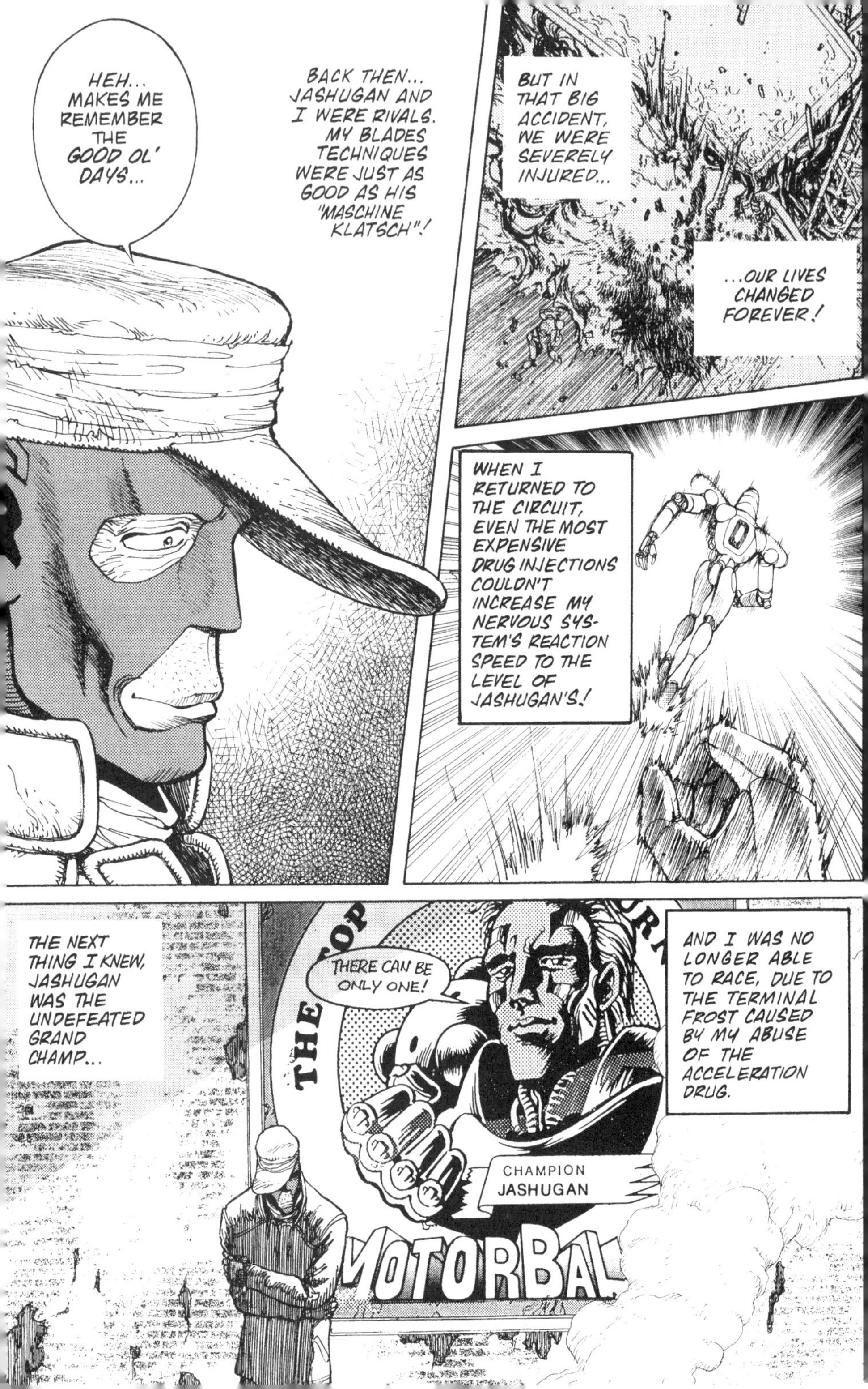
HEH... MAKES ME REMEMBER THE GOOD OL' DAYS...
BACK THEN... JASHUGAN AND I WERE RIVALS. MY BLADES TECHNIQUES WERE JUST AS GOOD AS HIS "MASCHINE KLATSCH"!
BUT IN THAT BIG ACCIDENT, WE WERE SEVERELY INJURED...
...OUR LIVES CHANGED FOREVER!
WHEN I RETURNED TO THE CIRCUIT, EVEN THE MOST EXPENSIVE DRUG INJECTIONS COULDN'T INCREASE MY NERVOUS SYS-TEM'S REACTION SPEED TO THE LEVEL OF JASHUGAN'S!
THE NEXT THING I KNEW, JASHUGAN WAS THE UNDEFEATED GRAND CHAMP...
THERE CAN BE ONLY ONE!
CHAMPION JASHUGAN
MOTORBAL
AND I WAS NO LONGER ABLE TO RACE, DUE TO THE TERMINAL FROST CAUSED BY MY ABUSE OF THE ACCELERATION DRUG.

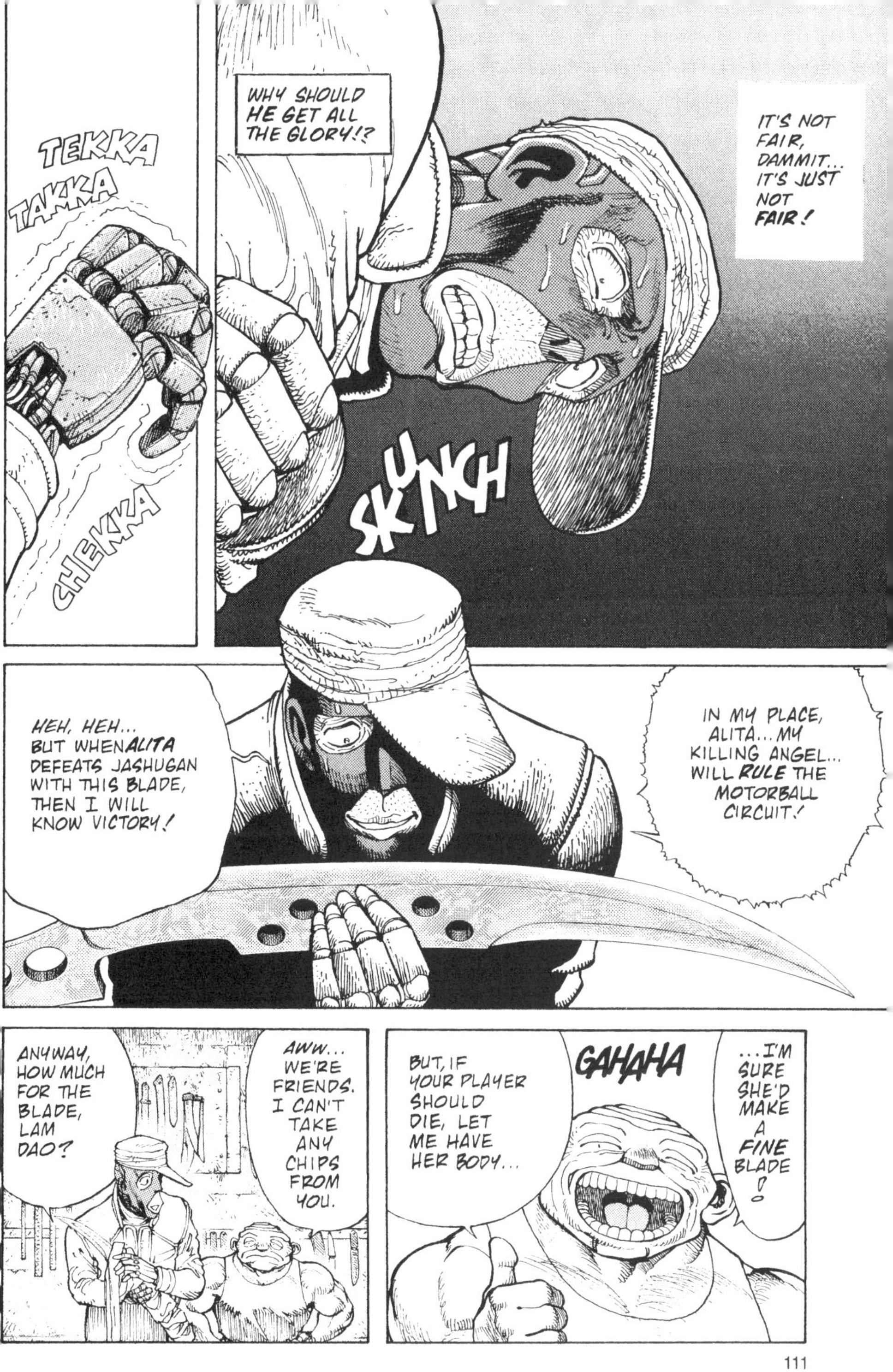
TEKKA
TAKKA
CHEKKA
WHY SHOULD HE GET ALL THE GLORY!?
IT'S NOT FAIR, DAMMIT... IT'S JUST NOT FAIR!
SKUNCH
HEH, HEH... BUT WHEN ALITA DEFEATS JASHUGAN WITH THIS BLADE, THEN I WILL KNOW VICTORY!
IN MY PLACE, ALITA... MY KILLING ANGEL... WILL RULE THE MOTORBALL CIRCUIT!
ANYWAY, HOW MUCH FOR THE BLADE, LAM DAO?
AWW... WE'RE FRIENDS. I CAN'T TAKE ANY CHIPS FROM YOU.
BUT, IF YOUR PLAYER SHOULD DIE, LET ME HAVE HER BODY...
GAHAHA
...I'M SURE SHE'D MAKE A FINE BLADE!

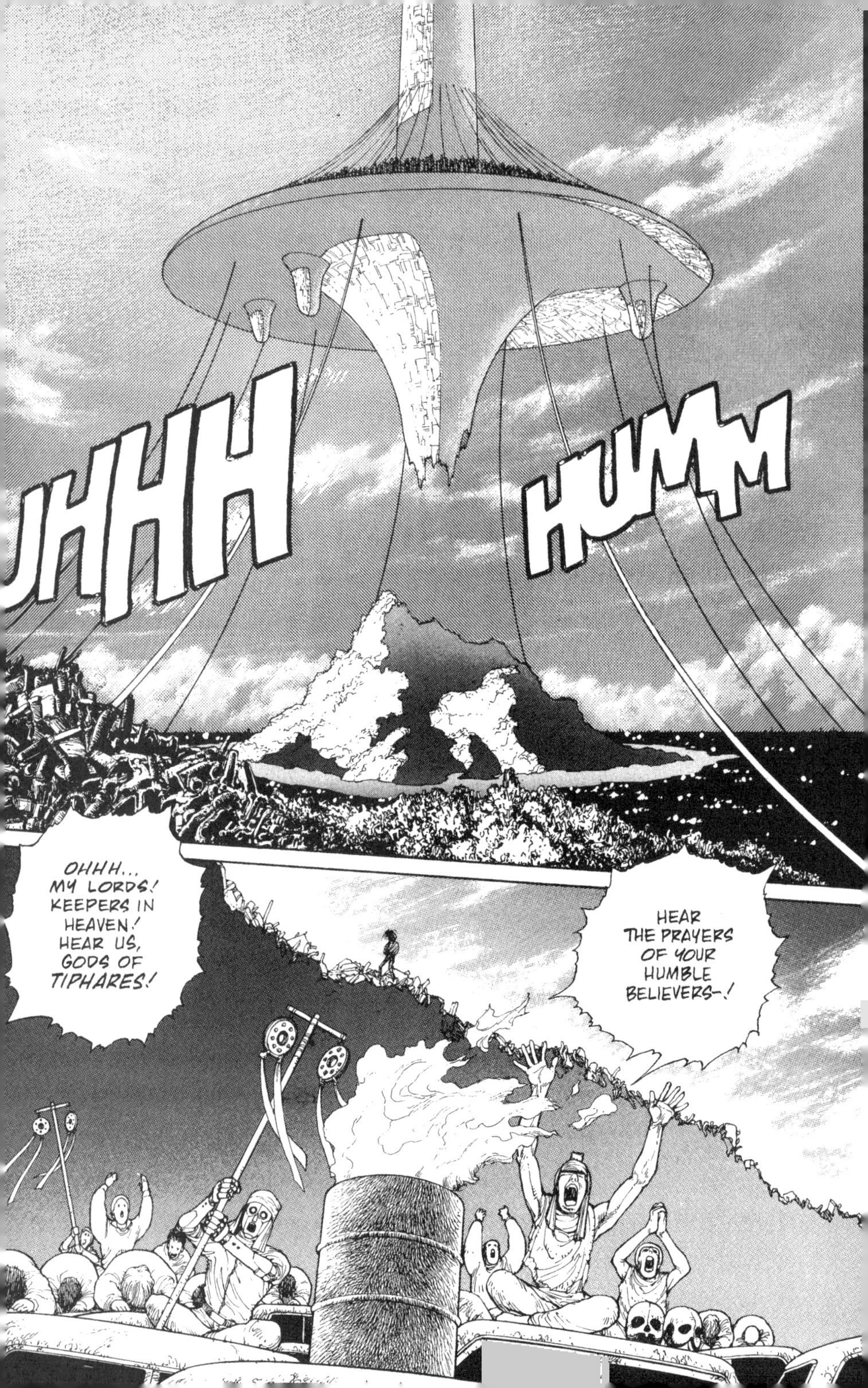
UHHH
HUMM
OHHH... MY LORDS! KEEPERS IN HEAVEN! HEAR US, GODS OF TIPHARES!
HEAR THE PRAYERS OF YOUR HUMBLE BELIEVERS-!

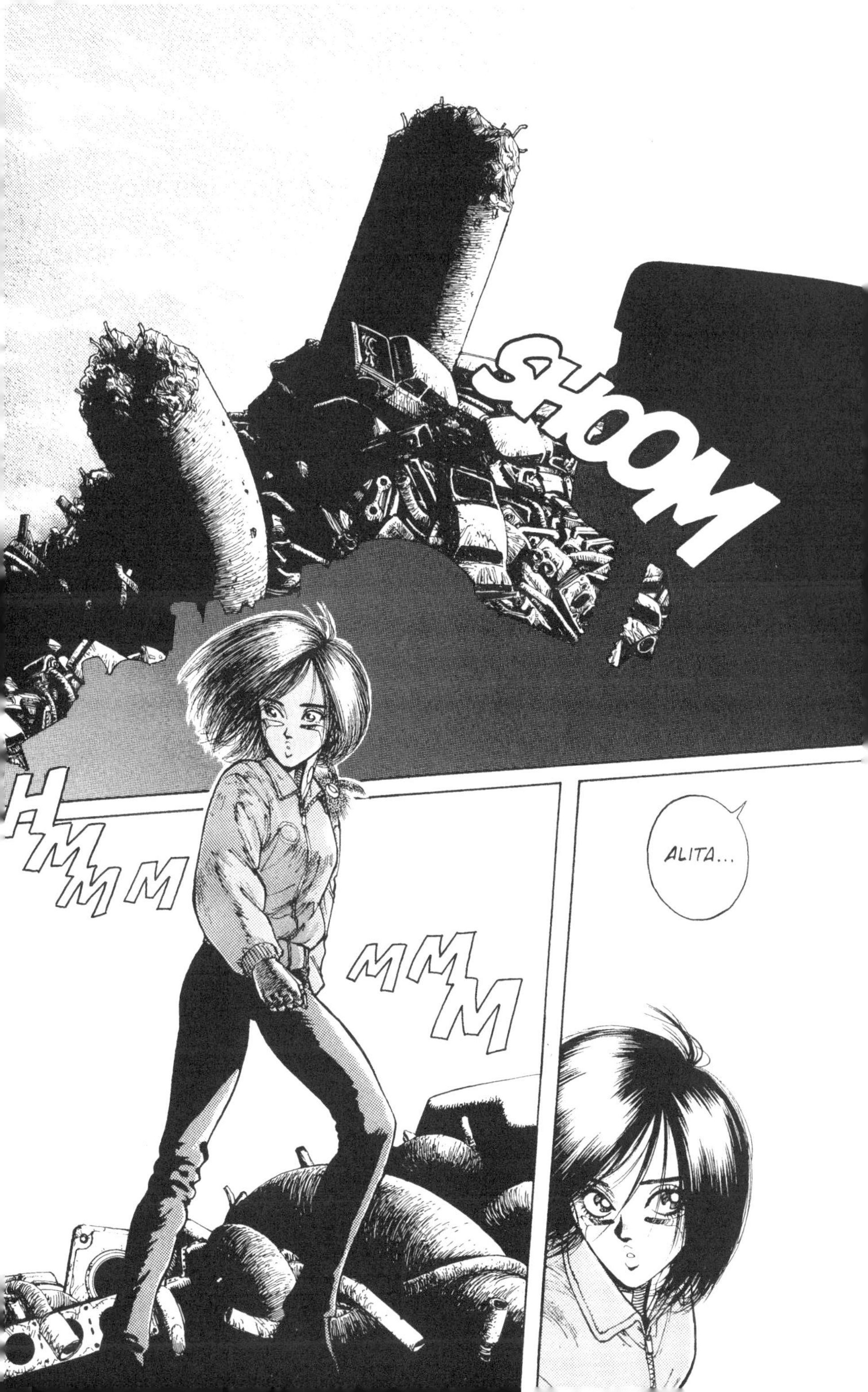
SHOOM
HMMMM
MMMM
ALITA...

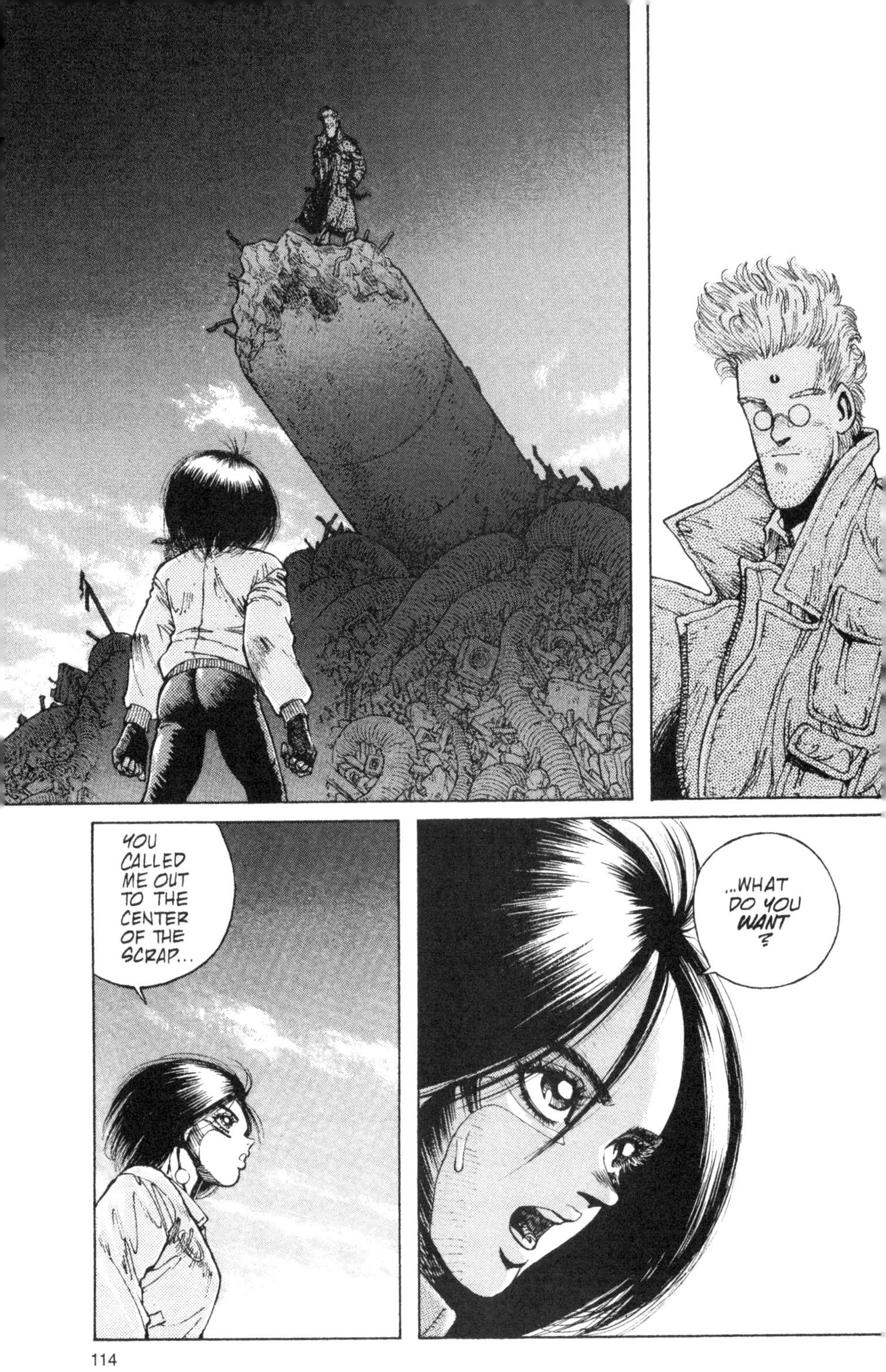
YOU CALLED ME OUT TO THE CENTER OF THE SCRAP...
...WHAT DO YOU *WANT*?

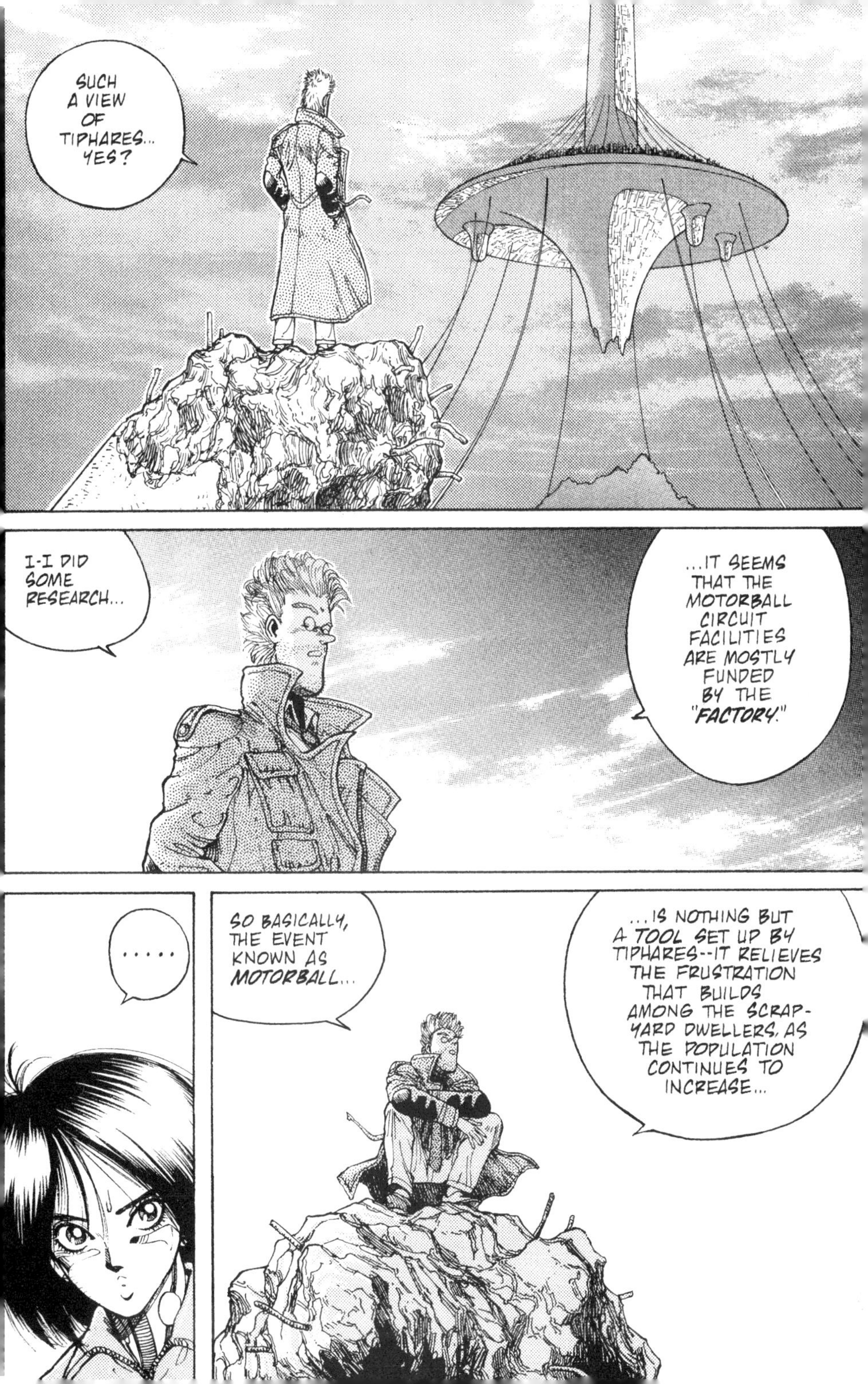
SUCH A VIEW OF TIPHARES... YES?
I-I DID SOME RESEARCH...
...IT SEEMS THAT THE MOTORBALL CIRCUIT FACILITIES ARE MOSTLY FUNDED BY THE "FACTORY."
.....
SO BASICALLY, THE EVENT KNOWN AS MOTORBALL...
...IS NOTHING BUT A TOOL SET UP BY TIPHARES--IT RELIEVES THE FRUSTRATION THAT BUILDS AMONG THE SCRAP-YARD DWELLERS, AS THE POPULATION CONTINUES TO INCREASE...

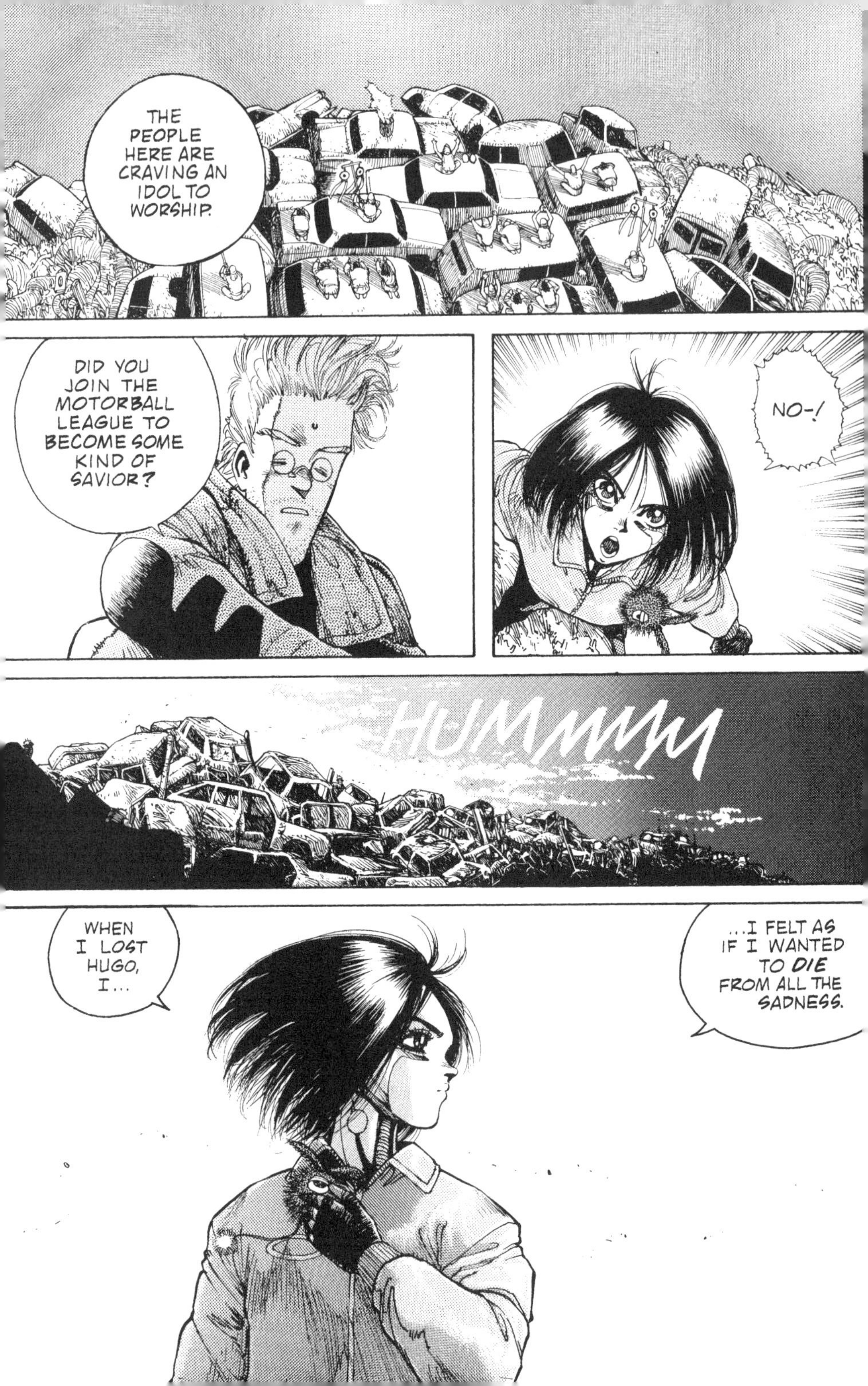
THE PEOPLE HERE ARE CRAVING AN IDOL TO WORSHIP.
DID YOU JOIN THE MOTORBALL LEAGUE TO BECOME SOME KIND OF SAVIOR?
NO-!
HUMMMM
WHEN I LOST HUGO, I...
...I FELT AS IF I WANTED TO *DIE* FROM ALL THE SADNESS.

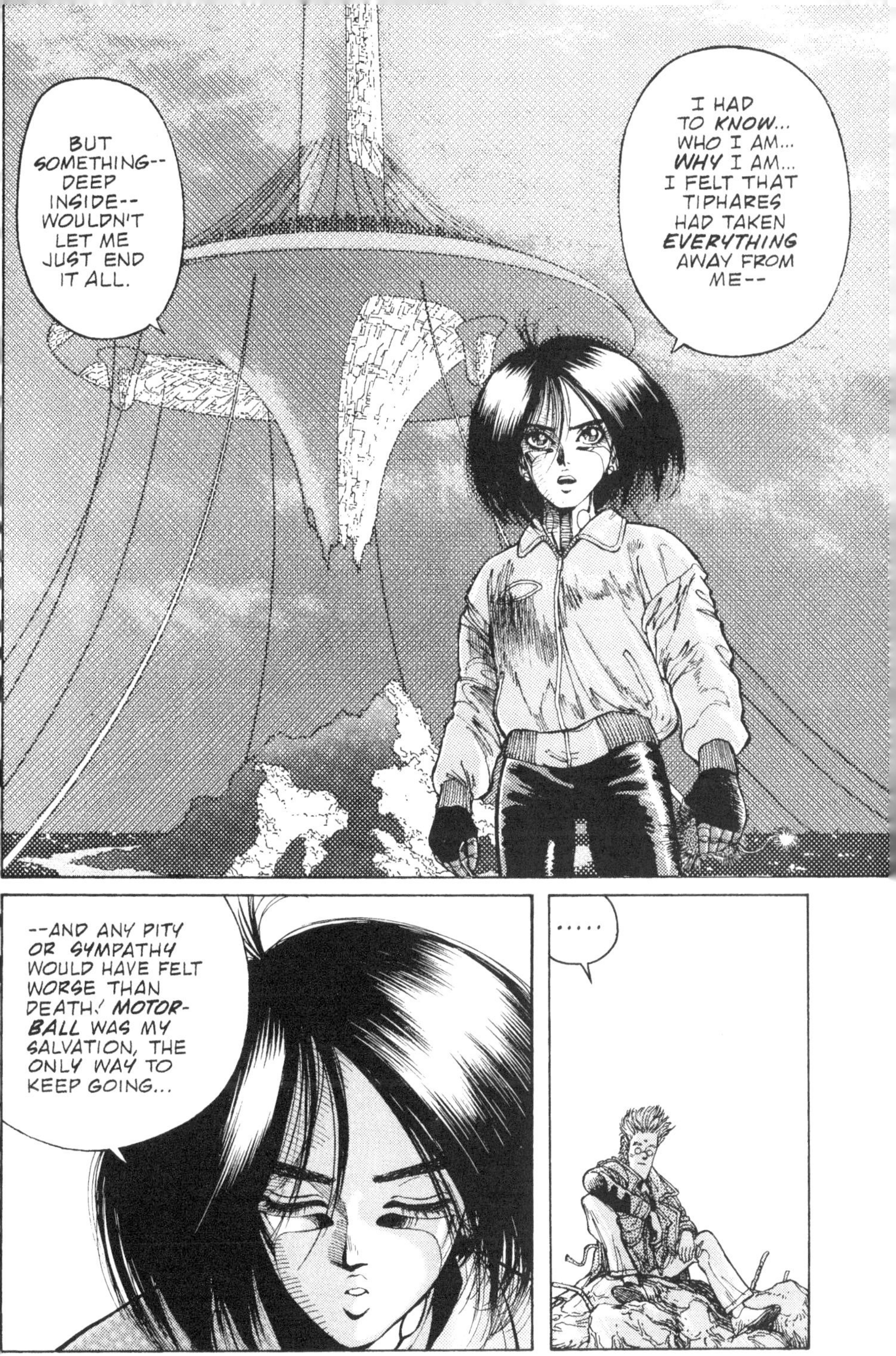
BUT SOMETHING-- DEEP INSIDE-- WOULDN'T LET ME JUST END IT ALL.
I HAD TO KNOW... WHO I AM... WHY I AM... I FELT THAT TIPHARES HAD TAKEN EVERYTHING AWAY FROM ME--
--AND ANY PITY OR SYMPATHY WOULD HAVE FELT WORSE THAN DEATH! MOTOR-BALL WAS MY SALVATION, THE ONLY WAY TO KEEP GOING...
.....

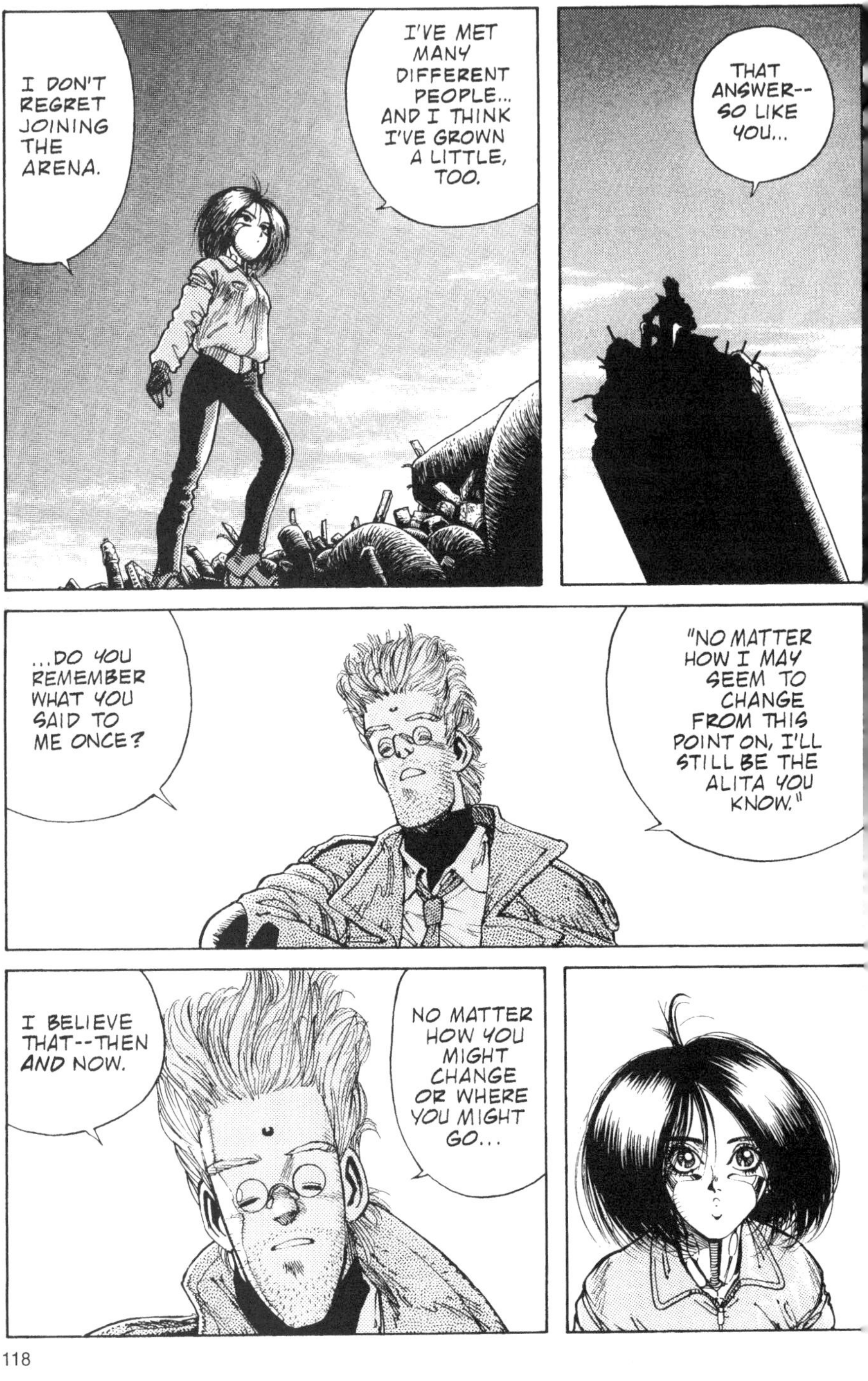
I DON'T REGRET JOINING THE ARENA.
I'VE MET MANY DIFFERENT PEOPLE... AND I THINK I'VE GROWN A LITTLE, TOO.
THAT ANSWER-- SO LIKE YOU...
...DO YOU REMEMBER WHAT YOU SAID TO ME ONCE?
"NO MATTER HOW I MAY SEEM TO CHANGE FROM THIS POINT ON, I'LL STILL BE THE ALITA YOU KNOW."
I BELIEVE THAT--THEN AND NOW.
NO MATTER HOW YOU MIGHT CHANGE OR WHERE YOU MIGHT GO...

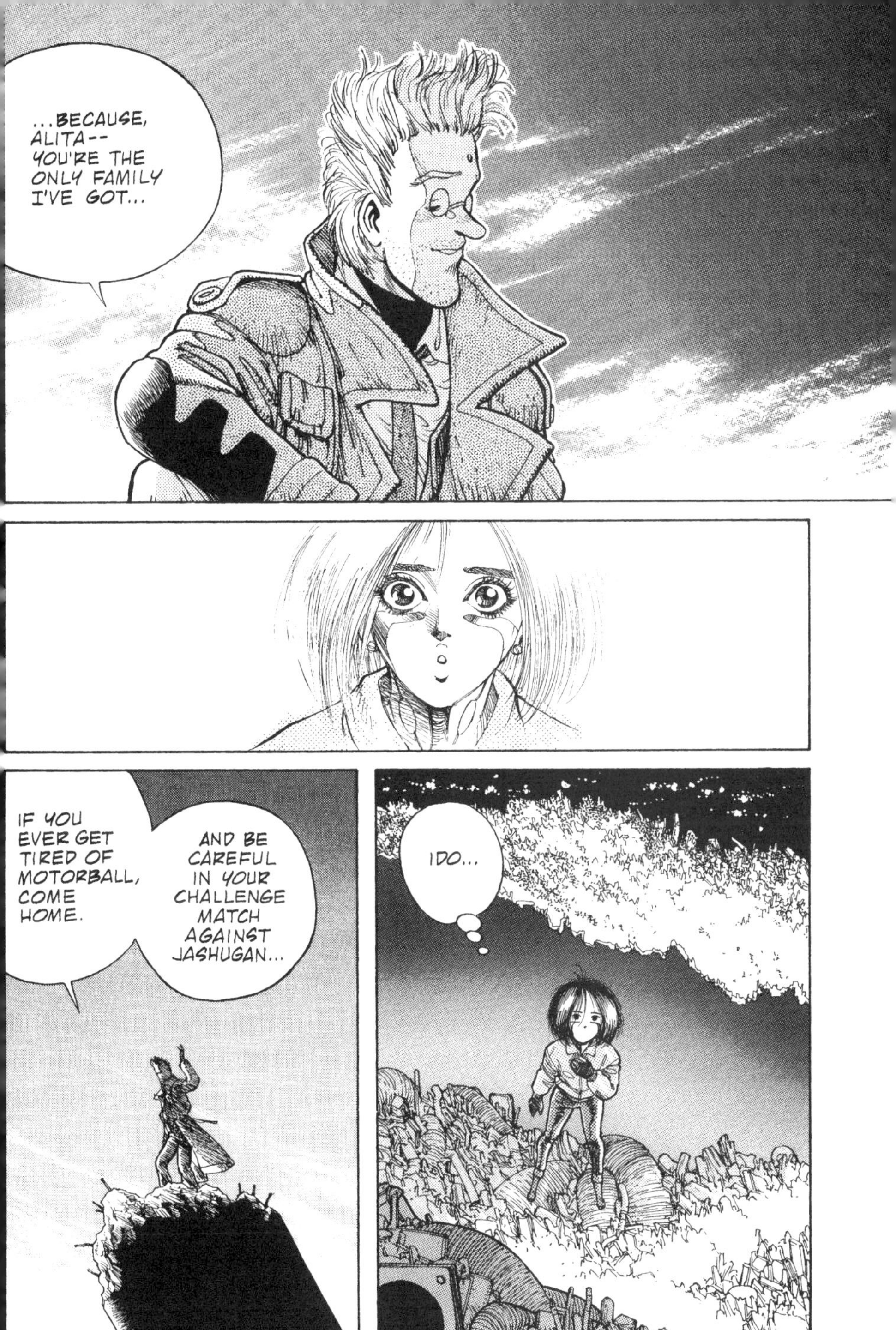
...BECAUSE, ALITA-- YOU'RE THE ONLY FAMILY I'VE GOT...
IF YOU EVER GET TIRED OF MOTORBALL, COME HOME.
AND BE CAREFUL IN YOUR CHALLENGE MATCH AGAINST JASHUGAN...
IDO...

SHRNCH

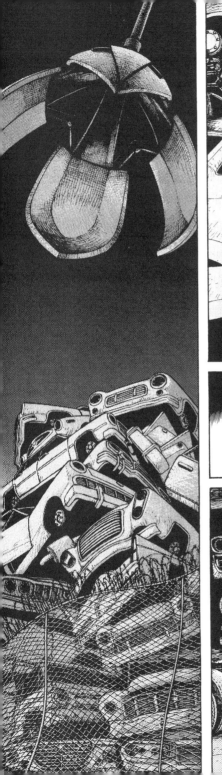

AH! IT IS *YOU*, JASHUGAN...

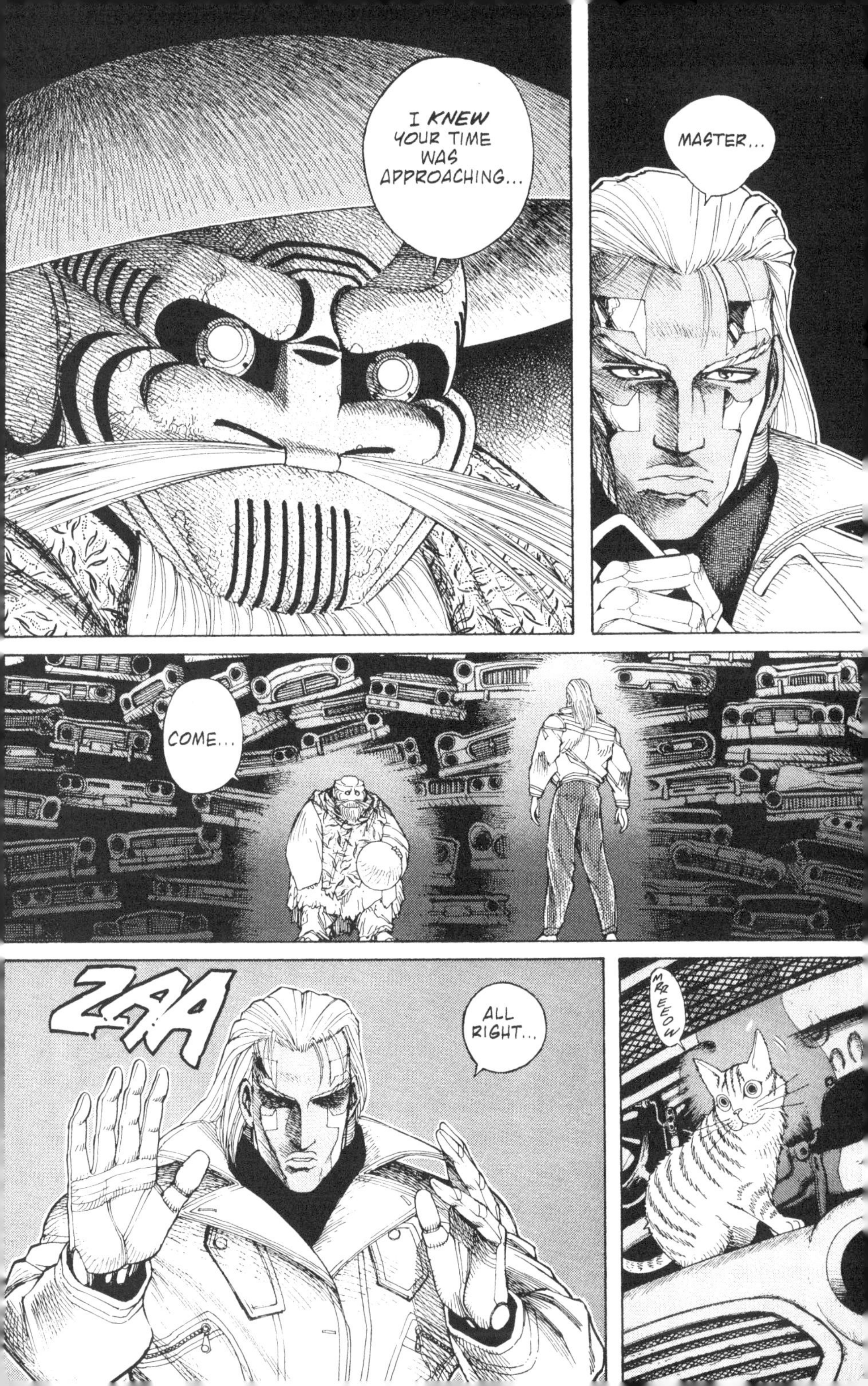
I KNEW YOUR TIME WAS APPROACHING...
MASTER...
COME...
ZAA
ALL RIGHT...
MRREEOW

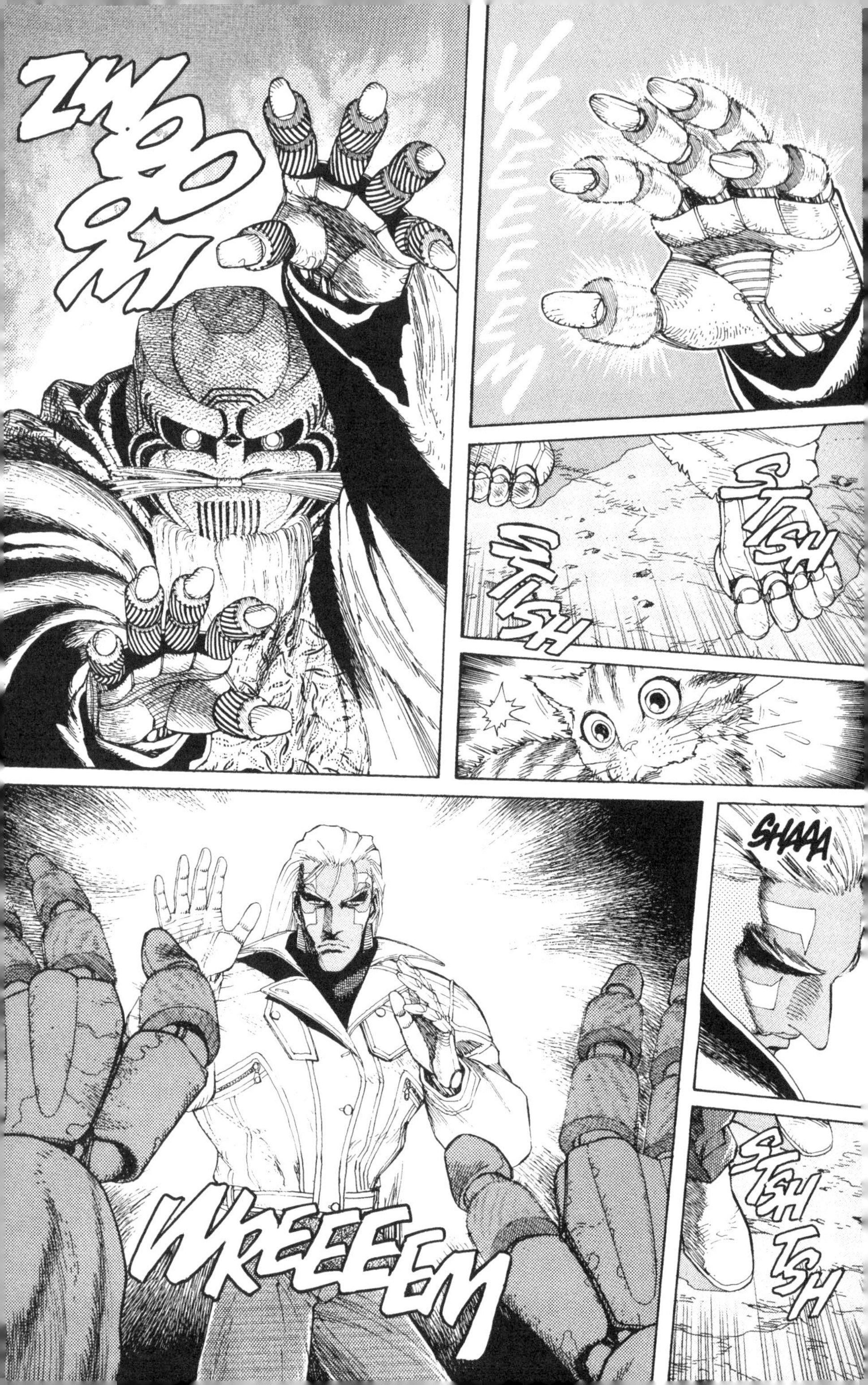
ZWOOOM
VREEEEEM
STISH
STISH
SHAAA
WREEEEM
STISH TSH

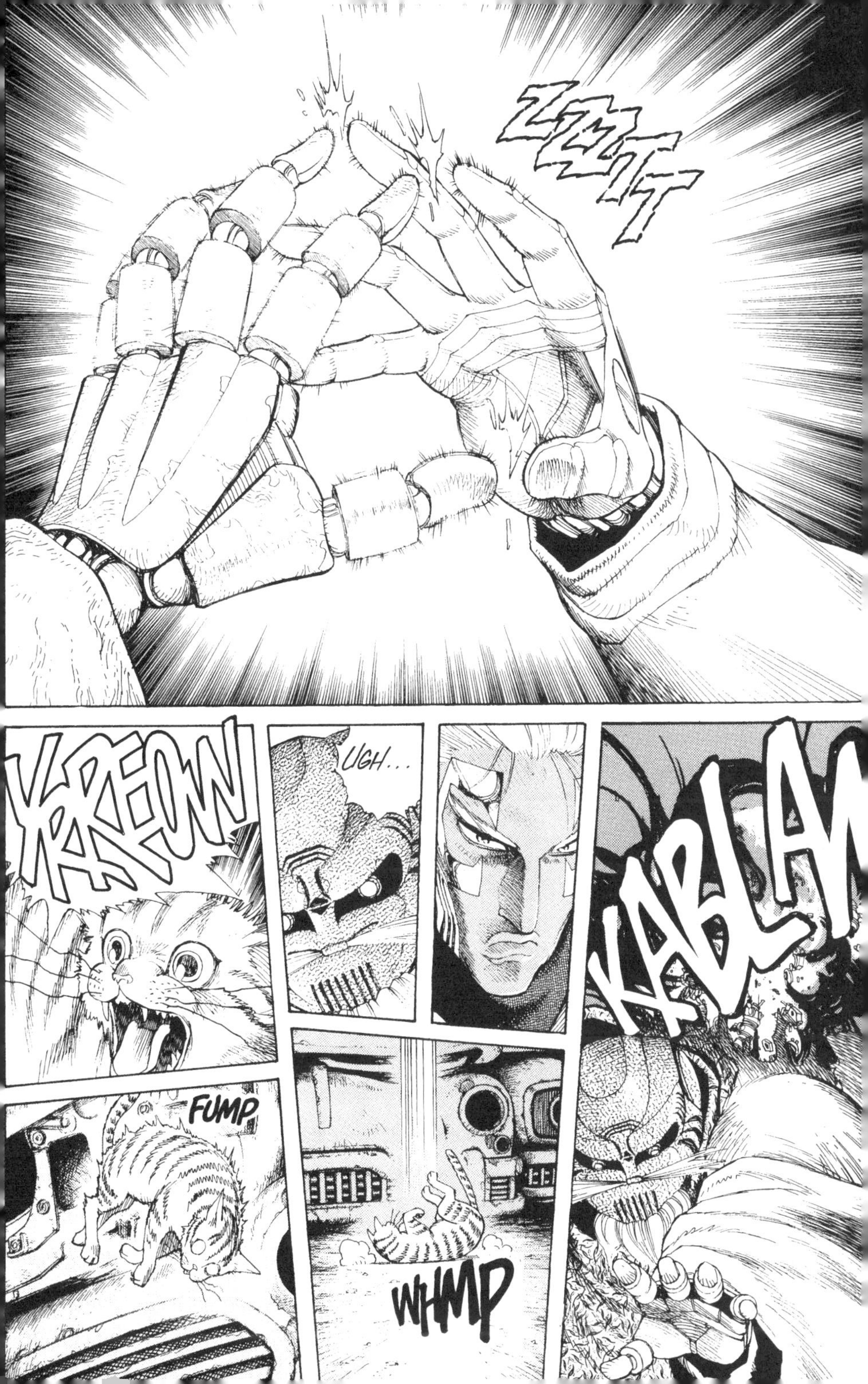
ZZZTT
KRREOWN
UGH...
FUMP
WHMP
KABLA

M-MAGNIFICENT! YOU'VE MASTERED THE **CHI** TECHNIQUE OF REFLECTIVE RESONANCE*..

KREK

TEK

KACHEK

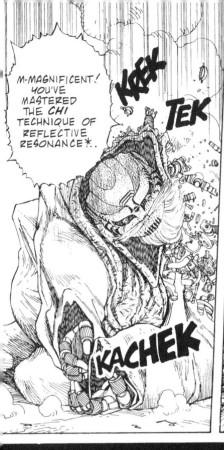

BUT I STILL SENSE SOMETHING **BOTHERING** YOU...

.....

I **FEAR**...

...MY ABSOLUTE **DEATH.**

I CAN'T BELIEVE I'M HEARING THIS FROM YOU...!

THE SECRET OF MASCHINE KLATSCH IS TO SYNCHRONIZE WITH THE ROTATING MACHINE--

--AND **MACHINES** DO NOT **FEAR DEATH!**

*BY MATCHING THE OPPONENT'S FLOW OF "CHI," THE VITAL LIFE FORCE IN THE BODY SAID TO BE REGULATED BY ACUPUNCTURE, AN INCREDIBLY DESTRUCTIVE VIBRATORY FEEDBACK IS CREATED.

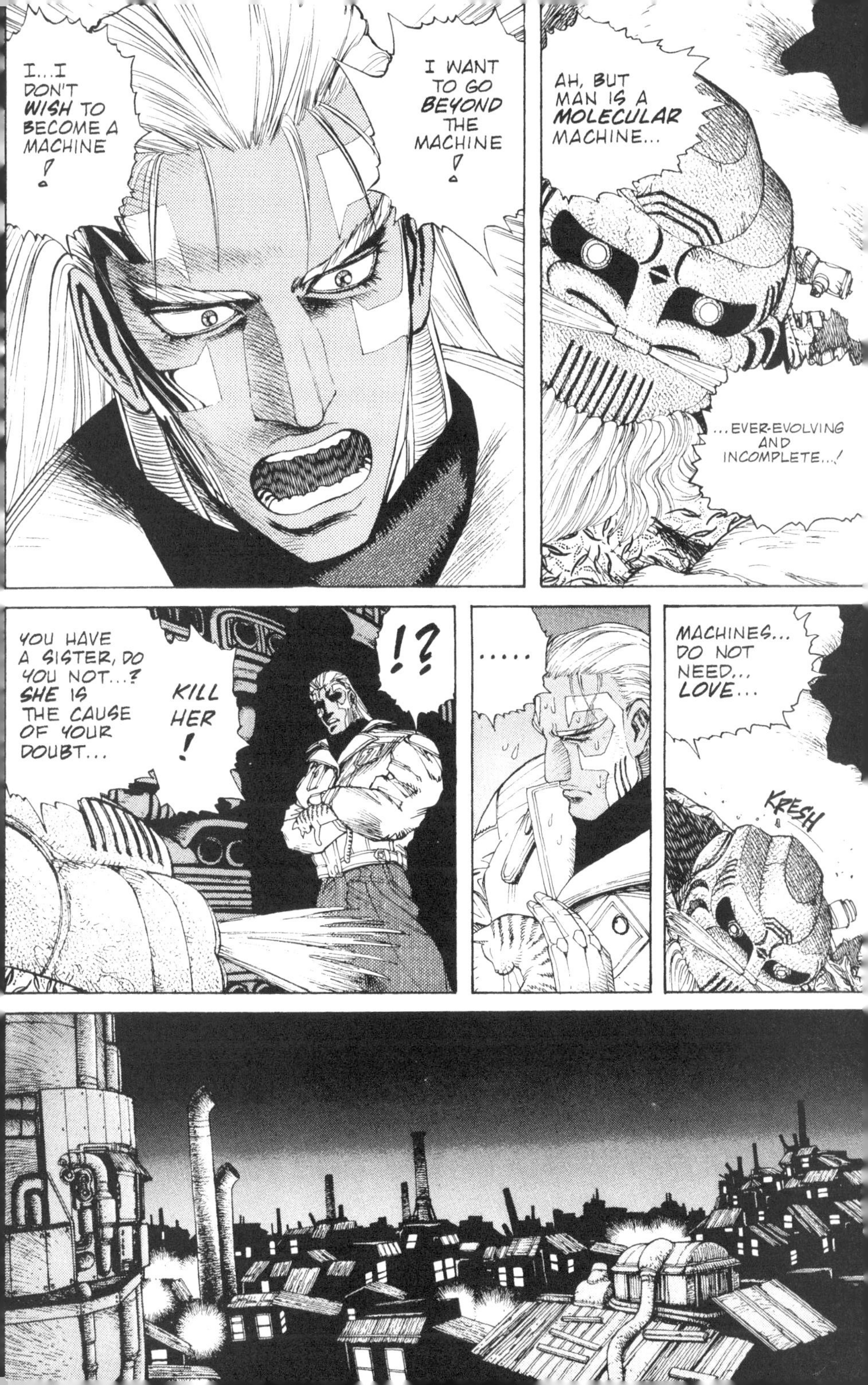
I...I DON'T WISH TO BECOME A MACHINE!
I WANT TO GO BEYOND THE MACHINE!
AH, BUT MAN IS A MOLECULAR MACHINE...
...EVER-EVOLVING AND INCOMPLETE...!
YOU HAVE A SISTER, DO YOU NOT...? SHE IS THE CAUSE OF YOUR DOUBT...
KILL HER!
!?
.....
MACHINES... DO NOT NEED... LOVE...
KRESH

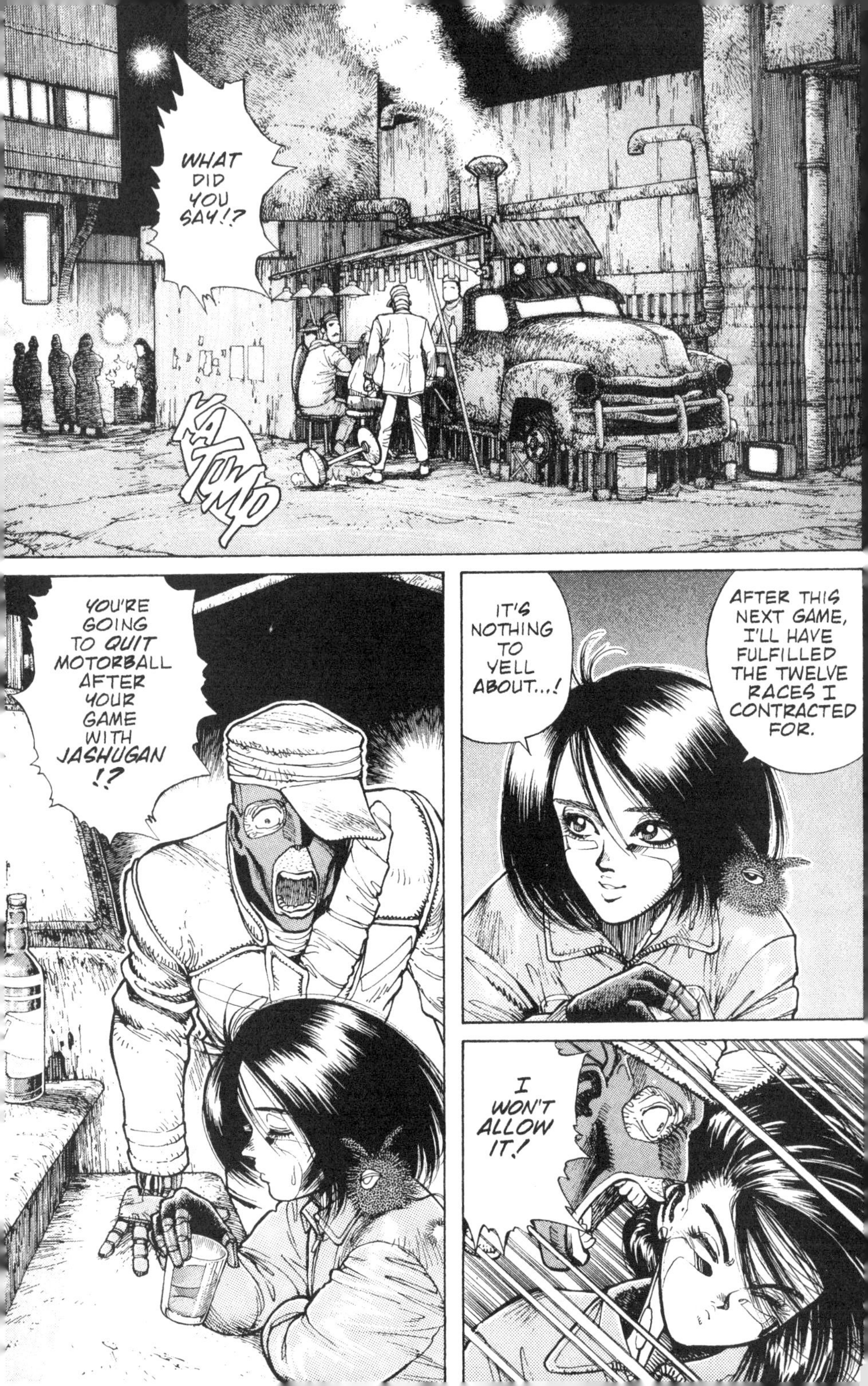
WHAT DID YOU SAY!?
KA-TOMP
YOU'RE GOING TO QUIT MOTORBALL AFTER YOUR GAME WITH JASHUGAN!?
IT'S NOTHING TO YELL ABOUT...!
AFTER THIS NEXT GAME, I'LL HAVE FULFILLED THE TWELVE RACES I CONTRACTED FOR.
I WON'T ALLOW IT!

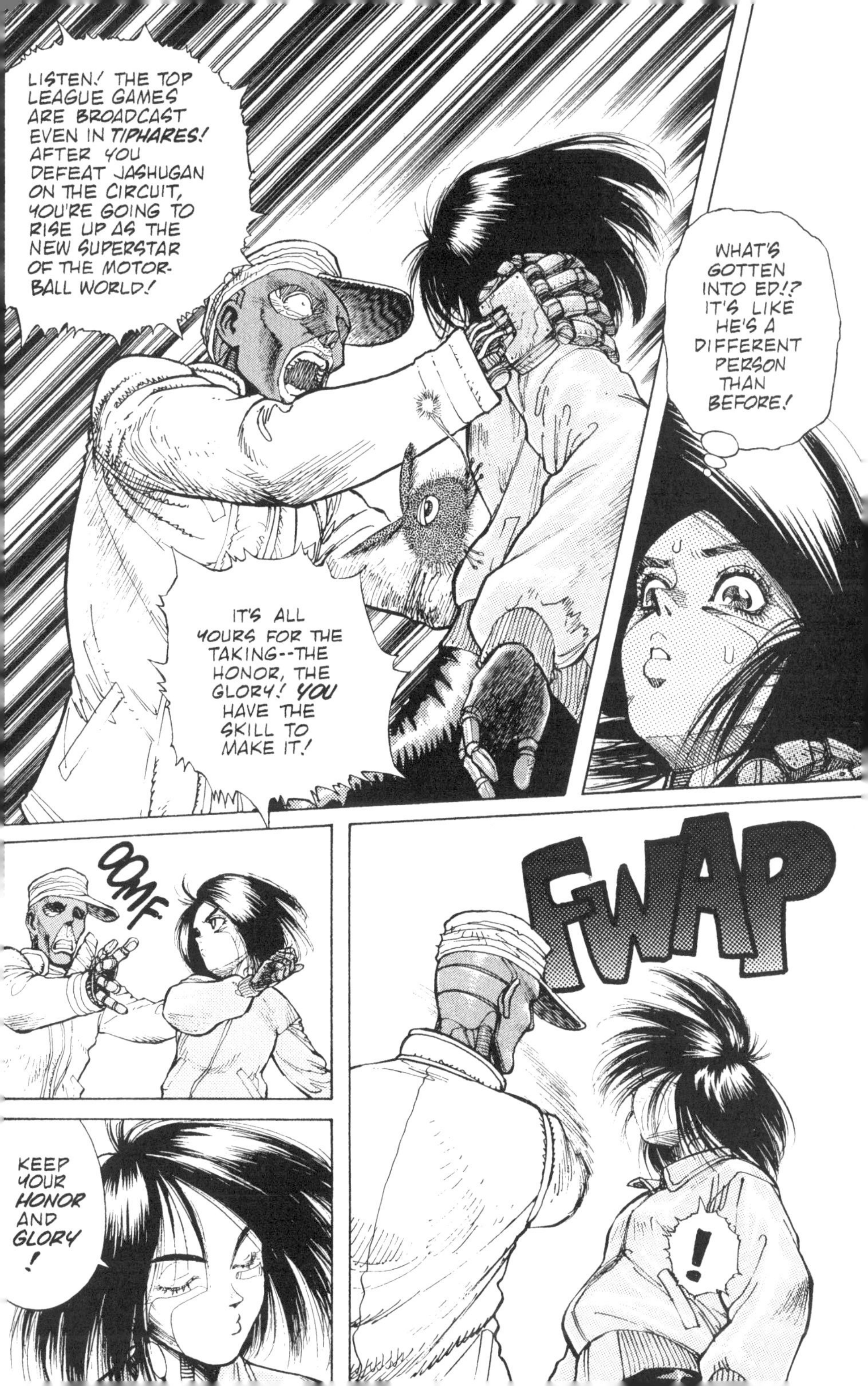
LISTEN! THE TOP LEAGUE GAMES ARE BROADCAST EVEN IN *TIPHARES!* AFTER YOU DEFEAT JASHUGAN ON THE CIRCUIT, YOU'RE GOING TO RISE UP AS THE NEW SUPERSTAR OF THE MOTOR-BALL WORLD!
IT'S ALL YOURS FOR THE TAKING--THE HONOR, THE GLORY! *YOU* HAVE THE SKILL TO MAKE IT!
WHAT'S GOTTEN INTO ED!? IT'S LIKE HE'S A DIFFERENT PERSON THAN BEFORE!
OOMF
KEEP YOUR *HONOR* AND *GLORY*!
FWAP
!

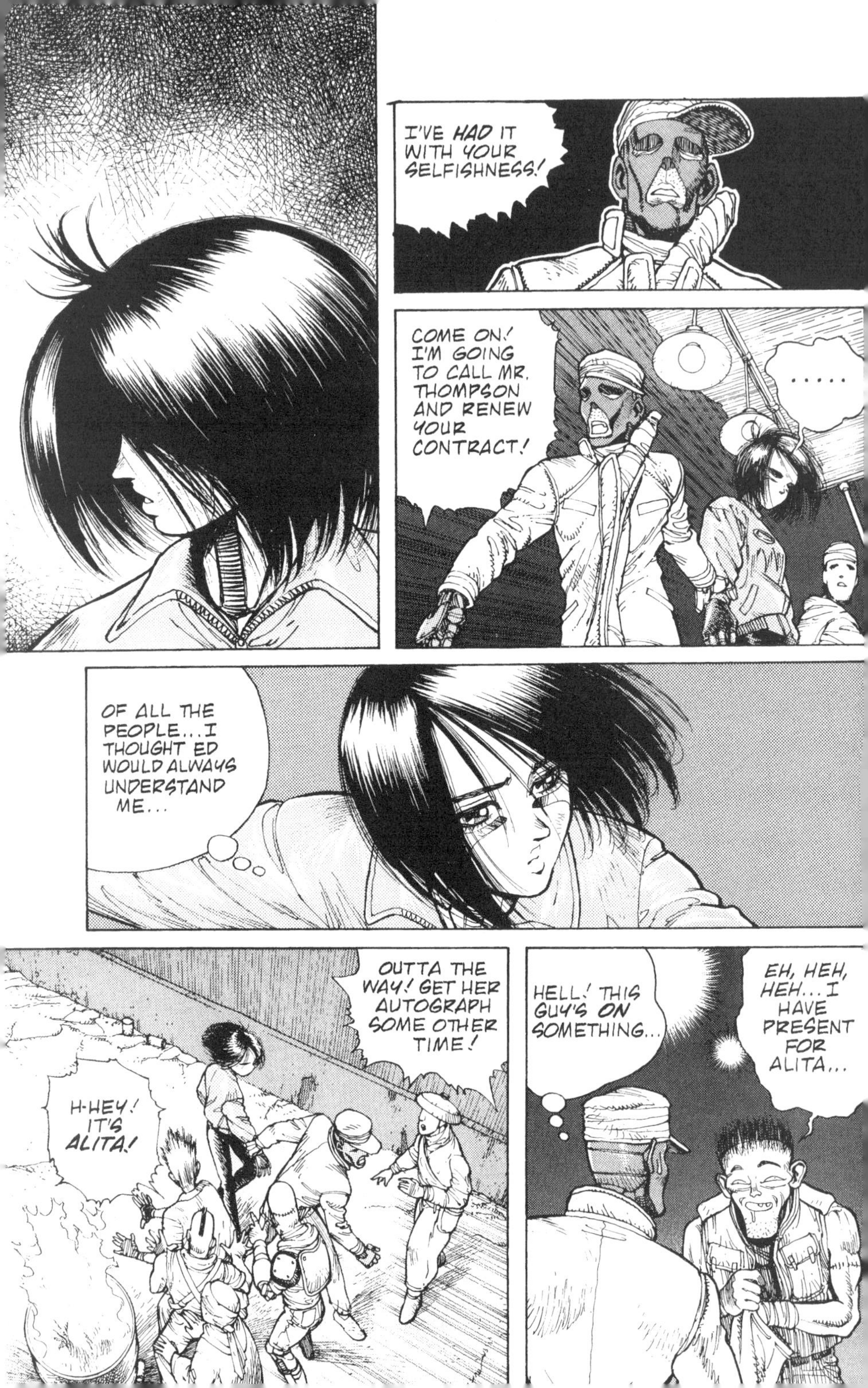
I'VE HAD IT WITH YOUR SELFISHNESS!
COME ON! I'M GOING TO CALL MR. THOMPSON AND RENEW YOUR CONTRACT!
.....
OF ALL THE PEOPLE...I THOUGHT ED WOULD ALWAYS UNDERSTAND ME...
OUTTA THE WAY! GET HER AUTOGRAPH SOME OTHER TIME!
H-HEY! IT'S ALITA!
HELL! THIS GUY'S ON SOMETHING...
EH, HEH, HEH... I HAVE PRESENT FOR ALITA...

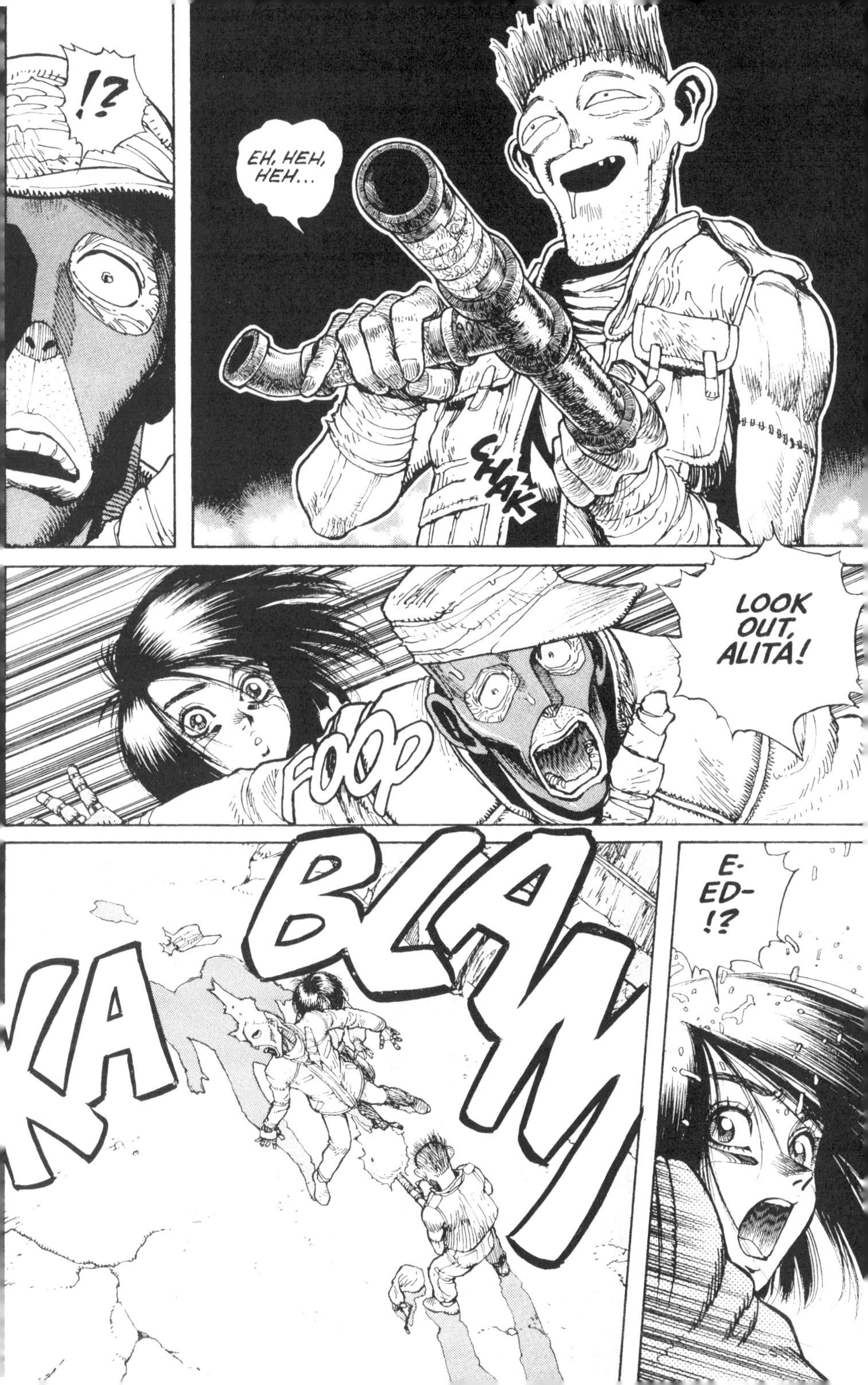
!?
EH, HEH, HEH...
CHAK
LOOK OUT, ALITA!
FOOP
BLAM
KA
E-ED-!?

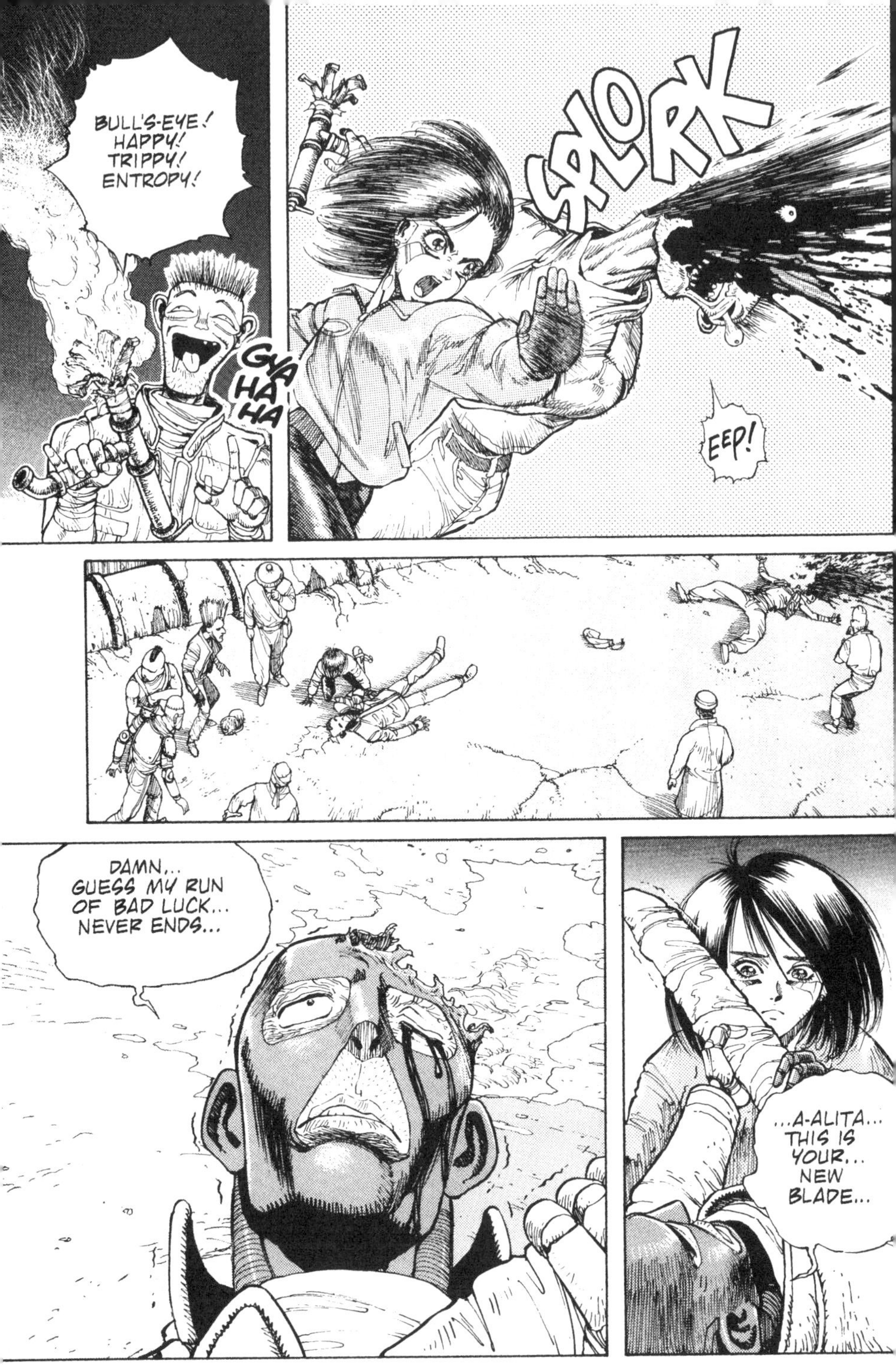
BULL'S-EYE! HAPPY! TRIPPY! ENTROPY!
GYA HA HA HA
SPLORK
EEP!
DAMN... GUESS MY RUN OF BAD LUCK... NEVER ENDS...
...A-ALITA... THIS IS YOUR... NEW BLADE...

...LISTEN... DON'T YOU DARE LOSE...

D-DAMN... MY ARM...

CHEKKA CHEKKA TEKKA

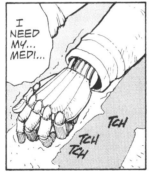

I NEED MY... MEDI...

TCH TCH TCH

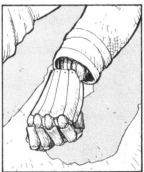

OUTSIDER
Race 4: Mystery Dance

AGRIPPA
CIR CUIT

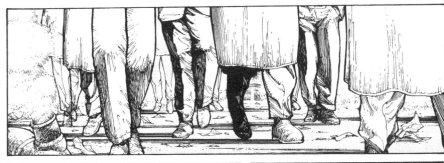

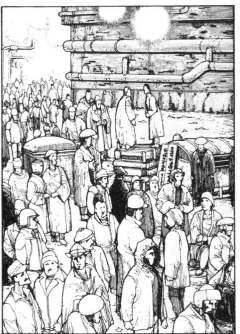

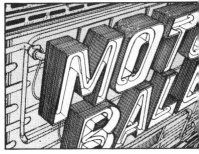

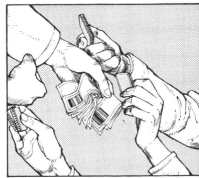

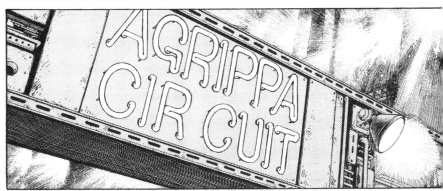

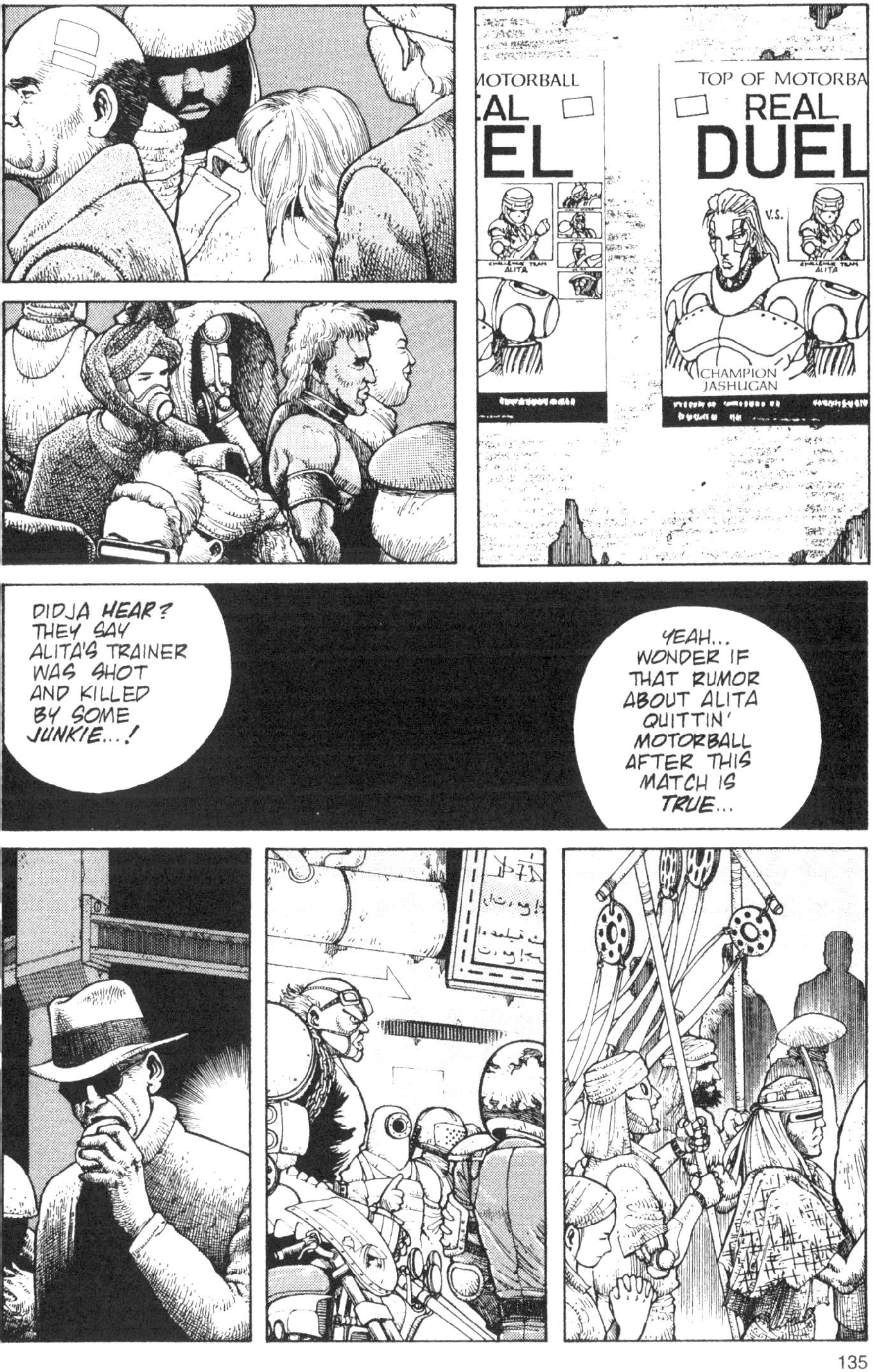

OTORBALL
AL
EL
ALITA
TOP OF MOTORBA
REAL
DUEL
V.S.
ALITA
CHAMPION JASHUGAN
DIDJA HEAR? THEY SAY ALITA'S TRAINER WAS SHOT AND KILLED BY SOME JUNKIE...!
YEAH... WONDER IF THAT RUMOR ABOUT ALITA QUITTIN' MOTORBALL AFTER THIS MATCH IS TRUE...

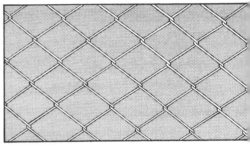

WOW-- CHECK THE HANDICAP REPORT! JASHU-GAN IS REALLY SICK... IN *NO* CONDITION TO RACE!

I HEARD THAT THE *REAL* JASHUGAN IS ALREADY DEAD! THE ONE THAT'S RACING IS ACTUALLY AN ANDROID BUILT BY *TIPHARES*...

FIRE PROHIBITED

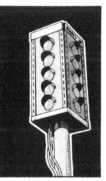

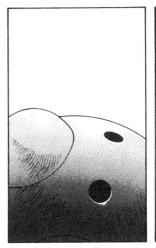

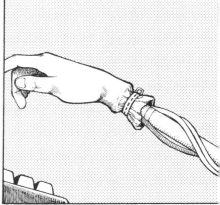

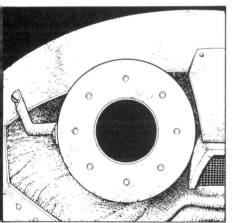

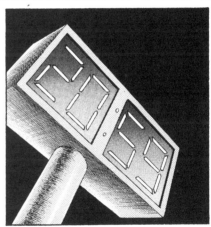

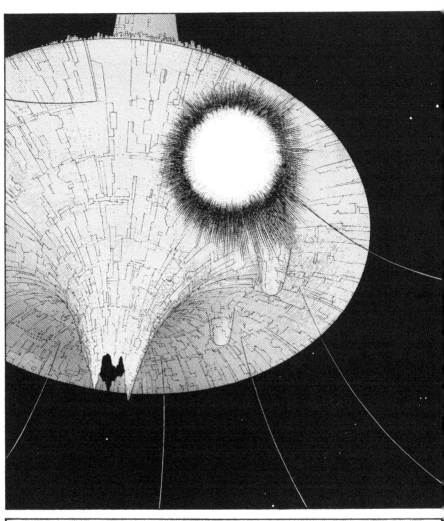

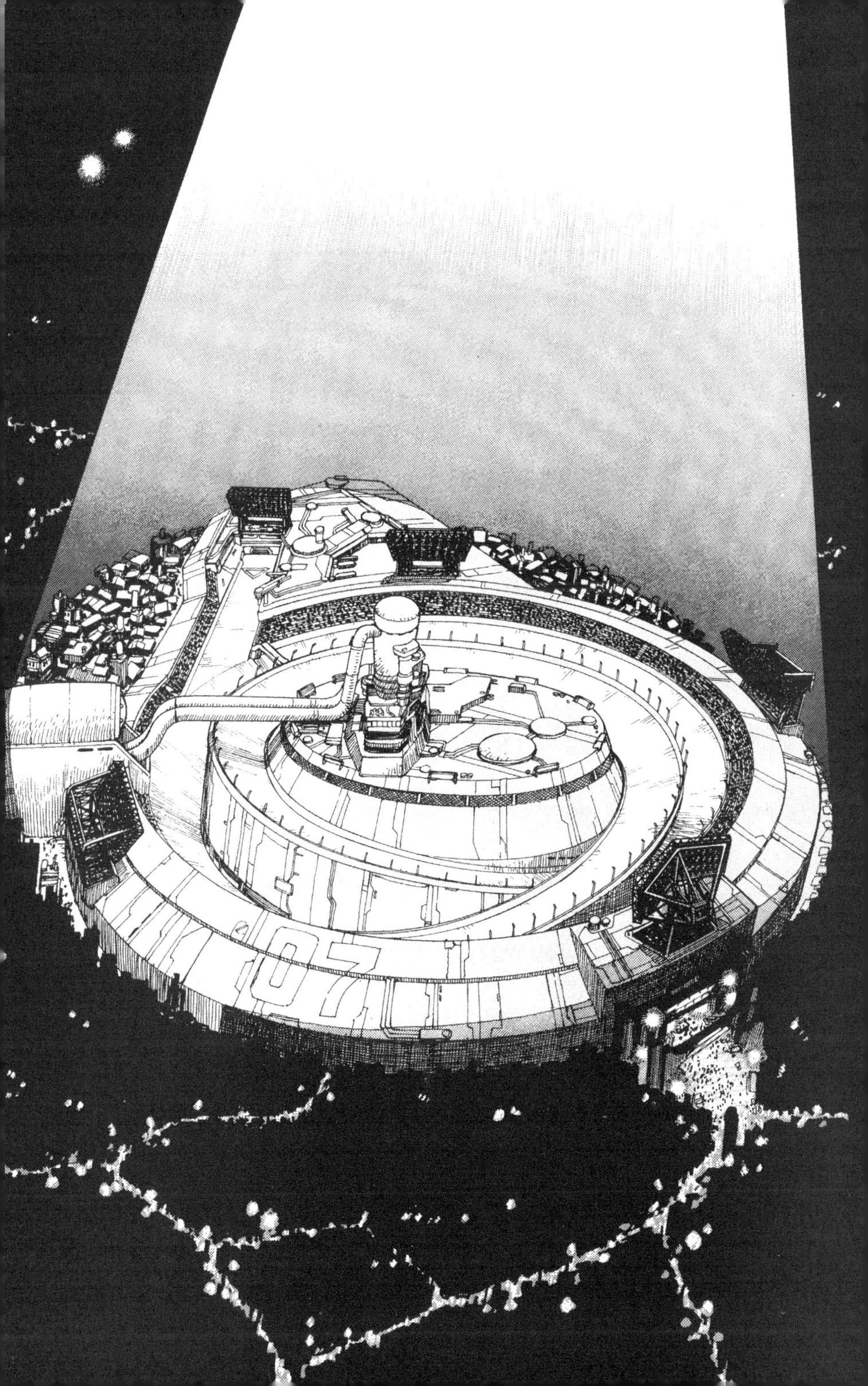
07

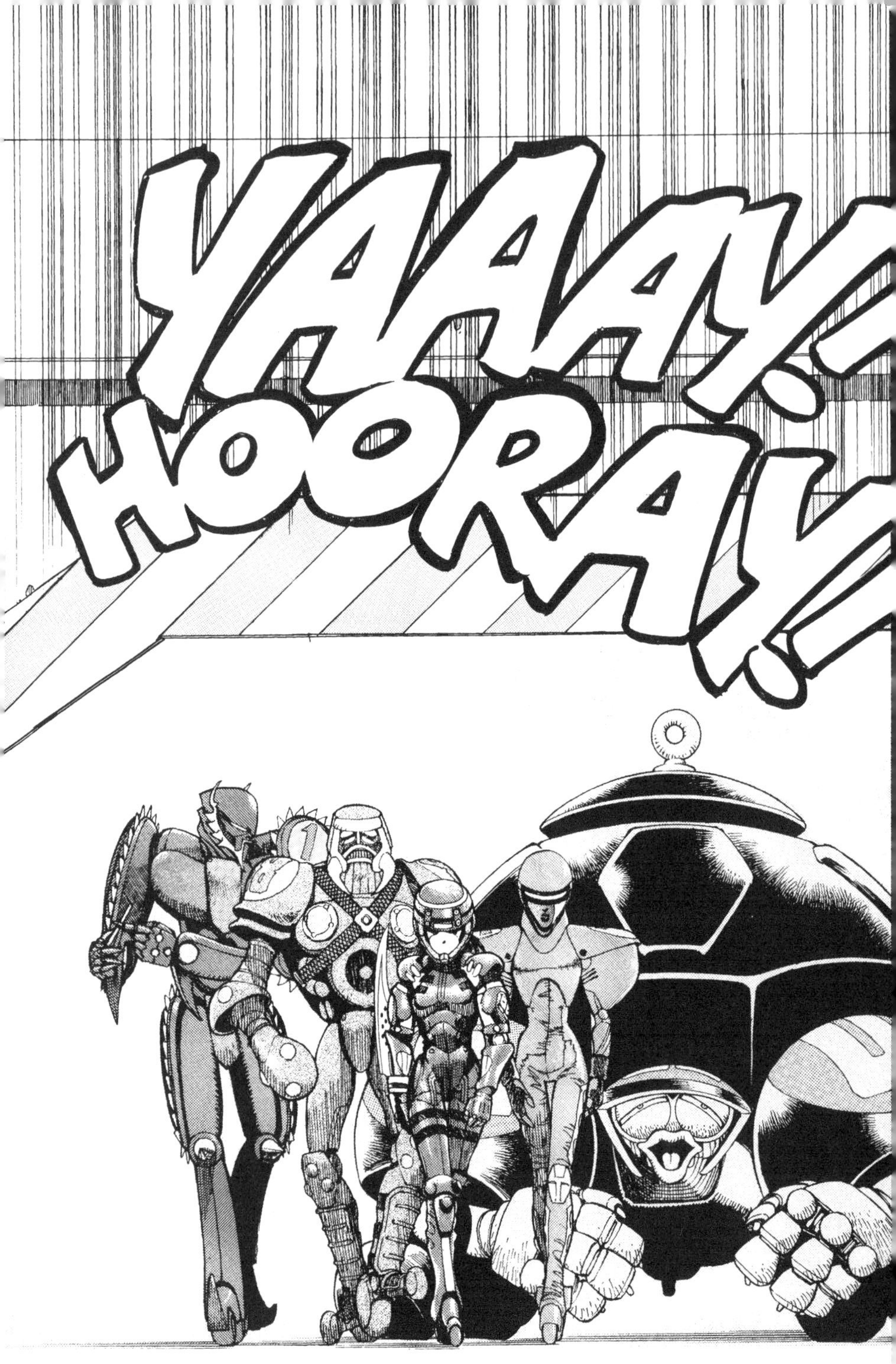
YAAAY!
HOORAY!

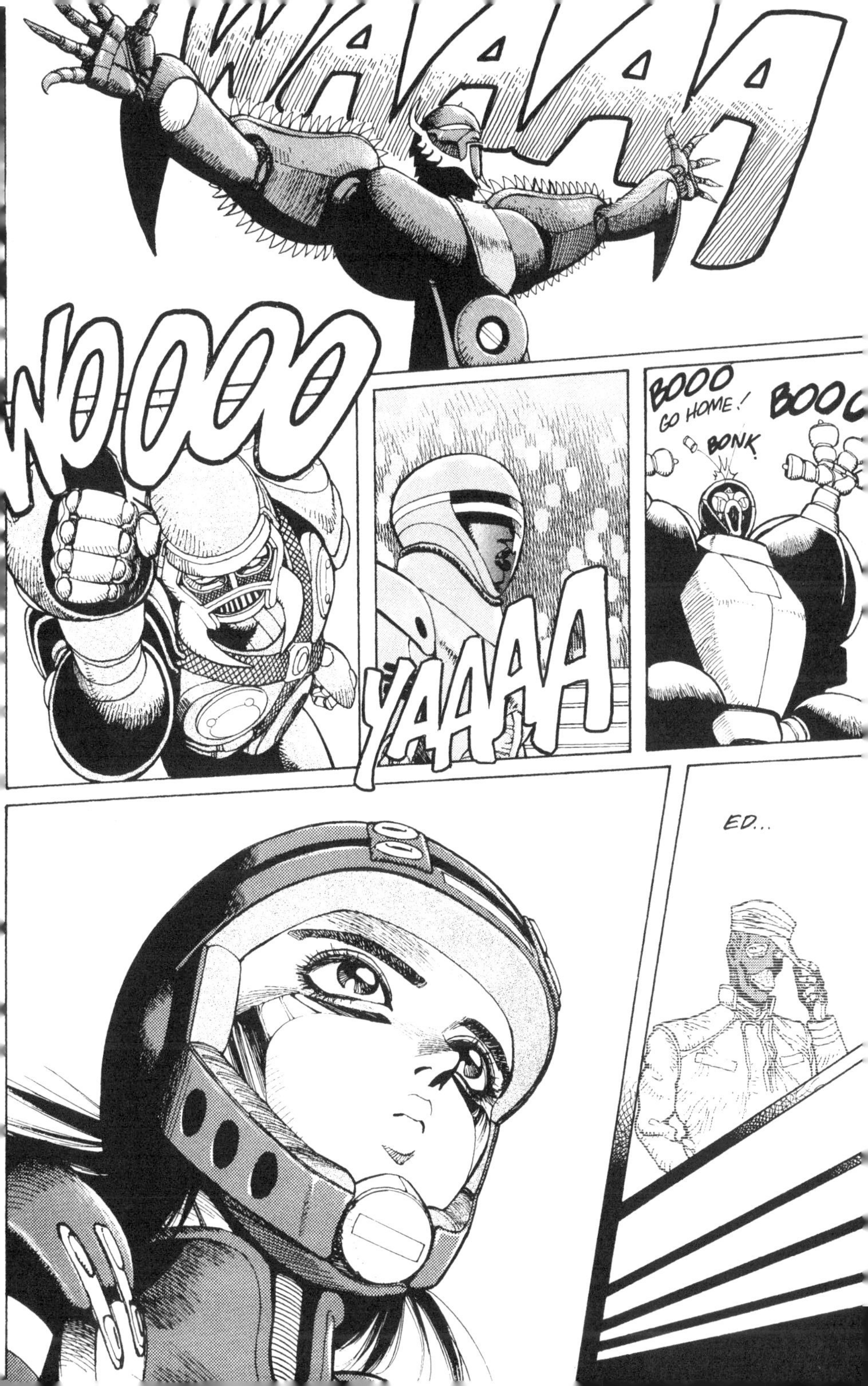
WAAAA
WOOOO
YAAAA
BOOO
GO HOME!
BONK
BOOO
ED...

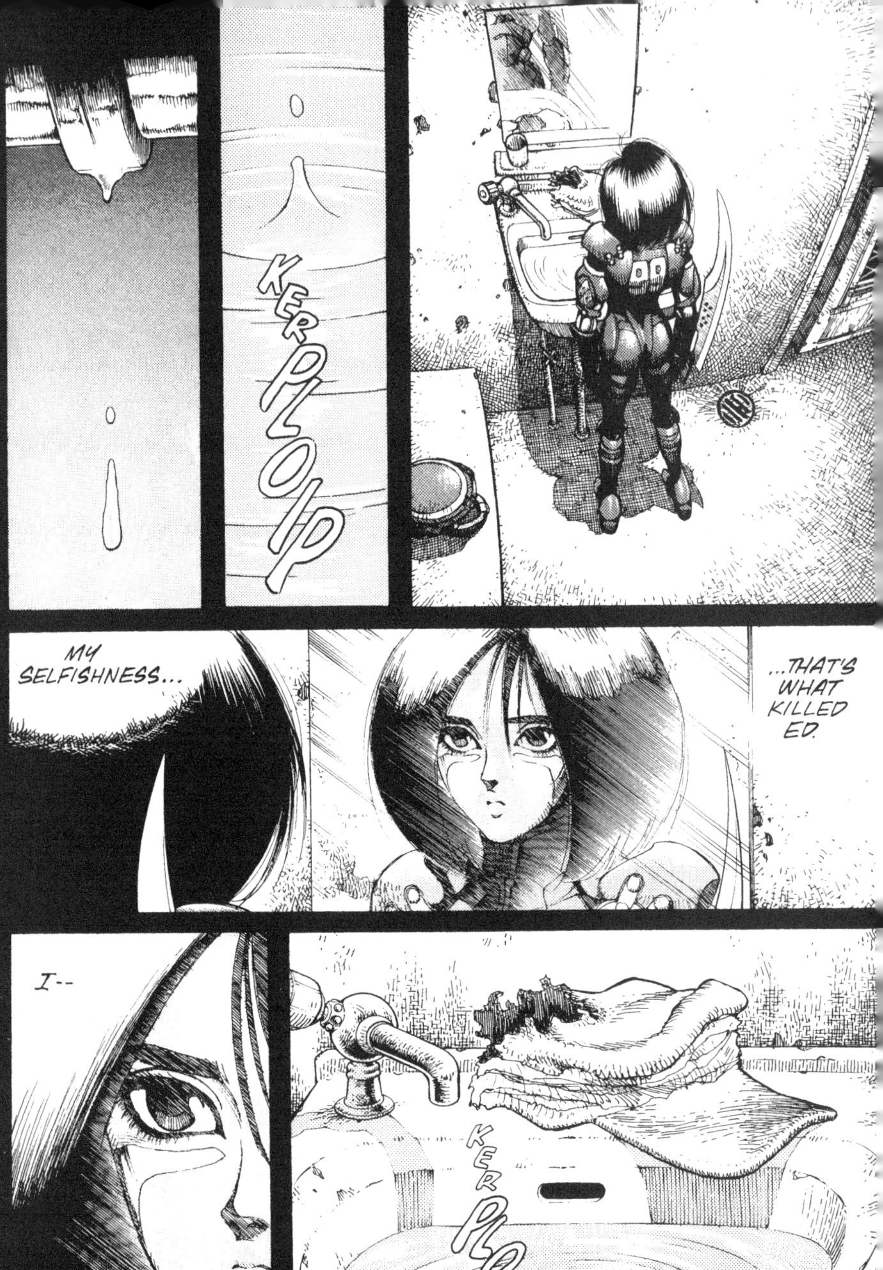
KERPLOIP
MY SELFISHNESS...
...THAT'S WHAT KILLED ED.
I--
KERPLOIP

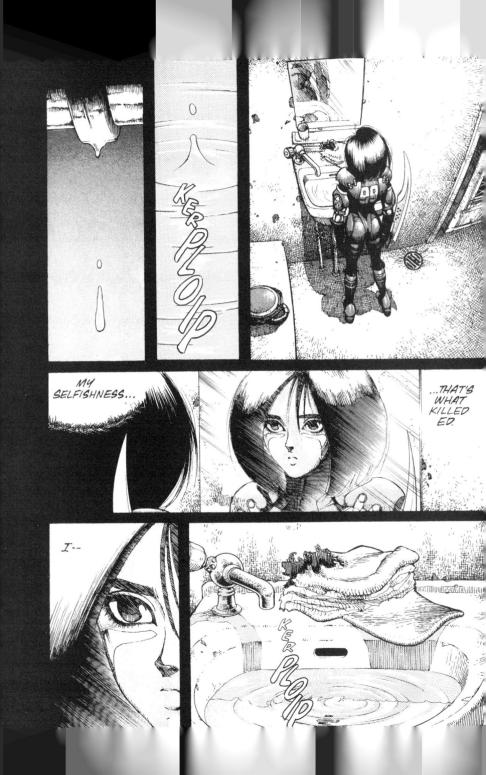

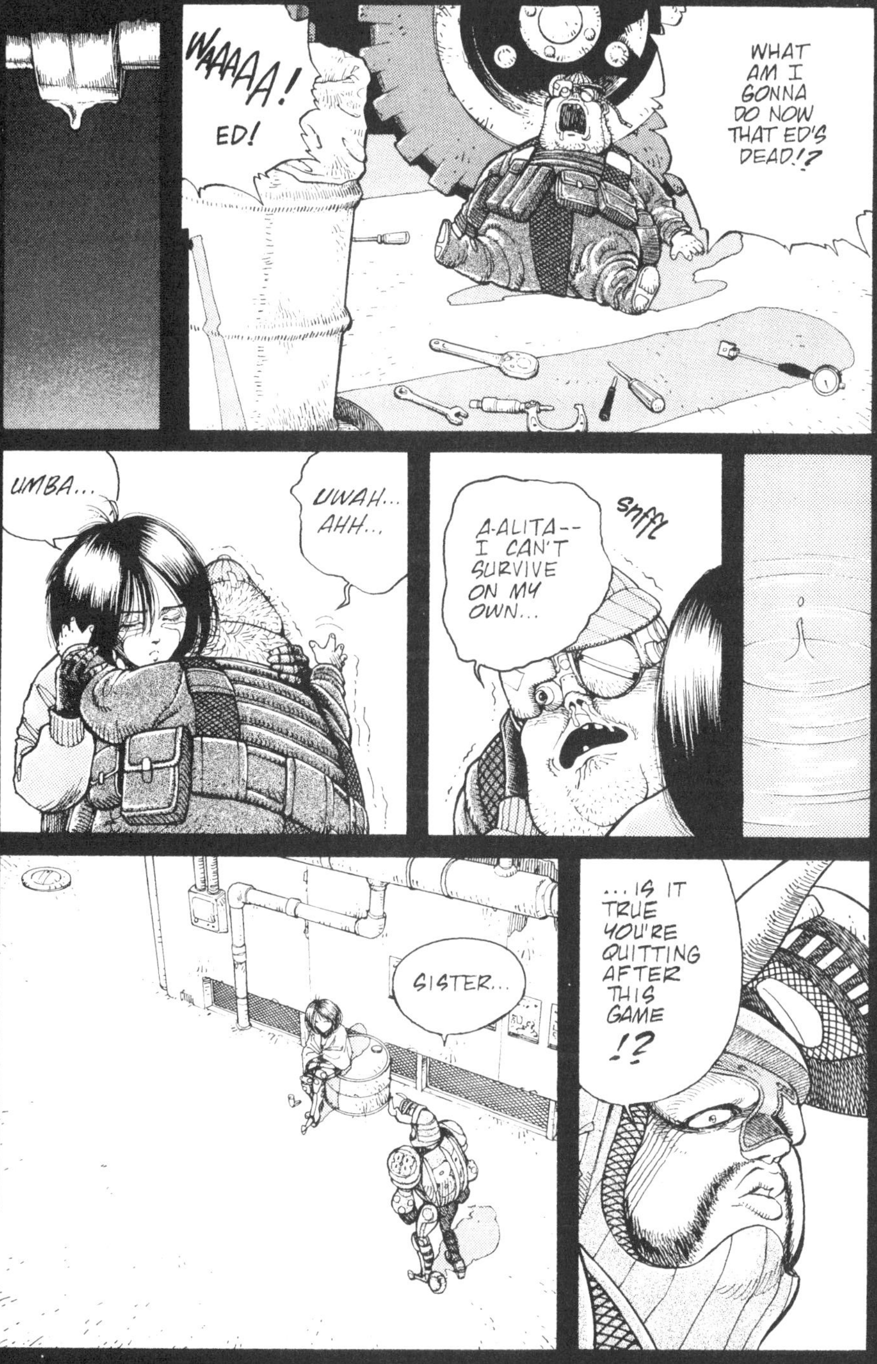
WAAAAAA!
ED!
WHAT AM I GONNA DO NOW THAT ED'S DEAD!?
UMBA...
UWAH... AHH...
A-ALITA-- I CAN'T SURVIVE ON MY OWN...
Snffl
SISTER...
...IS IT TRUE YOU'RE QUITTING AFTER THIS GAME !?

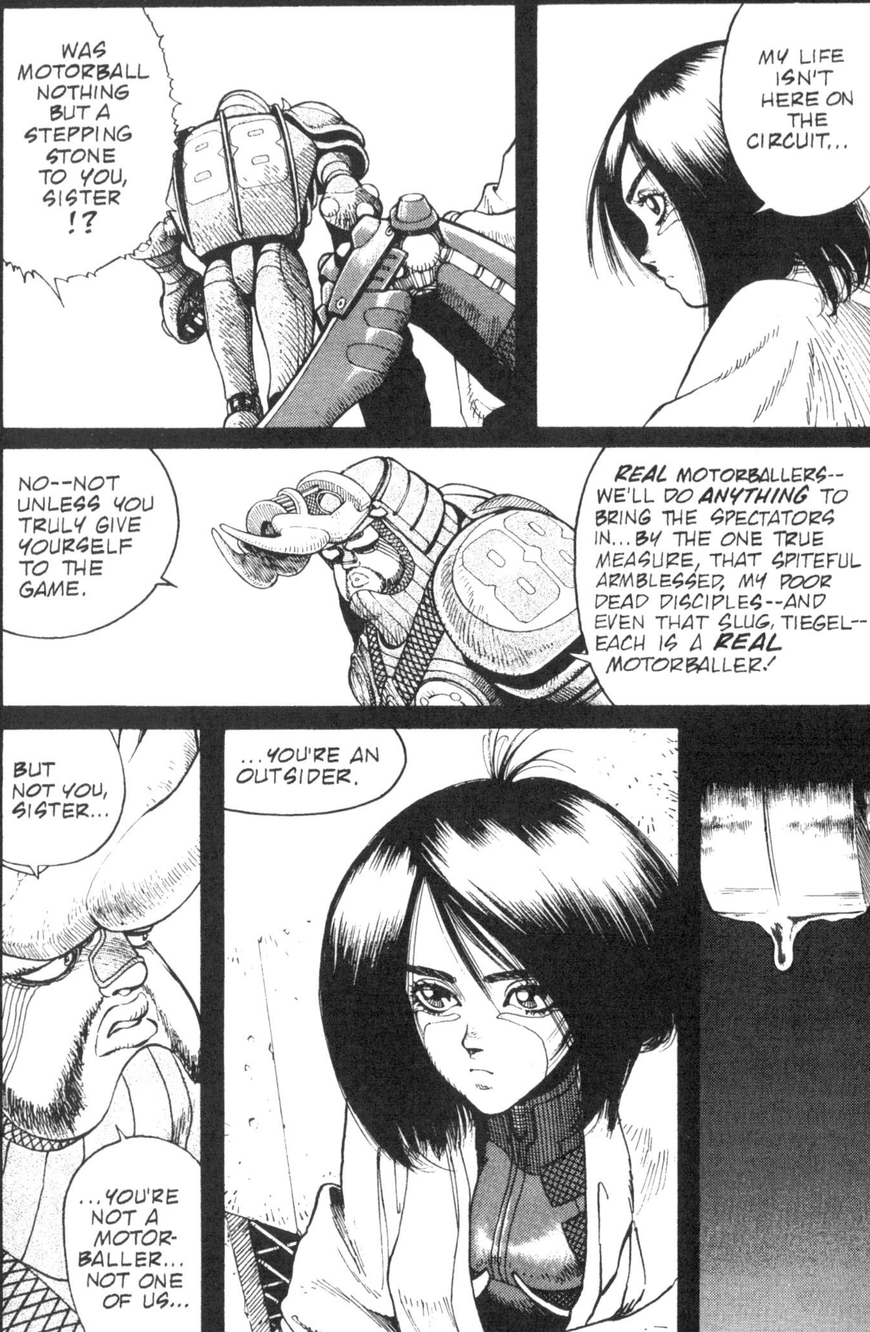
WAS MOTORBALL NOTHING BUT A STEPPING STONE TO YOU, SISTER !?
MY LIFE ISN'T HERE ON THE CIRCUIT...
NO--NOT UNLESS YOU TRULY GIVE YOURSELF TO THE GAME.
REAL MOTORBALLERS--WE'LL DO ANYTHING TO BRING THE SPECTATORS IN... BY THE ONE TRUE MEASURE, THAT SPITEFUL ARMBLESSED, MY POOR DEAD DISCIPLES--AND EVEN THAT SLUG, TIEGEL--EACH IS A REAL MOTORBALLER!
BUT NOT YOU, SISTER...
...YOU'RE NOT A MOTOR-BALLER... NOT ONE OF US...
...YOU'RE AN OUTSIDER.

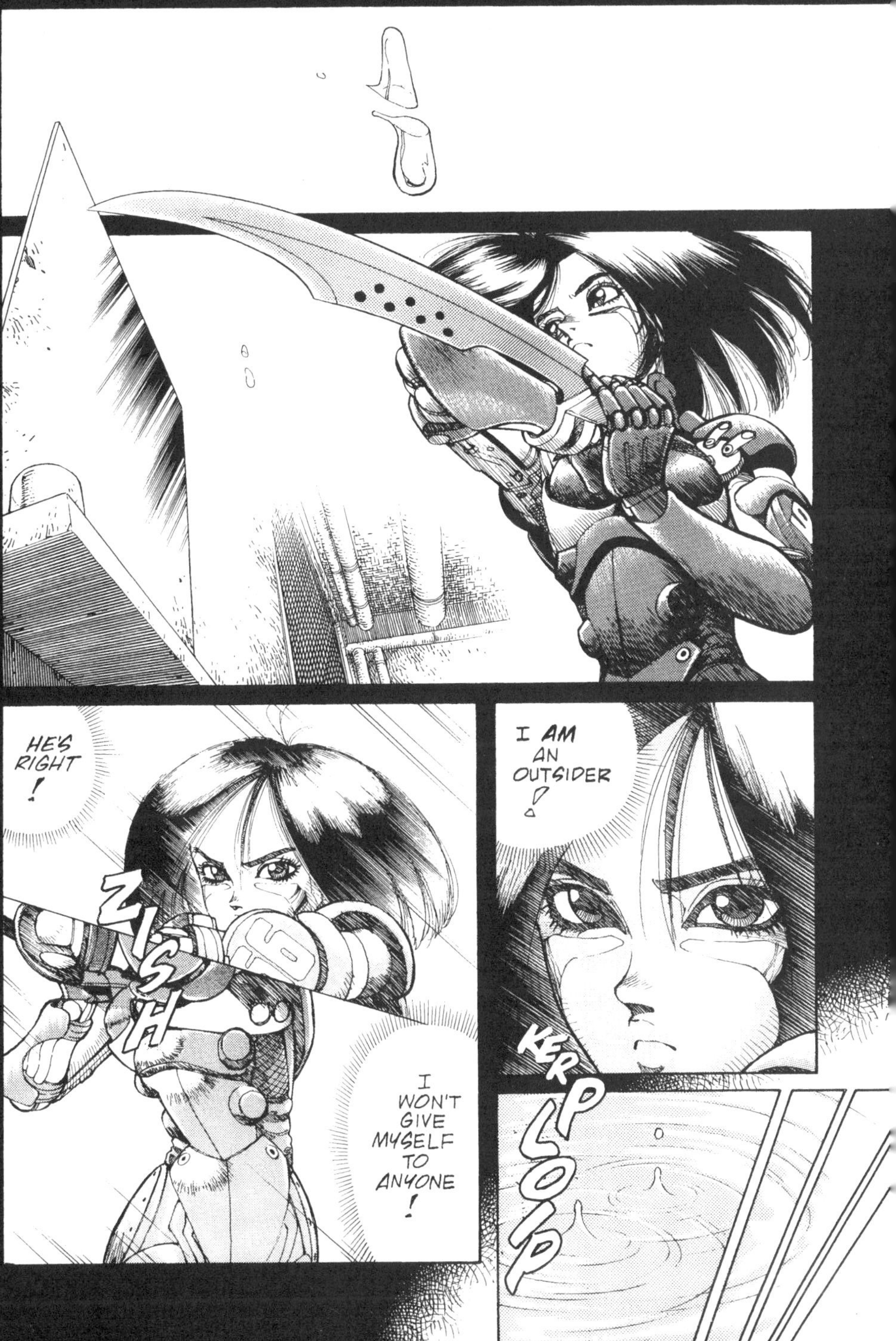
HE'S RIGHT!
ZISH
I WON'T GIVE MYSELF TO ANYONE!
I AM AN OUTSIDER!
KERPLOP

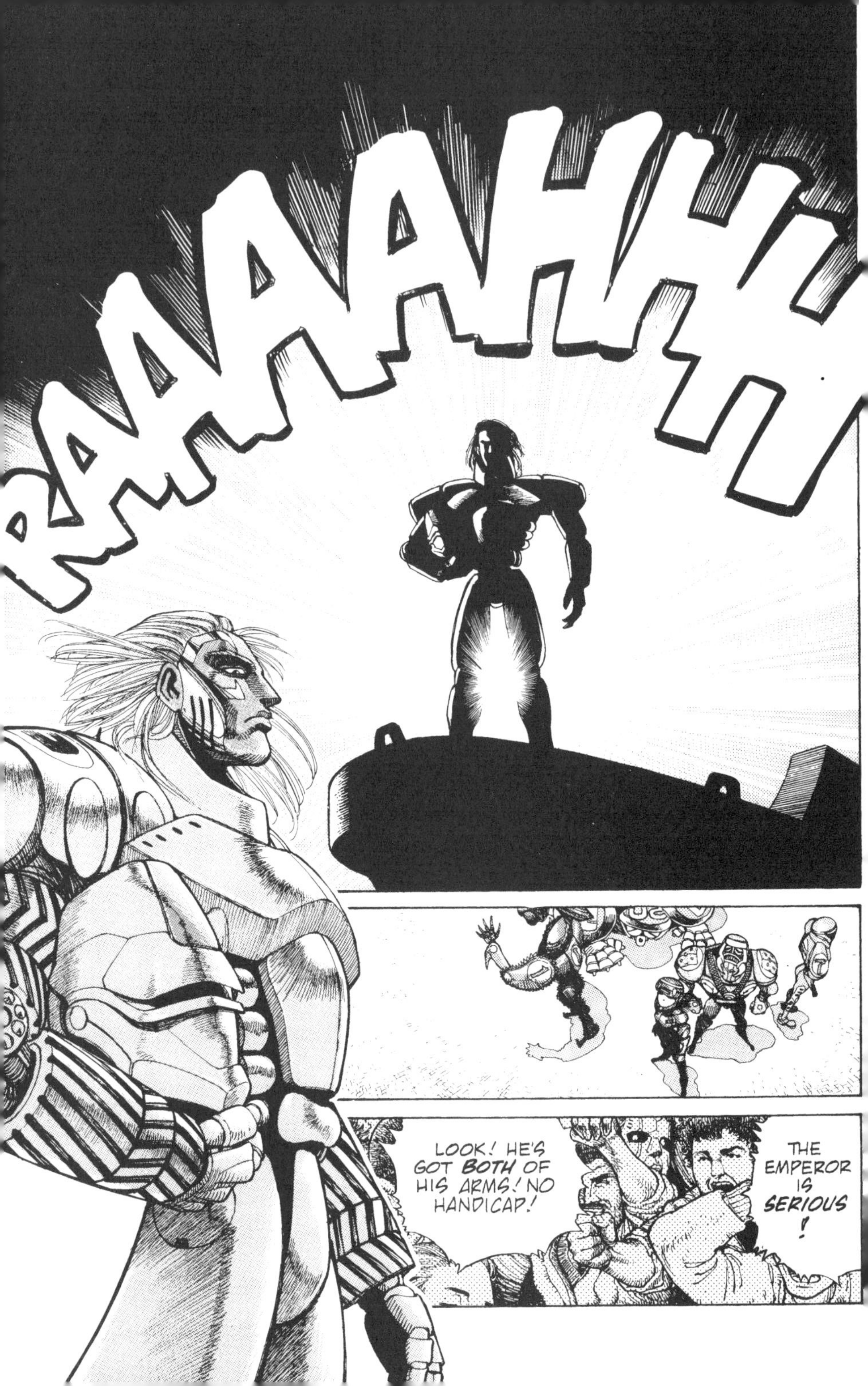
RAAAAHHH!
LOOK! HE'S GOT **BOTH** OF HIS ARMS! NO HANDICAP!
THE EMPEROR IS **SERIOUS**!

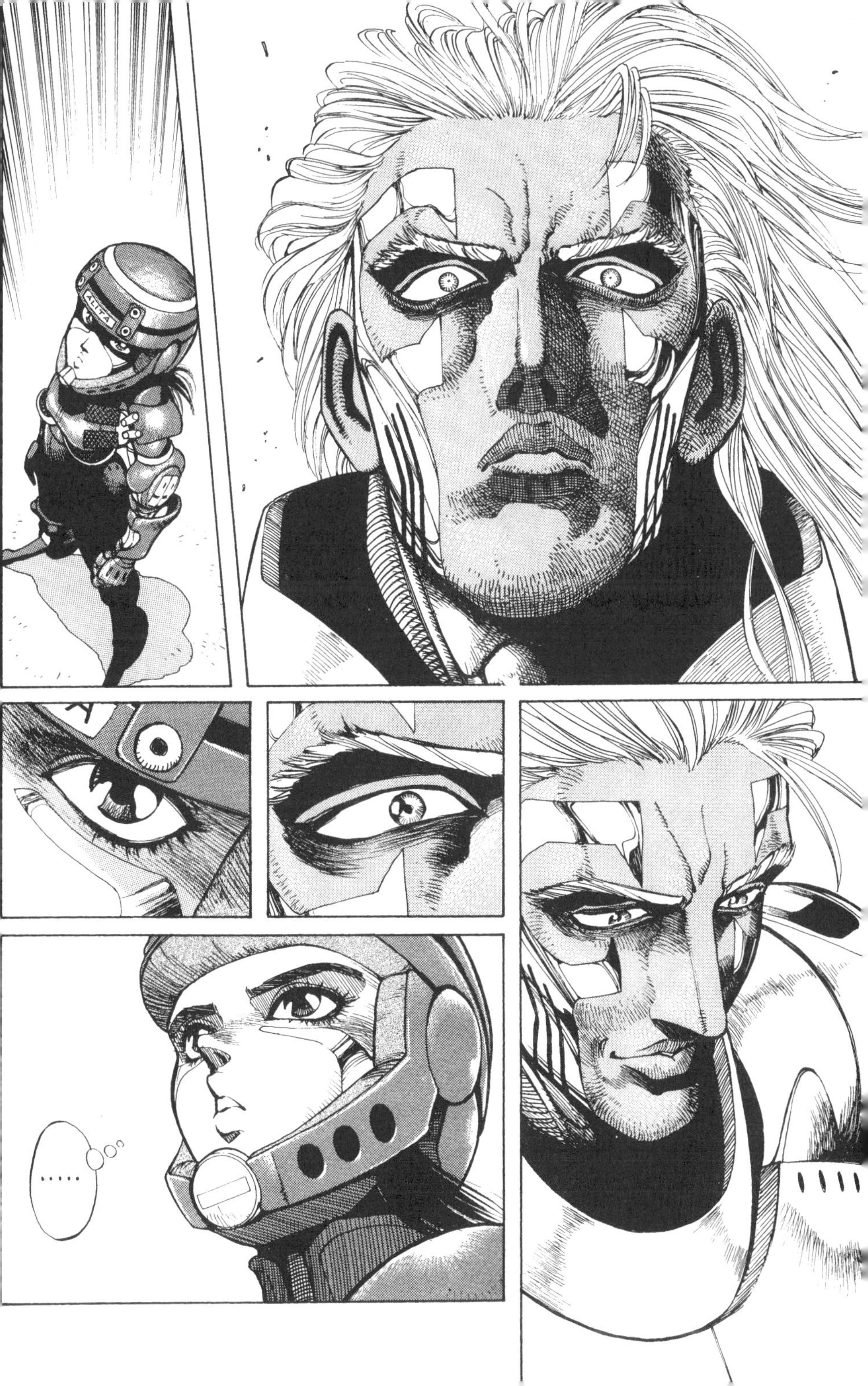
ALITA
.....

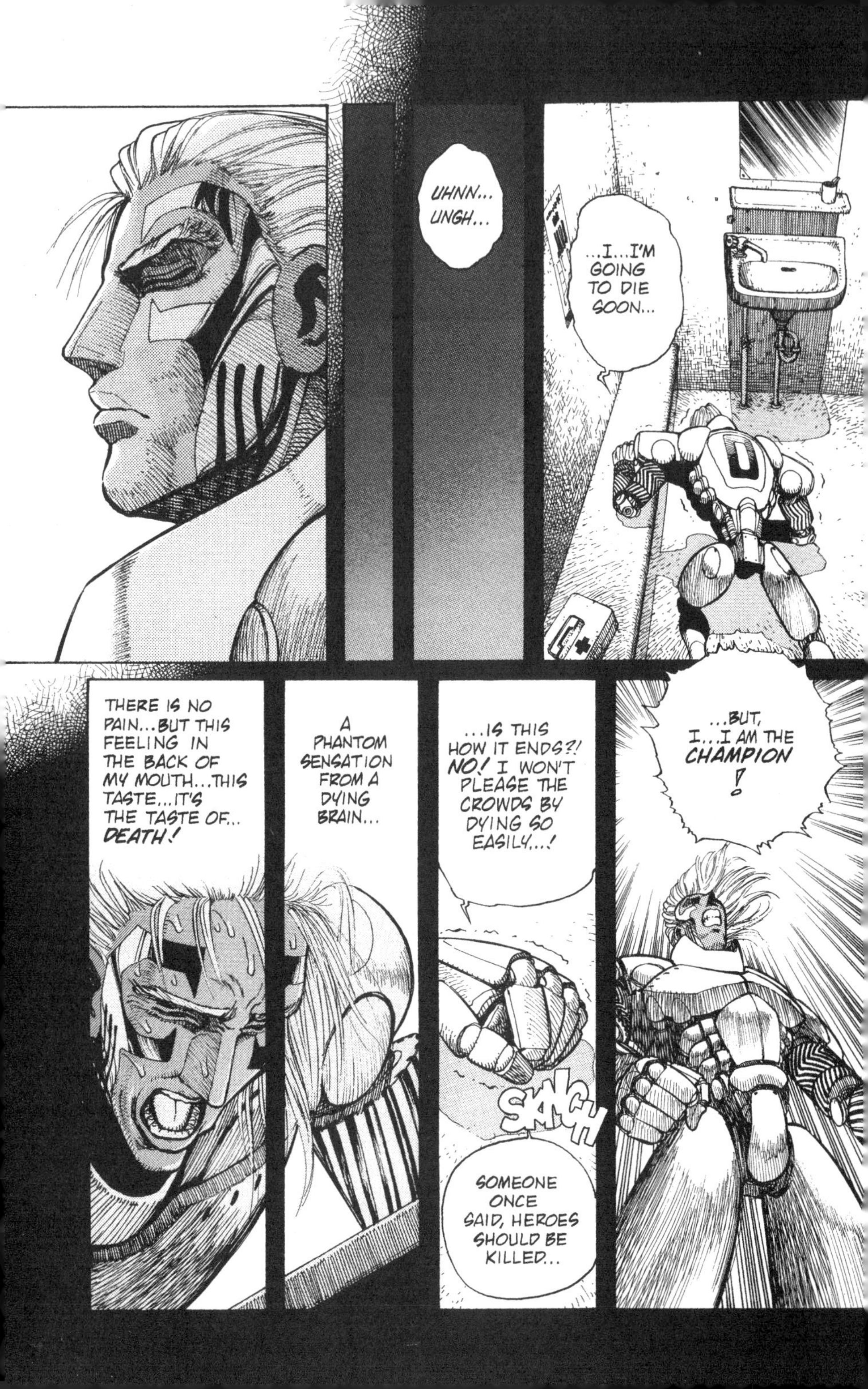
UHNN... UNGH...
...I...I'M GOING TO DIE SOON...
THERE IS NO PAIN...BUT THIS FEELING IN THE BACK OF MY MOUTH...THIS TASTE...IT'S THE TASTE OF... DEATH!
A PHANTOM SENSATION FROM A DYING BRAIN...
...IS THIS HOW IT ENDS?! NO! I WON'T PLEASE THE CROWDS BY DYING SO EASILY...!
SKANCH
SOMEONE ONCE SAID, HEROES SHOULD BE KILLED...
...BUT, I...I AM THE CHAMPION!

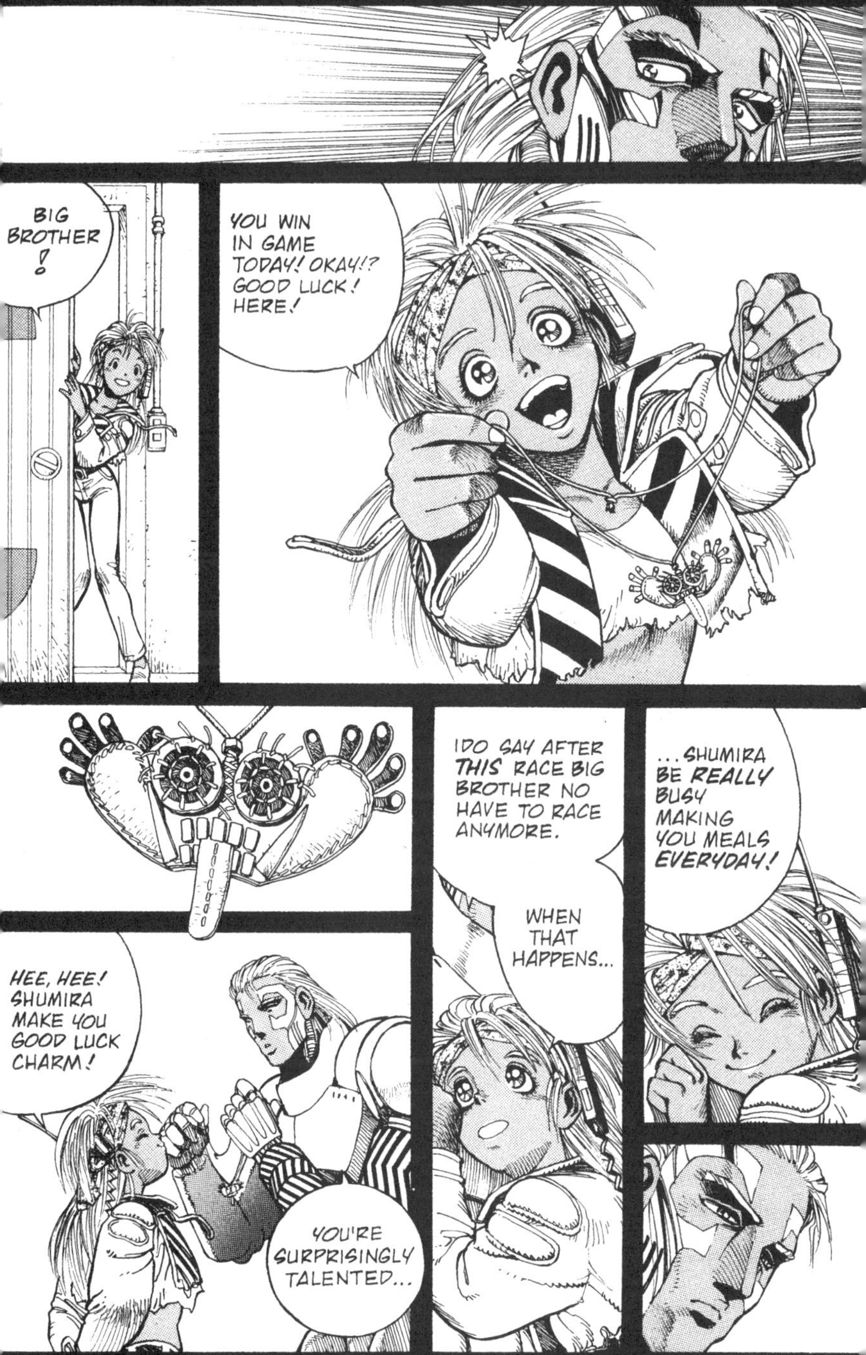
BIG BROTHER!
YOU WIN IN GAME TODAY! OKAY!? GOOD LUCK! HERE!
HEE, HEE! SHUMIRA MAKE YOU GOOD LUCK CHARM!
YOU'RE SURPRISINGLY TALENTED...
I DO SAY AFTER THIS RACE BIG BROTHER NO HAVE TO RACE ANYMORE.
WHEN THAT HAPPENS...
...SHUMIRA BE REALLY BUSY MAKING YOU MEALS EVERYDAY!

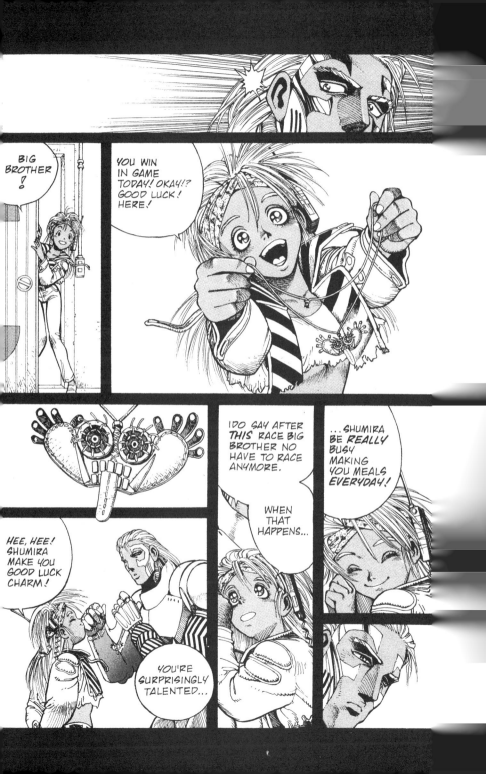

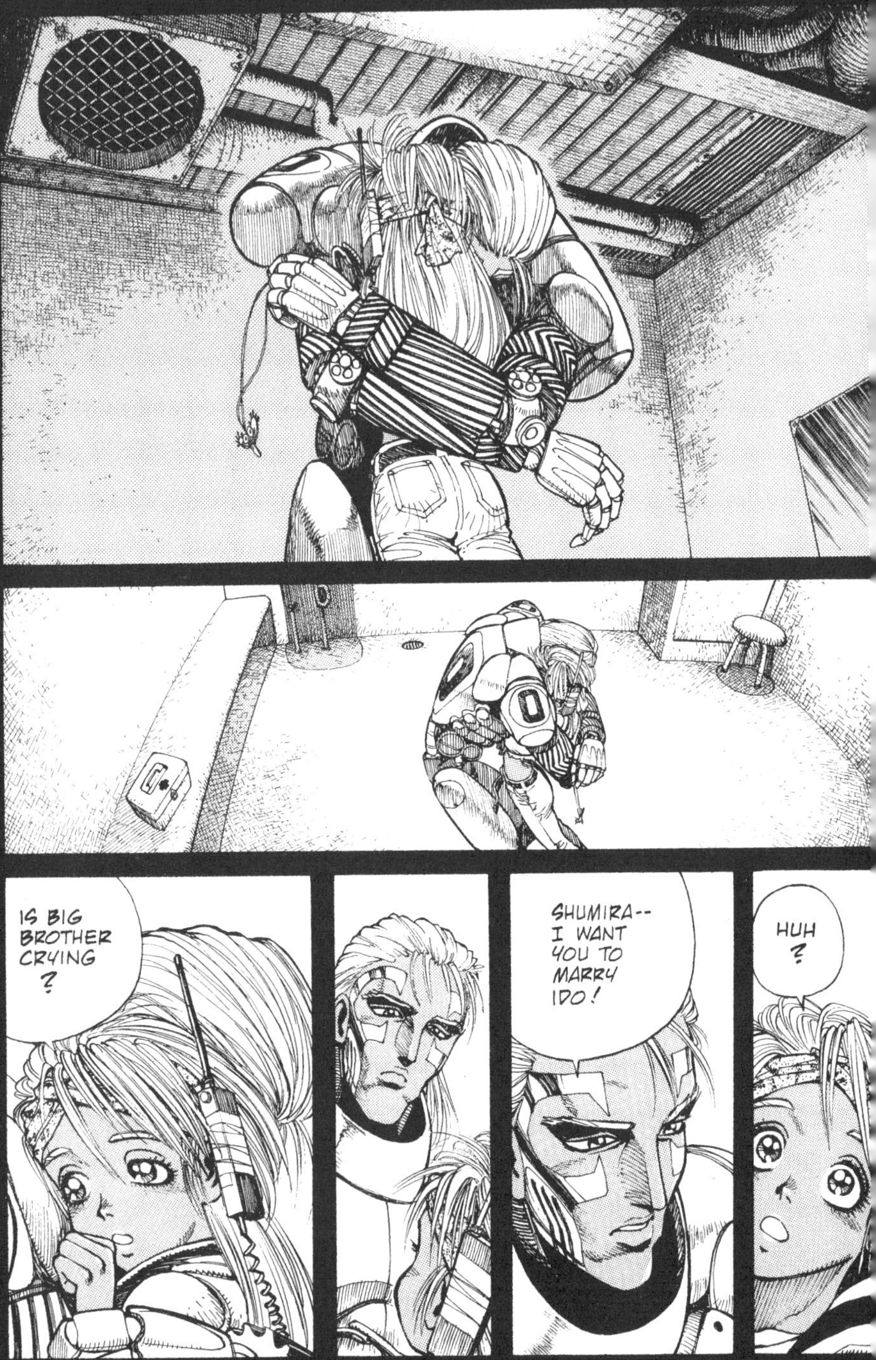
IS BIG BROTHER CRYING ?
SHUMIRA-- I WANT YOU TO MARRY IDO !
HUH ?

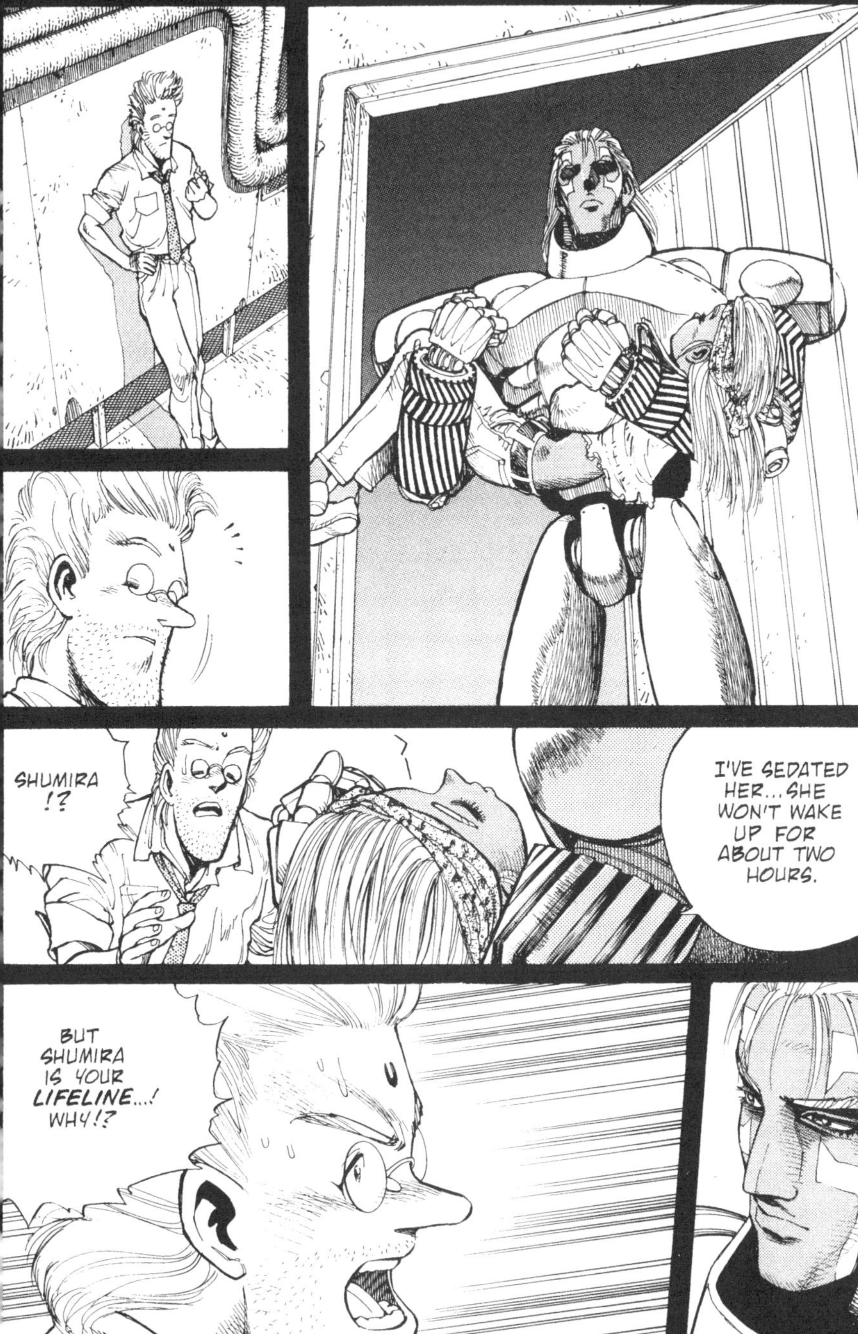
SHUMIRA !?
I'VE SEDATED HER... SHE WON'T WAKE UP FOR ABOUT TWO HOURS.
BUT SHUMIRA IS YOUR ***LIFELINE***...! WHY!?

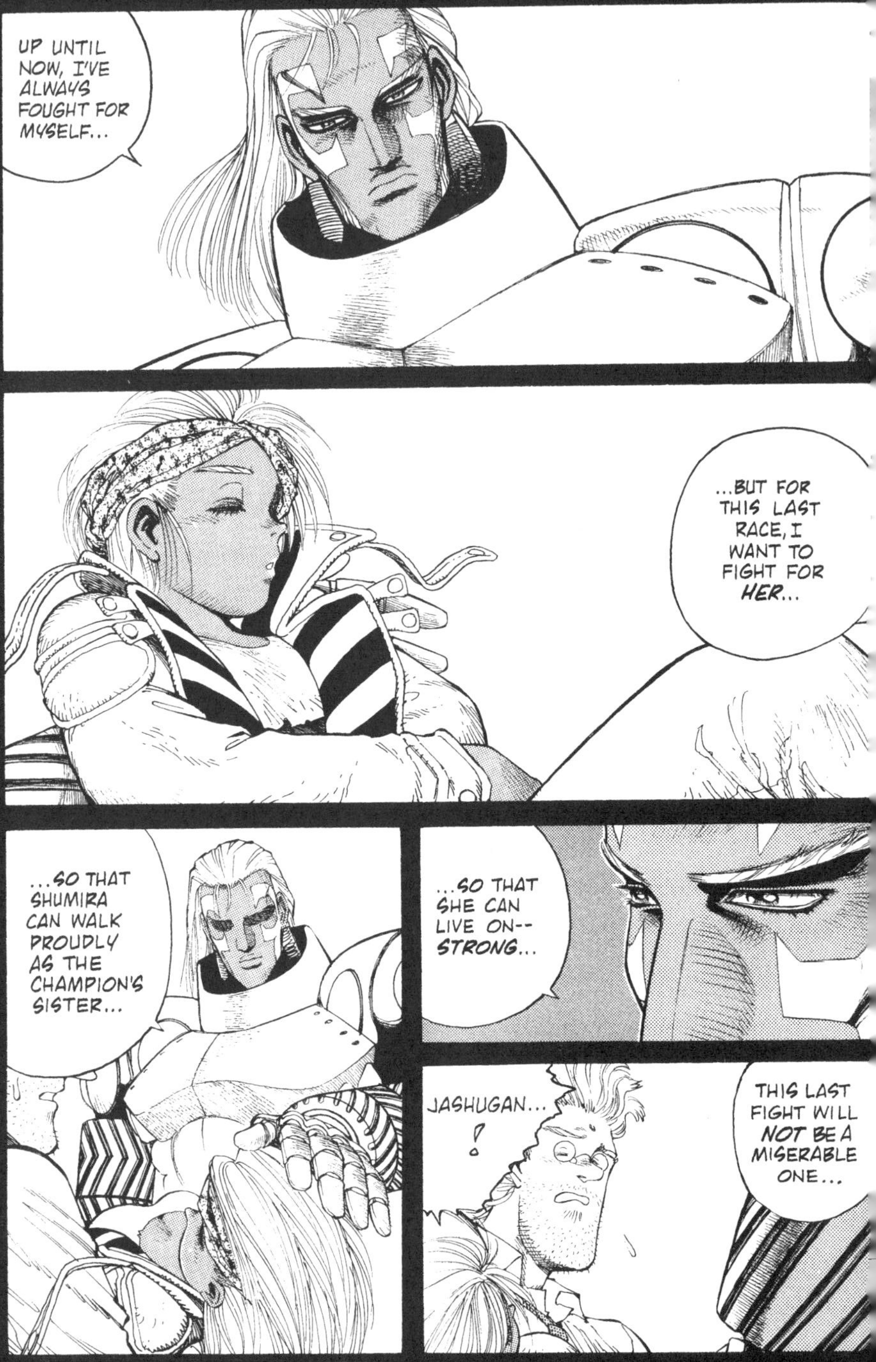
UP UNTIL NOW, I'VE ALWAYS FOUGHT FOR MYSELF...
...BUT FOR THIS LAST RACE, I WANT TO FIGHT FOR *HER*...
...SO THAT SHUMIRA CAN WALK PROUDLY AS THE CHAMPION'S SISTER...
...SO THAT SHE CAN LIVE ON-- *STRONG*...
JASHUGAN...
!
THIS LAST FIGHT WILL *NOT* BE A MISERABLE ONE...

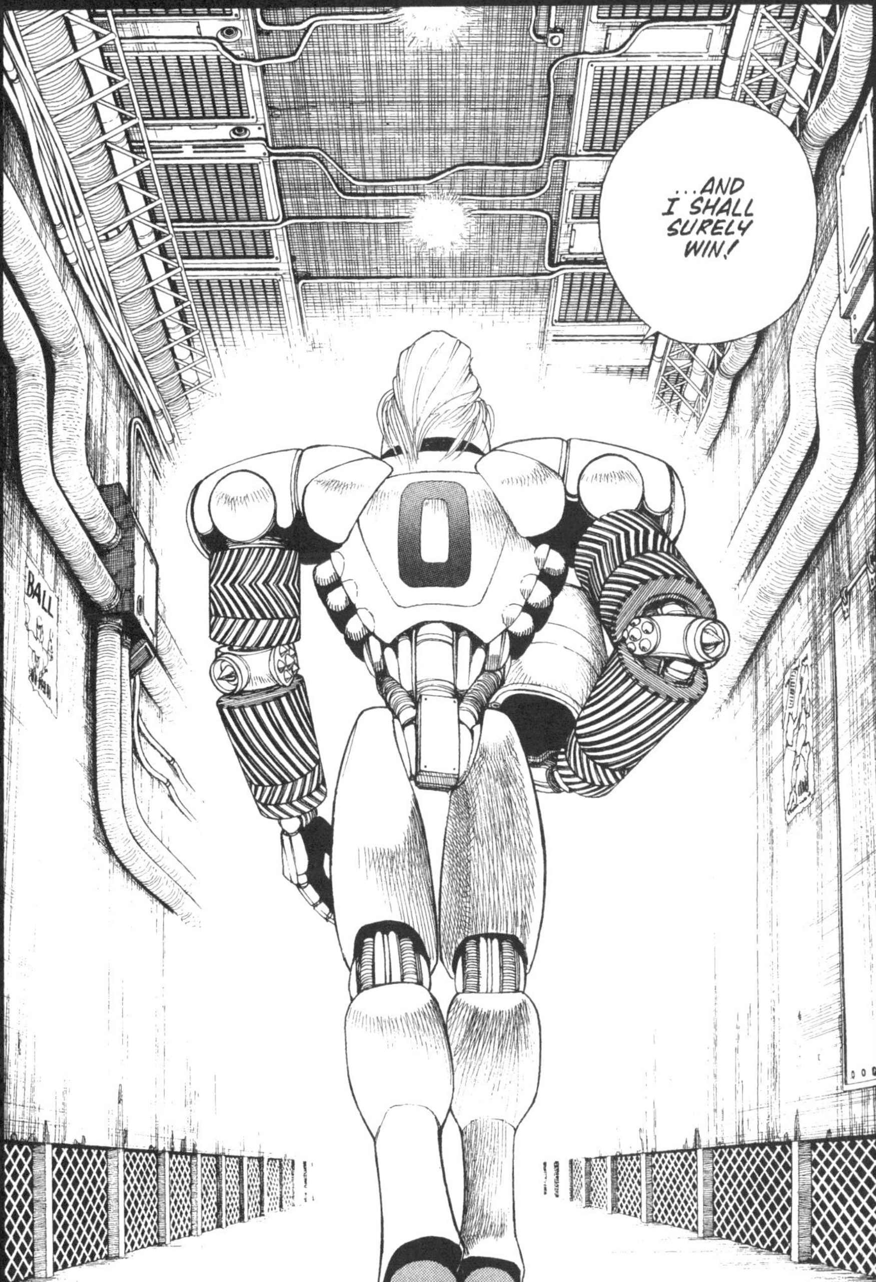
...AND I SHALL SURELY WIN!
BALL

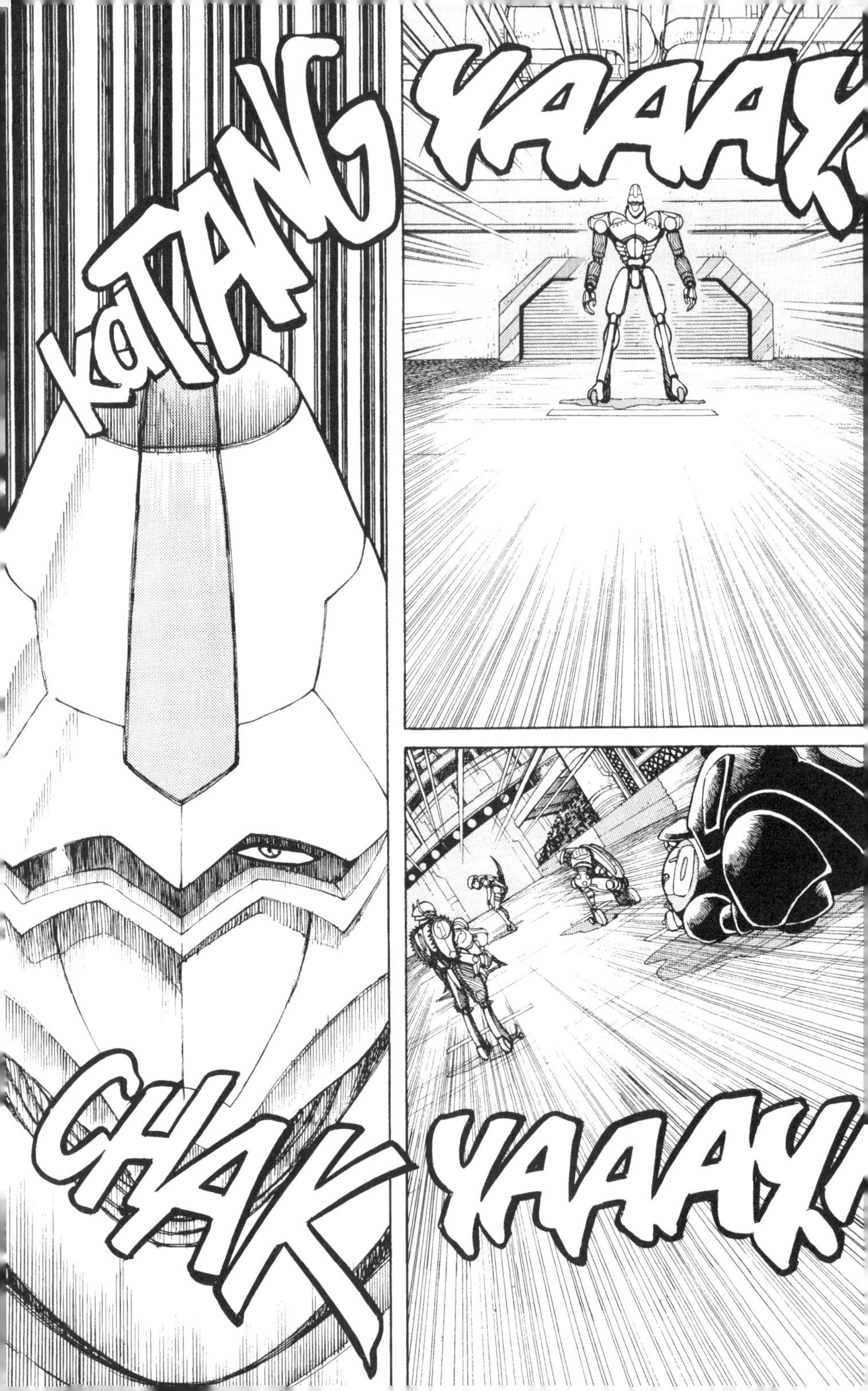
KaTANG
CHAK
YAAAAY
YAAAAY

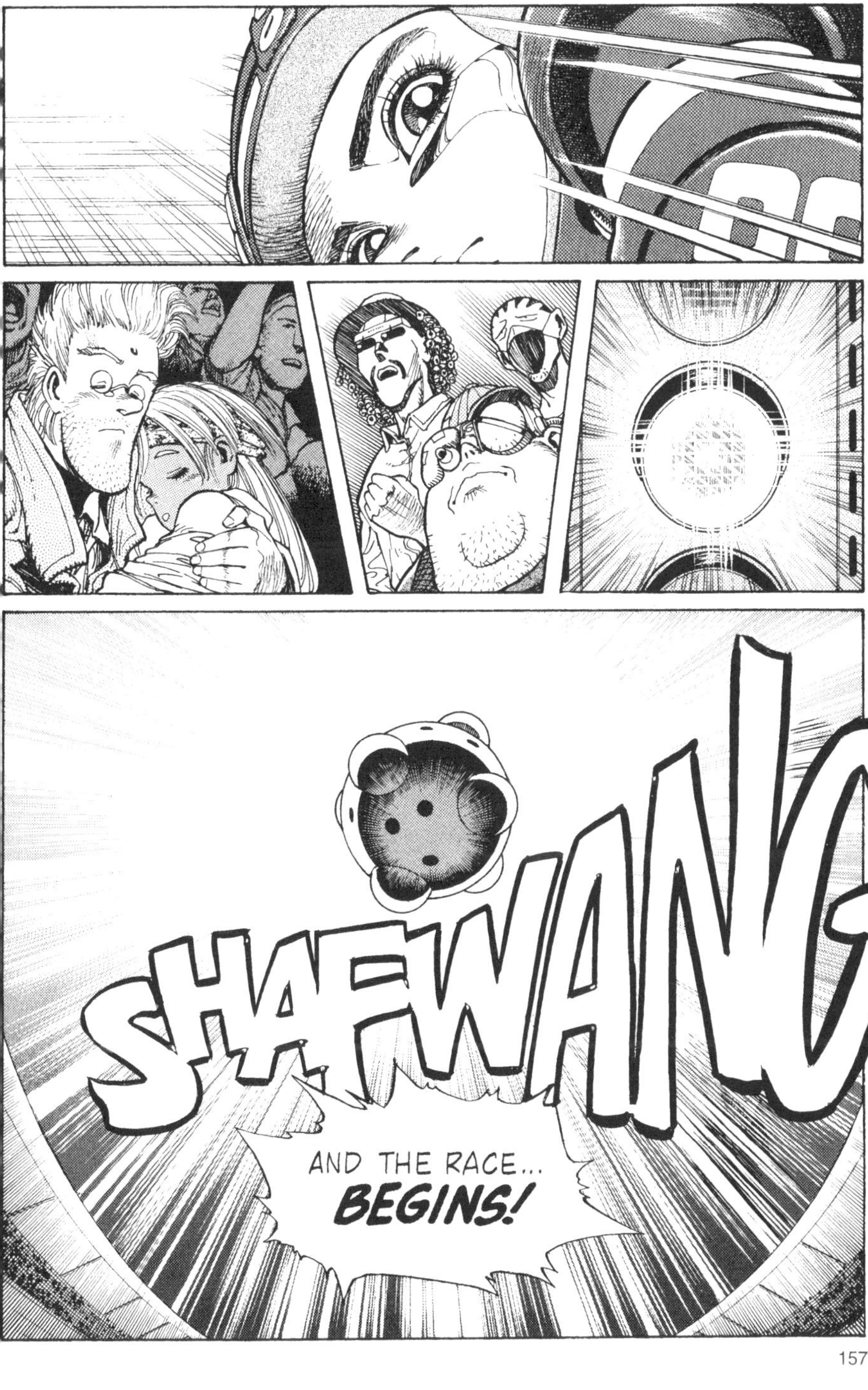
SHAFWANG
AND THE RACE... BEGINS!

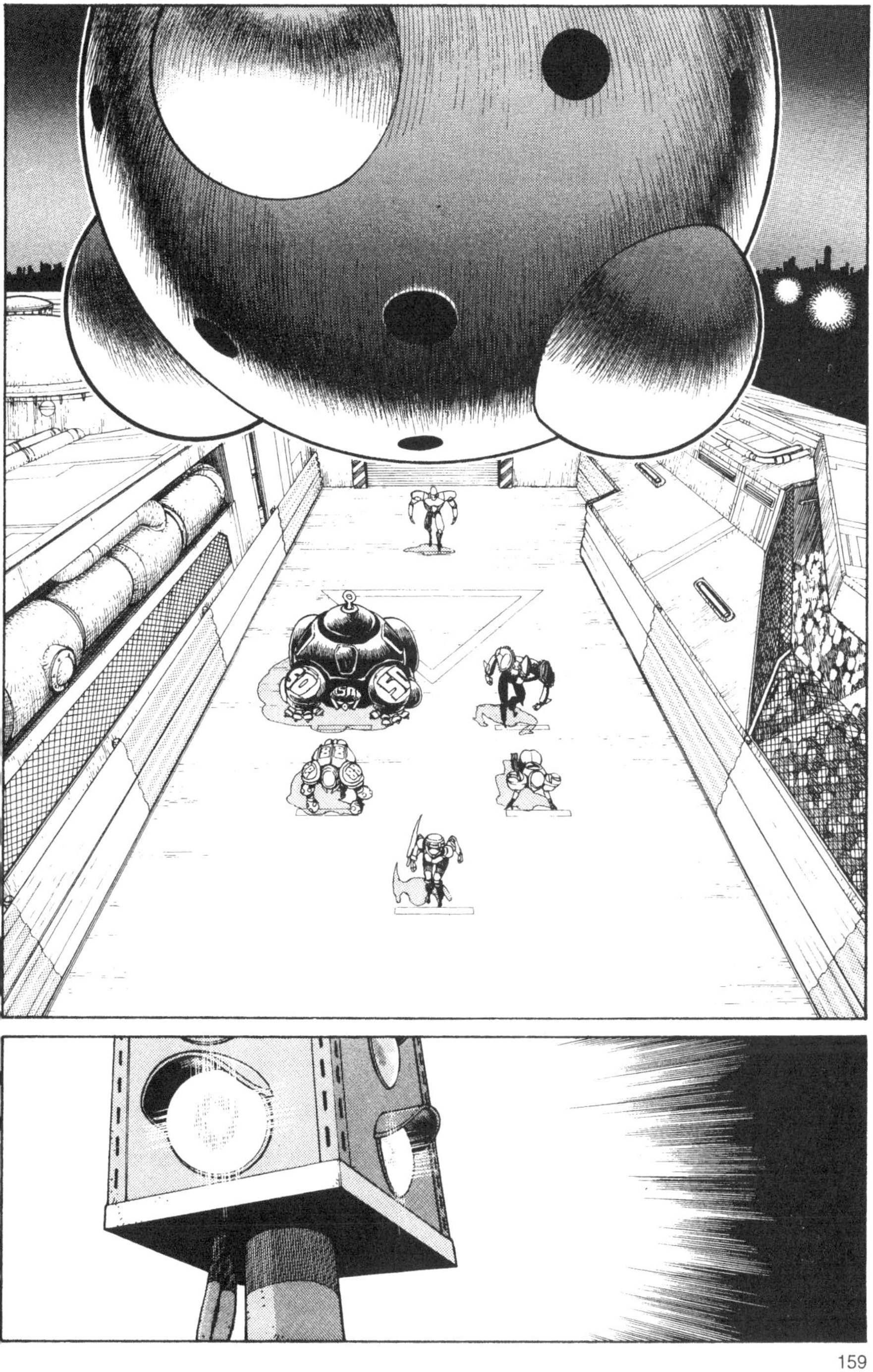

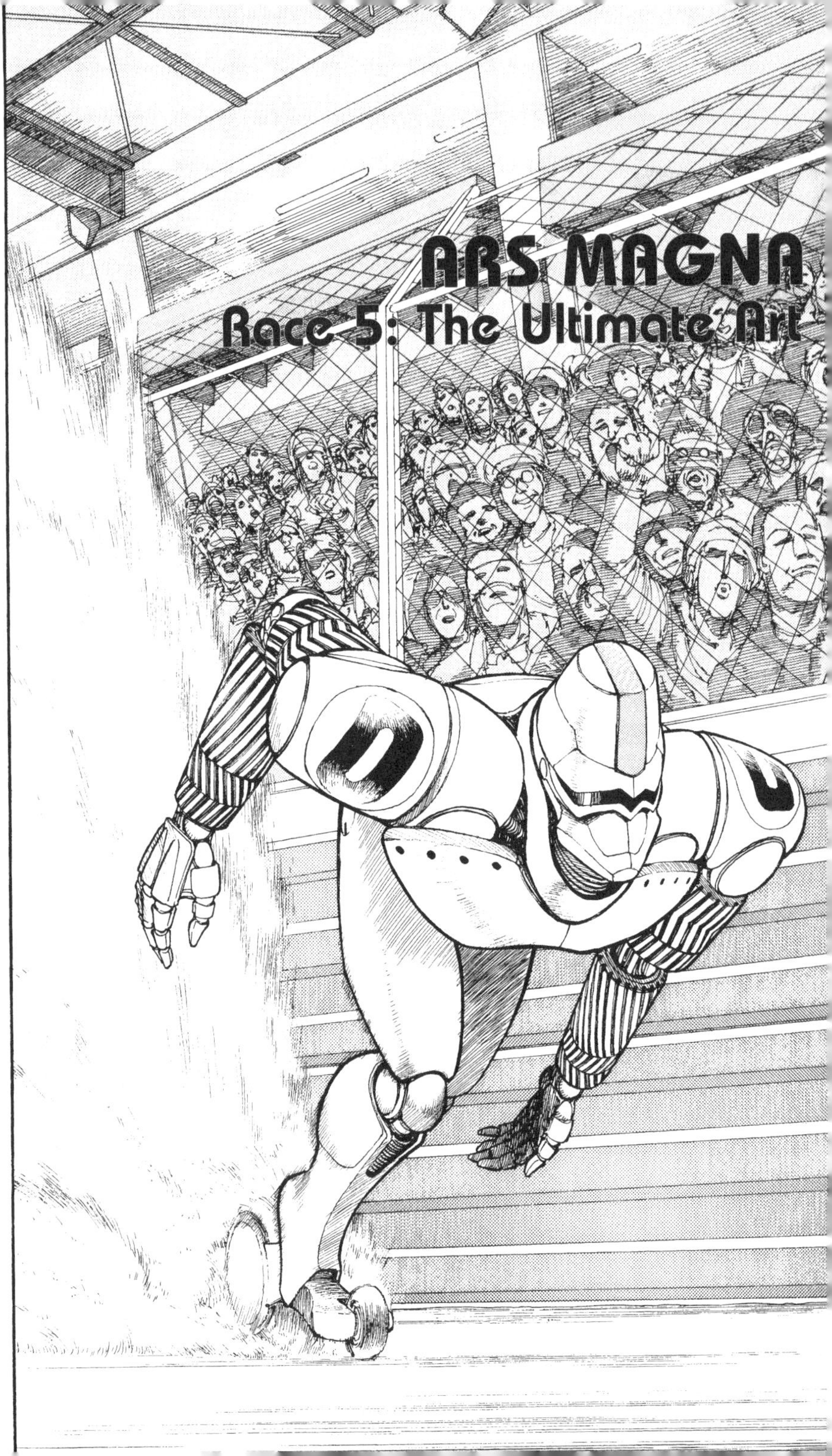
ARS MAGNA
Race 5: The Ultimate Art

ARE YOU WATCHING, TIPHARES !?

DO YOU SEE ME !?

THE TIME I HAVE LEFT IS **SHORT**...

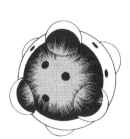

...BUT TO THAT LAST MOMENT, I **WILL** FIGHT ON AS THE CHAMPION!

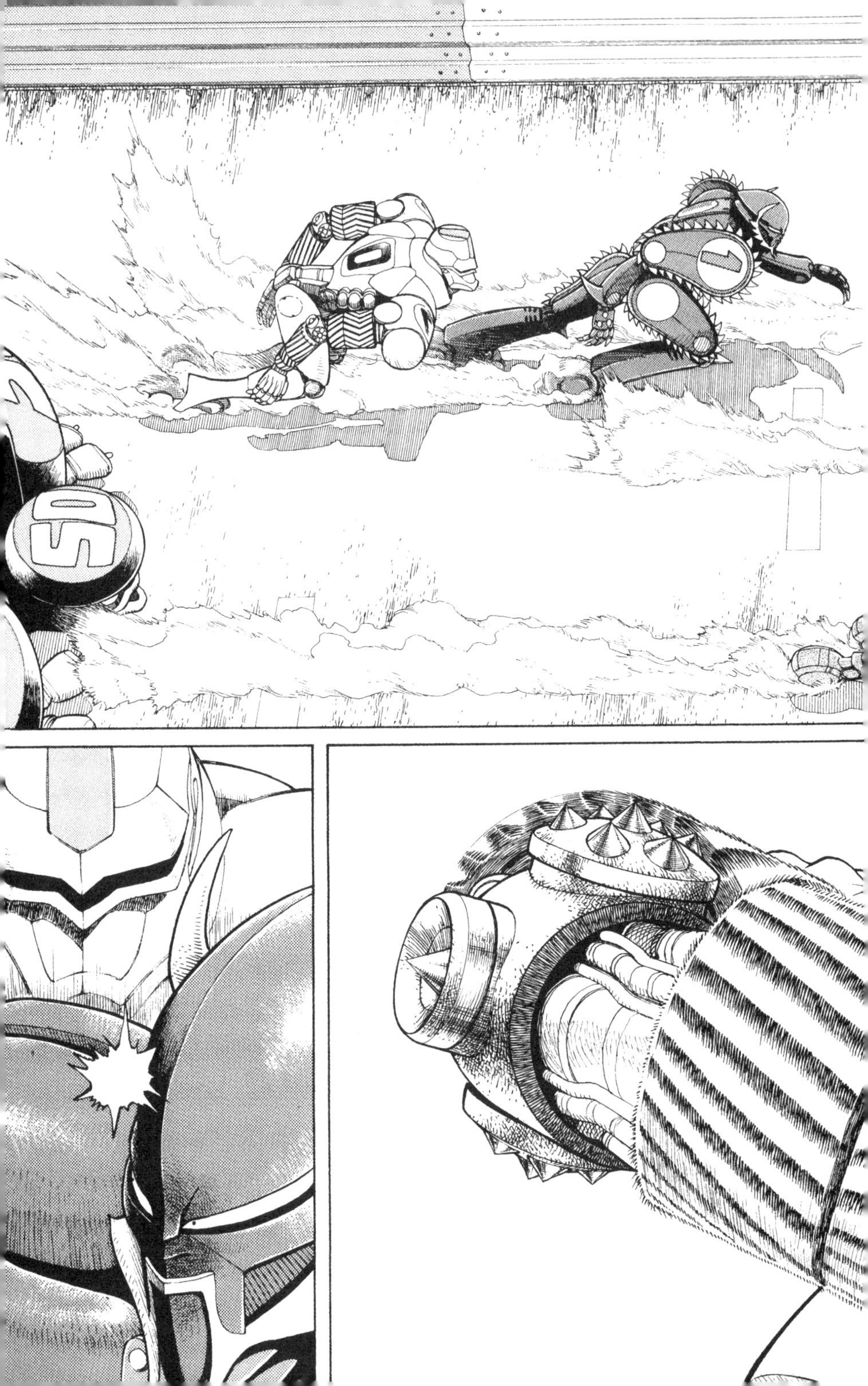
SD

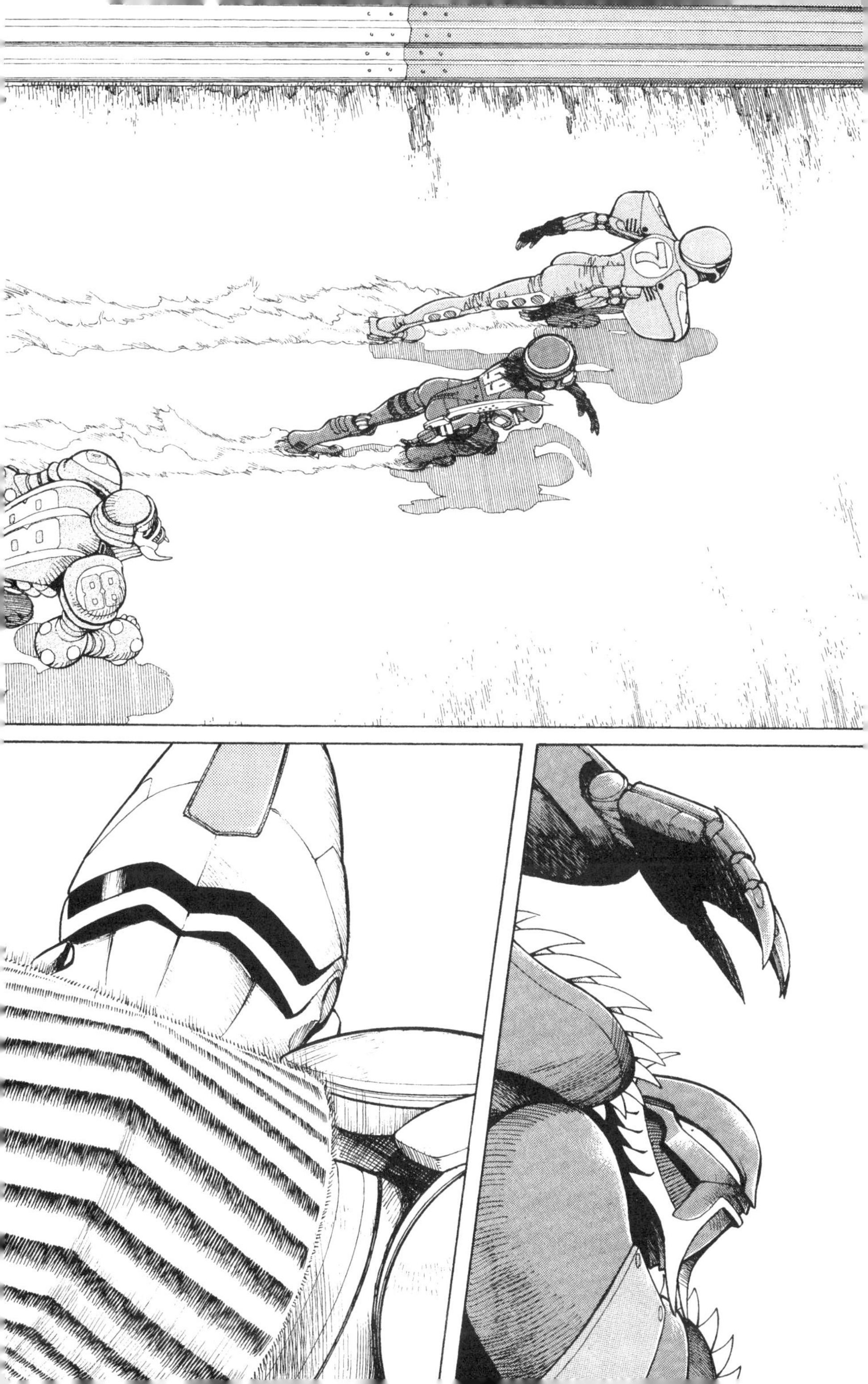

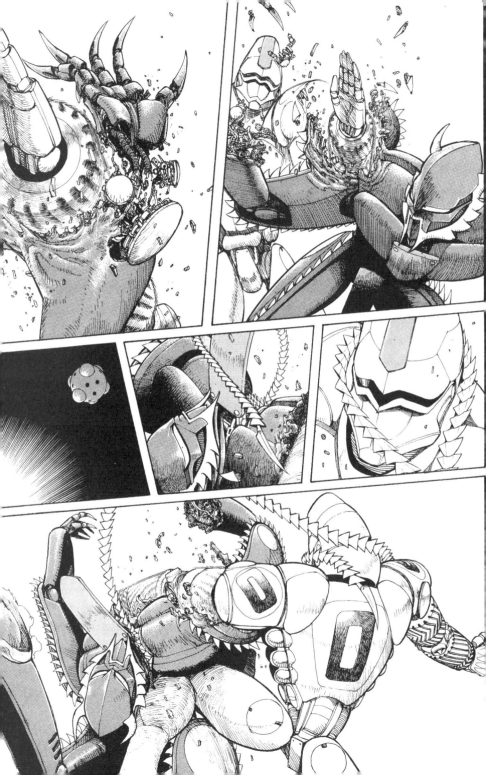

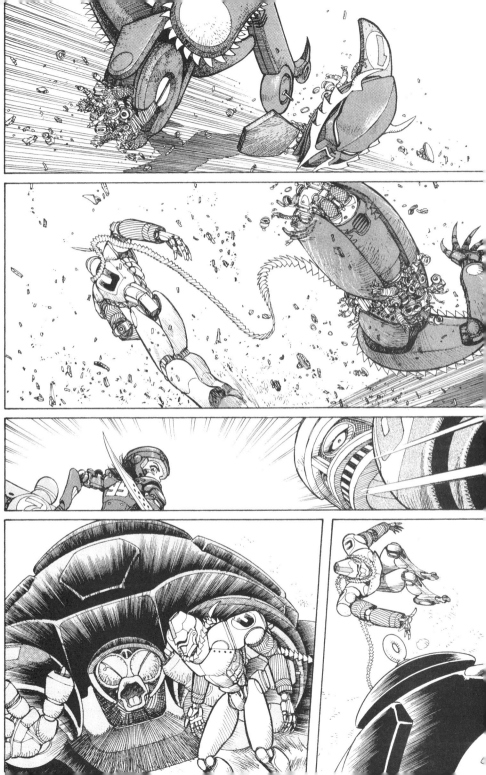

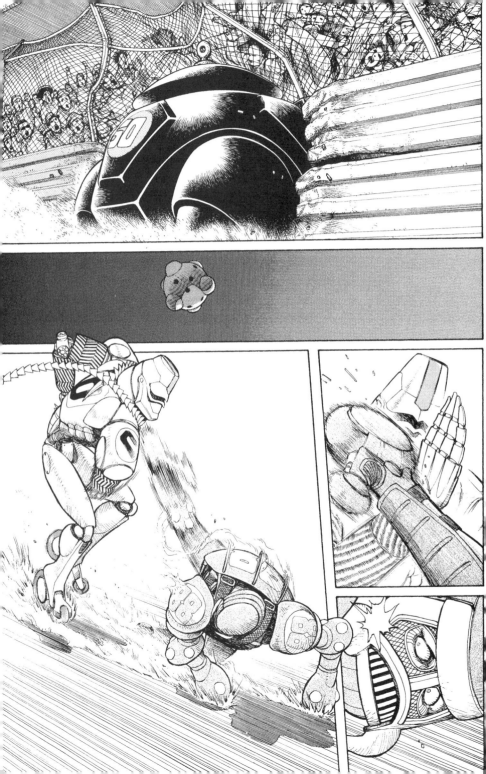

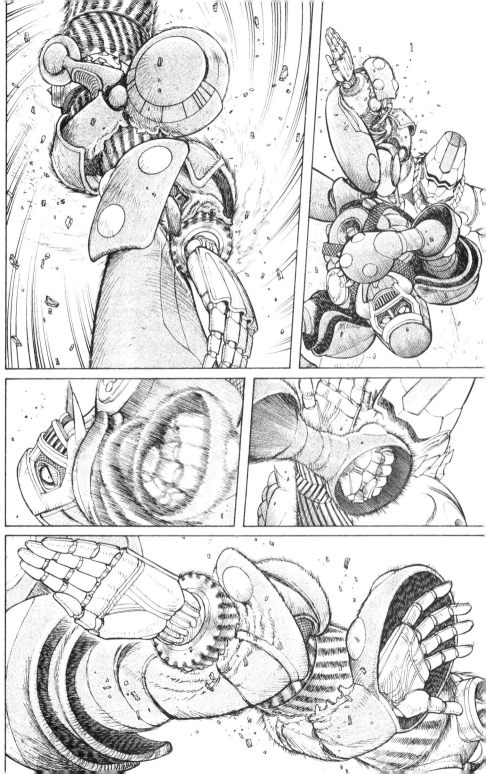

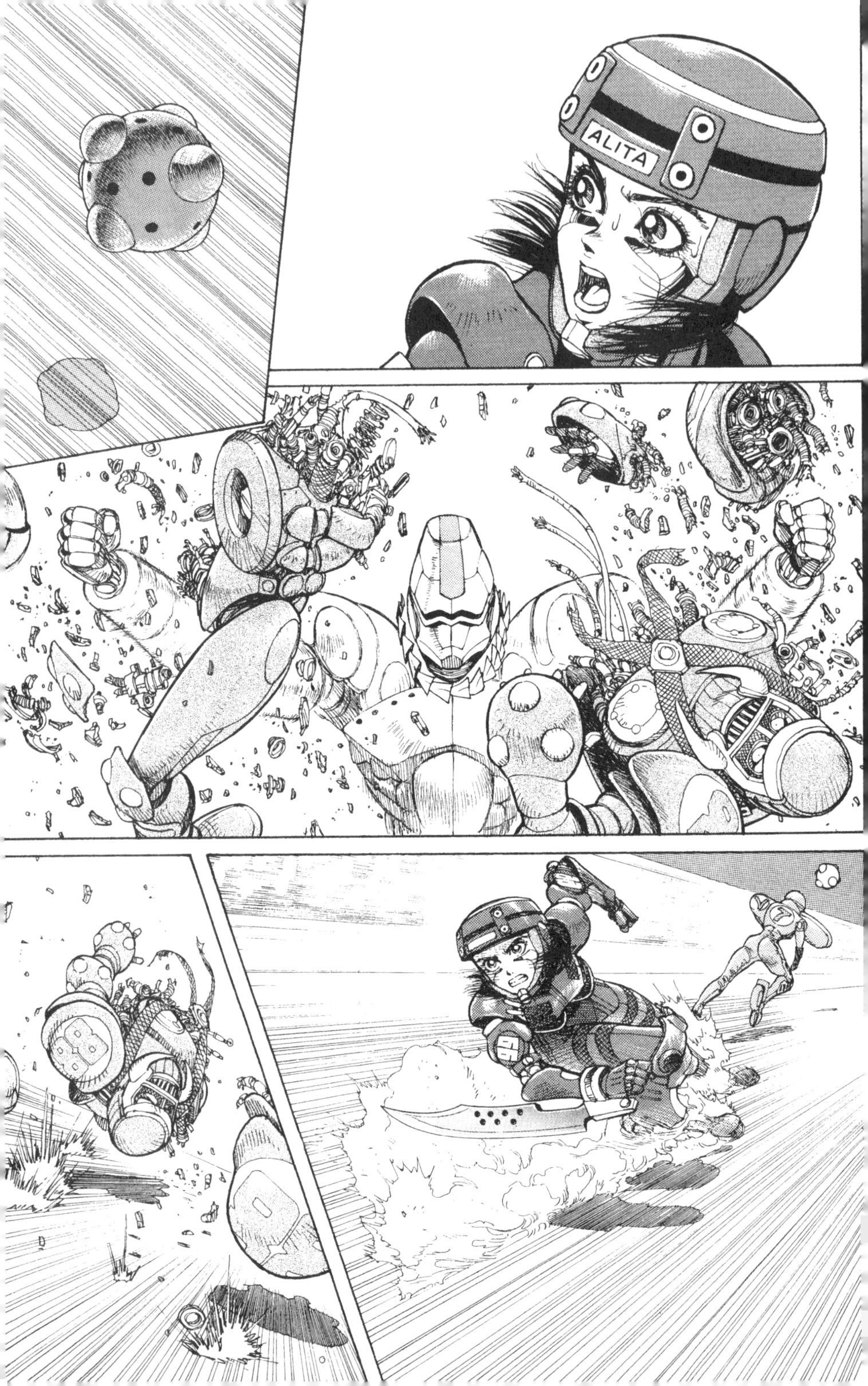
ALITA

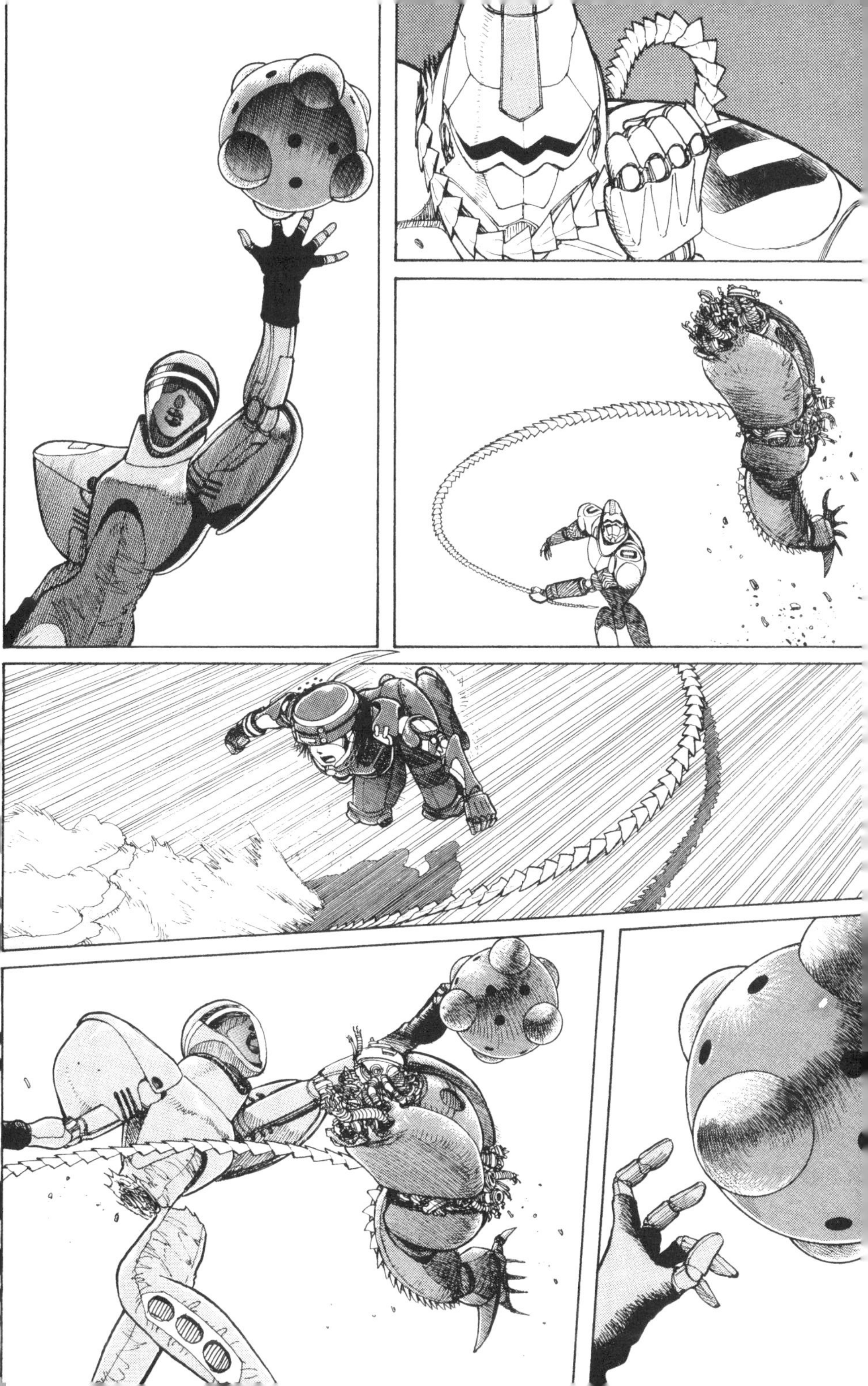

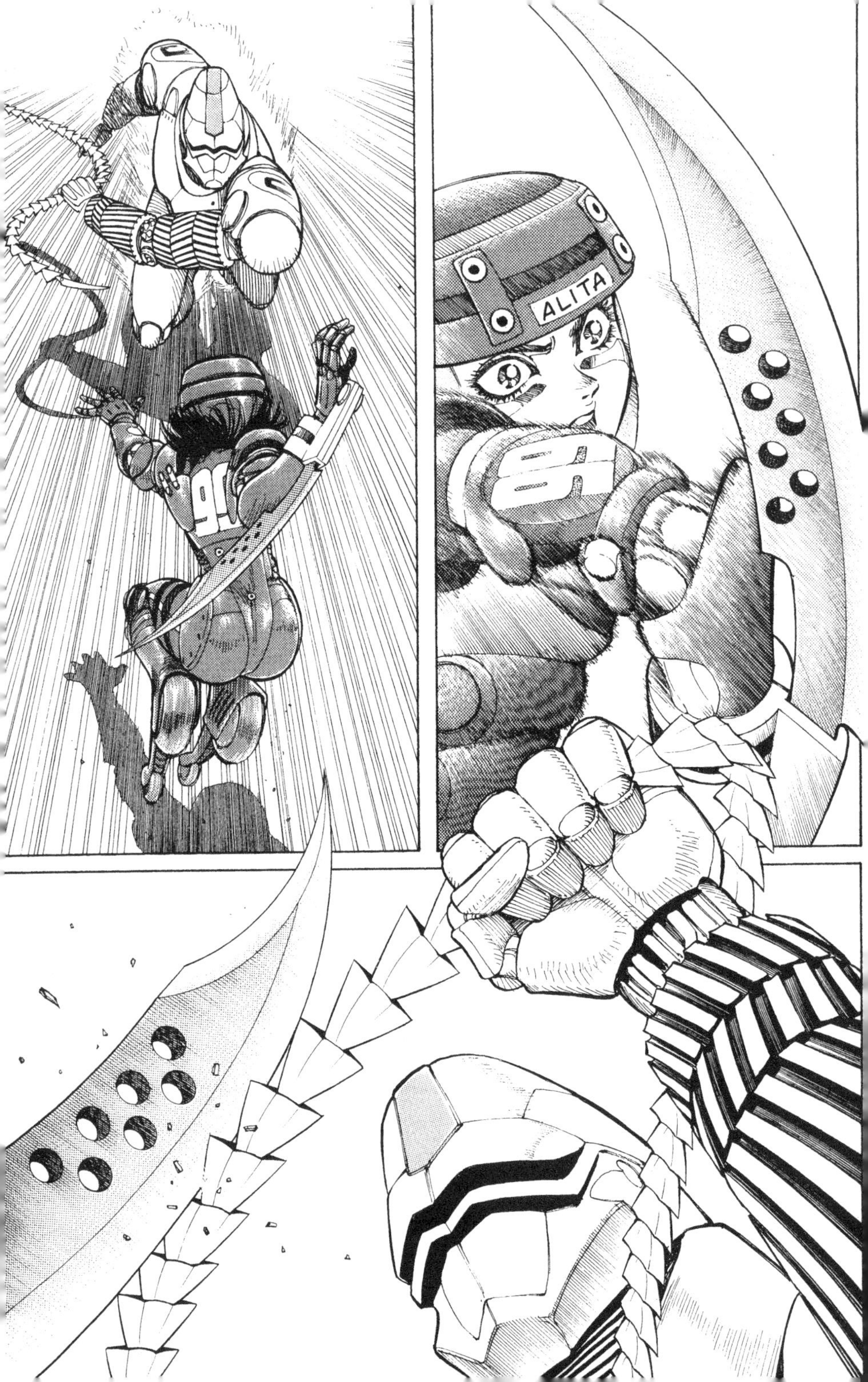
ALITA

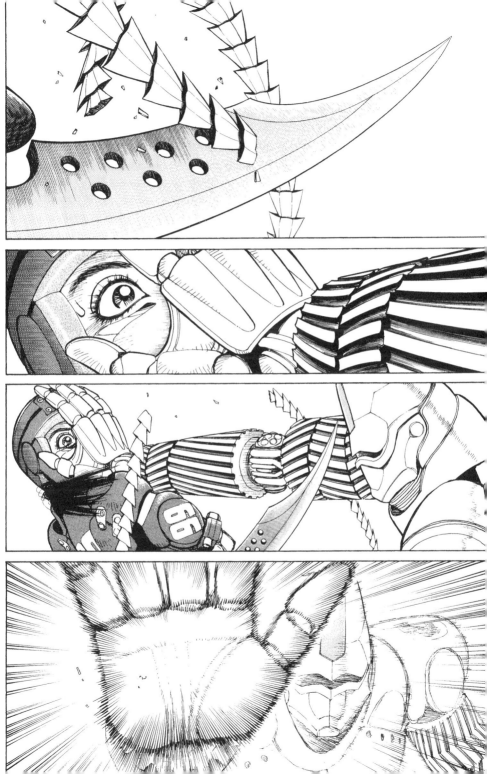

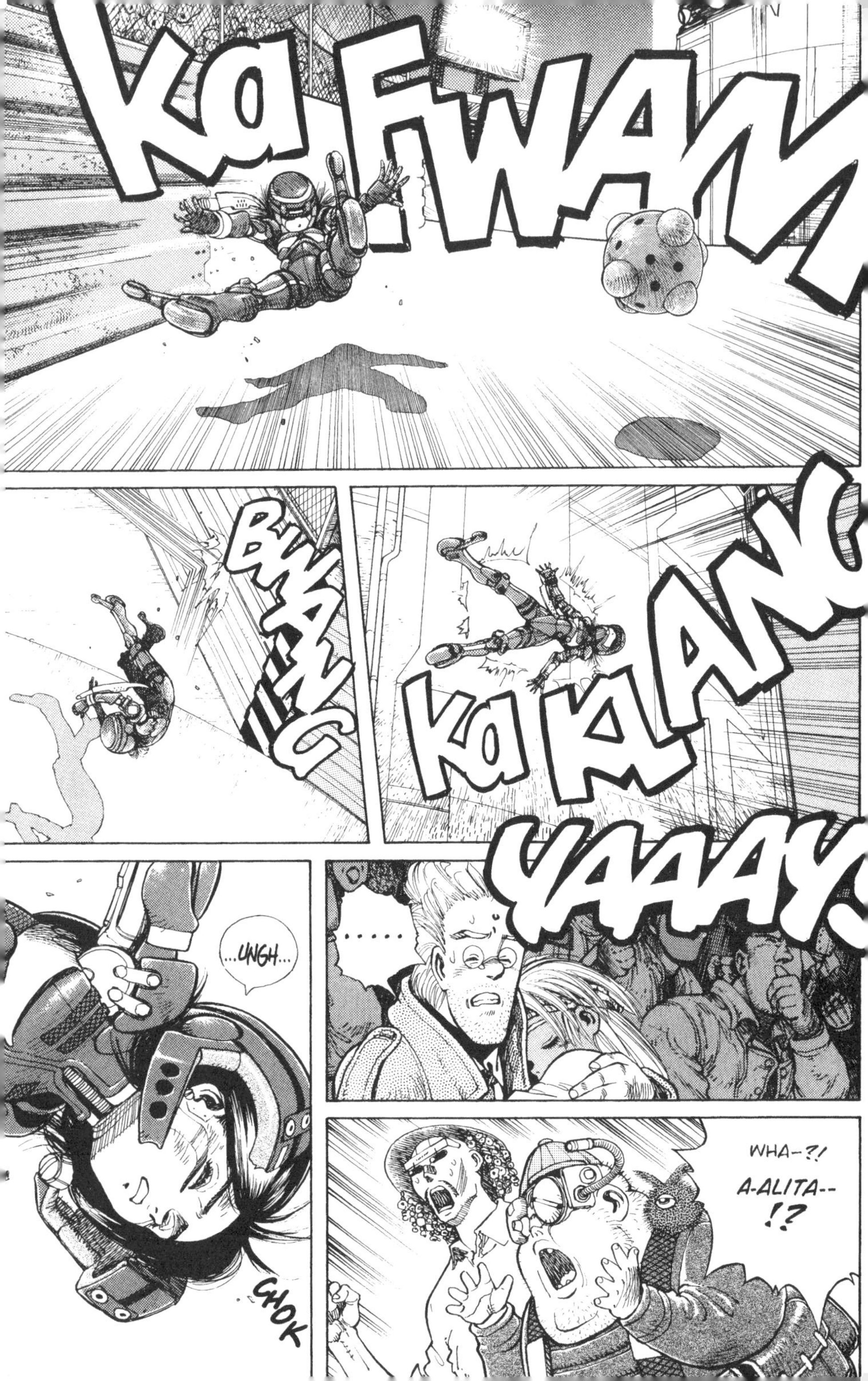
KAFWAM
BWAMG
KAKLANG
YAAAY!
...UNGH...
.....
CHOK
WHA--?!
A-ALITA--
!?

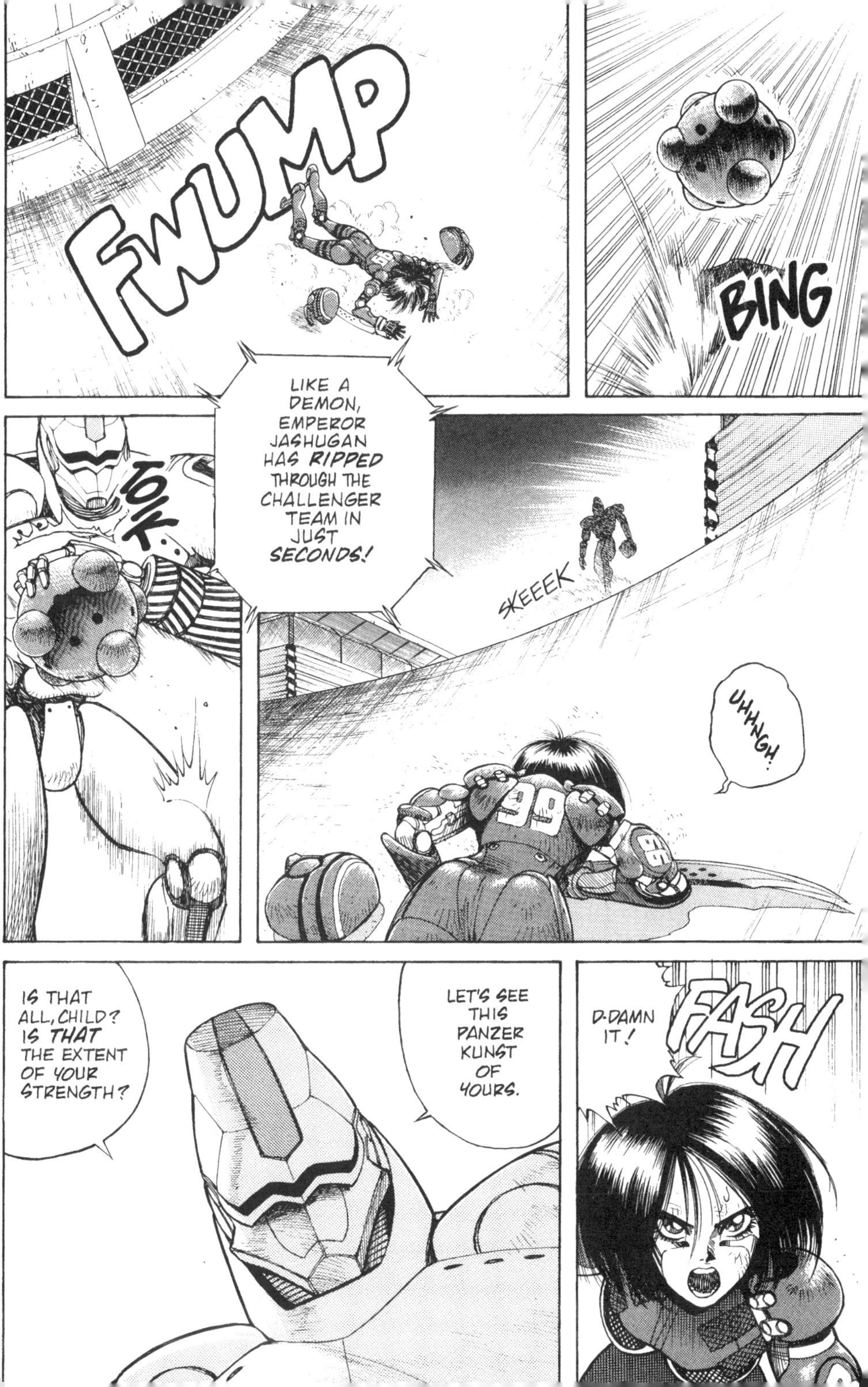
FWUMP
BING
LIKE A DEMON, EMPEROR JASHUGAN HAS *RIPPED* THROUGH THE CHALLENGER TEAM IN JUST *SECONDS!*
TOIK
SKEEEK
UHHNGH!
IS THAT ALL, CHILD? IS *THAT* THE EXTENT OF YOUR STRENGTH?
LET'S SEE THIS PANZER KUNST OF YOURS.
D-DAMN IT!
FASH

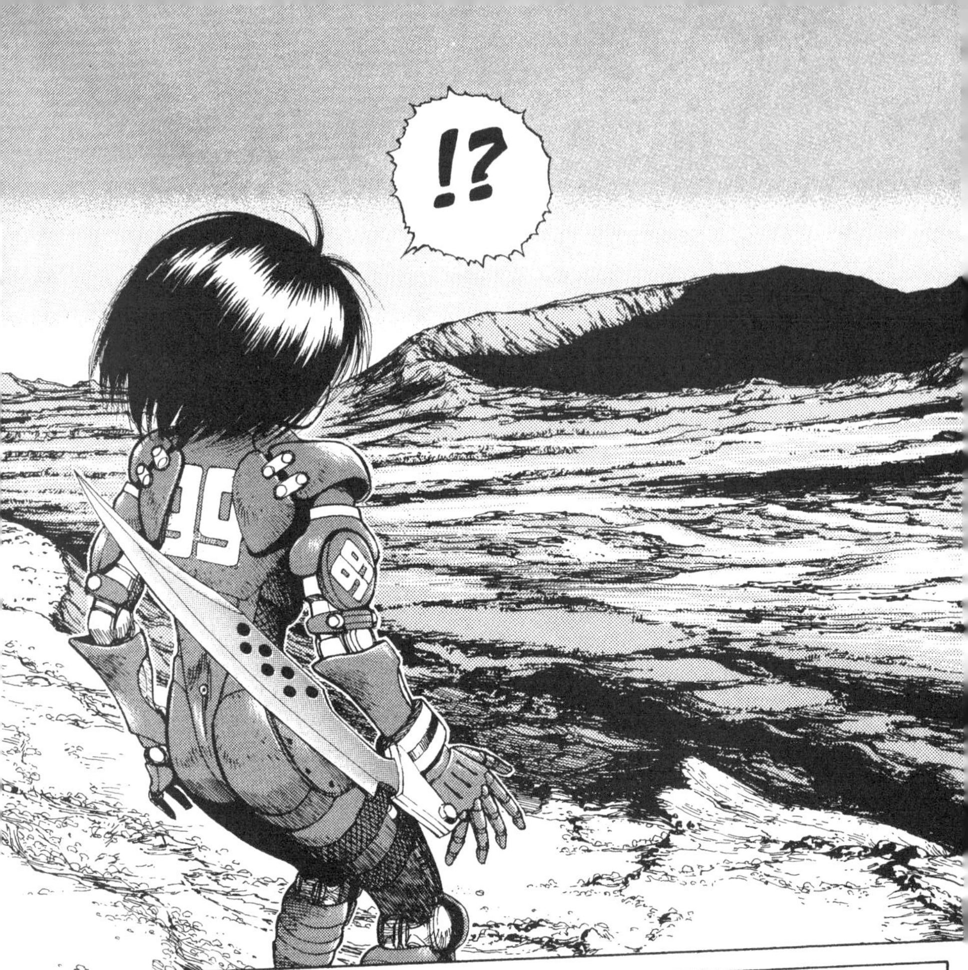
!?

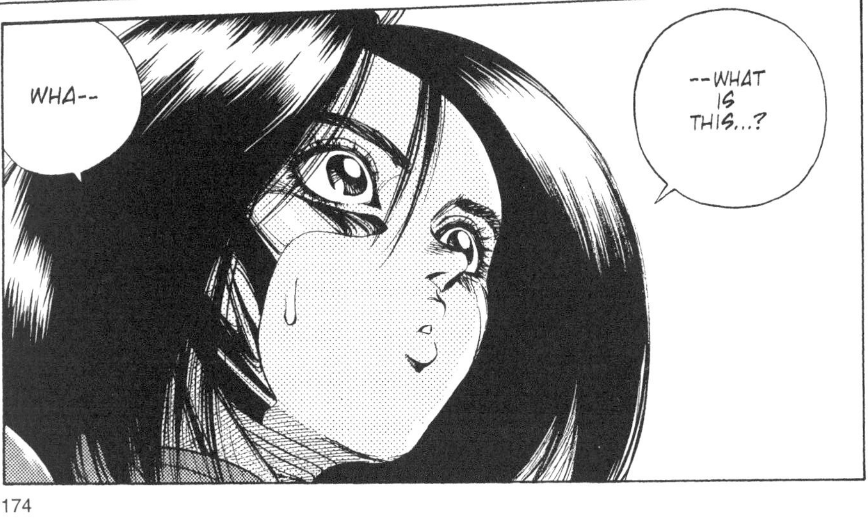
WHA--
--WHAT IS THIS...?

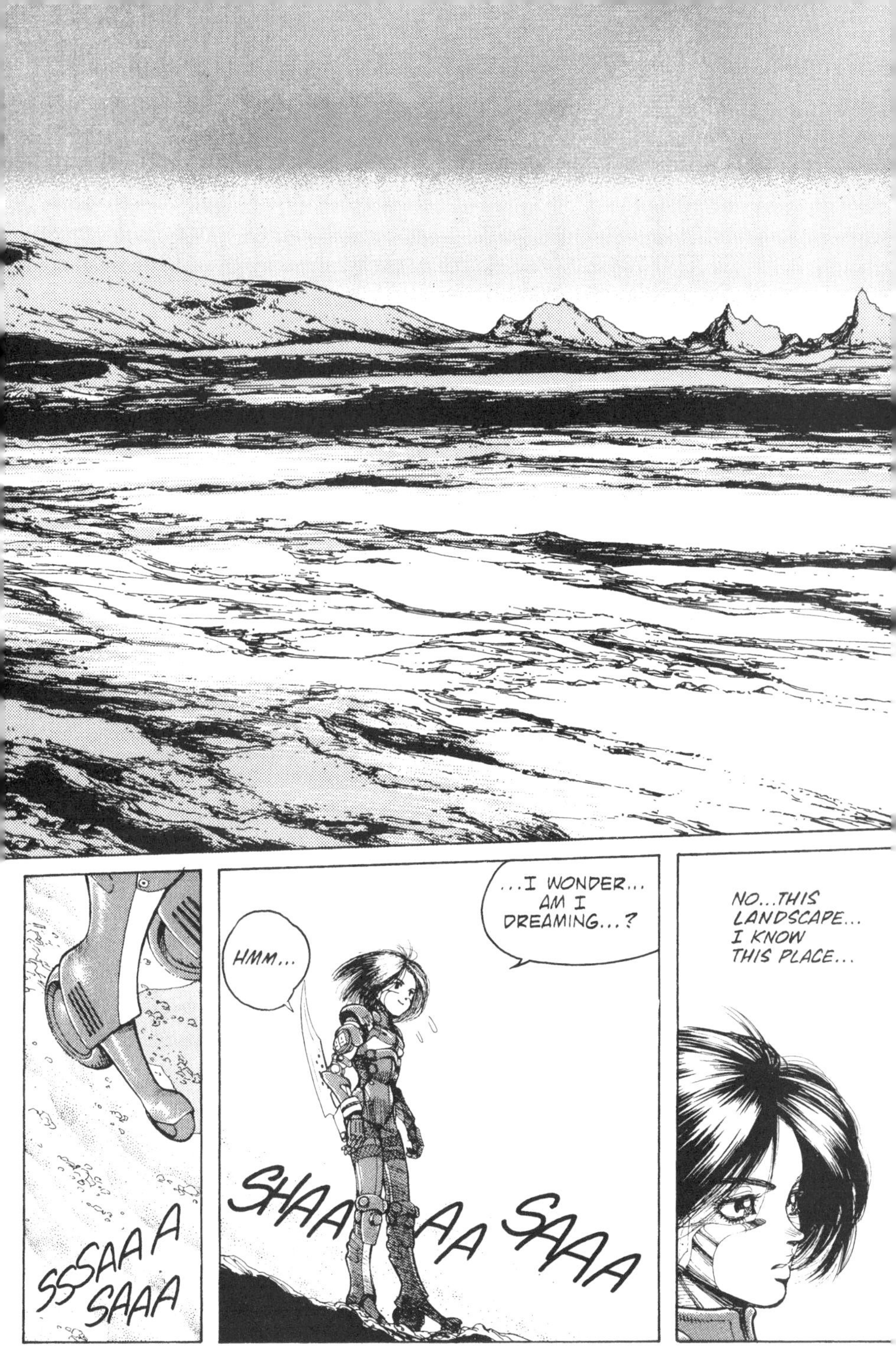
SSSAAA
SAAA
HMM...
...I WONDER... AM I DREAMING...?
SHAAAAA
SAAA
NO...THIS LANDSCAPE... I KNOW THIS PLACE...

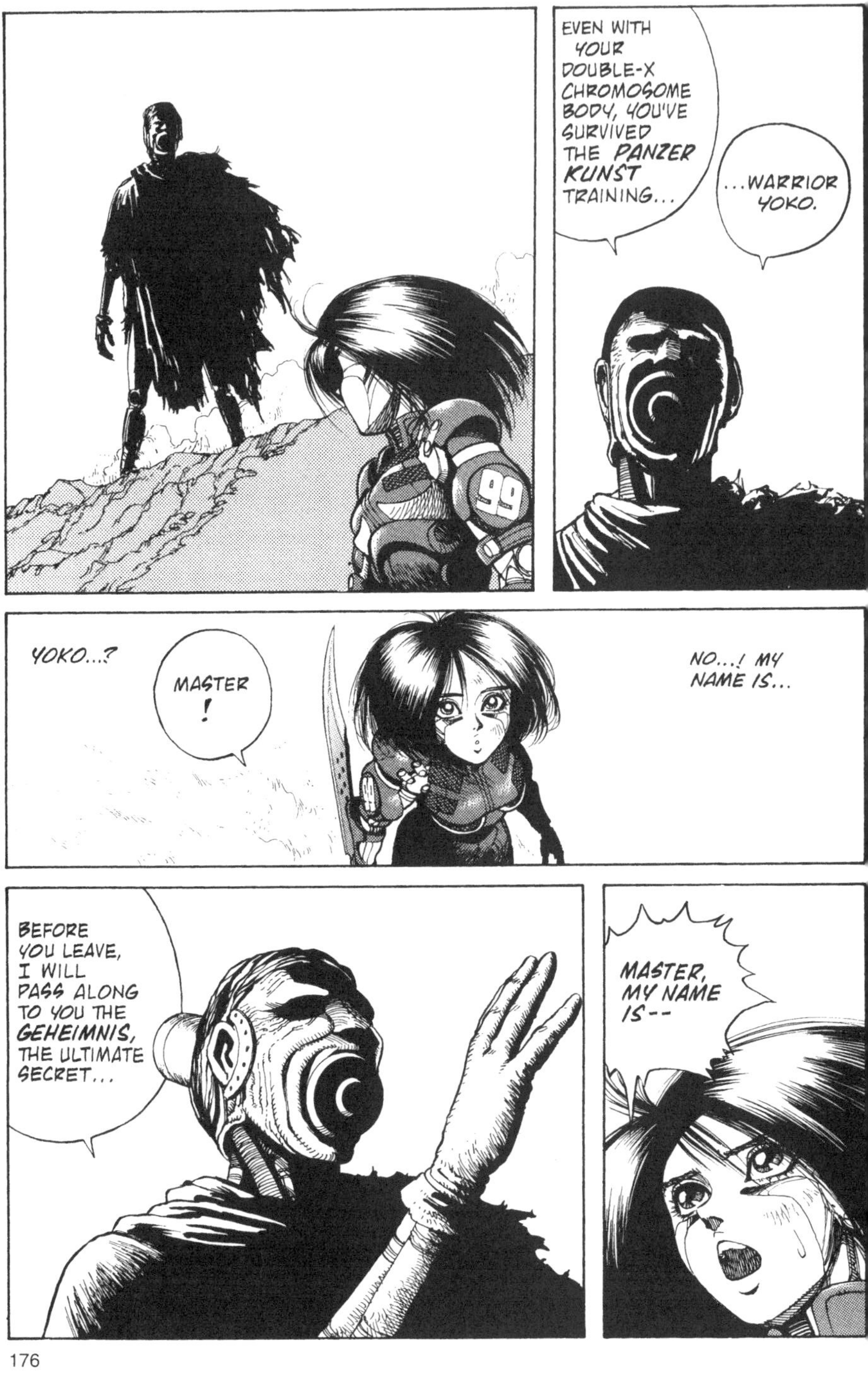
EVEN WITH YOUR DOUBLE-X CHROMOSOME BODY, YOU'VE SURVIVED THE PANZER KUNST TRAINING...
...WARRIOR YOKO.
YOKO...?
MASTER!
NO...! MY NAME IS...
BEFORE YOU LEAVE, I WILL PASS ALONG TO YOU THE GEHEIMNIS, THE ULTIMATE SECRET...
MASTER, MY NAME IS--

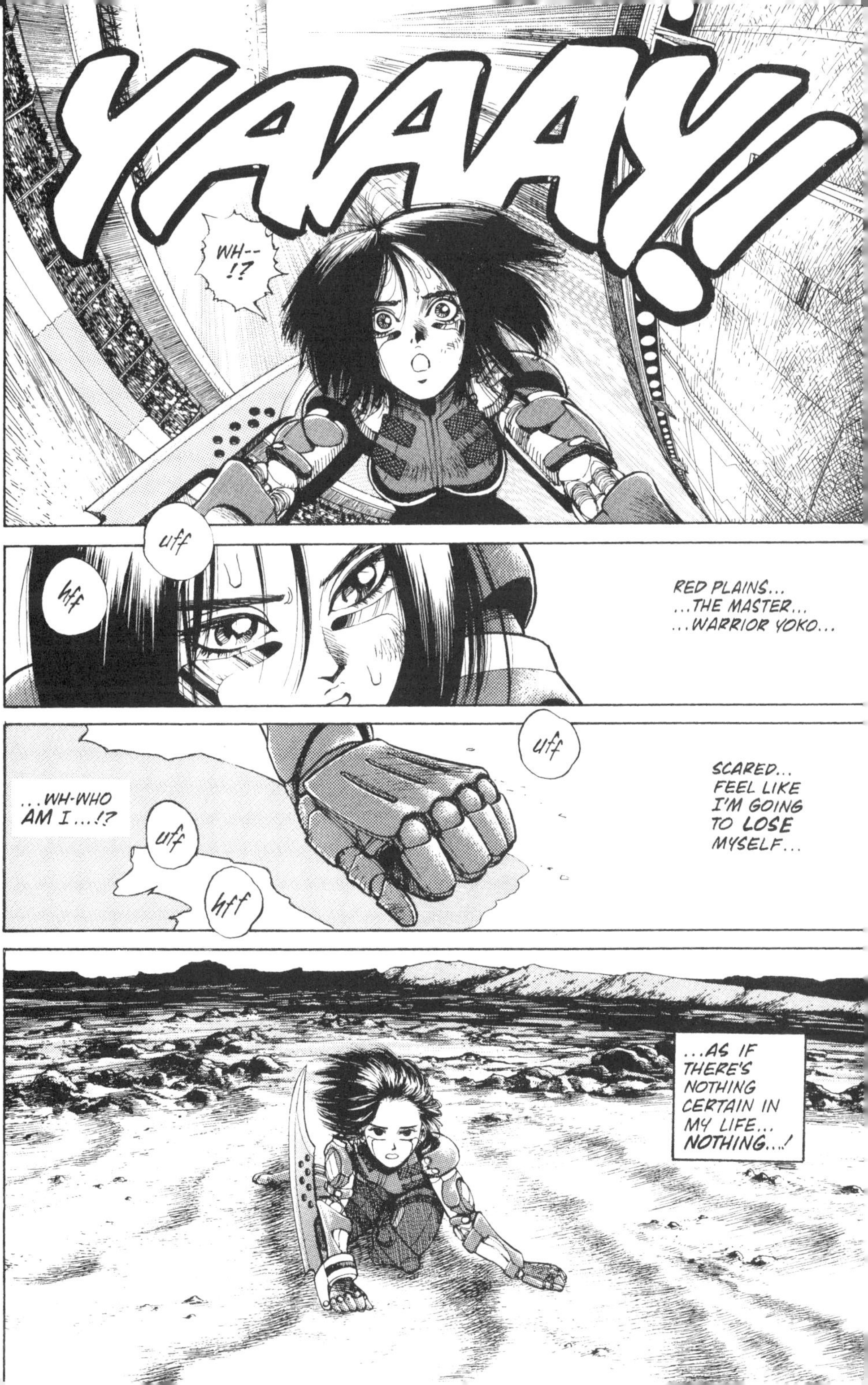
YAAAY!!
WH-- !?
uff
hff
RED PLAINS... ...THE MASTER... ...WARRIOR YOKO...
...WH-WHO AM I...!?
uff
uff
hff
SCARED... FEEL LIKE I'M GOING TO LOSE MYSELF...
...AS IF THERE'S NOTHING CERTAIN IN MY LIFE... NOTHING...!

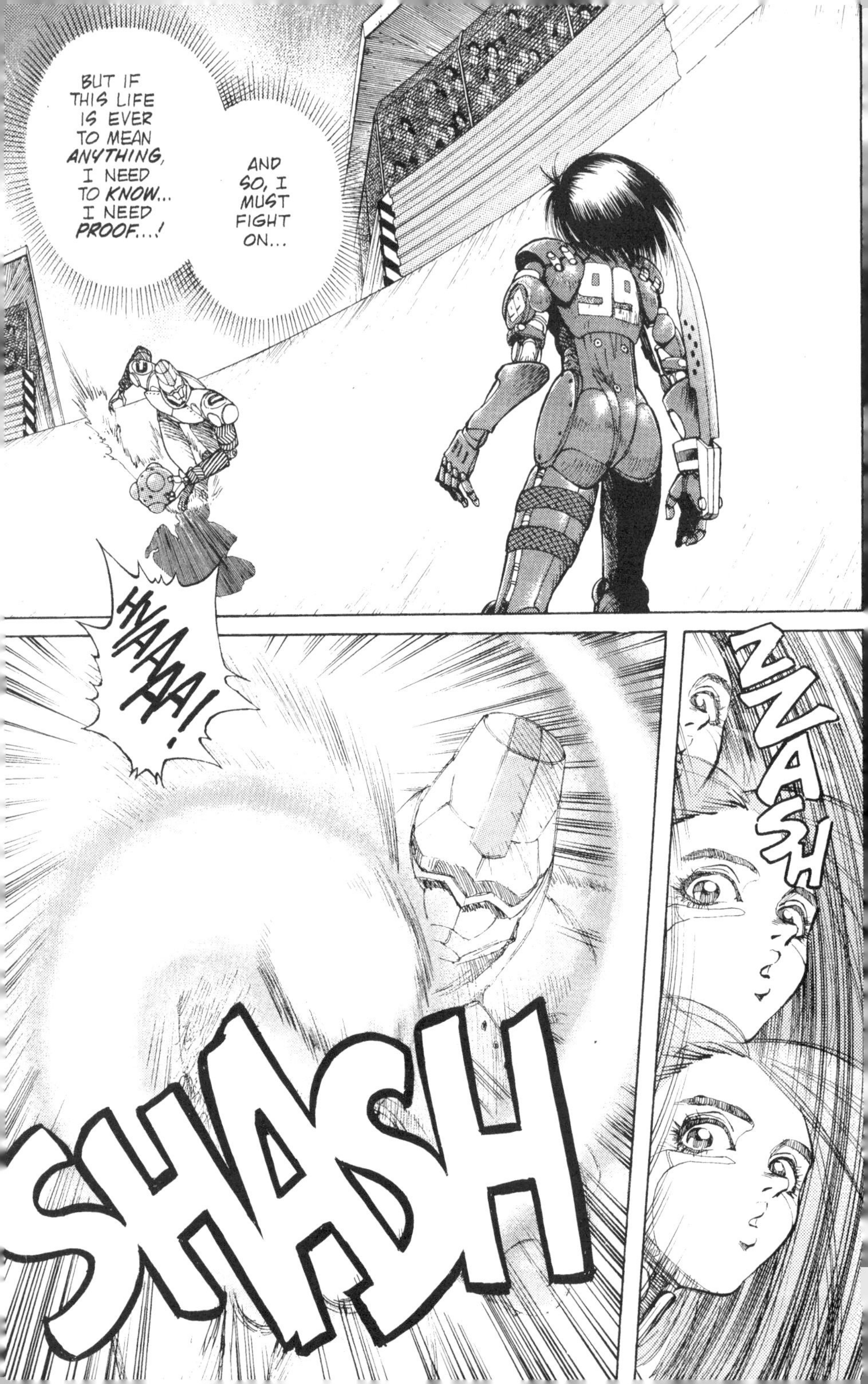
BUT IF THIS LIFE IS EVER TO MEAN *ANYTHING*, I NEED TO *KNOW*... I NEED *PROOF*...!
AND SO, I MUST FIGHT ON...
HYAAAAA!
SHASH
NNASH

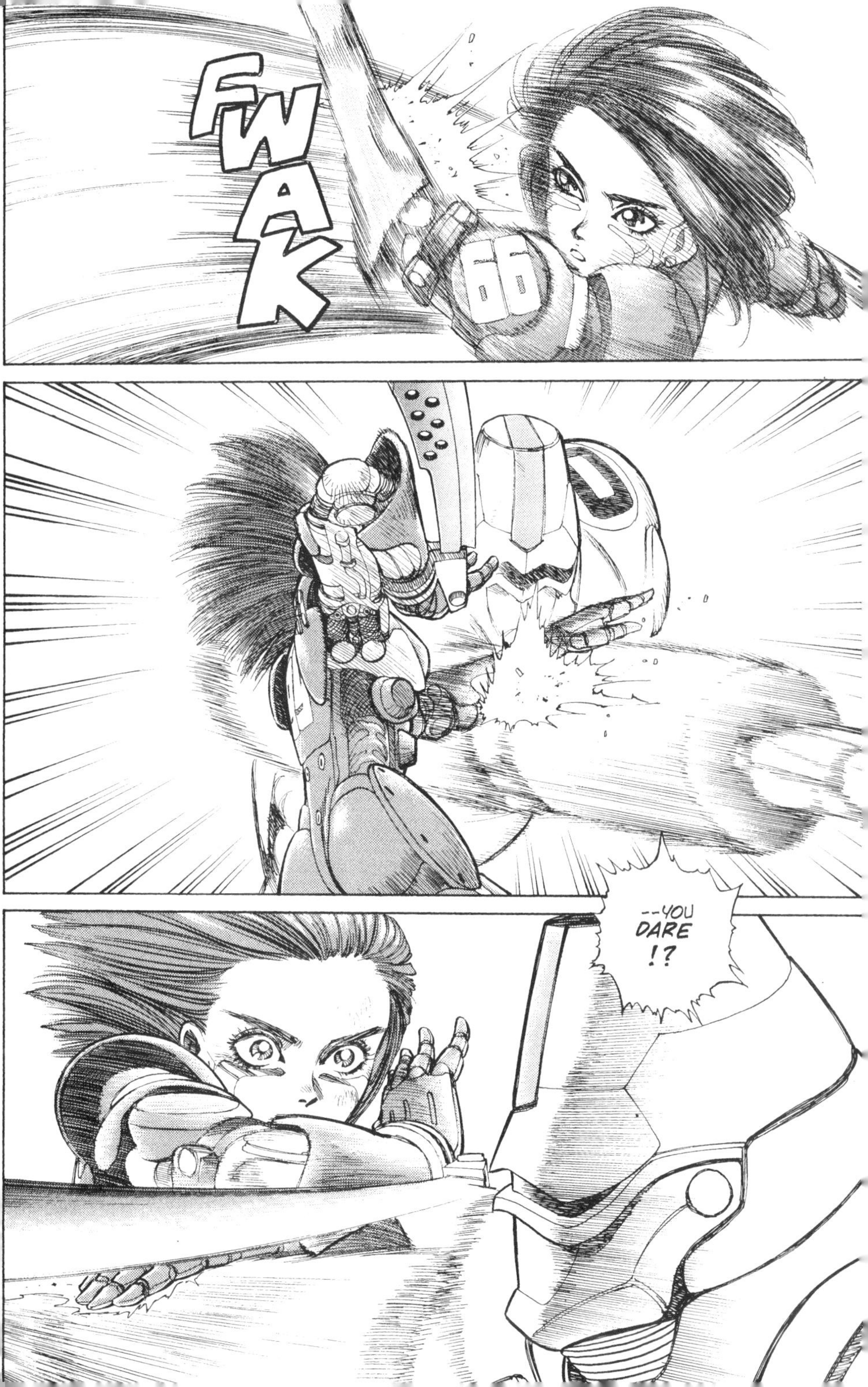
FWAK
--YOU DARE !?

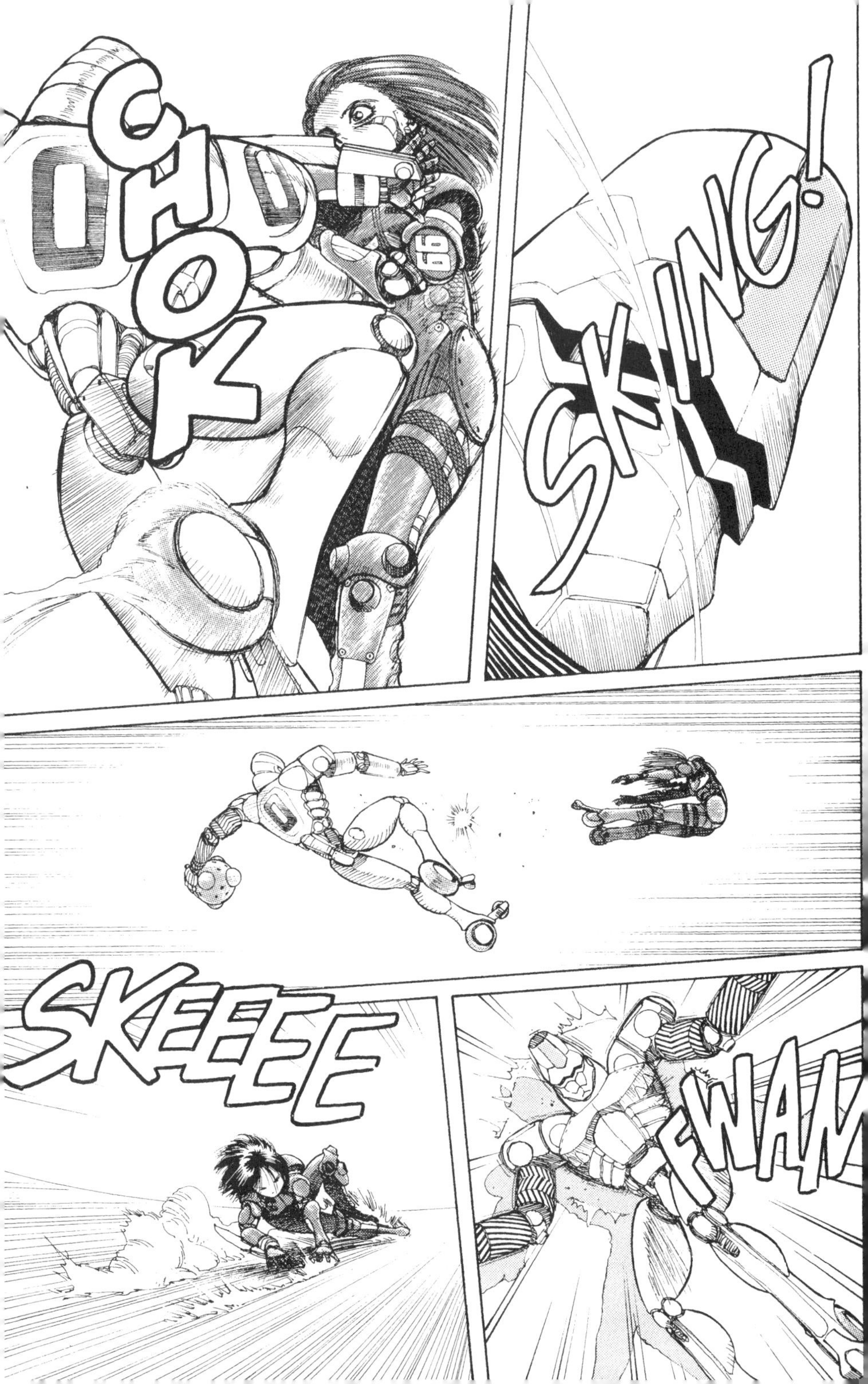
CHOOK
SKYING!
SKEEEE
FWAM

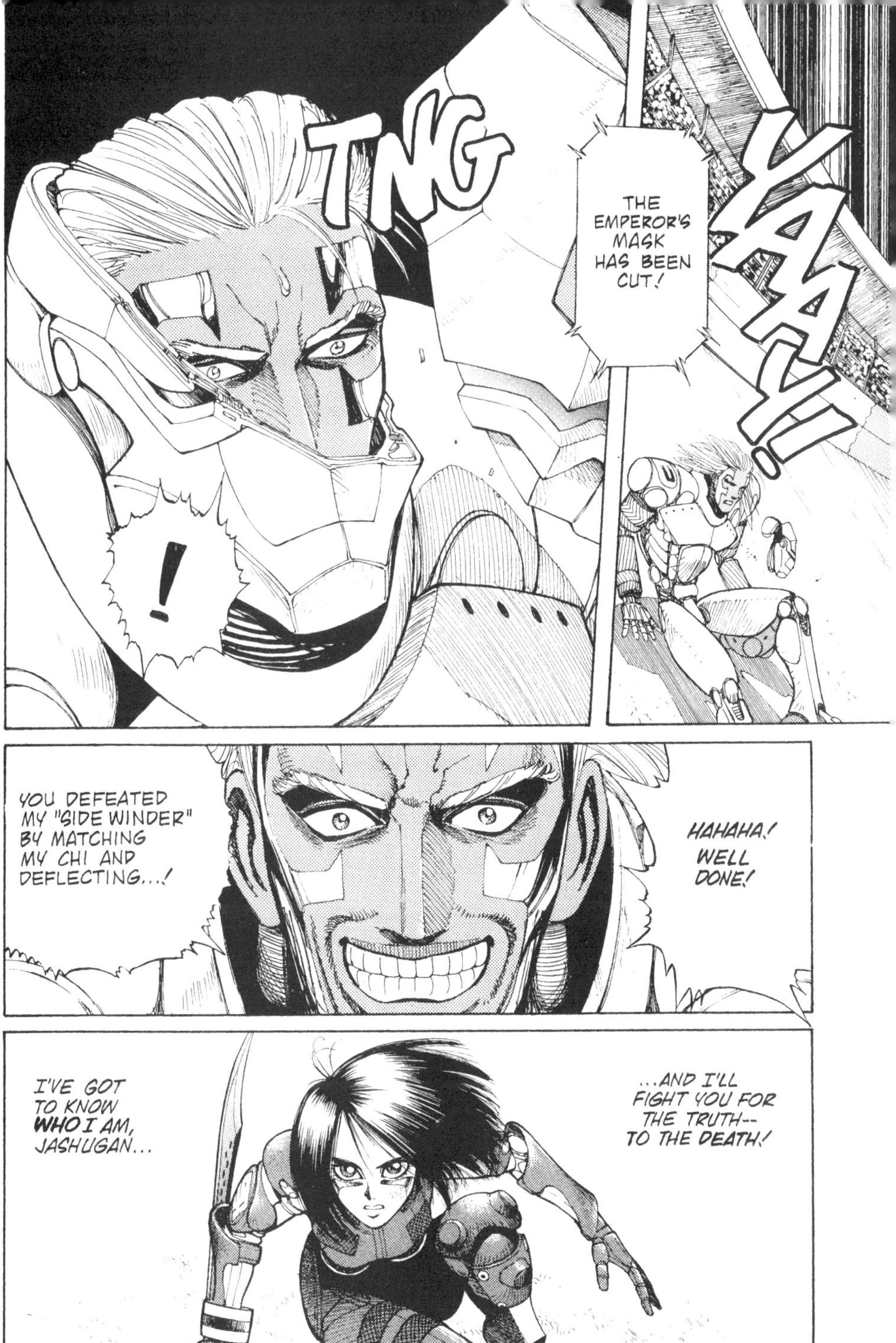
TNG
!
THE EMPEROR'S MASK HAS BEEN CUT!
YAAAY!!
YOU DEFEATED MY "SIDE WINDER" BY MATCHING MY CHI AND DEFLECTING...!
HAHAHA! WELL DONE!
I'VE GOT TO KNOW **WHO** I AM, JASHUGAN...
...AND I'LL FIGHT YOU FOR THE TRUTH-- TO THE DEATH!

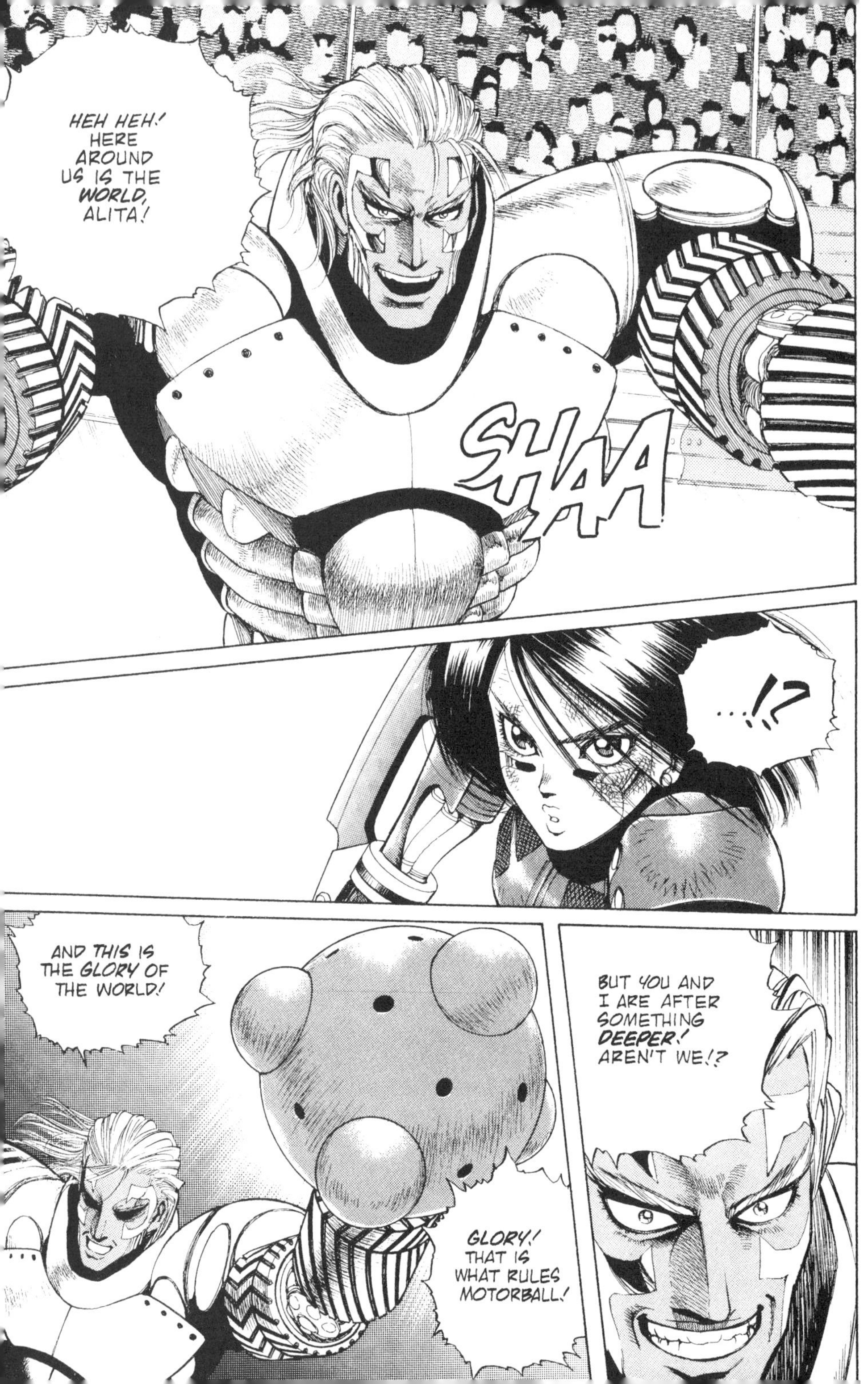
HEH HEH! HERE AROUND US IS THE WORLD, ALITA!
SHAA
...!?
AND THIS IS THE GLORY OF THE WORLD!
GLORY! THAT IS WHAT RULES MOTORBALL!
BUT YOU AND I ARE AFTER SOMETHING DEEPER! AREN'T WE!?

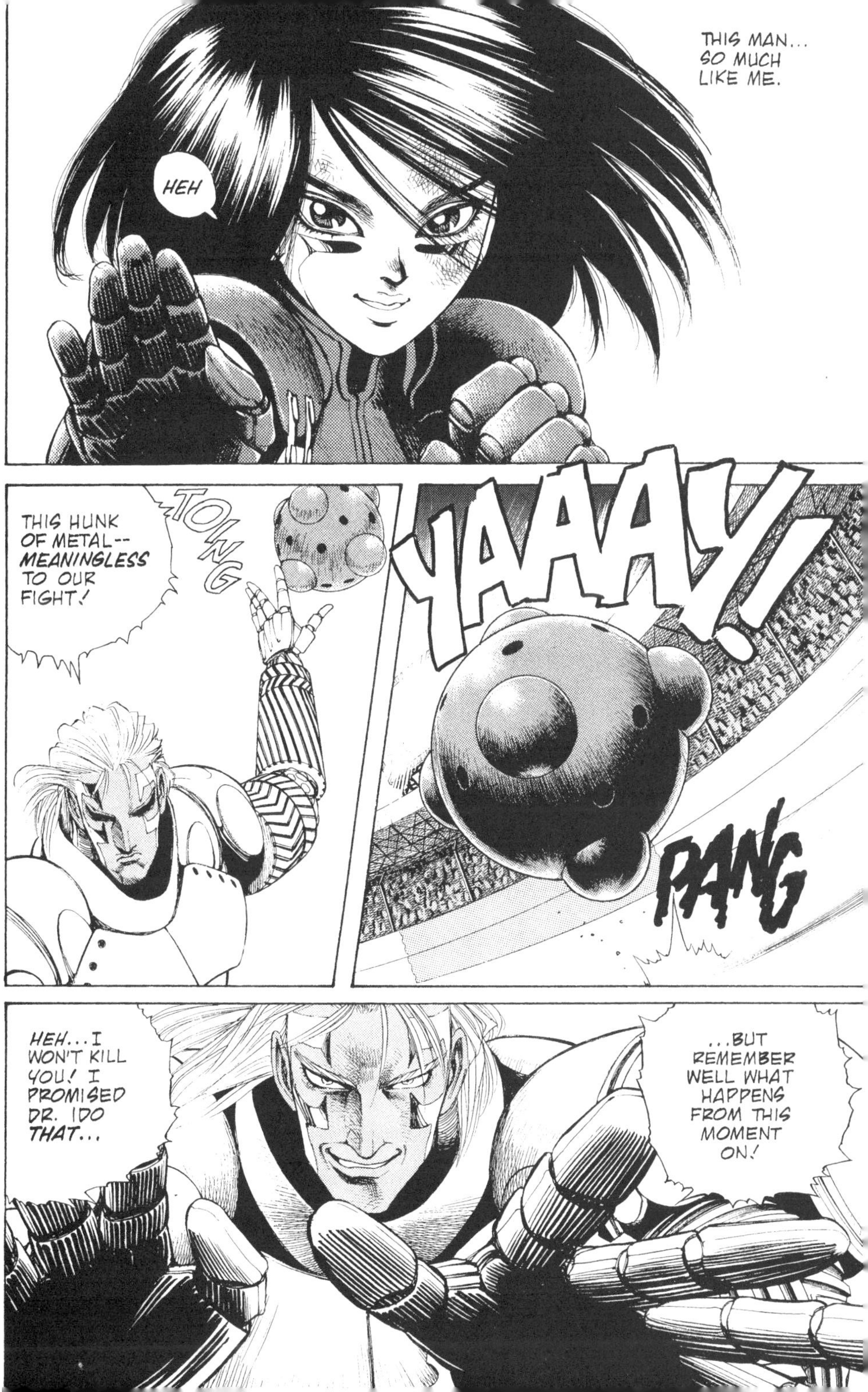
HEH
THIS MAN... SO MUCH LIKE ME.
THIS HUNK OF METAL-- MEANINGLESS TO OUR FIGHT!
TOING
YAAAY!
BANG
HEH... I WON'T KILL YOU! I PROMISED DR. IDO THAT...
...BUT REMEMBER WELL WHAT HAPPENS FROM THIS MOMENT ON!

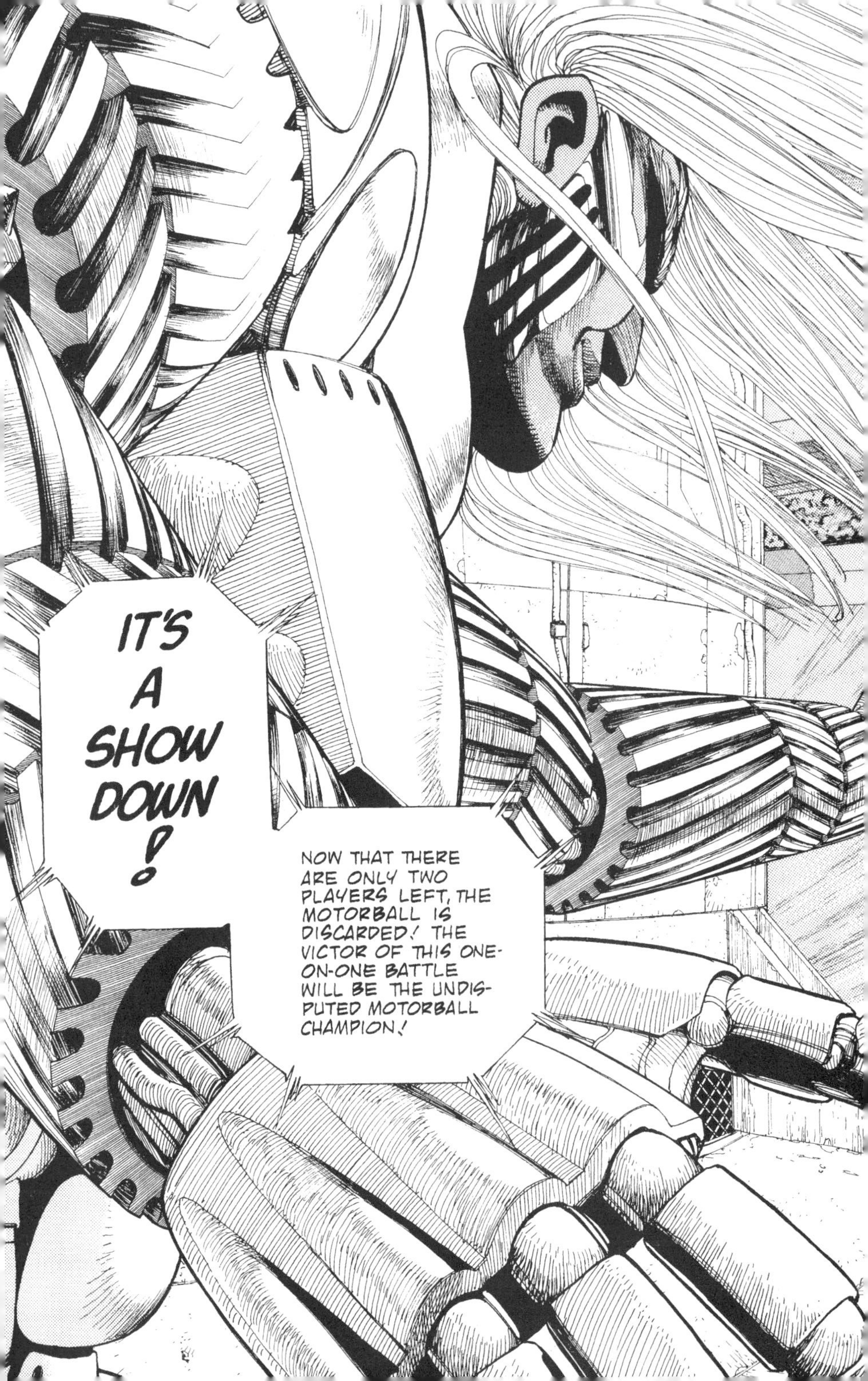
IT'S A SHOW DOWN!
NOW THAT THERE ARE ONLY TWO PLAYERS LEFT, THE MOTORBALL IS DISCARDED! THE VICTOR OF THIS ONE-ON-ONE BATTLE WILL BE THE UNDISPUTED MOTORBALL CHAMPION!

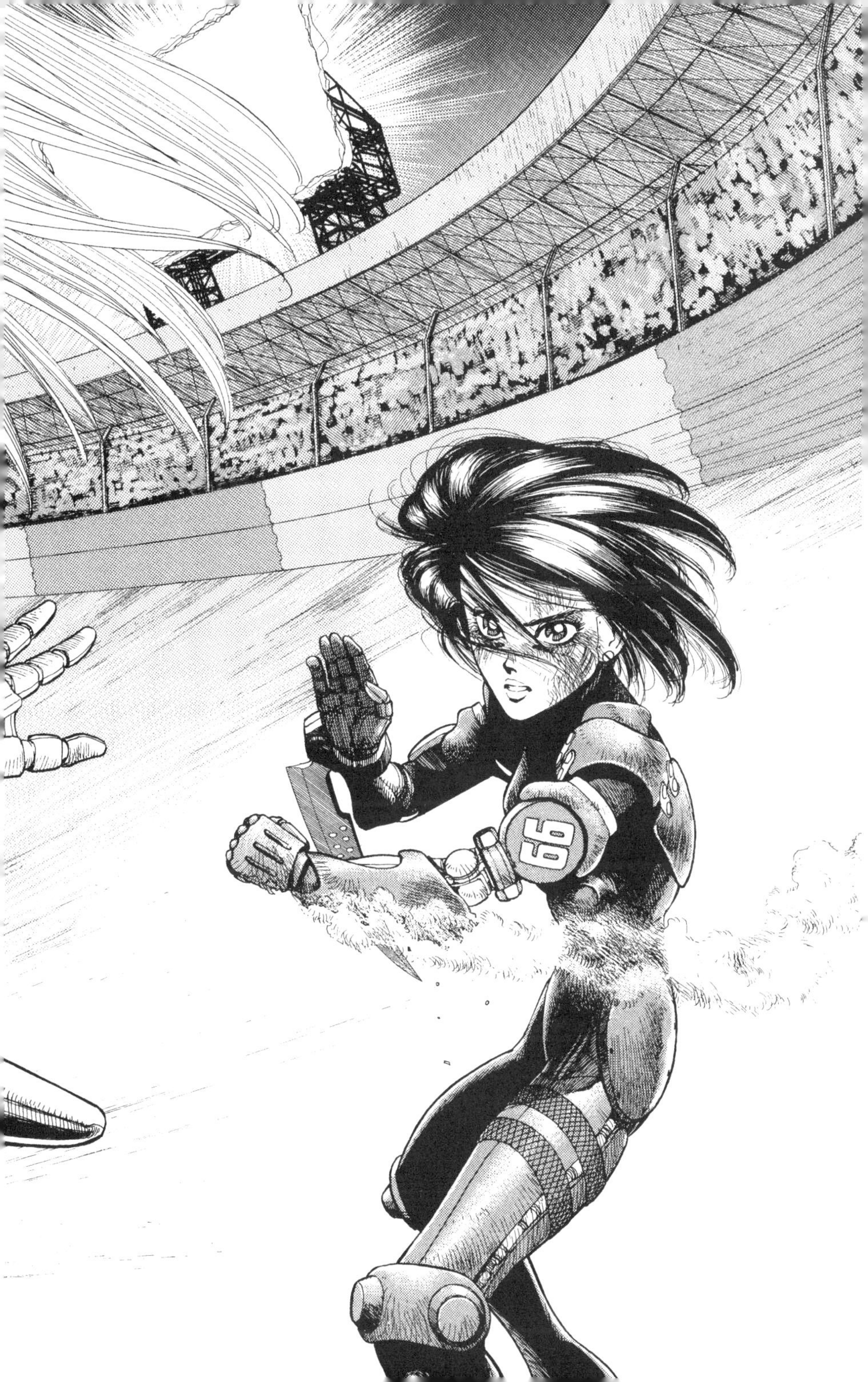

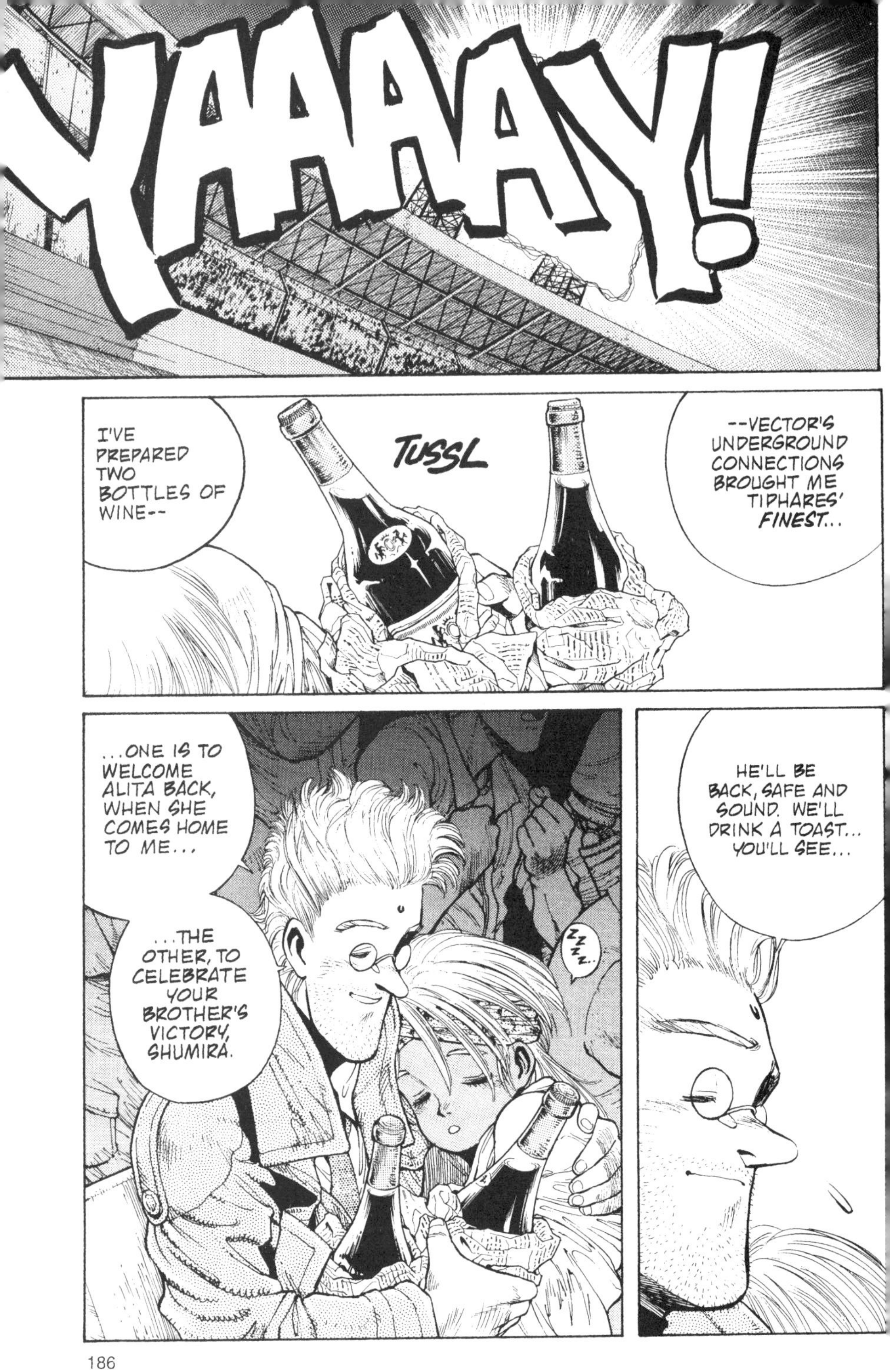
YAAAAY!
I'VE PREPARED TWO BOTTLES OF WINE--
TUSSL
--VECTOR'S UNDERGROUND CONNECTIONS BROUGHT ME TIPHARES' FINEST...
...ONE IS TO WELCOME ALITA BACK, WHEN SHE COMES HOME TO ME...
...THE OTHER, TO CELEBRATE YOUR BROTHER'S VICTORY, SHUMIRA.
ZZZ...
HE'LL BE BACK, SAFE AND SOUND. WE'LL DRINK A TOAST... YOU'LL SEE...

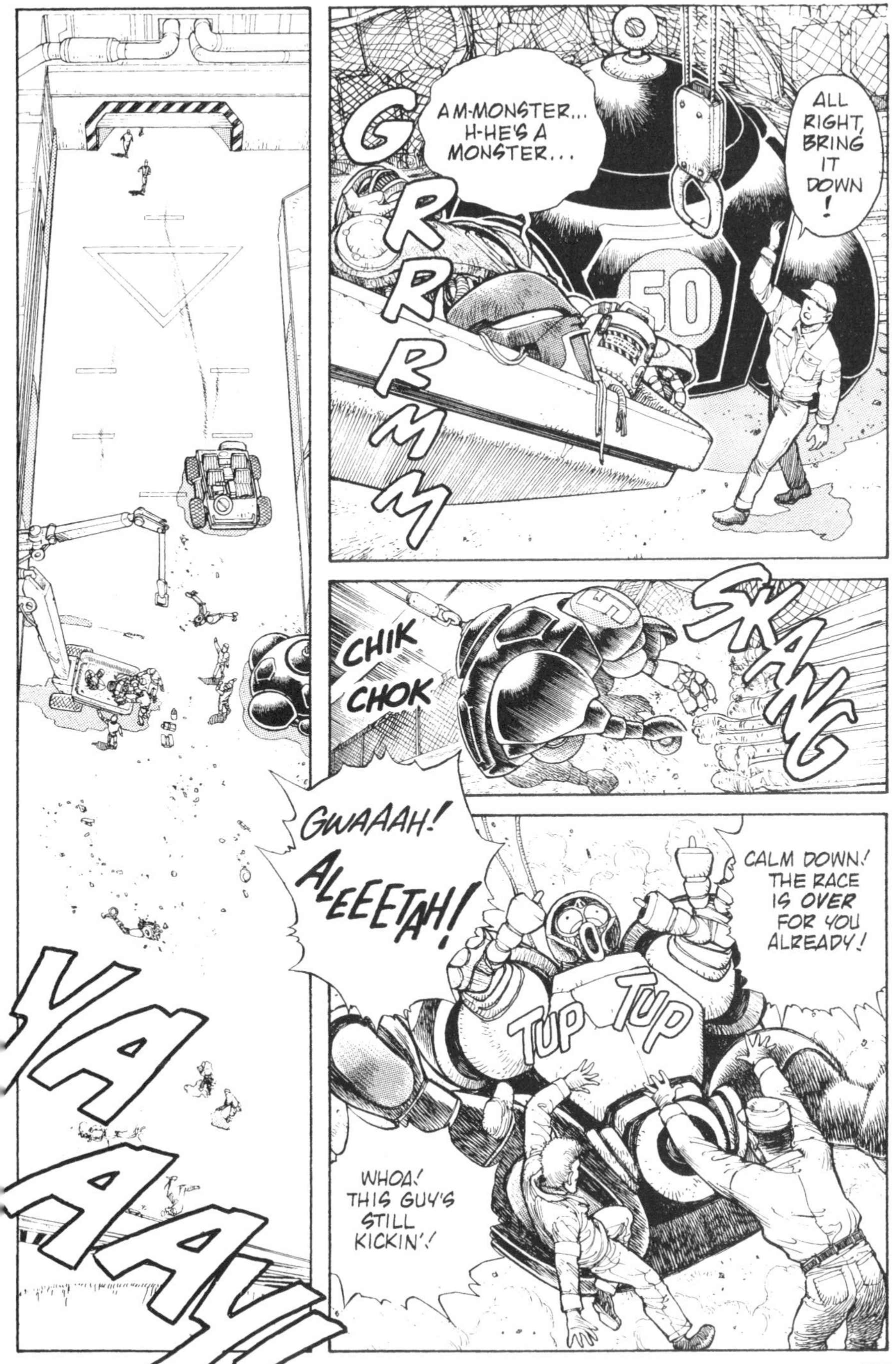
YAAAAAH!
GRRRMMM
AM-MONSTER... H-HE'S A MONSTER...
ALL RIGHT, BRING IT DOWN!
CHIK CHOK
SKANG
GWAAAH!
ALEEEETAH!
CALM DOWN! THE RACE IS OVER FOR YOU ALREADY!
TUP TUP
WHOA! THIS GUY'S STILL KICKIN'!

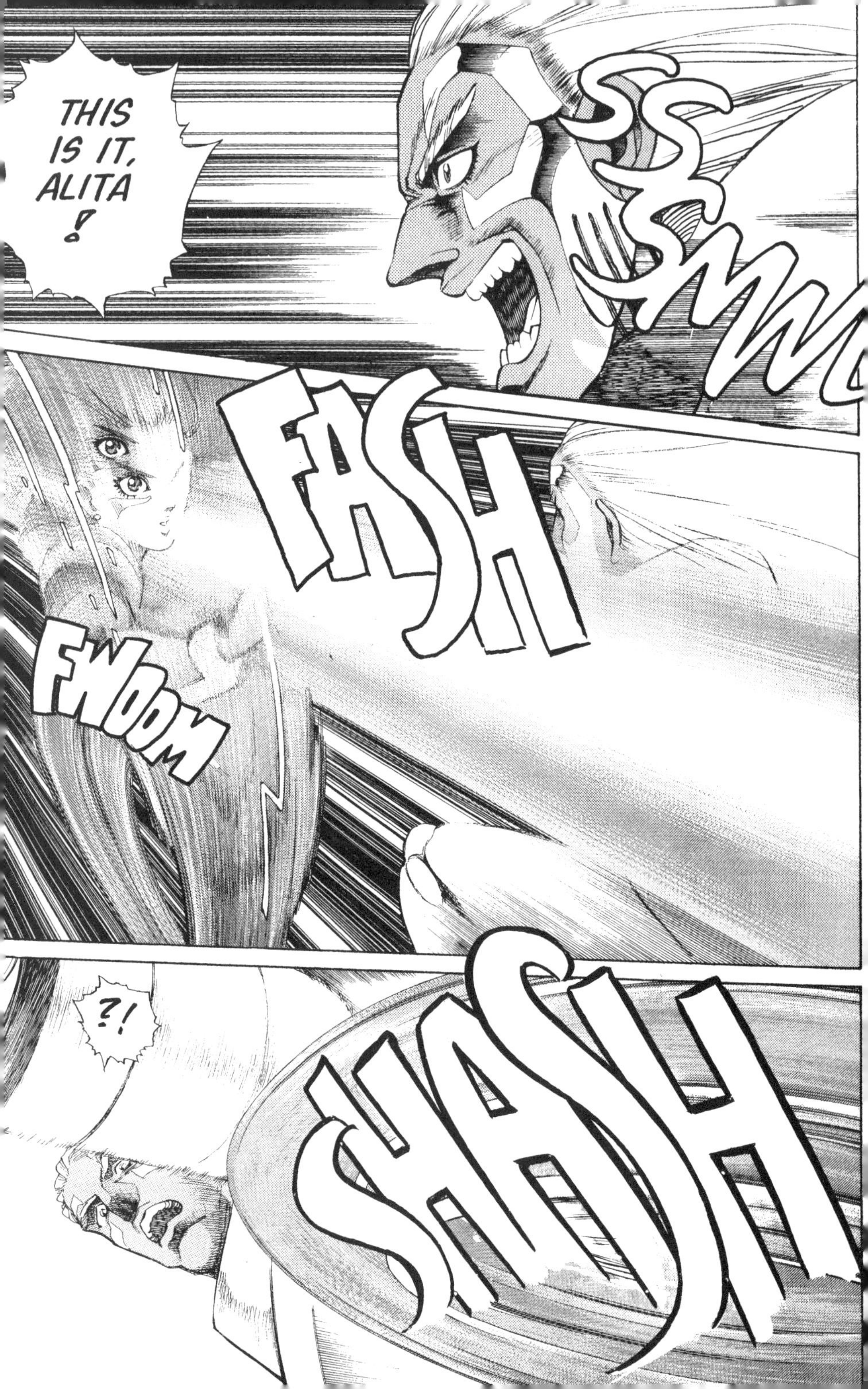
THIS IS IT, ALITA!
SSSHWOO
FASH
FWOOM
?!
SHASH

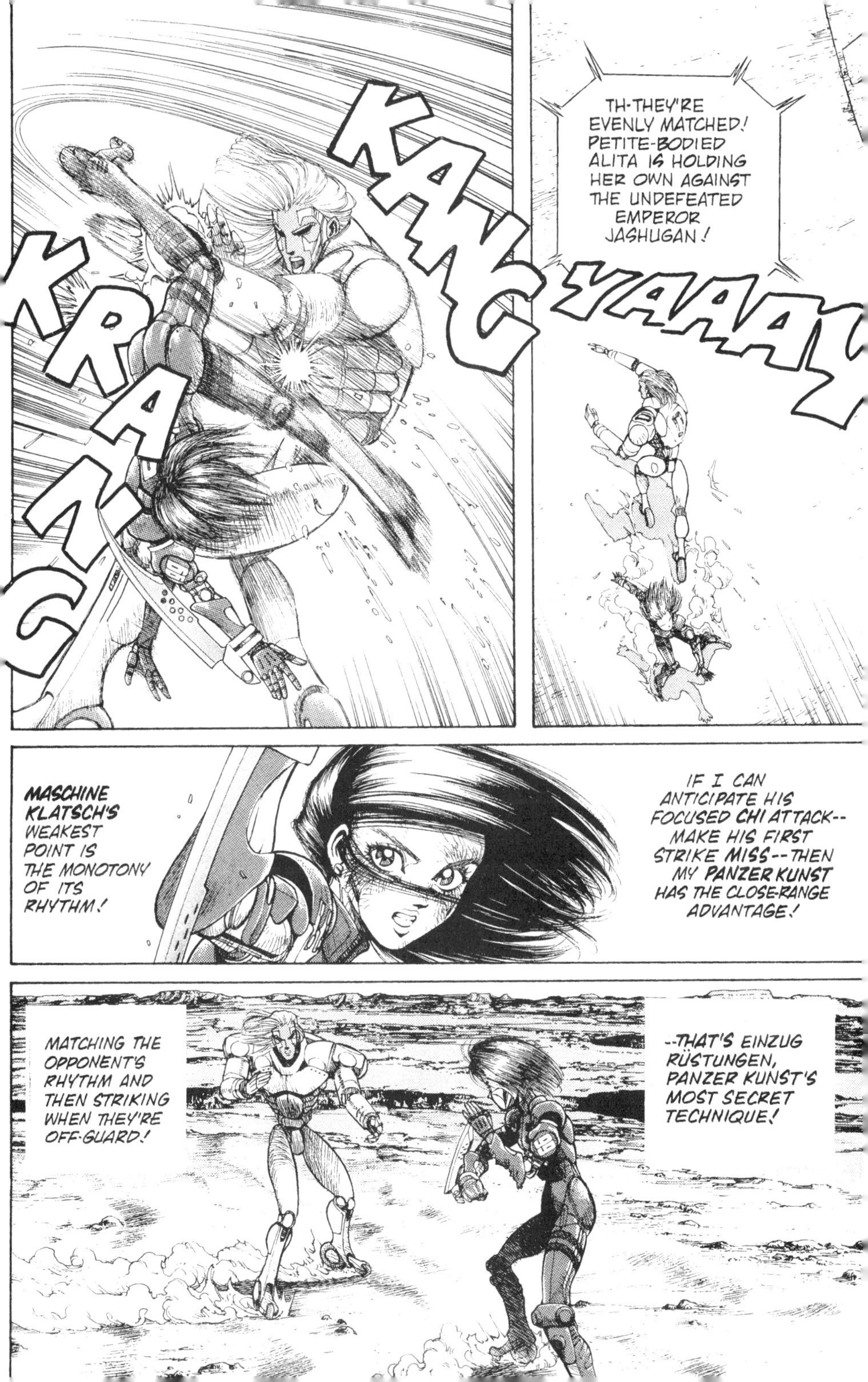
KRAANG
KANG
TH-THEY'RE EVENLY MATCHED! PETITE-BODIED ALITA IS HOLDING HER OWN AGAINST THE UNDEFEATED EMPEROR JASHUGAN!
YAAAAY
MASCHINE KLATSCH'S WEAKEST POINT IS THE MONOTONY OF ITS RHYTHM!
IF I CAN ANTICIPATE HIS FOCUSED CHI ATTACK-- MAKE HIS FIRST STRIKE MISS--THEN MY PANZER KUNST HAS THE CLOSE-RANGE ADVANTAGE!
MATCHING THE OPPONENT'S RHYTHM AND THEN STRIKING WHEN THEY'RE OFF-GUARD!
--THAT'S EINZUG RÜSTUNGEN, PANZER KUNST'S MOST SECRET TECHNIQUE!

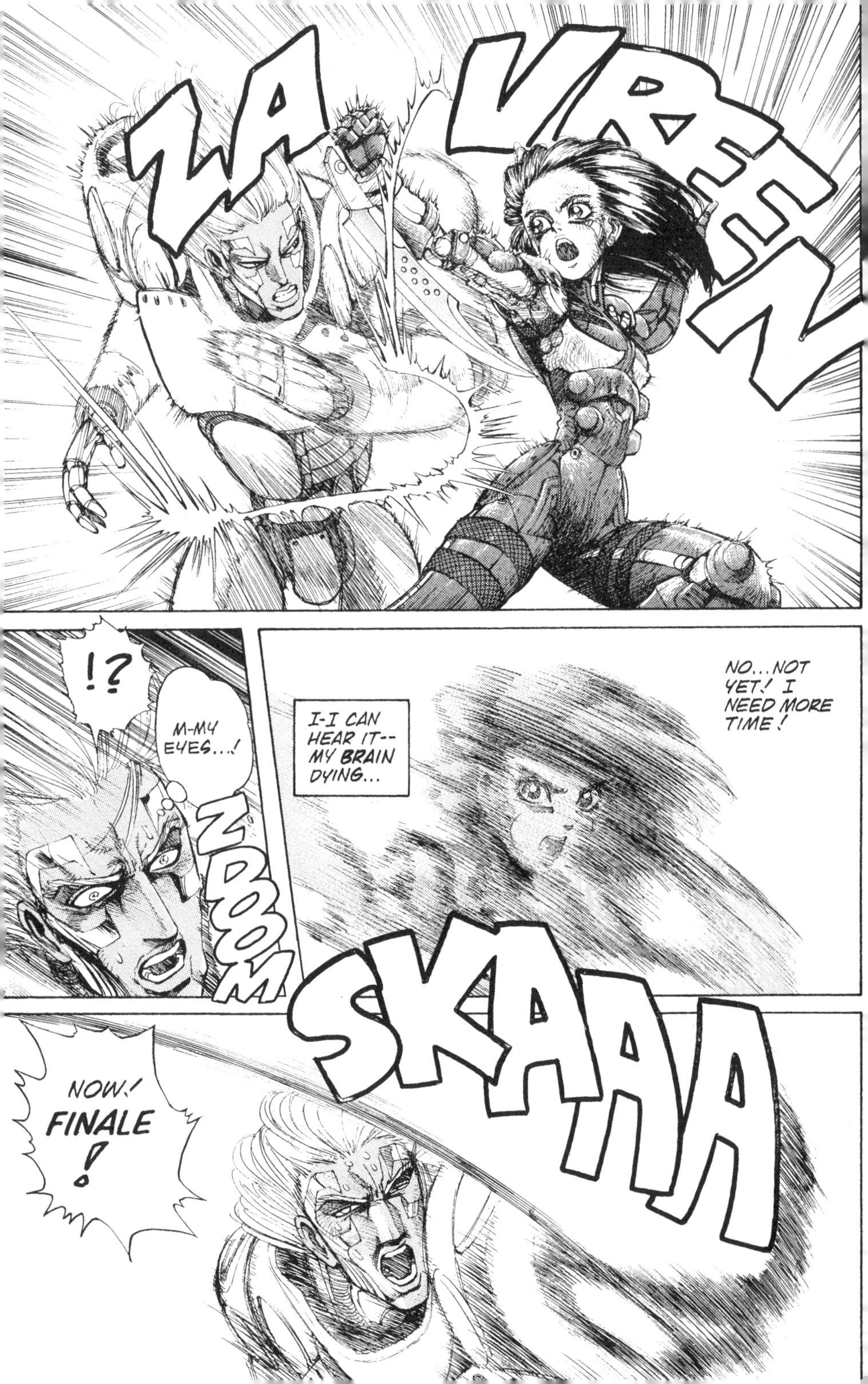

ZA
VRAHN
!?
M-MY EYES...!
ZDOOOM
I-I CAN HEAR IT-- MY BRAIN DYING...
NO...NOT YET! I NEED MORE TIME!
SKAAAA
NOW! FINALE!

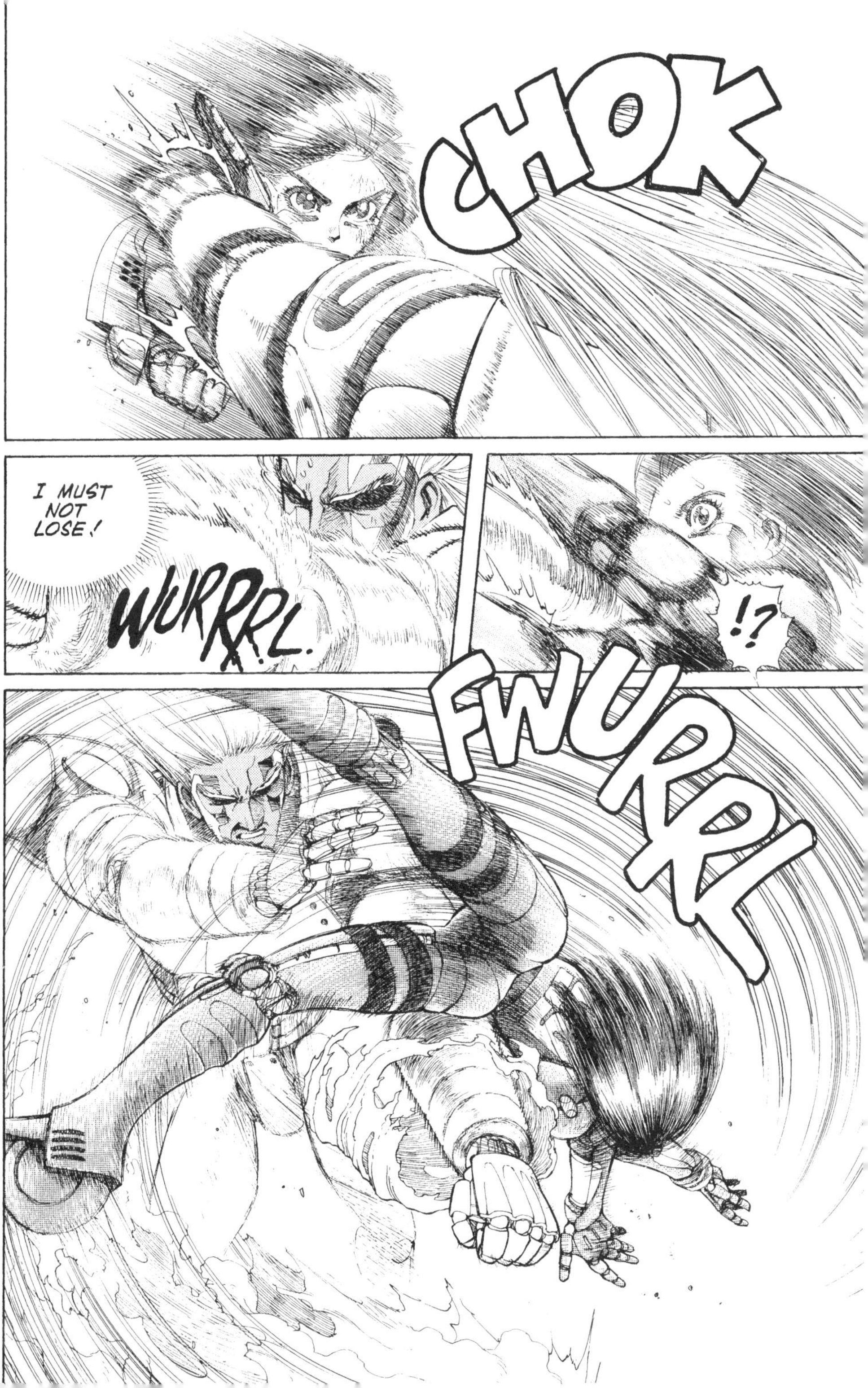
CHOK
I MUST NOT LOSE!
WURRRL.
!?
FWURRL

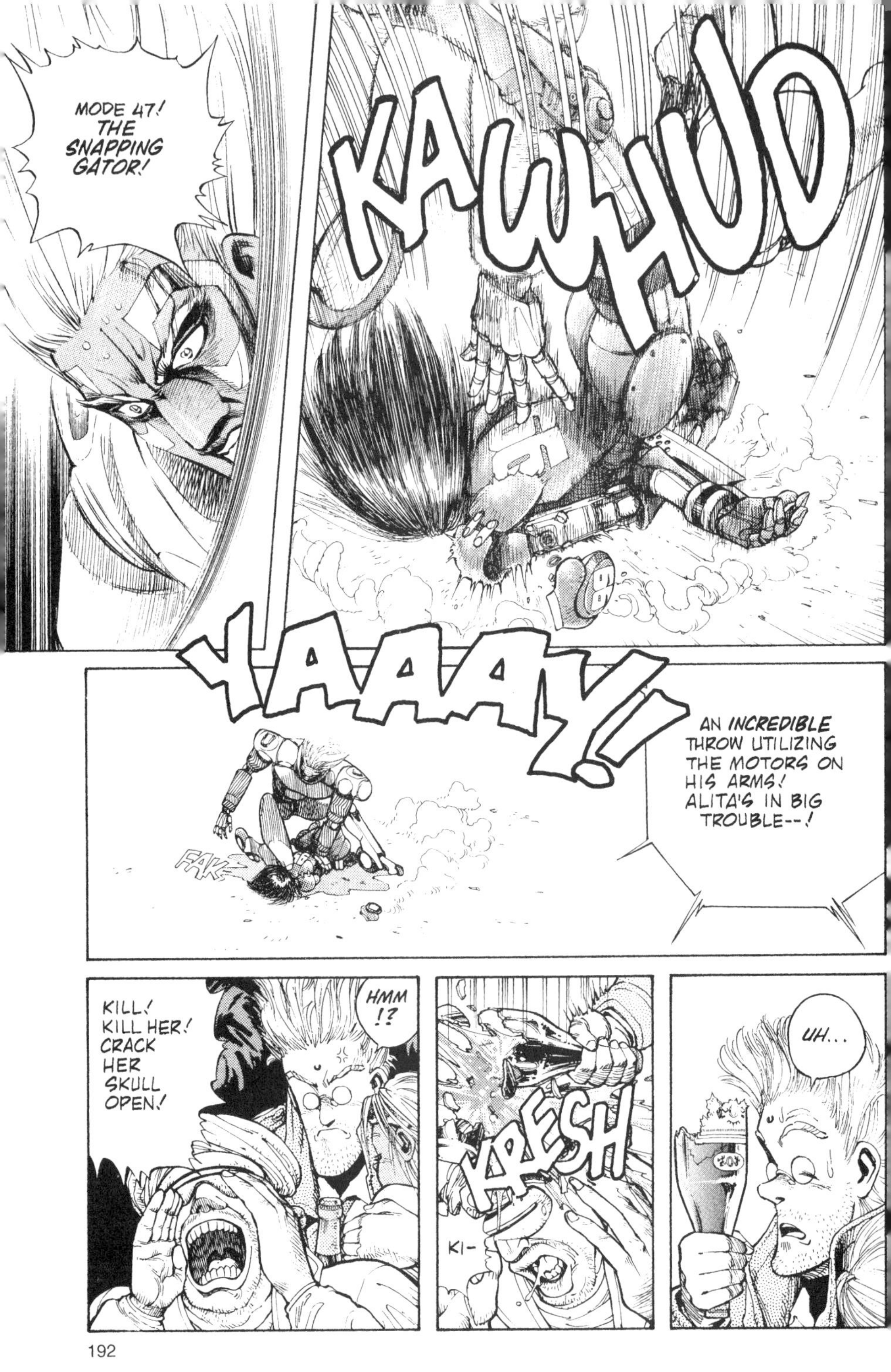
MODE 47! THE SNAPPING GATOR!
KAWHUD
YAAAY!!
AN INCREDIBLE THROW UTILIZING THE MOTORS ON HIS ARMS! ALITA'S IN BIG TROUBLE--!
FAK
KILL! KILL HER! CRACK HER SKULL OPEN!
HMM !?
KRESH
KI-
UH...

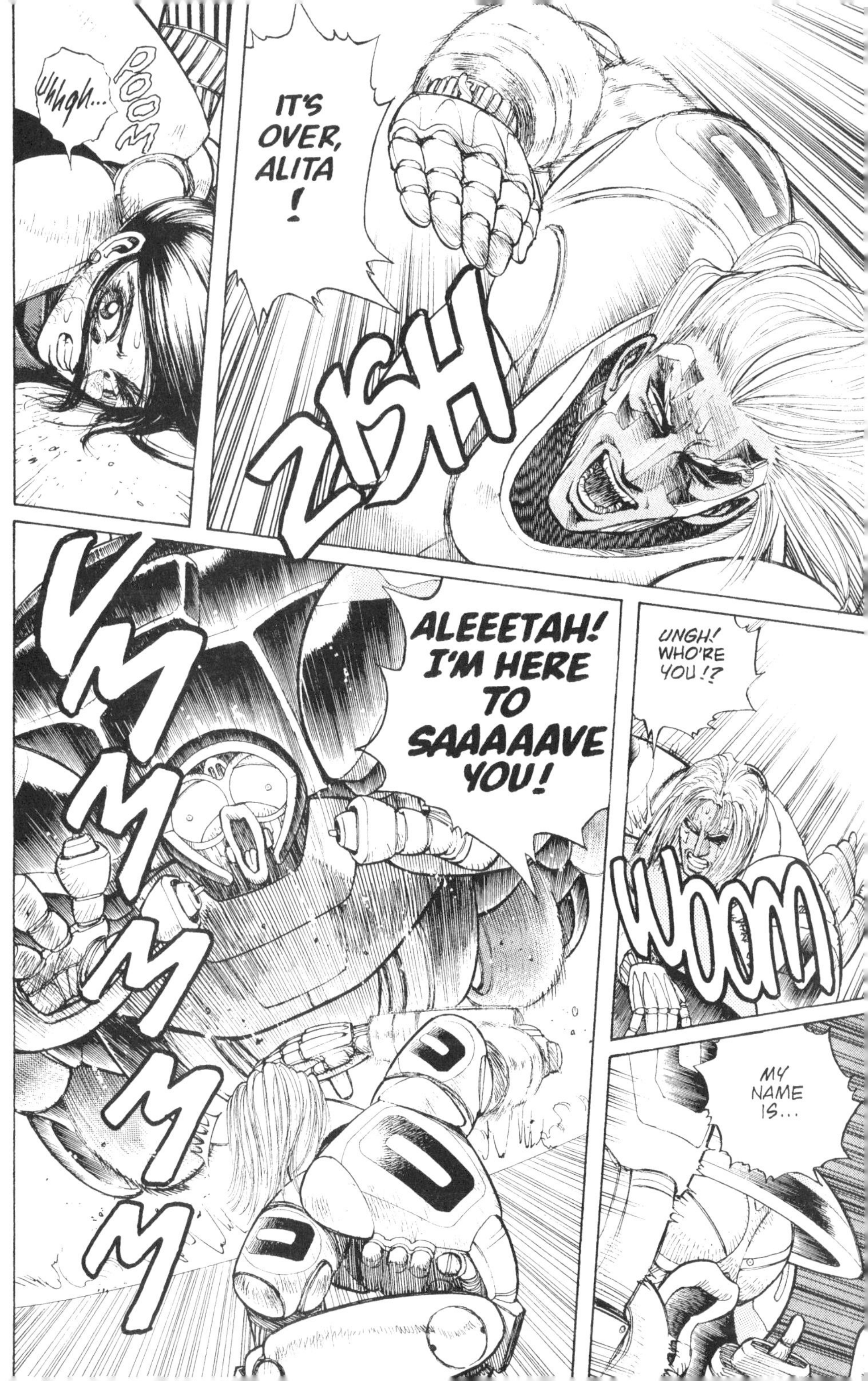
Uhhgh...
DOOOM
IT'S OVER, ALITA!
ZASH
VMMMMMM
ALEEETAH! I'M HERE TO SAAAAAVE YOU!
UNGH! WHO'RE YOU!?
WHOOM
MY NAME IS...

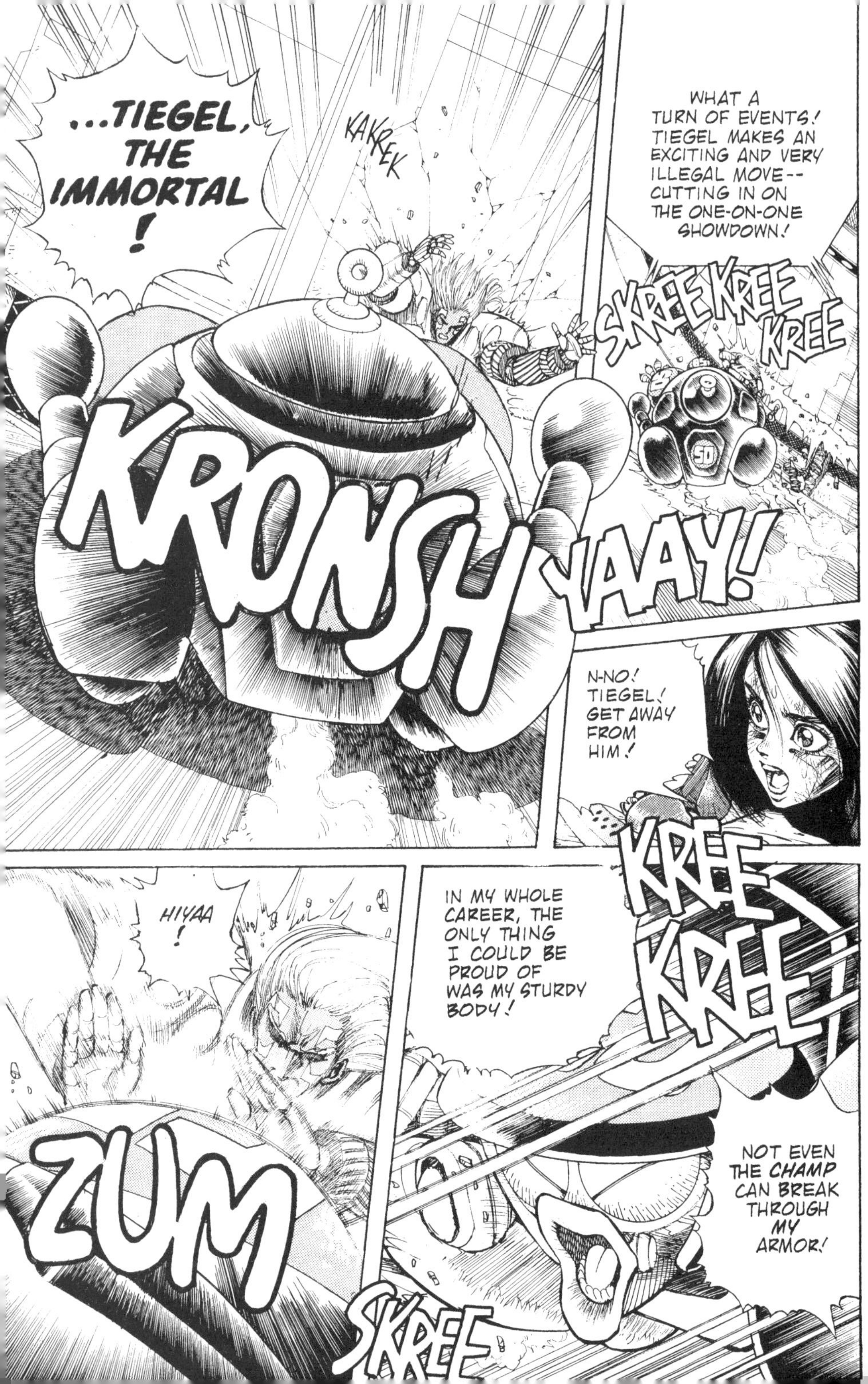
...TIEGEL, THE IMMORTAL !
KAKREK
KRONSH
WHAT A TURN OF EVENTS! TIEGEL MAKES AN EXCITING AND VERY ILLEGAL MOVE-- CUTTING IN ON THE ONE-ON-ONE SHOWDOWN!
SKREE KREE KREE
YAAAY!
N-NO! TIEGEL! GET AWAY FROM HIM!
HIYAA !
ZUM
IN MY WHOLE CAREER, THE ONLY THING I COULD BE PROUD OF WAS MY STURDY BODY!
KREE KREE KREE
NOT EVEN THE *CHAMP* CAN BREAK THROUGH MY ARMOR!
SKREE

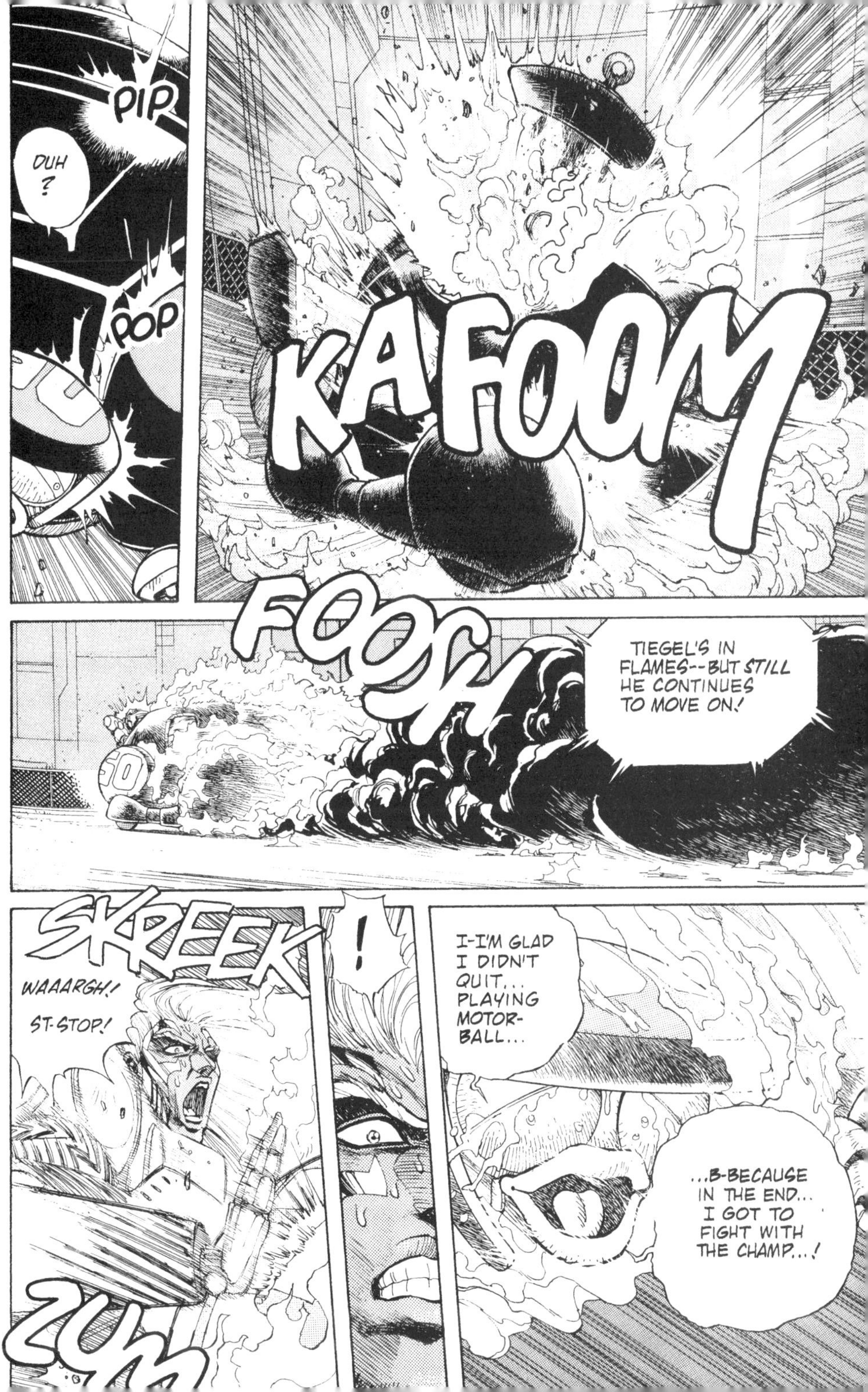
PIP
DUH ?
POP
KAFOOM
FOOSH
TIEGEL'S IN FLAMES--BUT STILL HE CONTINUES TO MOVE ON!
SKREEK
WAAARGH!
ST-STOP!
ZUM
!
I-I'M GLAD I DIDN'T QUIT... PLAYING MOTOR-BALL...
...B-BECAUSE IN THE END... I GOT TO FIGHT WITH THE CHAMP...!

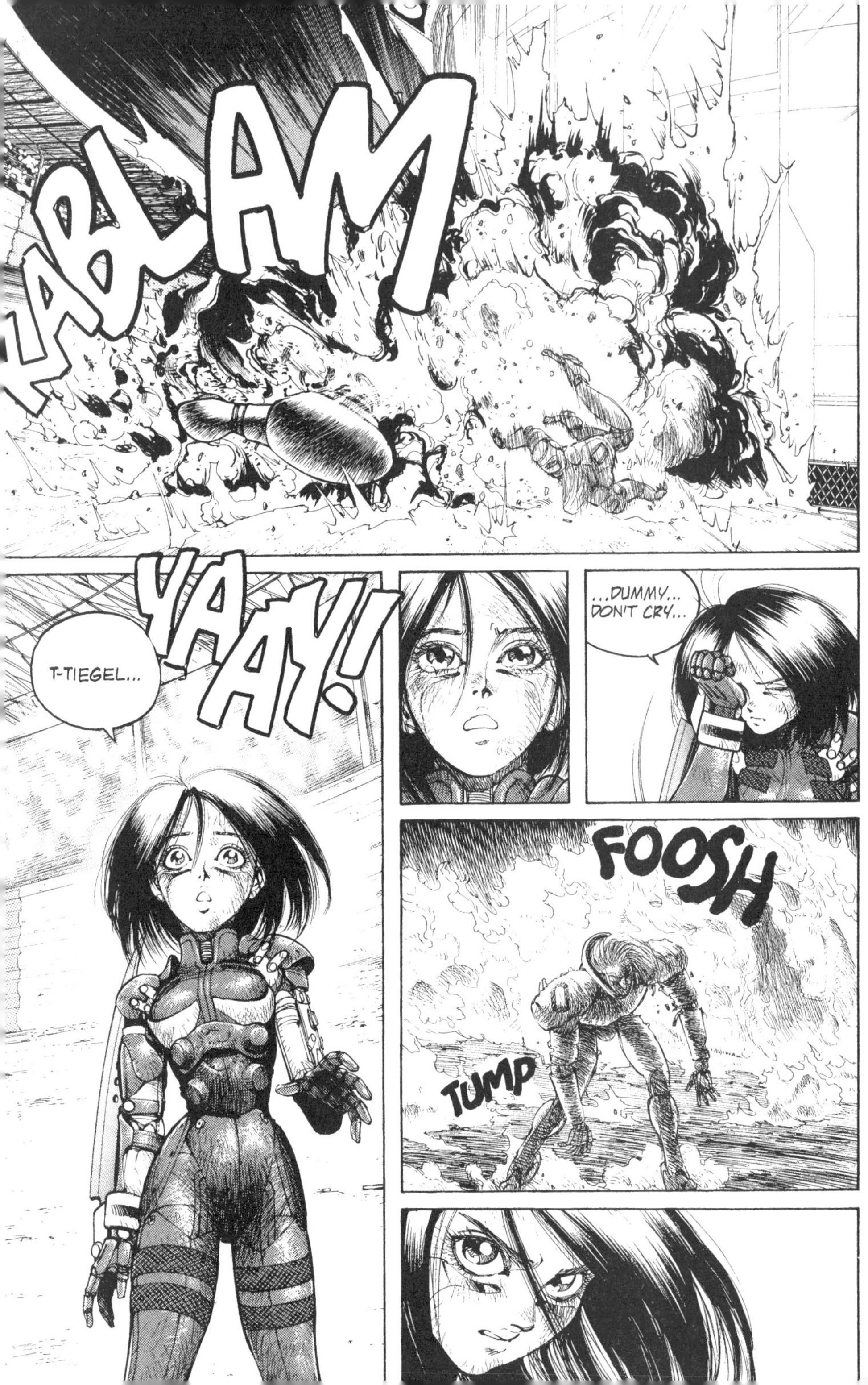
KABLAM
YAAAY!
T-TIEGEL...
...DUMMY... DON'T CRY...
FOOSH
TUMP

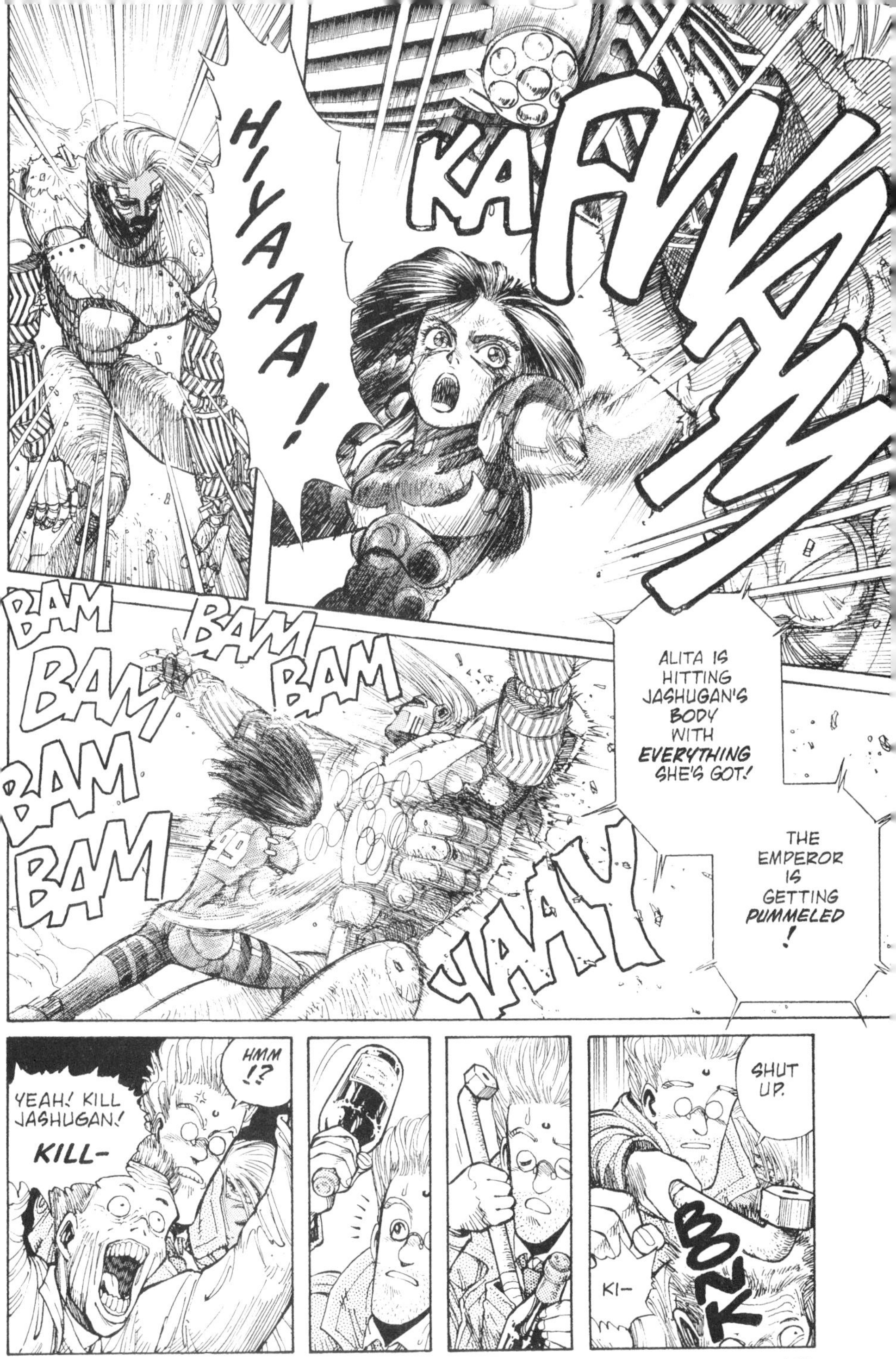
HIYAAAA!
KAFWAM
BAM BAM BAM BAM BAM BAM
ALITA IS HITTING JASHUGAN'S BODY WITH EVERYTHING SHE'S GOT!
YAAAY
THE EMPEROR IS GETTING PUMMELED!
YEAH! KILL JASHUGAN! KILL-
HMM !?
SHUT UP.
KI-
BONK

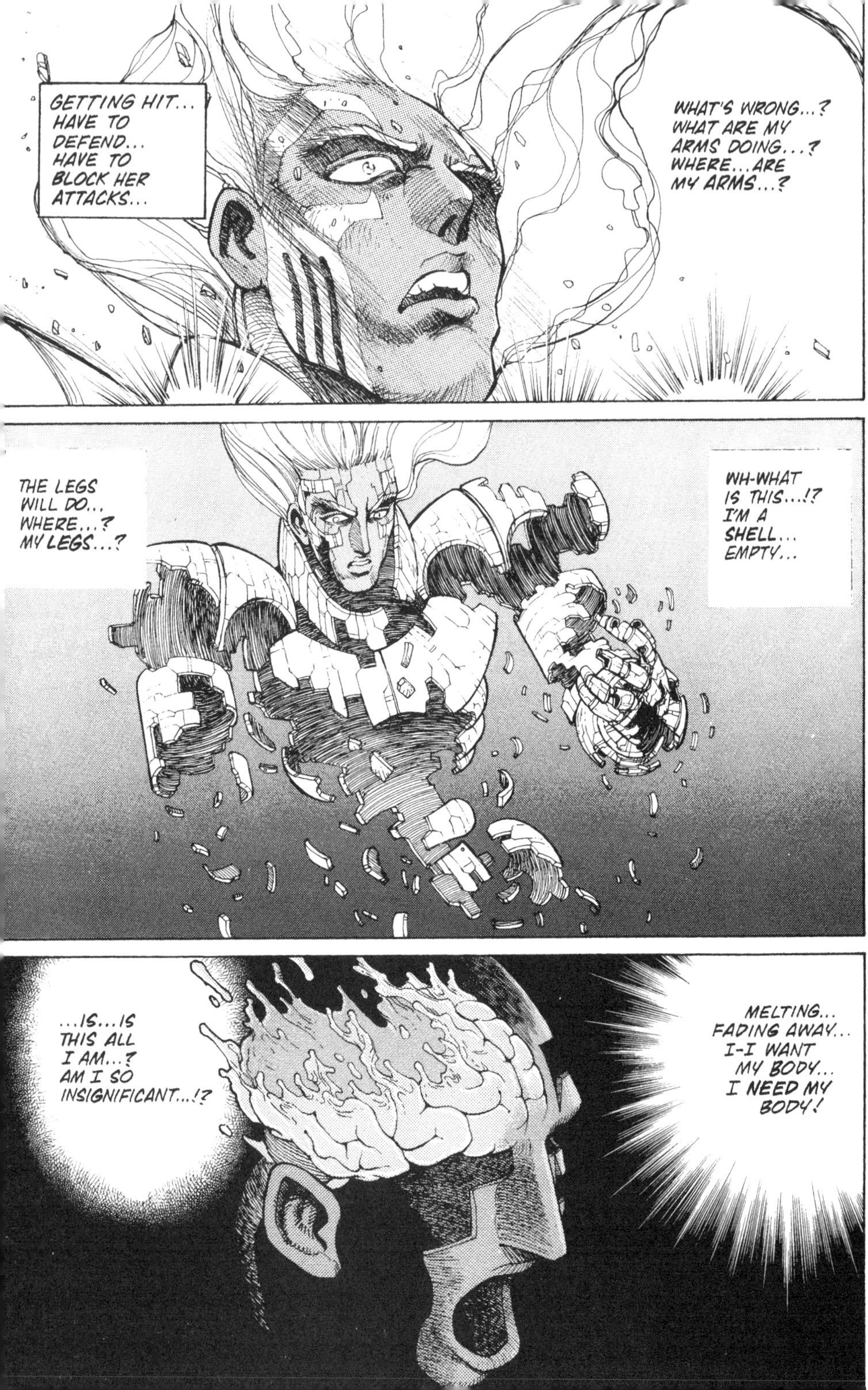
GETTING HIT... HAVE TO DEFEND... HAVE TO BLOCK HER ATTACKS...
WHAT'S WRONG...? WHAT ARE MY ARMS DOING...? WHERE...ARE MY ARMS...?
THE LEGS WILL DO... WHERE...? MY LEGS...?
WH-WHAT IS THIS...!? I'M A SHELL... EMPTY...
...IS...IS THIS ALL I AM...? AM I SO INSIGNIFICANT...!?
MELTING... FADING AWAY... I-I WANT MY BODY... I NEED MY BODY!

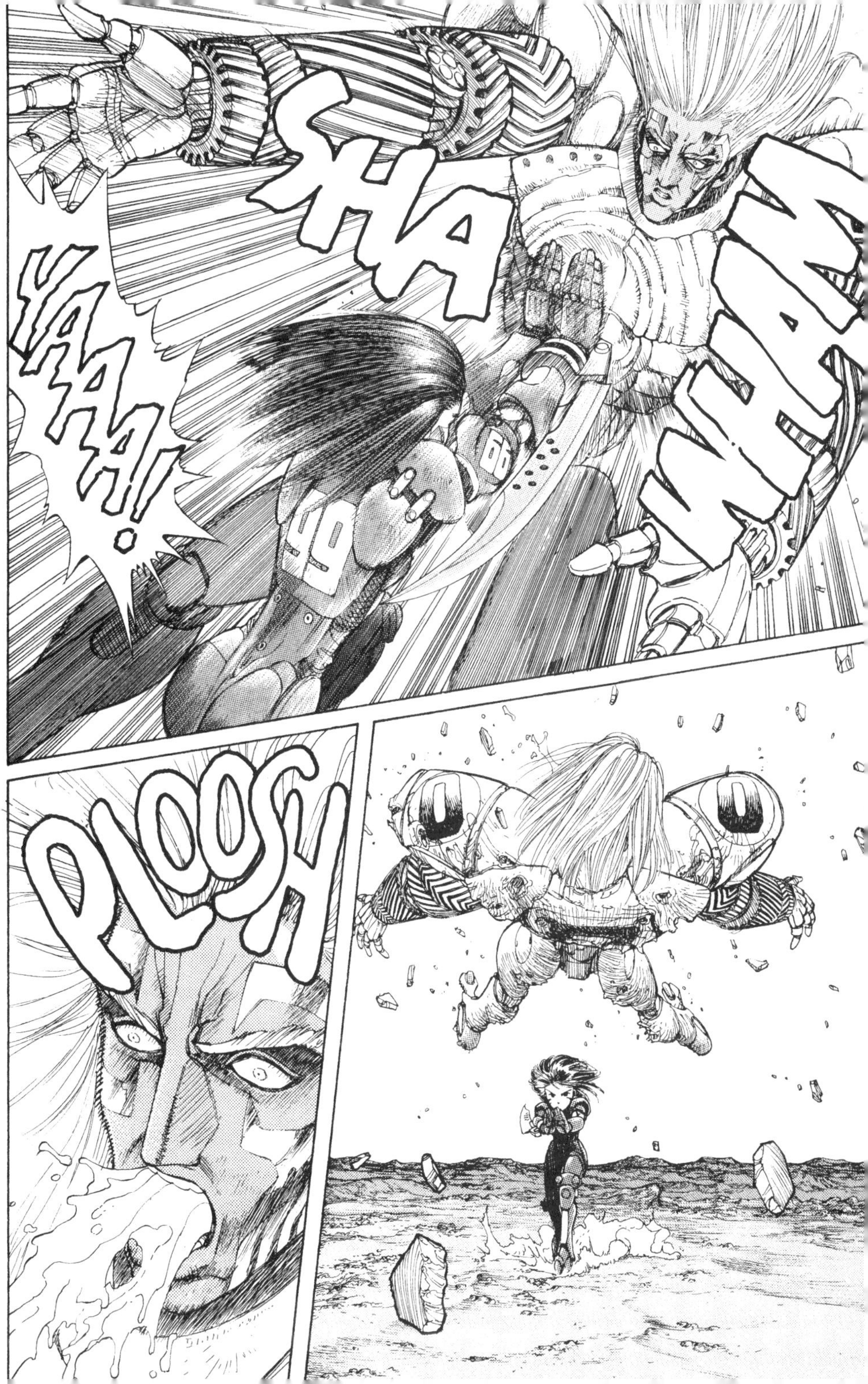
YAAA!
SHA
WHA
PLOOSH

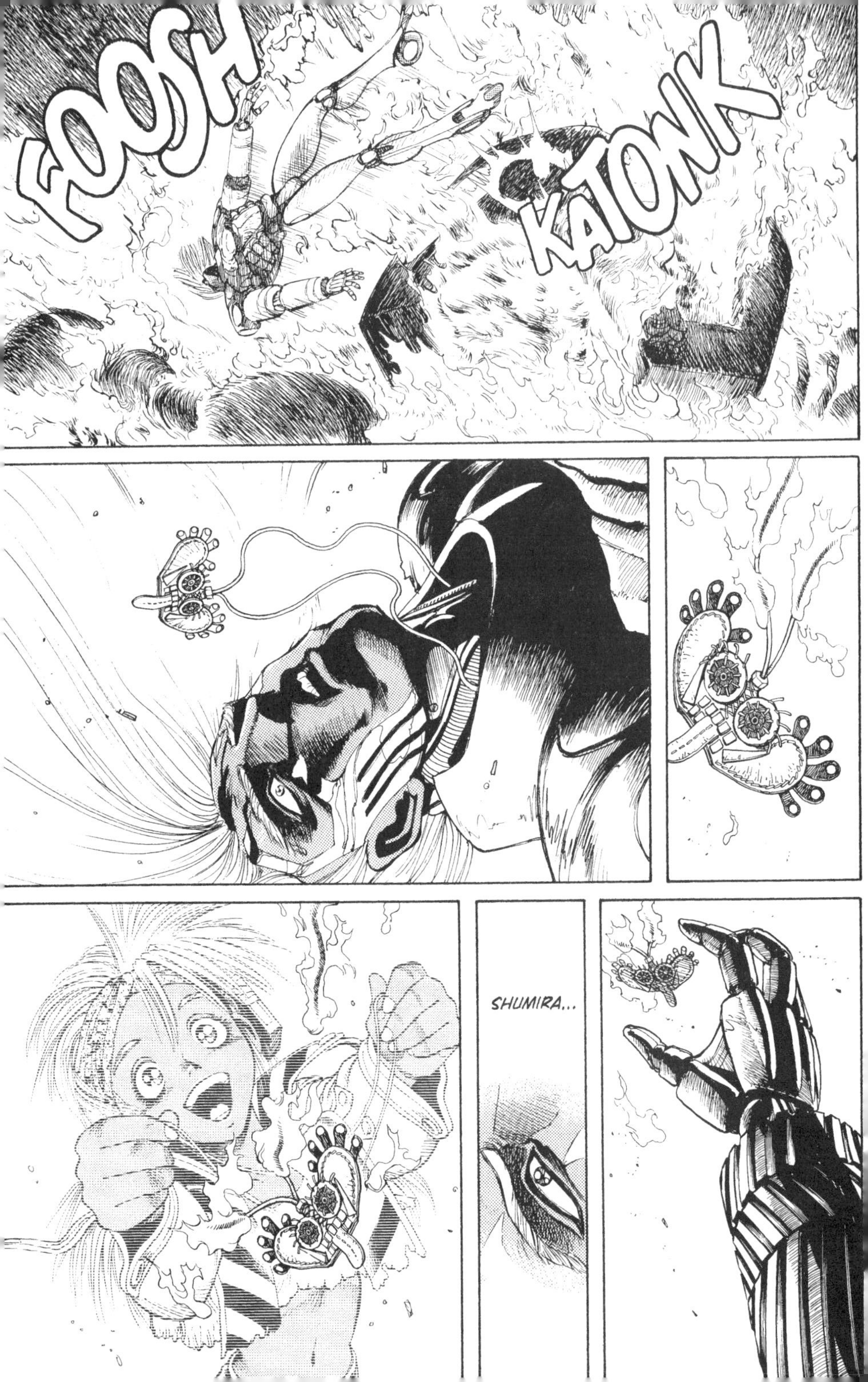
FOOSH
KATONK
SHUMIRA...

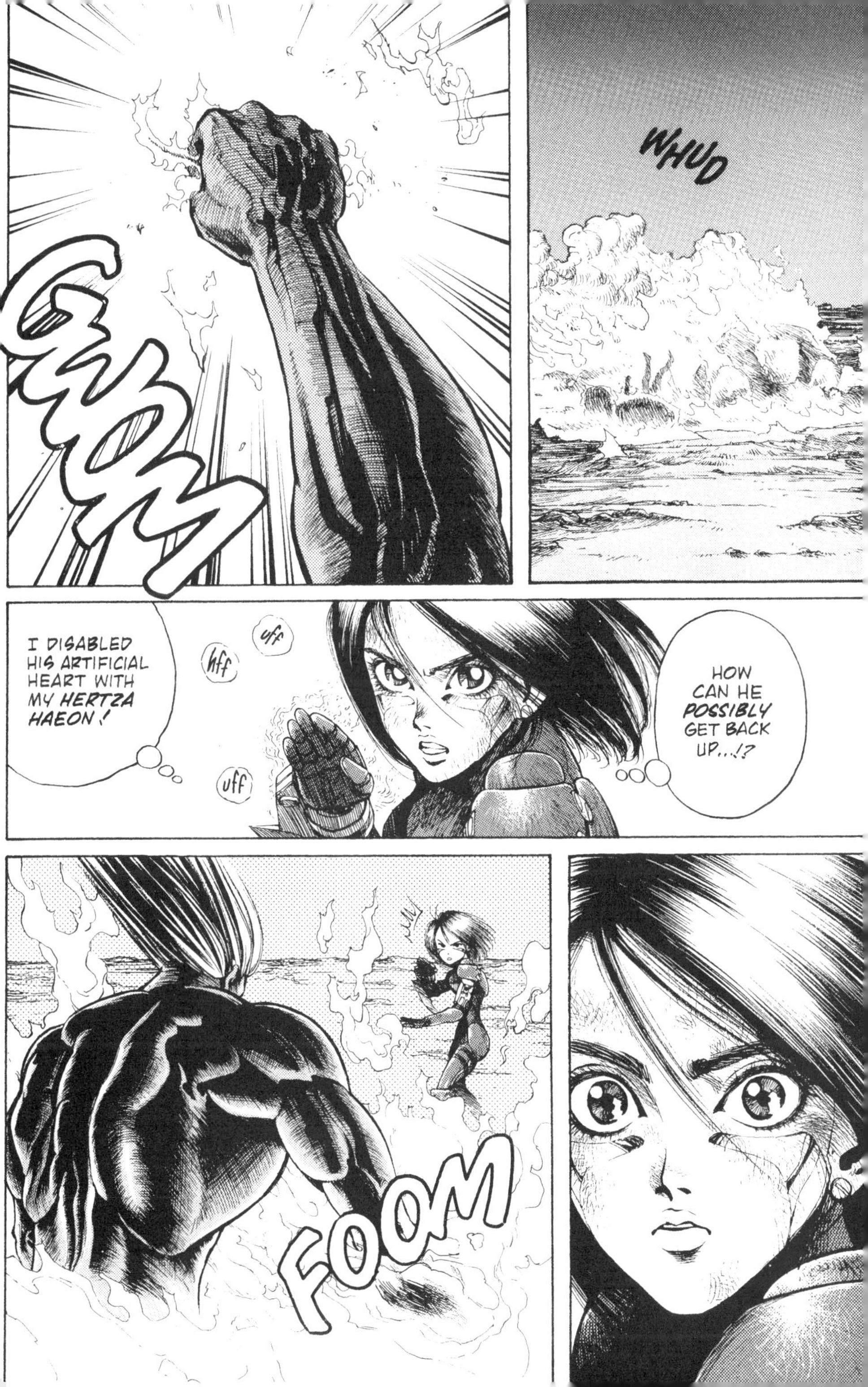
GWOM
WHUD
I DISABLED HIS ARTIFICIAL HEART WITH MY HERTZA HAEON!
hff
uff
uff
HOW CAN HE POSSIBLY GET BACK UP...!?
FOOM

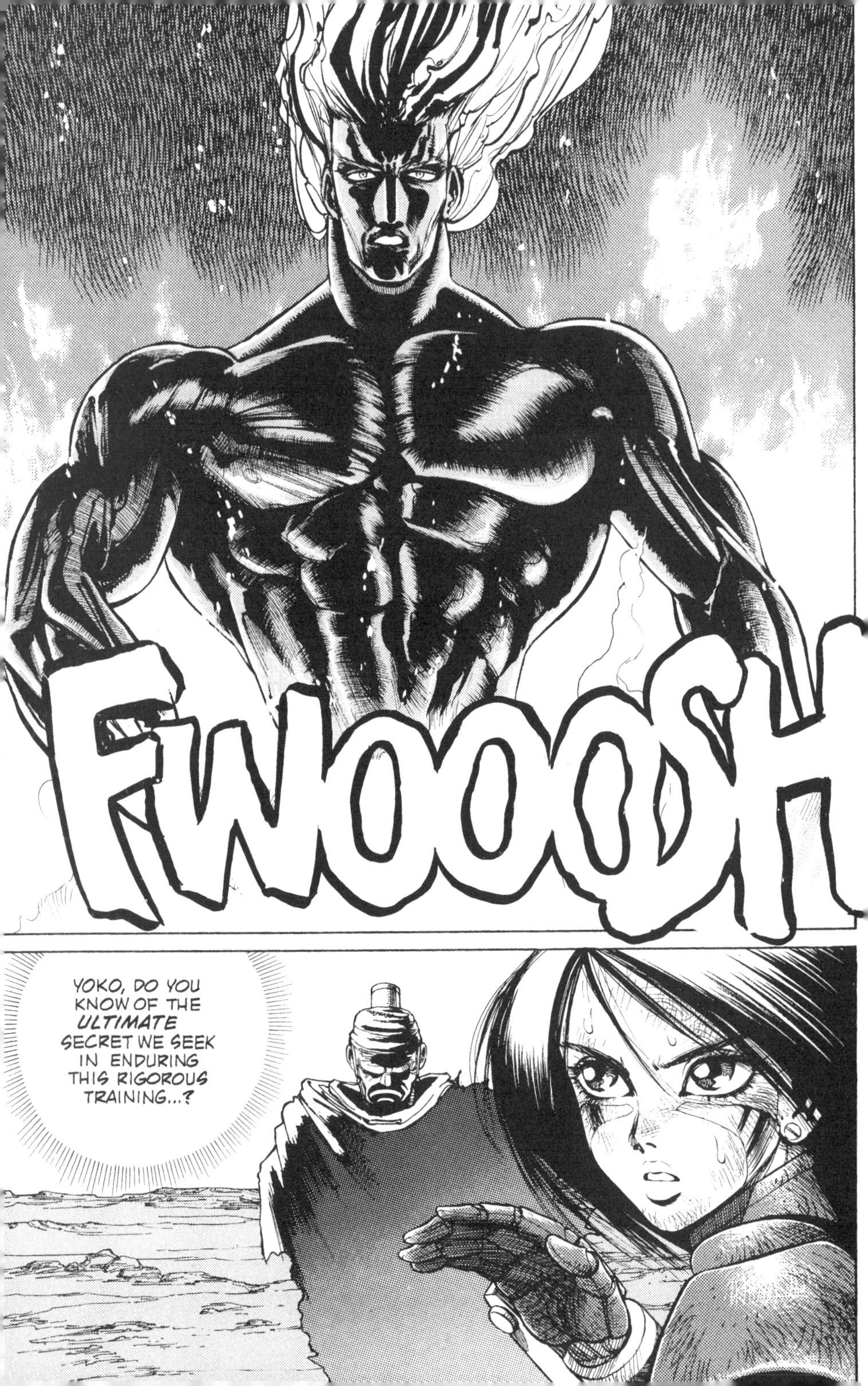
FWOOOSH
YOKO, DO YOU KNOW OF THE *ULTIMATE* SECRET WE SEEK IN ENDURING THIS RIGOROUS TRAINING...?

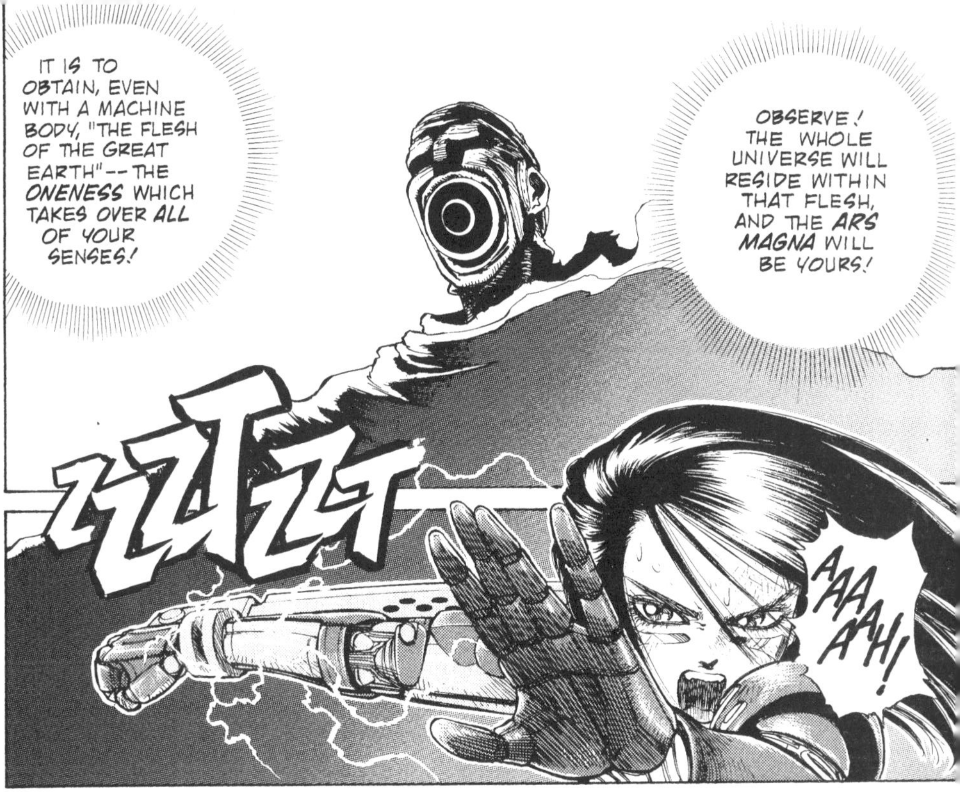
IT IS TO OBTAIN, EVEN WITH A MACHINE BODY, "THE FLESH OF THE GREAT EARTH"-- THE ONENESS WHICH TAKES OVER ALL OF YOUR SENSES!
OBSERVE! THE WHOLE UNIVERSE WILL RESIDE WITHIN THAT FLESH, AND THE ARS MAGNA WILL BE YOURS!
ZZZZZT
AAAAAH!
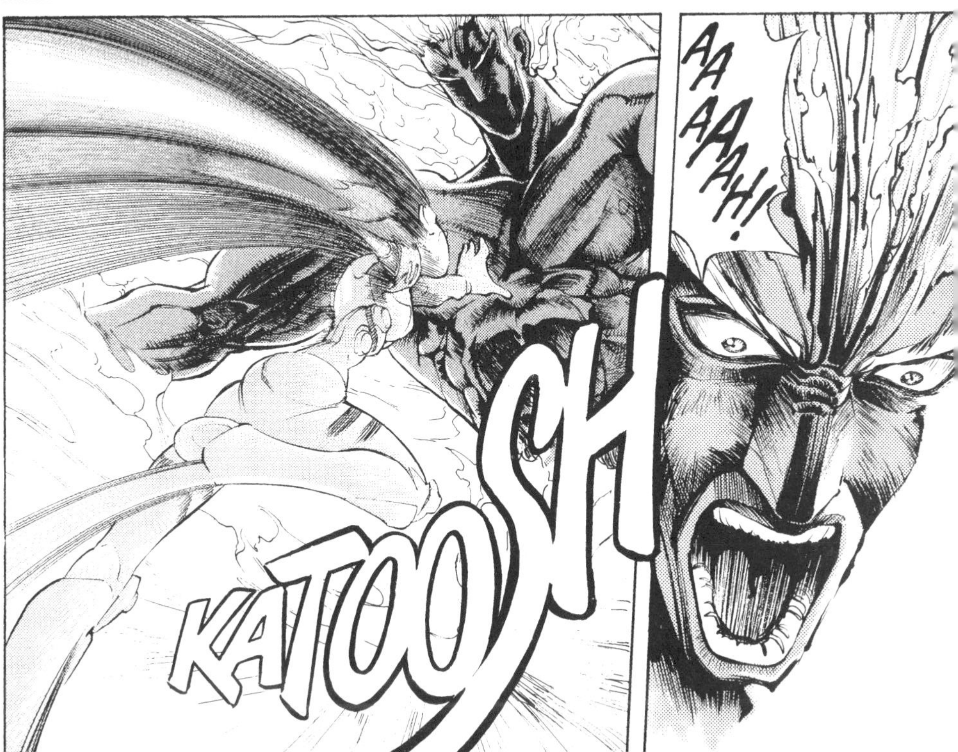
AAAAAH!
KATOOSH

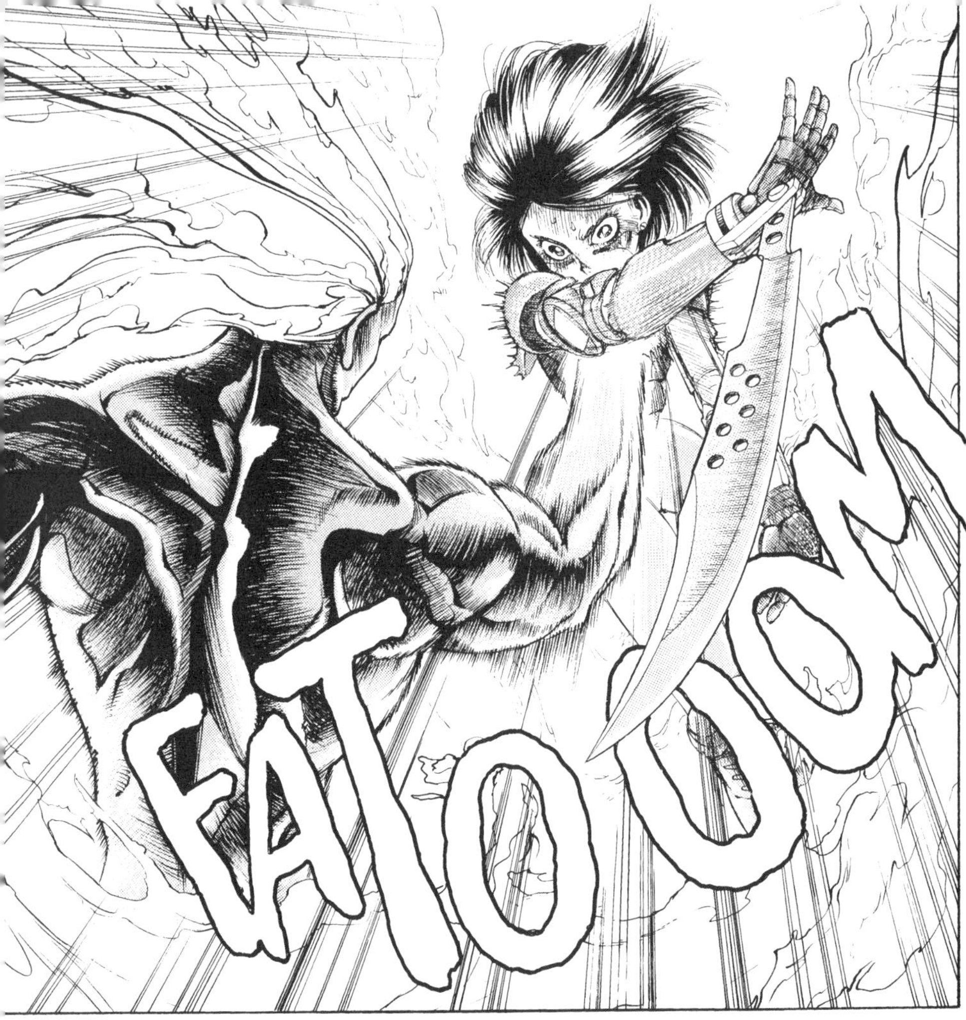
FATOOOM

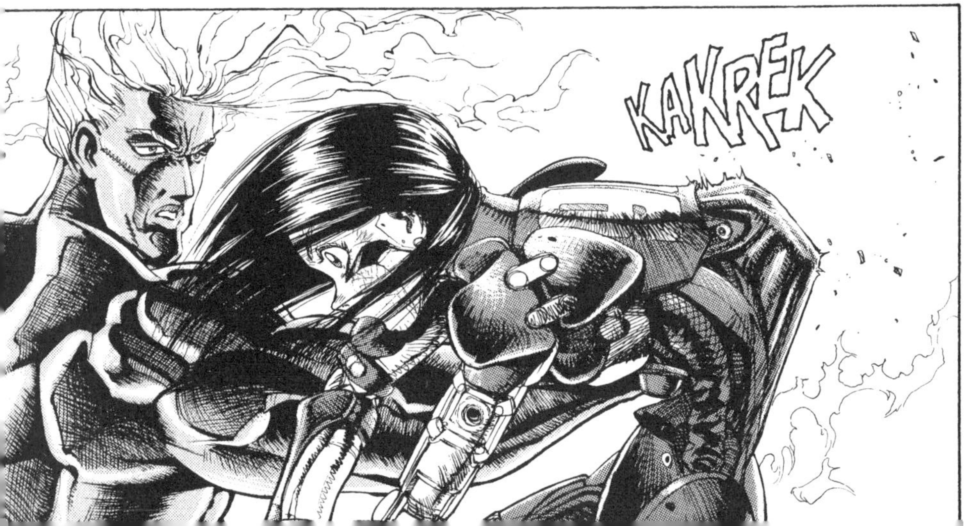
KAKREK

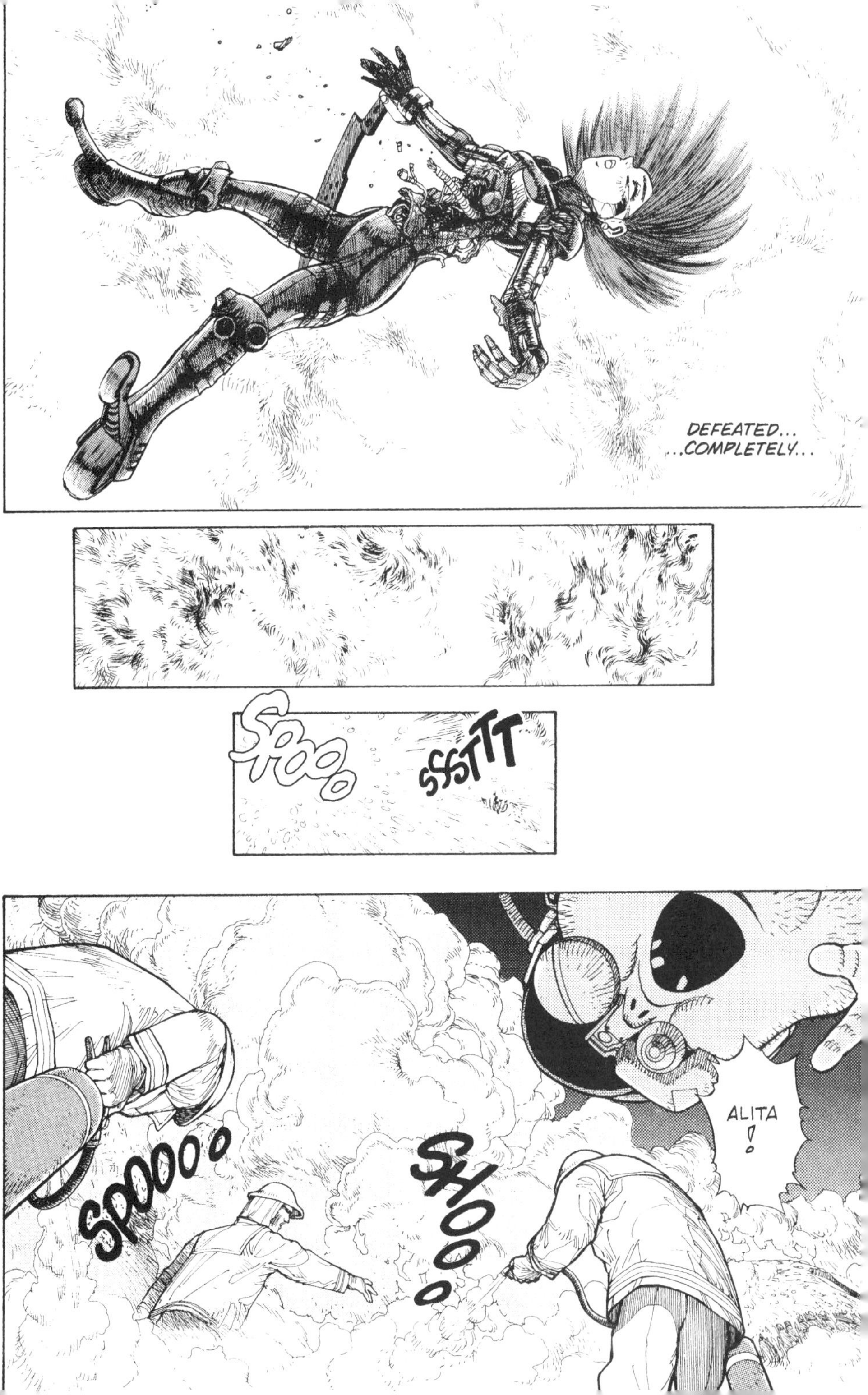
DEFEATED...
...COMPLETELY...
SPOOo
SSSTTT
SPOOOo
SHOOOo
ALITA!

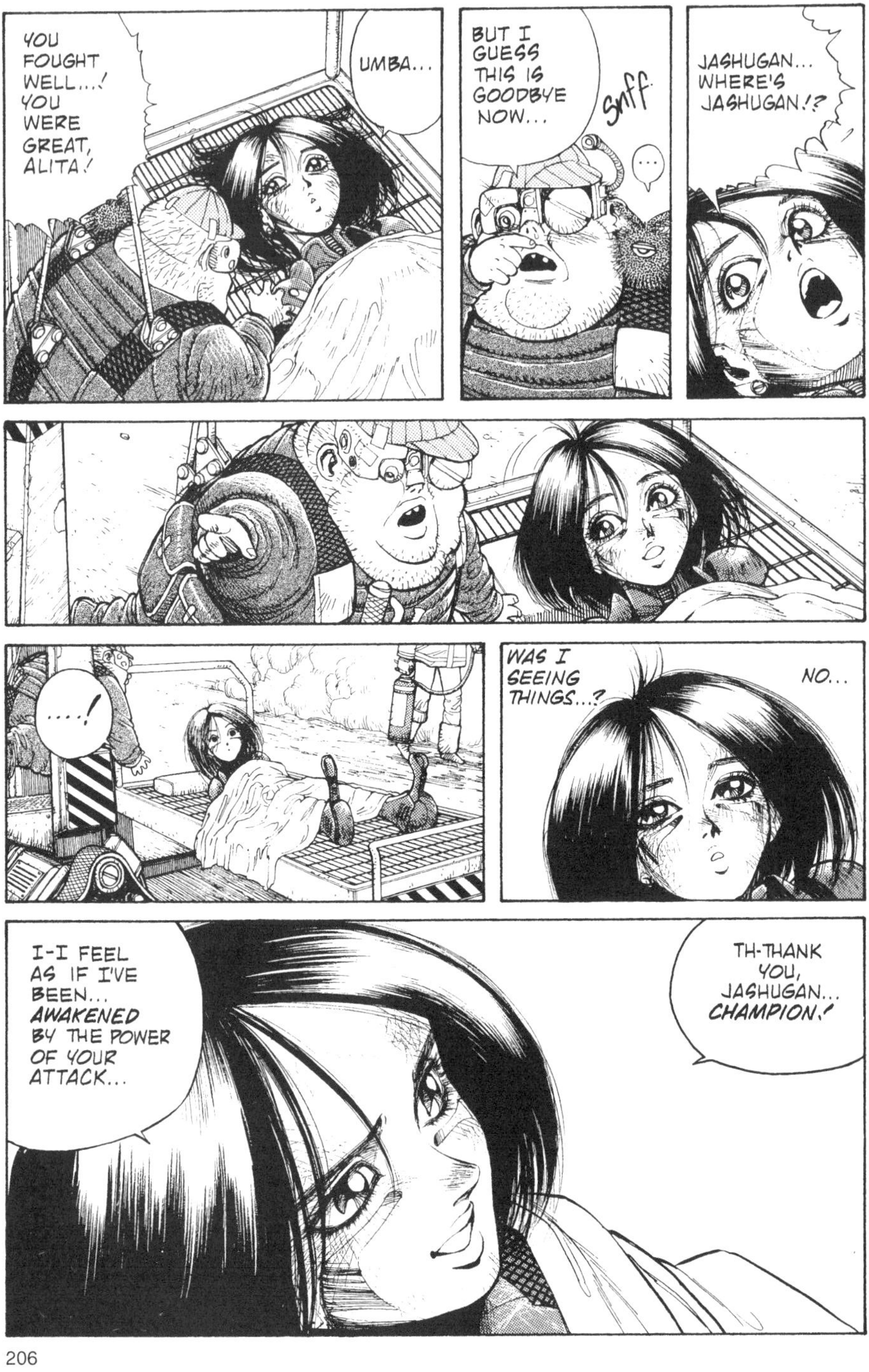
YOU FOUGHT WELL...! YOU WERE GREAT, ALITA!
UMBA...
BUT I GUESS THIS IS GOODBYE NOW...
SNFF
...
JASHUGAN... WHERE'S JASHUGAN!?
....!
WAS I SEEING THINGS...?
NO...
I-I FEEL AS IF I'VE BEEN... **AWAKENED** BY THE POWER OF YOUR ATTACK...
TH-THANK YOU, JASHUGAN... **CHAMPION!**

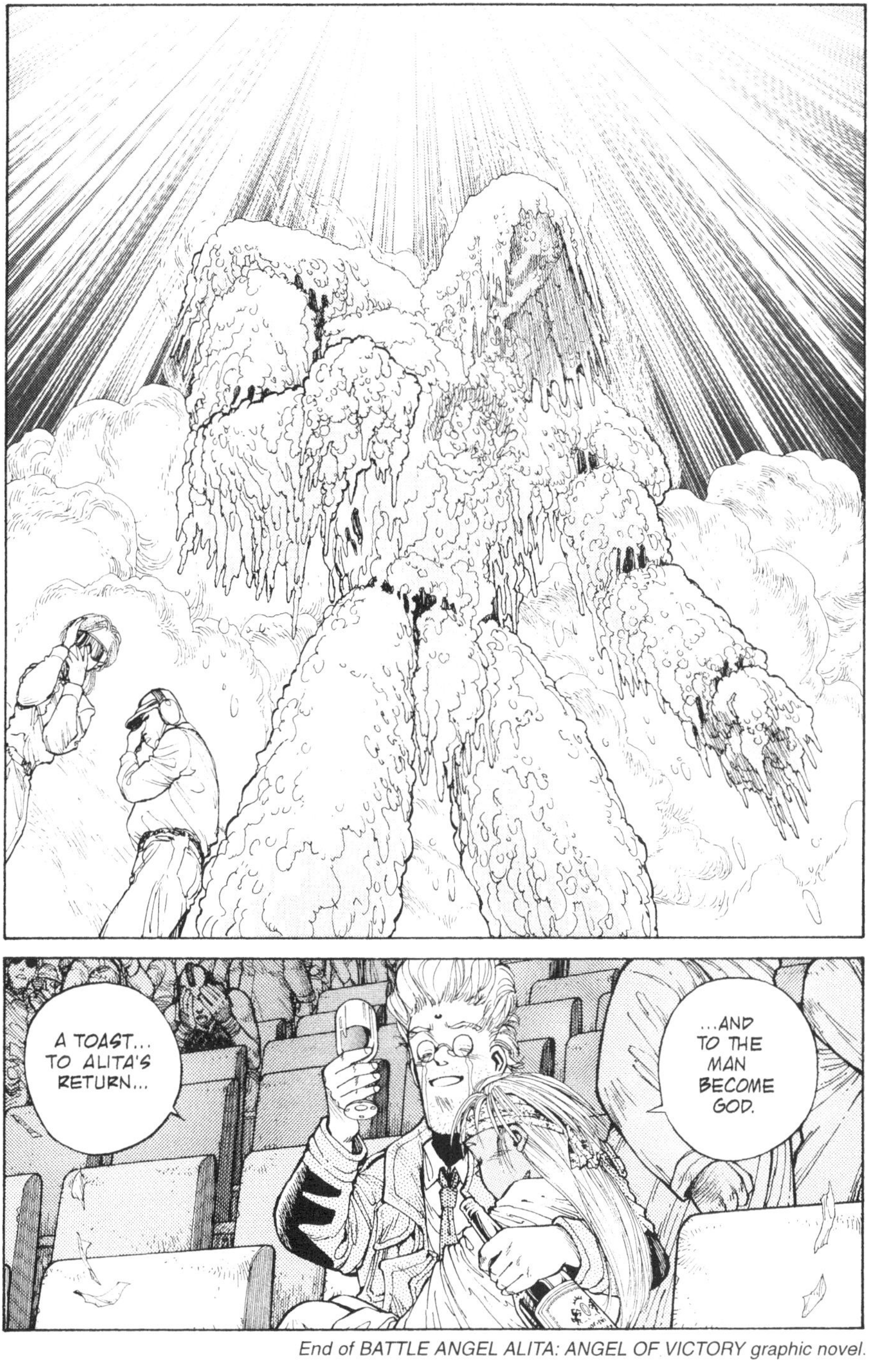
A TOAST... TO ALITA'S RETURN...
...AND TO THE MAN BECOME GOD.

End of BATTLE ANGEL ALITA: ANGEL OF VICTORY graphic novel.

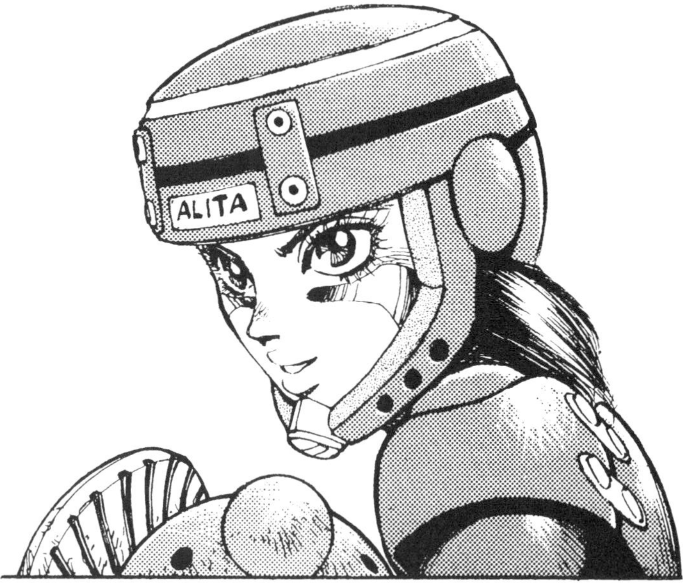
ALITA